Mary's Way

Romantic Love as a Path to God

MICHELLE RIOS RICE HENNELLY
& R. KEVIN HENNELLY

OUR LADY OF LIGHT
PUBLICATIONS

Santa Fe, New Mexico

Published by:
  Our Lady of Light Publications
  PO Box 6323
  Santa Fe, NM 87502
  LadyofLightPress@aol.com

Line art and cover design: Meaghan Drone Hennelly
Book design and production: Janice St. Marie

Printed in the United States of America on acid-free recycled paper

DISCLAIMER
This book is designed to provide information in regard to the subject matter covered. The purpose of this book is to educate. The authors, editors, and publisher shall have neither liability nor responsibility to any person or entity with respect to any perceived loss or damage caused, directly or indirectly, by the information contained in this book.

Publisher's Cataloging-in-Publication Data
Hennelly, Michelle Rios Rice

  Mary's way : romantic love as a path to God / Michelle Rios Rice
  Hennelly & R. Kevin Hennelly. — 1st ed. — Santa Fe, N. M. : Our
  Lady of Light Publications, 2004.

    p. ; cm.

    ISBN: 0-9742162-5-9

    1. Spiritual life. 2. Love–Religious aspects. 3. Sex–Religious
  aspects. 4. Man-woman relationships–Religious aspects. 5. Mary,
  Blessed Virgin, Saint, I. Hennelly, R. Kevin. II. Title.

BL626.4 .H46 2004   2003107196
291.5/677–dc21   0401

10 9 8 7 6 5 4 3 2 1

With great love,
we dedicate this book as a humble offering
to Mary, the Queen of Light,
who sustains all life and carries the earth
and all her creatures within her womb,
as we thank her for her illuminating presence,
for her enlightening teachings,
and for her blissful, blazing, eternal essence
with which she so graciously fills our hearts.
We honor her for guiding us on the path of beauty
and for bestowing her grace upon us.

Contents

Preface

The Cosmic Goddess, known throughout the ages by many different names, is appearing to ordinary people like me, Michelle, all over the world. I call her Mary because this is how she is best known to me. She is coming with gifts, teachings, and knowings so that we, the people of this planet, can enter consciously into the greatest spiritual revolution of all time. This revolution, which will affect us personally and collectively as individuals, couples, families, and nations, is about love, its power, and its return into everyone and everything. She is teaching us how to lift the veil of illusion, see truth, and expand our hearts into a virgin state of sacredness. She is showing us the way to become who and what we truly are.

Mary's appearances to me are everything that is mysterious, but what about love isn't mysterious? Just as the love between two lovers cannot be seen or captured in words, neither can Mary nor the experience of her. We try to fit our experiences into words, a concept, a language. But divine love cannot be seen or explained in ordinary terms. It is seen and explained by the intellect of the heart, which is love. Only love can grasp love, and only the divine can grasp the divine. All else is a mere reflection of the awesome majesty of divine love. Mary is divine love, pure and unconditional, and only in the purity of the divine love that dwells deep within our hearts will we truly know her.

So, as my story goes, I was in a meditation sanctuary nestled in one of my favorite spots in the northern New Mexico forest. It is so clean and untouched by the hustle and bustle of ordinary life that one can sense the magic of the dazzling inner play of oneness that sustains all living beings. It is felt in the towering majesty of the trees as they speak to you and in the poetic songs of the birds. The sanctuary itself is an amazing building. Large, round, and about thirty feet tall, it has several sizable rectangular windows, each with three giant three-foot prisms. The windows are situated to capture the rays of the sun throughout the day. As the sunlight passes through the windows, a kaleidoscope of rainbow colors, alive in silence and beauty, is created and fills the sanctuary. It is a holy place indeed and a perfect setting for Our Lady of Light to appear.

As I sat on the ground as I had done so many times before in this God-filled place, I began my open-eye meditation and entered into the eternal peace within. Suddenly, to my left and about ten feet above the ground appeared a woman surrounded by a vibrating white light of fire. It was streaming everywhere, bringing everything alive with its most miraculous vibration and sensation. She and her light were as bright as a million suns. At once she said to me, "Do not fear. I am Our Lady of Light. You can call me Our Lady of Light. I will come to you every day for the rest of your life." She stayed there for a short time. She spoke no other words, but I felt an unspoken language of fiery transformative love.

When I returned to my ordinary awareness, I knew that what had just happened was real, yet I was in a state of total shock. My heart raced, set ablaze with a burning fire, and my mind was shattered into a million tiny pieces. Nothing in my life would ever be the same. You see, when Mary touches your heart with her passionate, fiery, creative, nurturing love, your Sacred Heart opens and you enter into rivers of eternal golden love. The alchemical process of life and its lessons enters into the fiery purity of divine love and you taste and can become who you really are.

My husband Kevin and I pray, meditate, and do spiritual practices together. I receive the loving messages from Mary daily. At times, Jesus or Joseph also appear, either alone or, more often, alongside Mary in a glow of oneness. Kevin writes down their messages, as we work together to disseminate them as the team Mary asked us to be on her mission. We are the messengers, not the message. Mary's messages come from the mother of ALL. We do not do this work for ourselves, as anyone who has seriously taken on the spiritual path knows. It is a magical path, but also a most difficult one which takes a tremendous amount of work. It calls for the shattering and letting go of all that is old in order to make way for love. While some may be interested in the details of our life and the experiences of the visions, what is most important is to believe in the unbelievable, to see what is unseen by ordinary eyes, and to live and know from within the hidden chambers of our hearts where, as Mary reminds us, we are divine.

We have written *Mary's Way* because Mary asked us to. The messages, which are reproduced verbatim, are the most important part of the book. We have tried to organize the messages in a way in which they tell the larger story that Mary is revealing. The reader will find, however, that Mary is not revealing just one story, but many. The thread that ties them together is Mary herself: her life and her love.

Many of the visions occurred in Cristo Rey Church in Santa Fe, New Mexico. This church is a holy place, and the presence of the "old faith," which existed in Santa Fe for many years, can still be felt there.

As you read along, your heart and higher mind will tell you what you need to learn, hear, and see from this book. It is not for us to convince you of the truth of the messages, change your mind, or alter your beliefs. Mary will speak to you directly, opening the door to new ways of being as her teachings remind you of things your Higher Self and the Sacred Heart within you already know. Enjoy and Injoy the Cosmic Mother's love and teachings.

Introduction

In these extraordinary times, the Cosmic Goddess, best known in Western culture as Mary, the mother of Jesus, is appearing to increasing numbers of people around the world. Although she has come to people continually over the past two thousand years, never before have her appearances been as frequent or her messages as urgent. Her messages that are the subject of this book address a broad range of topics, including the historically unprecedented transition the earth and her people are currently undergoing. But, most importantly, her messages are about love. Mary says that she is "desperately" trying to awaken us to love and to the unlimited possibilities that love can bring to us and to our world. She affirms repeatedly in the visions that "In love, all things are possible. In love, one sees all realities and all truths. In love, one is free."

We encounter one of our most profound experiences of love when we fall in love. Mary wants us to know what this experience is really about and its untapped potential to initiate us into the freedom and bliss of divine love. When we are in love, our hearts are open to another, bringing us into contact with something much greater than ourselves. At such times, the spark of our divine essence is ignited, and a magical energy comes alive within us. This energy awakens in us a sense of the divine because, according to Mary, it is divine. It holds for us, she explains, the possibility of becoming one with our divine essence, one with the beloved, and one with God. Romantic love is thus about the fulfillment of our highest purpose: to live in oneness with the divine.

Mary identifies romantic love not only as a spiritual path but, for many people, as the most direct path to God. She shares her own experience of love and relationship when she walked the earth as the spouse of Joseph and the mother of Jesus so that we can fully understand the unlimited possibilities that romantic love holds for us. With words of great beauty and tenderness, she reveals how her and Joseph's love for each other brought them into oneness with their own divinity, with each other, and with God. Correcting distortions and half-truths about her life and love, Mary discloses this information because she knows that we are like her and that deep within we desire to love and be loved and, ultimately, to become love.

Unfortunately, few people see romantic love as a spiritual path. In today's world, romantic love is too often trivialized and confused with false and misleading portrayals of love disseminated through the media and the entertainment industry. Disjoined from any sense of the sacred, such notions of romantic love lead many people astray, causing them to squander one of the greatest opportunities they have to draw closer to God and fulfill their life purpose. It is out of concern for these digressions and the harm that results from them that Mary comes to us with a deepened understanding of romantic love and the place it is meant to have in our lives. She tell us that romantic love was a sacred path for her and that it can be a sacred path for us.

Mary's messages, along with messages from Jesus, address another facet of romantic love fundamental to us as spiritual beings: sexual energy. They explain that sexual energy is the most powerful force within us and is deeply linked, in ways few people understand, to our spirituality. This energy is not only the fire that kindles our spirituality: In many ways it is our spirituality. How we relate to this fire shapes our destinies as spiritual beings. Referring to it as essential to our spirituality, Ronald Rolheiser writes in *The Holy Longing: The Search for a Christian Spirituality*:

> Hence, spirituality is not about serenely picking or rationally choosing certain spiritual activities like going to church, praying or meditating, reading spiritual books, or setting off on some explicit spiritual quest. It is far more basic than that. Long before we do anything explicitly religious at all, we have to do something about the fire that burns within us. What we do with that fire, how we channel it, is our spirituality. Thus, we all have a spirituality whether we want one or not, whether we are religious or not.[1]

Mary tells us that our sexual energy is meant to be joined with the energy of love that flows from our hearts. When this merging of sexual and vital energies occurs, the combined energies become a creative, healing, and blissful force with the power to heighten our consciousness and lift us into union with the divine. Sexual energy, however, is poorly understood and widely misused. According to Mary, the consequences of its misuse are staggering. Sexual intimacy that is not an expression of love erodes our spiritual potential, estranges us from the truth of who and what we are, and impairs our ability to unite with God.

Mary's messages inform us about the nature of sexual energy and how it impacts every facet of our lives. So important is the proper understanding and use of this energy that Mary reveals she and Joseph were, and still are, lovers. Lest we still fail to grasp its power and the magnitude of its influence, Mary tells us that sexual energy is the energy of the Holy Spirit. This enlightened perspective gives rise to critical questions: Are societies worldwide on the brink of destruction because they have dishonored and abused one of the most sacred forces in the universe? If so, how might we remedy the miasma of sexual misuse that pervades our lives and world? In teaching us the purpose for which sexual energy is intended, Mary is giving us the opportunity to restore this energy to its rightful place in God's plan for us to be one with Him and remedy one of the greatest maladies afflicting humankind today.

Mary and Jesus also provide a perspective on marriage that takes it out of the realm of the profane and into that of the sacred. When a marriage is not lived as sacred, according to Mary, it becomes yet another impediment to love and to the union of two souls with each other and with God. Mary and Jesus explain what constitutes a marriage and what marriage is meant to be for us as spiritual beings. They tell us that, when romantic love is sealed within the sacred union of marriage, the marriage can become, in Mary's words, "the great vehicle for two souls to return to God."

However, for romantic love to reach its highest expression, lovers must do more than open their hearts to each other and bring their sexual energy to life in them within a sacred bond of love. Mary says that lovers also must be willing to travel together on a journey of love that will take them out of the ordinary and into the extraordinary. Again offering her own life as an example, she urges lovers to risk everything in order to gain what their hearts truly desire. This journey, she says, consists of the following four tasks which, in one form or another, belong to all spiritual paths:

- Loving God above all else.
- Living a holy life.
- Letting go of all that is not love.
- Facing darkness while becoming light.

Mary's messages about romantic love, sexual energy, and lovers' dedication of their lives and relationship to becoming pure love culminate in teachings about the wisdom of the heart. When we open our hearts, we open them not only to joy but to sorrow, as did Mary in her life as the mother of Jesus. Both Mary and Jesus guide us to the realization that love and suffering are the experiences that touch us most profoundly, bringing us to a deeper wisdom of the heart and to the truth and freedom that we desire. These messages, in turn, are preparing us for the birth of a new consciousness on this planet and the dawn of an era which Mary describes as an Age of Light. Mary says we are meant to live a heaven on earth, which will only be possible when we become pure love. Mary reminds us that we are living in a world of both light and darkness and that each soul has to choose between them. Thus, whether we walk with Mary into this new world will depend on the choices each of us makes. She comes, as she has many times before, to awaken us to truth and guide us out of darkness and into the light.

Mary's Way is as much about Mary as it is about her messages.[2] Her life as recorded in Scripture is but a small part of a much grander picture of who and what she is. In the visions, she identifies herself as the Cosmic Goddess who has been active throughout the ages in the unfolding of God's plan. She also calls herself the Divine Mother who has come in various forms to bring light and love to her children of every race, culture, ethnicity, religion, and gender and to guide them back to their divine origins. As she teaches us about herself, she cautions us not to mistake any one form or manifestation of her for all that she is. Rather than being preoccupied with the different forms in which she appears to people or the different names that people give her, she asks us to open our hearts to the truth of who and what she is so we can come to know the truth of who and what we are. This self-discovery follows naturally, she assures us, because she is like us and we are like her.

Although no name or appellation can capture the vastness of her being and no single religion can fully convey the depth and breadth of her teachings, Mary asks in these visions to be known as Our Lady of Light or the Queen of Light. While the theme of love is timeless, she knows that we are struggling to love and be loved in a period of our history when the world is increasingly engulfed in darkness. Indeed, she comes at this time of world darkness not only to bring light, but to teach us how to use it to become pure love and unite with God. Light, according to Our Lady, is the manifestation of God's love, and by learning its use for spiritual attainment we can join with her to dispel the darkness of the world.

Mary's way is not for the faint of heart. It calls for a full commitment to oneself, to one's beloved, and to love. It is, moreover, not only for those called to romantic love as a spiritual path. It is for all those who wish to be in love with love and to know God, as does Mary, as the ultimate lover. For all seekers of truth, Mary's way insists on an open mind willing to challenge basic beliefs about ourselves, the world, and God. In the end, romantic love as a path to God, while a bold proposition, leads to the healing and truth so desperately needed in today's world. Those who dare to follow this path cannot help but encounter disappointments, setbacks, and seemingly formidable obstacles, but Mary promises that we need not walk it alone. As she reminded the fearful Juan Diego, the Aztec Indian to whom she appeared as Our Lady of Guadalupe in 1531: *Cuix amo nican nicà nimoNantzin* ("Am I not right here who is your Mother?").[3]

While reading Mary's words, feel her love vibrate in the core of your being. Like the radiating circles formed by pebbles tossed into a still pond, let her words ripple through your soul, announcing her presence and her invitation to take an extraordinary journey with her. By whatever name you choose to call her, reach out to her as she reaches out to you and draw comfort from her offer to accompany you along the way:

Take my hand and walk with me. There will be no regrets.
Do not fear. It is only love that is awaiting you and all who
join in love.

PART ONE

The Spiritual Nature of Romantic Love

CHAPTER ONE

Romantic Love

 SOMEWHERE WITHIN US, we long to join with and become one with something greater. We may not always feel this longing, but it is natural to us, as the great spiritual masters and sages teach. This longing speaks to our innermost truth and is closely connected to the purpose for which we have come into this world.

Romantic love is about this truth and purpose. Throughout the ages, romantic love has been at the center of the human experience. It fascinates and intrigues, enchants and compels, drawing lovers toward a oneness with something inexplicably greater than themselves, as reflected in Old Testament psalms, ancient Greek myths, the verses of Rumi, and the works of Shakespeare. For when we fall in love, we encounter something extraordinary. An energy comes alive within us, lifting us out of our ordinary awareness as we begin to see ourselves, our beloved, and the world as if through new eyes. This energy is the pure love, the divine essence, that dwells within us. As if imprisoned, it is set free, and we feel a magic, joy, bliss, and freedom that we may never have known before.

This energy carries us into uncharted realms. Enthralled with the beloved, we fall in love with love; and when we fall in love with love, we fall in love with God. This occurs, Mary tells us, because "God's highest expression is love," and as we come alive in love, God comes alive in us. We then begin to awaken to the truth of who and what we are and to our highest purpose.

While we may not recognize it as such, romantic love is the experience that brings most of us closest to God. This accounts for why we are occupied with romantic love, why we long for it, and why we are devastated upon losing it. Yet too often we fail to recognize romantic love for the gift that it is. Seldom do we bow in awe before the miracle unfolding in our midst or recognize the grace flowing in and around us. Instead, we too readily see it as an aberration, something incidental to our life, and limit its potential to take us from the ordinary to the extraordinary. For what is romantic love if it is not the journey from human to divine love?

Mary tells us that romantic love has the potential to take us from human to divine love and lift us to the majestic heights at which we are meant to live as children of God. There we would discover that at our core we are mystics meant to be one with our divine essence, the beloved, and God. Mary says that "the children of the light are meant to live a heaven on earth" and that romantic love is a path to that heaven. When we embrace romantic love as a sacred calling, we are on that path. As we travel further along it, we learn that divine love is not what we become, but what we already are.

Love's Urgent Longings

Were you ever drawn into a relationship wondering if your feelings were of romantic love or perhaps something else? Distinguishing romantic love from other forms of attraction is not always easy. We are complex beings with many levels of experience and diverse personal histories. Our relationships reflect this complexity as they touch each of us differently on physical, emotional, mental, and spiritual levels. Adding to the difficulty, popular culture inundates us with distorted views of love and relationship that mislead us as to the true nature of romantic love. Further, romantic love holds certain ineffable qualities that make it hard to define.

It seems, nevertheless, that there are three salient characteristics of romantic love that set it apart. These characteristics, which will be experienced by persons in different measure on the basis of their unique personalities and histories, are not meant to be a definition of romantic love. They simply help to distinguish romantic love from similar experiences that may be mistaken for it.

The first characteristic of romantic love is that it opens the lovers' hearts to the spark of divine love that is their essence. This divine love dwells within us in what Mary calls the hidden chamber of the heart, which sits beyond the depth of the energy center located near to the physical heart.[1] Being in love opens us to this sacred space, which Mary calls the Sacred Heart, and connects us to its divine energy. It is the flow of this divine essence that accounts for the heightened sense of beauty, magic, bliss, and freedom we feel when we are in love. In several visions, Mary has shown this place of pure love within her heart, revealing an endless expanse of light and beauty.

The second characteristic of romantic love is the desire it engenders to become one with the beloved. This merging can occur on different levels. It occurs physically and energetically during love-making. It may also occur with the lovers becoming one at the level of their divine essence.

The third characteristic of romantic love is the transcendent feeling it evokes. The vibration of divine love, which Mary says is the highest vibration we can experience, lifts us into a higher consciousness. We experience this transcendence most poignantly in those ecstatic moments when we feel most connected to the beloved. For some people, these moments define on a personal level what romantic love is. At these times, which we want to hold onto forever, we begin to glimpse the truth of who and what we are.

Romantic love, in its essence, is a spiritual experience that wells up from deep within us. The desire underlying romantic love is the same desire we find in the spiritual longing for union with the divine. The Spanish mystic San Juan de la Cruz, in his classic work *The Dark Night of the Soul*, wrote of this when he described his journey to God beginning "One dark night, fired by love's urgent longings."[2] We all feel at times these urgent longings, although we may not recognize them for what they are: a desire to become one with something greater than ourselves.

Mystics of all traditions characterize this union as a piercing fire in the depths of the soul and identify it as God. As ordinary as we may seem, we too are called to the mystical union that kindles this fire. We are born to be as God—pure, holy, and on fire with love. This is what we become when we, together with that other special person, open ourselves to the eternal love that dwells within our hearts. It is what awaits us when we surrender completely to love and love's urgent longings.

The Knowing of the Heart

Romantic love can easily be confused with other experiences. For example, relationships based primarily on psychological projection are often mistaken for romantic love. Psychological projection occurs when we perceive parts of ourselves in another person. While such projections invariably accompany genuine feelings of romantic love to some degree, they cannot form the basis of romantic love. The reason for this, according to Mary, is found in the difference between the knowing that comes from the heart and the knowing that comes from the mind.[3]

Psychological projection results from perceiving ourselves and others through the lens of the mind. We literally project onto someone some content or contents of our minds. But what are the contents of the mind? They are concepts, ideas, thoughts, and memories governed by various mental processes. They are not love and, Mary tells us, they actually hinder us in loving:

> When one puts understanding or a concept on love, one places limitations on it. With love there is no limitation.

She further states that we cannot grasp love through the mind, but only by being love:

> Love cannot be understood. Love cannot be put into words. Love cannot be held or grasped. Love can only be.

We are love when we open to the pure love of the Sacred Heart and merge with that love. This does not occur through the mind or by virtue of the contents of the mind. Rather, it occurs when we free ourselves of the mind and open our hearts. Again stating that divine love cannot be grasped through concepts, Mary distinguishes human from divine love:

> There is only one thing that is real, one thing that truly matters and is worth pursuing, and that is love. Love is a word, and one has concepts as to what love is. But here we are not talking about concepts. We are talking about the divine, and the divine cannot be put into a concept. The divine is love, and all human love is a reflection of divine love. But divine love is greater than all human love put together. Human love is a way for human beings to experience the divine, but it is not the complete essence until one becomes it. This is the path of all human beings. Some choose to reject this path, but it is the path you are meant to follow.

The path of divine love to which we are all called, then, is not a path of the mind, but of the heart. Mary identifies it as the only path that will lead us to truth:

> There is only one truth and that is the truth of love. If you succeed completely in knowing love, you know God and you become like God. You can create miracles because all the power and all the truth and all the knowing are in love. And love is God, and God is in all things.

Thus, whereas relationships based primarily on projection entangle us in illusions, those based on the heart open us to truth. When the heart opens, we begin to see through what Mary calls the "eyes of love" the truth of who we are and who the beloved is. Then the projections fall away as we recognize them for what they are: the masks and props belonging to the dramas of our minds and having nothing to do with love. Some say that love is blind, but this is not true. It is when we perceive others through the clouded lens of our projections, and not through the clear eyes of love, that we are unable to see the truth of love in others and in ourselves.

Projections also contribute to the misplaced emotions, such as those associated to possessiveness or fears of betrayal, rejection, or loss, that are often present in relationships. When we love another, we have no desire to control them or hold them back from being all that they can be. It is not to say that in our humanness we may not at times be naive, misinterpret situations, or allow projections to dislodge us temporarily from the vibration of love in our hearts. But one of the great blessings of romantic love is its ability to liberate us from the mind's illusions by drawing us into the truth of the heart. As Mary explains, "When your hearts are pure, your minds will be pure, too."

It may be difficult for some people to accept, especially in today's world where the mind is considered by many to be the arbiter of truth, that truth is not found through the mind. Mary is not speaking figuratively when she asserts that the way to truth is not through the mind, but through the intellect of the heart:

> There is one true knowing, the knowing that sits deep inside the intellect of the heart. This is the knowing of love, the intimate and true knowing of all things.

This is not the way of knowing just for love and the things of love. It is the way of knowing that will serve us in every aspect of our lives. The more we open our hearts, the more we access the intellect of the heart. Then, according to Mary, we come at last to the true knowing of all things.

Love's Hidden Treasure

We desire to love and be loved in a pure way, yet most of us believe such a thing is impossible. Mary observes, "All souls are called to become pure love, but few believe it." Conditioned by countless erroneous concepts, we believe instead that we are unworthy of love, that we will be disappointed or hurt by love, that we will give but not receive love, or receive it but be unable to give it—in short, that pure love is beyond our reach. Out of a fear of being hurt, we build elaborate defenses to love and put our egos in charge of maintaining them. We then ask ourselves how realistic is it to become pure love and to commit our lives to that goal.

Mary knows that we desire to love and be loved in a pure way. She also knows that the ego and the mind have a tenacious hold over most of us. She reminds us that pure love is our birthright attainable in the here and now and tells us that by giving ourselves totally to love we free ourselves from the fears of the ego and illusions of the mind and enter into the heart of pure love. She thus urges:

> Open your hearts deeper and deeper. Open them to the truth, and you shall understand that with love there is no need. When you go deep enough, you find that you, too, have a Sacred Heart. It is the heart of pure love, of the highest intellect, the greatest knowing, and undying passion. It is the seed of truth that sits within everyone.

What does it mean to become pure love? It signifies being filled completely with the energy of love flowing from the Sacred Heart within us. It is within the Sacred Heart that we merge with our essence of pure love and light and become filled with its vibration, which Mary identifies as the vibration of God. Mary explains:

> When you reach the place of pure love and light, you shed all that is not God, all that is not divine. You become your divine essence. You are love energy.

Relationship is natural to us, and in the most intimate of relationships we have the opportunity to move into the vibration of divine love. But this is a qualitatively different sort of love than the human love with which we are most familiar. In human love we feel a sympathetic vibration with others that may be mistaken for pure love. But, if our love were pure, our intimate relationships, our families, and our lives would be very different. Commenting on this disparity, Mary observes:

So few know love. Many claim to know love, but they do not. Parents do not love children. Children do not love their parents. To love means to love without expectation. Loving another, really loving another, means loving as I love.

Pure love sits within our hearts without expectations, conditions, agendas, or judgements. It is virgin in its purity. We experience it at different times in our lives, and our souls know that it is the way we are meant to be: pure in all we are. Everyone who has fallen in love has felt this virgin love within them and knows that it holds the key to what their lives are about.

To become pure love, then, is to discover the hidden treasure of the Sacred Heart. It is to be filled with its vibration, which carries us beyond thoughts and emotions and into mystical union with the beloved and with God. This union is the culmination of the quest that lies at the heart of romantic love. Mary explains what happens when we enter fully into the vibration of pure love:

> You have to empty the mind and open the heart. In the vibration of love, you know all things. You become all things. In divine love, in pure love, you go into oneness with the other and with God.

Mary's view of romantic love clearly marks it as sacramental. A devotion of the highest order, it becomes an occasion for grace, the energy of divine love, to enter and transform us. It is this energy that will bring us to the miracle of pure love where we will live the "heaven on earth" that Mary, as did her Son two thousand years ago, calls us to.

Healing Our Deepest Wound

Our deepest wound, according to Mary, is our separation from God. All other wounds stem from this primordial wound. We can see it reflected in the pain we cause ourselves and others as we act it out in different ways. We seek peace, security, and love, often in ways and places that are familiar to us. But does what we find bring the deeper healing we desire? We will find this healing, Mary says, only when we return to God:

True healing and true health come from being one with God.
If you become one with God, you are not sick on any level.

Romantic love can be a path to this healing. As our hearts open to another and we move closer to the Sacred Heart, our separation from God gradually melts away as the vibration of divine love dissolves all that is not love within us. We begin to discover the truth of who and what we are and desire to return to the fullness of this truth. It is the truth that we first experienced at the dawn of our existence.

According to Mary, each soul is created together with another soul "from the same breath of God." Both souls come into being joined together in a single ball of pure light. They then separate into two distinct spheres of light, both carrying the "breath of God" as their essence. Two souls created together in this way are sometimes called "twin flames," although Mary has not used this term. She simply wants us to know that at the beginning of our existence we were one with God and another soul in an intimate bond of love. The memory of this original state of perfection, as well as its loss, are imprinted on our souls. While our minds may not remember, our souls do and long to return to this lost paradise.

Mary tells us that God likewise longs for us to join with our beloved and Him in the ecstasy of pure love. It is because of His longing for us and the vastness of His love that Mary calls God "the ultimate lover." She adds that bliss is God's experience of pure love, which is precisely what we long to recover in romantic love.

How did we lose this original state of perfection? We lost it at some point in our soul's journey when we allowed something other than love to enter us and chose to identify with it. Trapped in the resulting illusion of separateness, we proceeded to make it our reality, forgetting who we were and where we came from. We continue to hold this illusion in our minds, and the ego works to convince us that our separation from God, and not our oneness with Him, is our truth. But as Jesus points out:

It is the mind that separates. It is the ego that separates. It is
not truth. Truth is love. Love is light. Love is free.

The mind and ego are none of the things that Jesus says are truth. They are not love, they are not light, and they are not free. Instead, they produce the endless illusions that keep us separated from truth and lead us astray, even in the midst of romantic love. This is why romantic love so often does not bring the fulfillment we desire. Instead of giving ourselves completely to love, we lose ourselves in the fears of the ego and the illusions of the mind. We then remain caught in a low level of energy that, like a thick molasses, prevents us from sustaining the higher vibration of love. Mary says that we must emancipate ourselves from the tyranny of the ego and mind if we are to be free to love and join with God.

Romantic love, when lived as a sacred path, has the power to set us free. When we open to the pure love within us, the veils of darkness that cloud our consciousness and blind us to truth begin to lift. We sense once again our original state of perfection, sometimes as a soft murmur and at other times as a bolt of lightning. Our longing intensifies as we move closer to retrieving something lost in the mists of time—the original romance of two souls joined in love with God.

CHAPTER TWO

Virgin Lover, Virgin Goddess

 MARY DOES NOT FIT NEATLY into any category. We think we know her, and then she reveals more about her herself. With each new revelation, we come to see more fully the grandeur of her being, from her humble submission to God's call for her to be the mother of His Son to her awesome majesty as the Queen of Heaven and Earth. We learn that there are many facets to her, some of which are beyond our comprehension. We call her Mary but we could call her by many other names, for indeed she is known by many other names.

It is especially difficult to know Mary as she was during her life as the mother of Jesus because the historical record of her life is limited. The most authoritative sources are the Gospels, but their accuracy is uncertain and subject to ongoing debate among New Testament scholars. Mary reveals in the visions information about herself and her relationship with Joseph that broadens and in some ways alters our limited understanding of her based on Scripture. These disclosures also contradict some commonly held beliefs about her.

Why is Mary bringing forth this information now? One reason is that she no longer wants to be known within the limited context in which she is traditionally seen. She states that she will no longer be confined within this view:

> I am far more than any church can teach or preach. I am coming to teach the world who I am.

A second reason relates to Mary's unparalleled influence as the model of feminine virtue in the Western world for the past two thousand years. Our understanding of her has played an immeasurable role in shaping Western consciousness. How we see her has influenced in countless ways how we see ourselves. Thus, significant shifts in our view of Mary have major implications for how we view ourselves. As her revelations indicate, she should indeed be revered as the model of feminine virtue, but not for all the reasons she has been.

A third reason Mary is sharing information about herself is that she wants us to know that we are like her. As she reveals who she is, she reveals who we are, and we discover that her truth is also our truth. Thus, as we listen to her messages and come to know her intimately, we will come to know ourselves in a new way. We will find that we, too, in the depths of our souls are unfathomable oceans of love.

We are still left with the question why Mary is revealing this information about herself now. This information forms part of a larger story unfolding across the globe in which Mary is emerging as a central figure. She is telling people around the world, in visions and locutions, that the events occurring on the global stage, both natural and man-made, will bring an end to the world as we know it and give birth to a new era of light and a consciousness of love. As a beacon of light shining in a sea of darkness, she comes to teach us who she is and to guide us into this new world.

Mary in the Gospels

Mary is mentioned only a few times in the Gospels. Her story begins with the appearance of the angel Gabriel when she was betrothed to Joseph and probably in her early or mid-teens, since it was Jewish custom at that time for girls to be engaged at that age. Gabriel announces to her that God had chosen her to be the mother of His Son. Mary asks how this could be since she is still a virgin. Gabriel explains that she would conceive through the Holy Spirit and concludes his visitation with the message, "For nothing will be impossible with God."[1]

Mary assents to God's call and later, in a song of praise known as the *Magnificat*, extols God's greatness and her own humility. After the birth of Jesus in Bethlehem and the visit of the Magi, she and Joseph flee to Egypt with Jesus to escape from Herod, who sees Jesus as a threat to his rule and plans to kill Him. Afterwards, she appears in the Gospels only a few more times. The most striking of these appearances is at Jesus' crucifixion when she stands with two other courageous women at the foot of the cross and watches her Son die. Her heart is indeed pierced by a sword as Simeon had prophesied years earlier when Jesus was an infant.

This limited account of Mary in the Gospels leaves us wondering about this extraordinary being and wanting to know more about her. As if responding to this desire, she states:

> You want to know of me and who I am. I am a mother. I am a lover. I am a woman. I am a girl. I am pure. I am love. I am light. And I am divine. It is no secret who I am. I am like you in every way, and you are like me in every way.

Mary as Mother

Mary describes herself first as a mother. This should not come as a surprise, for being a mother was and is one of her most important roles. The mother carries and nurtures life into being. Mary was the mother of Jesus, and she is the spiritual mother of us all. She is our Divine Mother, and we are her divine children. As our Divine Mother, she tells us:

I am the mother of all mothers. I have a great love. My love
is like God's love, but it is also a motherly love.

Like God, Mary loves us unconditionally and, like a mother, she
nurtures, guides, and protects us. Also like a mother, she speaks to us in
words that sometimes are soft and gentle, bringing us comfort and con-
solation, and at other times strong and firm, telling us what we need to
know but may not want to hear. As she points out:

The role of a mother is varied. Sometimes a mother needs to
be firm, and sometimes a mother needs to be soft. A mother
must wear many hats, and I must do that.

As our Divine Mother, she sees us lost in a world of darkness and living
under veils of illusion. She wants us to be free. She wants to fill us with
her love so that we can transform ourselves, our lives, and our world into
love. For this reason, she came two thousand years ago, and she comes
today. We need only open ourselves to her to feel her presence and the
vibration of her love. Letting us know she is always with us, she says:

I am not just in churches. If you take the time, you will find
me, see me, and hear me everywhere.

Mary reminds us, as she has throughout the ages, that she will guide us
back to God if only we allow her. She will help us overcome the obstacles
that prevent us from loving and becoming love. She knows our longings and
fears, our hopes and desires. She knows the pain we carry, the mistakes and
missteps we have made. And she knows the love and beauty we carry within.
She wants none of her children, no matter who we are or what we have done,
to be separated from love and from God. She desires to help us to heal our
deepest wound, to fulfill our innermost desire, and to know that we too are
beings of light and love. Describing further her role as mother, she states:

As a mother, I love all my children and all souls equally. One
is not greater or better than another in terms of my love for

them. Some please me more than others. Some serve me more than others. But I love them all the same. You are all children, learning and growing, and all equal souls, learning and growing. Just as in your world, you look at your children and are wiser and help them see what they do not see and grow into what they need to grow into, I do the same.

Speaking of her unconditional love, even when her children hurt her and themselves, she adds:

A parent who is a loving parent does not ridicule because the child does not know. The parent patiently waits and guides and helps the child to grow in ways they need to grow and do what they need to do. This is what I do with all my children. Some want to listen and some do not. Those who do not listen hurt me and themselves, but I still love them the same. This, too, you must do.

Mary's love and guidance are illustrated in a dream in which a woman who had recently died at an elderly age appeared dressed in white and surrounded by pink and golden light. She had not had an easy life, but maintained a special devotion to Mary as her spiritual mother, which grew in her later years as she found more time to devote to prayer. This woman said that she was in heaven. Attributing this to Mary, she stated, "Mary takes care of her own." These few words capture what our relationship with Mary can mean for us. Like this woman, we are one of Mary's own. If we turn to her, she will take care of us too, regardless of our religious affiliation, spiritual background, or personal history.

In several messages, Mary speaks of a mother's role. Just as Mary brought the Light of Jesus into the world, she wants our light, the Divine Child within us, to be born into the world, too. She says it is the special role of the mother to spark this light in her child with love:

It is the mother's job to teach her children love. But, even if the mother does not teach the child love, the child is a soul with many experiences and knows love. Really, what a mother is to do is to spark the light in the child with love. Many mothers do not do this. This is part of the problem in your world.

Sadly, she points out that some mothers do just the opposite of sparking the light in their children:

There are bad mothers who want to lead their children into darkness and suffering. Then they stand back and watch their children suffer and blame the world for it.

Mary urges parents to look deep within their children for the meaning of their lives. Distinguishing different levels of meaning, she clarifies, "I am not talking about the meaning the mind gives. I am talking about the meaning of truth within."

She also maintains that the mother should be the spiritual teacher of the child and the family. She explains that a woman has an innate spiritual power that makes her uniquely qualified for this role and that the husband, who in other ways is also a spiritual anchor to the family, should support her in this. She points out that, if the mother does not do this, then the family will not be a spiritual unit, but a group of people tied together in ways and for purposes unrelated to their spiritual identities and deeper truth.

As the Divine Mother, her essence is love, and all her children carry within them this same essence. When we open to this light, like a magical fire, it consumes our illusions and darkness, making way for the birth of the Divine Child within us. Then we enter into her womb, the womb of love itself, where we discover that we are the same fiery essence, the same miracle of love.

In a vision of truly stunning proportions, Mary shows herself as the womb of all God's creation and with all creation contained within her. In the vision, God appears in the form of a man, and Mary appears where God's face would be. Her womb occupies the place of God's mouth, while the earth, all the beings of the earth, and her Son

Jesus Christ are enclosed within her womb. She speaks of the meaning of this vision:

> God impregnated me with the earth and the people of the earth because I am His favorite creation. I am the Mother of all beings. In order to come here (to the earth), you have to come through me.

Then, alluding to the anguish a mother feels when she sees her children suffer, she states:

> I suffer because I am the mother of all the souls and the earth. As with a mother who has love and good intentions for her children, the child has free will and the mother is not responsible for the child's decisions. But I suffer anyway when I see my children suffer and make wrong decisions.

Mary is the Cosmic Mother with all God's creation contained within her. Nothing exists without her as mother. As the Cosmic Mother, she manifests her love throughout all creation, and our life and being are her love. She is what nurtures and sustains us and all beings. As her cosmic children, we carry within us all that she is. Yet this is so much greater than we can grasp until we become like her. She thus entreats us to devote ourselves to her so that we too become pure love:

> I am the Cosmic Mother. I am greater than any concept, any word, any perception, any thought. I do not fit into any category. I am beyond words. I am beyond experience. I am the Cosmic Mother. I will do and bring great things. Honor me and you will be taken care of. Devote your heart, your soul, your mind, your body, and your time to me. Devote everything to me. I am the Cosmic Mother.

Until we are like her, we can only bow before the grandeur of this extraordinary being, who tells us:

I am Mother Mary.
I am the Mother of Heaven. I am the Mother of Light.
I am the Mother of Love. I am the Mother of Joy.
I am the Mother of Truth. I am the Mother of Peace.

Mary as Lover

Mary says that she is a lover. Whether Mary and Joseph were lovers has been a source of much controversy. Some believe they were, while others accept the traditional view that they were not. Responding to a request to confirm that she and Joseph were lovers, she states unequivocally that she was a lover and goes on to describe what love-making is meant to be:

I told you I was a lover. When two people make love, God is present with them and in them. Joseph and I, when we would make love, would experience the divine rather than just the flesh. You see, in love-making, two bodies become one. One. One. Do you hear what I am saying? One. In this being one, the experience of being complete with God allows a human being to be one with the other, to be one with God, and to experience divinity. True love-making is not the hunger of the flesh alone. It is not the appetite for lust and beauty. It is the desire for love and being one with God.

Speaking further of her and Joseph as lovers, she describes how lovers should approach love-making:

You must feel the oneness, feel the love, and feel God present in the every second of the love-making. This is what Joseph and I experienced while in the flesh.

She also points out that love-making continues after lovers pass over to the other side, indicating that she and Joseph are still lovers:

As you know, love-making continues once one has shed the body. But it is different because it is the merging of Spirit. Yet it is the same sensation you can relate to as an orgasm.

In another vision, Mary discloses that she and Joseph had children together after Jesus was born. This would be expected since they had sexual relations. These children were Jesus' half-siblings because Jesus, according to Mary, was conceived through the Holy Spirit. Pointing out that the truth that she and Joseph were lovers and parents of other children is not found in Scripture, she states:

The Scriptures have been written and rewritten over the years. They are not exact. The truth has been watered down and distorted. There is truth in them, but it is not exact. It is twisted. I was not a virgin. I had relations with Joseph, and Jesus had siblings.

People accustomed to the traditional view of Mary may find it hard to accept that Mary was and is a lover. But she tells us the belief that she and Joseph lived a celibate life together is erroneous. She wants us to know the truth of her life as the mother of Jesus, and there are many reasons for this. One reason is that the distortion of the truth about her and Joseph as lovers has contributed greatly to the denigration of sex and its role as a powerful spiritual force that is meant, as Mary explains, to bring us into union with God. In the Christian world, sex has been commonly associated with sin, darkness, and evil. While some people may claim that they do not view sex in these ways, the association runs deep within Christian culture and the Western psyche. It is probably fair to say that few people raised within Western culture manage to avoid the pernicious effects of distorted views of sex, which are based in part on the false teaching that Mary and Joseph never consummated their marriage or their love for each other.

Mary not only tells us that she was and is a lover, but also shares what love-making is meant to be: a way for lovers to become one with each other, join with God, and experience divinity. What she describes is what we long to experience in romantic love: the fulfillment of what San Juan de la Cruz calls "love's urgent longings." In the opening of our heart to that special other in sexual intimacy, our desire to be one with the other, with God, and with our own divine essence can be fulfilled. Mary tells us that love-making is one of the ways, and perhaps the principal way, for romantic love to reach its highest expression.

Mary beckons us to the sacredness of love-making. Offering us the example of her own life, she reminds us not only that love-making is a sacred act, but one of the most sacred acts we can experience. Her words also illuminate love-making as an experience that brings us back to the original state of perfection in which we were one in love with another soul and with God. As Mary gently guides us back to the truth of what love-making is meant to be, she is restoring love-making to its proper place in God's plan for us to know and become one with Him.

Love-making is sometimes seen as an impediment to reaching God, something to be dispensed with as we strive for spiritual attainment. Mary's revelation that she and Joseph were lovers broadens our understanding of them in a way that serves to heal the split many people experience between body and Spirit. Our desire for love and God can be experienced in the flesh and at the same time lift us beyond the flesh into Spirit. Mary thus affirms that love-making in the flesh is a vital part of who we are as spiritual beings and that God has given us love-making as a means for us to know Him and for Him to enter us in a very intimate way. The body becomes a temple of the divine, a vessel of light, in love-making, and we are spiritual beings engaged in a most sacred act when we come together in love with another in sexual intimacy. The beauty and wisdom of God creating us as beings of both flesh and Spirit are seen in Mary's revelation of what she and Joseph experienced as lovers. She is telling us that, in the most essential aspects of our humanness, we can come to know and experience God and, ultimately, become lovers with God.

Mary's message is love, and love does not separate or divide. Some will find it difficult to accept that Mary and Joseph were lovers, while others will feel the truth of what she is saying. She gives us this information not to divide, but to heal us of misguided notions of sexuality that too often separate us further from God instead of bringing us closer to Him. Anticipating diverse reactions to these revelations, she states that the two views of her, as a virgin and as a lover, are both correct:

> I was a virgin when I conceived. Thereafter, I was not a virgin. So those who call me Virgin Mary are not wrong, and those who do not believe I was a virgin are not wrong either.

She further states:

> Do not worry about what the Church thinks about these visions or their position on my virginity. There are many who believe in me and know that I was not and am not a virgin. I conceived of the Holy Spirit, and I had relations with Joseph. The Catholic Church will oppose this. In your book, it will cause some people disbelief. Do not worry about that and do not worry about them. They do not know the truth. My relationship with Joseph was full, and in every way I was a woman.

What does it mean to be virgin? This is where part of the problem in understanding Mary arises. Mary explains what it is to be virgin:

> I was virgin in my heart and in my mind and in my body because I was pure in my heart and in my mind and in my body because I am and was and always have been pure. This does not mean I did not have sexual relations. My relations with Joseph were virgin. My relations with Joseph were and are pure. This makes me virgin.

Being virgin, then, is not about having sexual relations or not. It is about purity of heart, mind, and body. When we are pure in these ways, we can be virgin in the most intimate of relations and, like Mary, be virgin lovers. As Mary has said, we are called to be pure. When we bring this purity to our love-making, we can experience the fullness of what love-making is meant to be and what we are meant to be. The purer we are in heart, mind, and body, the more God comes alive in us and in our love-making. The light of God can grow within us and become brighter than a thousand suns. We can become towers of God as the divine fire within us melts away darkness and illusions. Then, like Mary, we can come to know God as the ultimate love and the ultimate lover.

However ordinary or mundane our experiences of love-making may seem at times, we can still recognize the truth of love-making. Love-making is always a sacred act, unless we choose to make it something different. To be a lover in love is a profound gift, and to experience this love sexually, if not misused, can open us to a vibration of light and love in which we can not only experience God, but also the Virgin Goddess, the creative power of pure love, that dwells within each of us.

Mary as Woman and Girl

Lest we overlook the fullness of her life, Mary reminds us that she was also a woman and a girl and continues to carry these parts of herself that she experienced when she walked the earth. As a woman, she was humble and wise, yet strong and courageous. At a young age, she took on an immense task, the full magnitude of which we may never grasp. Hers was a spiritual calling of the highest order. The spiritual life involves many things, not the least of which is intense conflict between powerful forces of light and darkness. It is not for the faint of heart. Contrary to many popular images of her, Mary says that at times she had to be more than just sweet and innocent:

> The power of love is a force beyond compare. In my times on earth, I was not just sweet and innocent. My heart was innocent, but much that I had to do would not be considered innocent. But everything I did was out of love and love for God. I am a source of power. I am a source of strength. You too must be a source of power and a source of strength. Do not fear. Be it.

Mary also held the capacity for a depth of relationship between a woman and a man. Her description of the love between her and Joseph leaves no doubt that she loved deeply and shared herself fully as a woman.

As a woman, she also was and is deeply humble and obedient. Her response to the angel Gabriel stands as one of the most singular acts of humility and submission to a higher calling ever recorded: "Here I am, the servant of the Lord; let it be with me according to your word."[2] Similarly, in the *Magnificat* she proclaims that God "has looked with favor on the lowliness of his servant."[3] Her submission to God's will reflects a deep wisdom that usually comes later in life, if at all, when we realize that true wisdom lies in following God's will and not our own.

As the Queen of Heaven, she continues to be humble before God. In a remarkable testament to her humility, she says that she still bows down to God and urges us to do the same:

> I still bow down to God. You too must bow down to God. I do not mean to get on your knees. I mean in your heart and in every action bow down to Him. I still bow down to God even though I am like Him.

As she speaks, she crosses her hands over her heart, then folds them in front of her heart as in prayer, and finally extends them upward toward God. As she performs this gesture over and over again, she says that she did it when she walked the earth and still does it now. Then, amidst the scent of roses, she reminds us that to love is the only thing that truly matters:

> Offer all of your hearts and all of yourselves to God and to each other. There is only one thing that truly counts, one thing that truly matters, and that is to truly love.

She concludes by stating about the hand gesture she was doing, "This is the most holy gesture you can do with your hands. Do it often."

Mary also reveals how she appeared while on the earth, as well as certain aspects of her earthly life. Showing herself as she looked while on the earth, she says:

> The face that you see is my face when I was a young girl. In terms of the standards of outward beauty of your times, I would not be considered a raving beauty. But again, according to the standards of your times, I would not be considered very much. I could not read, and I did not have much. In the eyes of the people in your world, I would not be considered anything grand or great.

Then, smiling and extending her hands upward to God, she exclaims:

> But in God's eyes I was and am grand and great. In my heart I knew I loved. In my heart I was pure, pure in love, pure in truth. What you should want to work for and desire is that which is truly grand and great. All those things that are not love and that are not God are not grand and great. Live for God's way, with the divine, in the divine, and as the divine.

On another occasion, Mary again shows herself as she looked when she was on the earth. A golden light glows in and around her, while her face expresses great joy and great pain, leaving no doubt that she carried both deeply in her heart. Despite her suffering, Mary kept alive within her the innocence of a girl. In many visions, she delights the heart with an innocence mixed with humor and childlike playfulness. She points out that many children have an innocence to their love that is divine. She urges us to live and love with this innocence:

> It is the innocence of a child's love that all beings must carry, must know, and must display. It is the love that is innocent which will bring peace. Those souls who come in and love with a child's love—so innocent—their love is beauty, their love

is precious and kind and unconditional, and their love can warm the coldest heart.

The challenge for us, as it was for Mary, is to love with the innocence of a child in a world in which we encounter so much darkness and suffering. Her life stands as a model of how we can love with the innocence of a child even while experiencing great pain. She says that she knew her Son would be murdered and this was a terrible burden for her to carry as a mother. Yet, not only did she continue to love, she loved with the precious innocence of a child.

Mary exemplifies for both women and men alike the grace, power, and beauty of the feminine. When we honor the feminine and allow the feminine to be alive in us, we know this grace, power, and beauty. Conversely, when we fail to honor the feminine, these qualities are lost to us and the world. Mary embodied the feminine while she walked the earth and continues to embody it. Giving us the example of her life, she illumines what the feminine can be for us and our world. Indeed, as mother, lover, woman, and girl, she is the model of feminine virtue.

Mary as Pure, Love, and Light

Mary is pure, love, and light, and in our essence we, too, are all these. Yet we are not pure, love, and light in all of our being. We strive to achieve this God-like state on the spiritual path. So we are like Mary, but not like her. Mary makes this point when she speaks of her purity and what it means to be pure. Surrounded by a brilliant white light, with twelve stars circling her halo and an unusually powerful energy emanating from her, she declares:

> I am pure. I am strong and very powerful. I laugh and cry. I am like you. I am like every being. My being is different in that every part of me is pure. This does not mean what you think. It means pure in love. My entire being is God-like. This is what is when one is pure, pure in love. This does not mean that the dark side does not exist. It simply means that the dark side cannot tolerate my purity and my light, my

God-like existence. You see, I am pure. All pure. My way is
pure. My love is pure. My heart is pure.

Then, stating that God and she desire that we be pure, she continues:

But I can see all over that which is not pure. It is the desire
of God that all know and be the purity within. It is my desire
that all know and be the purity within.

The belief in Mary's purity has a long history. Officially recognized
by the Catholic Church in the Dogma of the Immaculate Conception, it
holds that Mary came into the world "preserved from all stain of sin."
Mary confirms this in a vision, stating:

I never fell from the side of God. I have always been at His
side and been in love with Him and loved Him above all
things. Because of my love for God, I came here and lived out
the play and had the human experiences, knowing I would
give birth to and lose my Son. I did this out of love for God.

She adds:

Few come into this life pure. I came into this life pure. I came
in ready to accept all God wanted me to do.

Although Mary was pure, it was up to her to remain pure. She says
that during her lifetime as the mother of Jesus she was tempted. Like
every soul who comes into this world, she was faced with choices between
light and darkness, especially at critical points in her life. She carried
what must have felt like the weight of the world on her shoulders from
the moment Gabriel came to her. In other words, she did not have a free
ride, even given her exalted role as the mother of God's Son. Yet, at every
turn she chose the light, maintaining the purity with which she came into
the world. She never ceased to be in love with God and to love God above
all else.

Mary often speaks of love, reminding us that God is love. In several messages, she distinguishes between love and religion. For example, identifying her religion as love, she states:

> Remember, my religion is love. Some of what religions teach is not true. But when they speak of love, they speak of truth. And this is my religion.

Cautioning us not to be caught up in the details of religion, she adds, "The details of one's religion are not God. God is love, and God's message is love." At another time, appearing alongside the face of the Buddha, she further asserts:

> The essence of all religions is the same. If anyone uses religion to separate people, they are not living the word of Christ, and they are not spreading love and light. Dogma is created by men, and it is not of the light in any religion.

Jesus similarly states that truth is found not in dogma but in love:

> It is not dogma that breathes the truth. It is love that breathes the truth. To love is the greatest truth. It is the greatest service. With love and in love, you see and know all things.

Mary contends that religions have failed to teach love. In a message in which she reiterates that she is love and speaks of what love is, she reproaches her Church for not teaching love:

> I am love and my Church should be teaching love. Love is not a form of control. Love is free. Love is alive. Love is peace. Love is all beauty. Love is all-encompassing. Love is truth. Love is light. Love is purity. Love is God.

Maintaining that all religions have fallen short in being and teaching love, she further declares:

There is one truth that all religions are meant to be and teach, which is love. Because of man's many flaws, they turn religion into something of their own will, which is not love.

According to Mary, when we become pure in love, we become light. She equates love with light and associates both with God. For example, she states, "God is light. God is love. When one is not in light or love, one is not in God." She likewise asserts, "Love is our Lord's way, and the way of light." At another time, she explains, "In love one sees and knows all things, one is the light, and one becomes the truth."

Mary is reminding us that light is the nature of pure love and God. It is a manifestation of divine love. It is what Jesus is and what He brought into the world. It is what the darkness cannot grasp or tolerate. It is also what the Kingdom of God is and what we will return to when we join with God. It is the light from which we were created and which we long to become. It is the light we will be if we so choose. It is what Mary is and what she calls each of us to:

> I am always present. Those who want to receive and know the light and become the light are welcome to the light. I am always looking for ways to awaken and reach my children.

One of the most striking aspects of Mary's appearances is the light with which she comes. In some visions, she appears in her essence of white light, while in others she appears surrounded by brilliant colors, including golds, violets, blues, and pinks. At other times, she fills the space in which she appears with radiant colors. She is showing us that she comes to bring light into a dark world and to teach us about light. It is vitally important, she says, that we understand the nature of light and its relation to love and God, especially now when the world is increasingly besieged by darkness. She notes that light and darkness have been in conflict since the beginning of time and this conflict is now reaching its climax and that in these precarious times turning to the light is increasingly a matter of survival on every level. Speaking of what the light can do for us, she explains:

The light can turn anything into light. If you become light,
you can make anything light around you.

Mary as Divine

Finally, what does Mary mean when she says she is divine? She is divine
in her essence of pure love and light, and she is one with God. This does
not mean, though, that she is God. Although she is one with God, she does
not lose her status as a discrete being. This is illustrated in visions in which
she appears as one with God or with Jesus, but she is still seen as distinct.
When we become one with God, we too will be divine, but will not lose
our unique identities.

Although she is not God, Mary has what can only be described as a very
special relation to Him. This is shown in a vision in which God appears in
the form of a man, with strong and powerful masculine features, and states:

> I am everywhere. I will come into you, and you can come into
> me any time you truly desire it.

From out of a narrow rectangle, extending from His mid-forehead to His
chin, Mary appears surrounded by an amber glow. Motioning to God, she
says, "I come from Him." Then God, responding to Mary, declares:

> She comes from me. The greatest beauty is that which comes
> from me. She is the love of all my loves.

So, while Mary refers to herself as divine, she is not saying she is God.
She bows before God and is the love of His loves, but she is not God.
Rather, she comes as what might be called a special emissary of God, as
His feminine side. In an extended message in which she speaks of her role
in today's world, Mary describes herself as the feminine side of God and
again reminds us that we cannot fully grasp who and what she is. She also
speaks of Jesus and their relationship:

> My Son came as man and came in the masculine form. But
> God is not masculine and God is not feminine. God is beyond

all concept. I come as the feminine side. I am the feminine side of God. But I am beyond all concept and all form. My Son is the light. I am the light. We are one. I come with the force of all of God. I come with the power of all of God. I come with the light of all of God. God and I are one. My Son and I are one. I am coming with new life, new possibility. I am coming with light. I am light. My Son came with light and new possibility. He shifted the balance and the darkness for the possibility of love and light to exist. I come to save my children. I am the Mother. It is the time of the Goddess. I am the Cosmic Goddess, the Queen of Heaven and Earth. I am the Queen of the Universe. I am the Queen of Light. I am the Queen of Love. I am the Queen of Peace. I am the Queen of Possibility. I am the Queen of Hope. I am the Queen, the Mother. I am the Mother of all, and I wrap my love and my light around all. It is those who love with an open heart who recognize and receive me. But I come for all. It is one simple thing I come to bring, and this is love. I am love and all loving. My Son and I are one. We have never been separated. We will always be one.

In another vision, in which Mary appears with God, Jesus, and the Holy Spirit, she again illustrates her special status in relation to God. The face of God appears. Mary is beneath Him, Jesus is beneath her, and the Holy Spirit is beneath the three of them. A stream of light flows from the Holy Spirit and moves upward carrying God, Mary, and Jesus.

As much as Mary reveals about herself, we cannot fully grasp the immensity of who and what she is, just as we cannot grasp the immensity of who and what we are. It is only when we enter fully into our essence of love and light that we will be able to know our own divinity and thereby know hers. She again reminds us of this when she appears larger-than-life on a cross, and in her face is the Eastern symbol of the yin-yang. As this symbol fades and the sun and moon appear in its place, she proclaims:

I am all things. I am positive and negative. I am masculine and feminine. I am beyond all that one perceives. I am in the face of God, and I am the light of God. I am coming as the Mother to try to save my children. It is by becoming pure in heart and pure in love that one becomes awake, that one knows that they are all and all is they, and that they are beyond anything which is perceived.

From the Ordinary to the Extraordinary

Mary is calling us to be like her, to move from the ordinary into the extraordinary. We may feel that we are ordinary, but Mary reminds us we are not. We have within us the purity, love, and light that she does. And, as souls created from the breath of God, our natures are divine like hers. Once again reminding us that we are like her in every way, she affirms:

You are like me. That is the beauty of all this. I was simply ordinary, and you have inside of you what I have inside of me.

It is possible for all of us to become divine, Mary says, but few of us can do it on our own. She explains, "To become a divine being, you need a divine being." Mary is offering herself to us, as her Son did, as that divine being. She comes to help us cross waters too deep for us to cross alone and to guide us to that seemingly distant shore where we too will know ourselves as pure love and once again be lovers joined as one with God.

CHAPTER THREE

An Untold Love Story

 MARY AND JOSEPH WERE CALLED BY GOD to fulfill a mission together as the parents of Jesus, and they fulfilled it impeccably. Yet their lives were about more than that mission. We learn from them that romantic love was and continues to be a vital part of their relationship. Based on what they share about their life together, it exemplifies how two souls can strive for and achieve a purity of love in a romantic relationship.

The relationship between Mary and Joseph is one of the great love stories of all time. A story of passion and commitment, it confirms what we sometimes feel deeply within ourselves: that romantic love in some mysterious way is connected to the miracle of divine love and to the purpose for which we are here. Standing in sharp relief to most contemporary models of romantic relationship, their relationship shows us how romantic love can be a path for lovers to move from human to divine love and join with God.

A Love That Is Pure

When we listen to Mary and Joseph describe their relationship and love for each other, we can sense that we are in the presence of something extraordinary. Mary speaks of the purity of their love for each other and how it was born out of their love of God:

> Joseph and I loved each other in a pure way. This is the way of God's love, not simply human love. In order to experience pure love, you must know God intimately, and He will be alive in you. Human love has a beauty. But human love is limited. This is where the problems come in. In human love, one does not love unconditionally. I honored, listened to, loved, and obeyed Joseph. This is what must be done in love that is pure.

As she goes on to talk of Joseph and their relationship, she further identifies the purity of their love with God:

> Joseph was an old man. He was a man who loved love. He loved me and gave to me and honored me and listened to me. He and I were one, one love. He was the strength. He was the pillar. But he did not make me any less. In divine love, in pure love, this is the case always. In that love you are everything to the other, and the other is everything to you. And in that love God is that everything.

Then, showing herself as she appeared while on the earth, she says that her and Joseph's love for each other made them who they are:

> Real love has nothing to do with outward beauty. Look at me. I was not what one would consider a beauty. Nor was Joseph what one would consider a beauty. On the other hand,

our love was so grand that all considered us a beauty. It was the love who made us who we are.

At another time, Joseph appears as a being of light, with distinct and clearly recognizable features. He is an older man, tall, thin, and handsome. His hair is brown, wavy, and mixed with some grey. His face is long, with fine lips and a well-defined chin with a beard. His nose is long, thin, and classic-looking. He speaks of his relationship to Mary, who is surrounded by light and standing near to him:

> I am always here. I am always with her. She is my love, my bride, my queen. I never let her out of my sight. I am here always. I am near her, with her, and in her always. She is my queen, my love, my other half. She is in me, and I am in her.

Mary responds:

> I am the Queen of Light. I am here to bring you light. The world has become so dim and dark. I am here to bring light. My love is vast.

She looks at Joseph and continues:

> For he is mine, and I am his. This has always been and will always be. We are one, and one we are. We are together always, always together. I come to bring light into the dark world, and he is with me and in me. This is the way it is to be. We are one, and one we are.

Joseph, turning to Mary, then says, "She is my love and my lady." He reaches his hand out toward her, and the light from each of them creates a ball of light around them, joining them as one. Joseph concludes by stating, "This is what always is and will always be."

On another occasion, Mary says that she and Joseph gave all their minds, bodies, and souls to each other and urges lovers to do the same:

Do not fear giving all your mind, your body, your soul. This
is what I did with Joseph and he with me.

Then, speaking of giving from the heart, she adds:

When your heart opens and you give all from the heart, God
is present and life lives in you. This is what Joseph and I have.

Mary acknowledges Joseph's role in what she accomplished in their
life together. In a beautiful testimony to his love of and devotion to her,
she says, "Joseph was the wind beneath my wings."

Mary explains that their love for each other became pure when they
began to see through the "eyes of God" or what she describes on other
occasions as "the eyes of love":

Joseph and I began to love purely and our love became pure
when we began to see through the eyes of God.

They could see through the eyes of God only by knowing God
intimately and by God being alive in them. This, Mary explains, made
their love pure and joined them together, while still on the human plane,
in a mystical union with each other and with God. In the purity of their
love, a distinction did not exist between their love for each other and for
God. Thus, when our love is pure, loving the beloved above all else is the
same as loving God above all else.

It is easy to overlook the fact that Mary and Joseph were human. Mary
reminds us that she and Joseph were people with ordinary experiences, yet
they still loved God above else, as Mary shares in the following message:

While we were on earth, we were people, people who suffered,
struggled, loved, laughed, cried, and ultimately loved God
above all things. Remember that we love each other above all
things because our love is God and our oneness is oneness
with God. This is truth, and it is true for you. I say to you:
Love is most important. Love!

Mary and Joseph achieved on a human level the original state of perfection in which they were one in love with each other and with God. Joseph states that Mary is his other half. Mary confirmed this in a vision, indicating that she and Joseph were created as one. Through the purity of their love, they came to experience, while in the flesh, the original state of oneness in which they were first created. Affirming her oneness with both Joseph and God, as well as with Christ, the incarnation of divine love, she states:

> I am one with God, and God is one with me. I am one with Christ, and Christ is one with me. I am one with Joseph, and Joseph is one with me. I am love.

God-Centered Lives

Mary and Joseph loved God above all else. Scripture tells us of their great love of God expressed in their selfless response to His calling and unwavering submission to His will. A hallmark of love of God is submission to His will, which means aligning ourselves with love, for God's will is love. Jesus reminds us of this when He says that the phrase in the *Our Father,* "Thy will be done," is asking that love be done. When we submit to God's will, when we bow before the power and beauty of love, then we come to know God intimately, as did Mary and Joseph.

Mary and Joseph were people who suffered, struggled, loved, laughed, and cried. Yet they loved God above else and gave all of themselves to God. Mary says of her experience of giving all to God:

> I too turned up to God and gave all to God, everything. Do you see who I am? I am the mother of Christ, and He was murdered on the cross. I suffered to see my Son die, and to know this was to come was deadly to a mother's heart. Yet I trusted in God and in God's love and truth. This, too, you must do.

Joseph likewise shares his experience:

Many things are untold and many truths have been hidden. I had my struggles, but my main focus was the will of God. A part of that was keeping Mary. She is my greatest love as woman, as wife, and as divine creature.

Their lives were centered on God, and the sacrifices they made are reflected in the details of their life. Mary describes their life as simple and at times impoverished. She says that she and Joseph had very little, but worried about the future far less than most people today who enjoy lives of great material abundance. Describing their life of material scarcity and at the same time reminding us that we are not of this world, she states:

> You are not your experiences, and you are not of this world. You must break free. When I was in human form, I had nothing. I had no bank account, no jewels, no sense of security in the human way. I had a child on the way, and I had nothing to offer him. When I turned for help, people turned me away. When my Son was born and He turned for help, people turned Him away. We struggled, and we did without.

She then presents scenes of her and Joseph's life. In the first scene, she is pregnant and asking people for food and being turned away. She next shows a dwelling where she and Joseph lived. Made of stone, it was a shack, not much more than a shelter, with a dirt floor and a wooden roof. It is obvious that they had very little. She is then at another location. She is very pregnant, and she and Joseph are seeking shelter. They walk from door to door, but no one takes them in. Each time they are refused, they simply turn away. They are very humble. It seems like a cold time of year because they are dressed in several layers of clothing. Their garments are simple and coarse and made from material that looks similar to gunny sack. In the final scene, she shows herself and Joseph with Jesus as a boy and again having little.

While having little in the material world, Mary and Joseph had everything in the spiritual world. They had a love of God and their love for each other. As Mary has said many times, love is the only thing that matters. There is a wisdom in what she is sharing with us about her life. It is not that poverty is a virtue. It is that, to the extent that we are entangled in the things of the world, we will find it all the more difficult to love.

Mary and Joseph lived a simple life, but it was not without peril. When Jesus was an infant, they fled into Egypt to save Jesus' life. Herod had learned of Jesus' birth and wanted to kill Him, believing Him to be a threat to his own rule. An angel told Joseph in a dream that Herod had intended to find and kill Jesus and that Joseph must take his family and flee immediately to Egypt. Joseph left for Egypt with Mary and Jesus the same night, saving Jesus from certain death. In a desperate attempt to destroy Jesus, Herod ordered all the children under the age of two in and around Bethlehem to be killed. Several years later, after Herod's death, an angel again came to Joseph in a dream and told him that it was safe for him and his family to return from Egypt.

As Mary and Joseph's story shows, the light does not go unchallenged. Mary and Joseph were beings of light and had in their care the Light of the world. They undoubtedly encountered many perils. Referring to the dangers of the spiritual path, Joseph speaks of the need for total commitment:

> In the world of Spirit there are many dangers. If one does not commit all to the path and to love, then one can be destroyed.

If Mary and Joseph had not committed all, they would not have succeeded in their mission or in their love for each other. But they did commit all, fulfilling their mission and sealing their love for eternity.

A Different Way

Mary and Joseph share the story of their love and life together because they want to bring healing to the spiritual malady at the heart of many people's lives. We desire love, and relationship is natural to us. We suffer greatly when we live without love or in a relationship in which love was never present or has waned. We also harm ourselves when we misuse love-making and fail to see its power to open us to the divine. Mary and Joseph are showing us a different way to approach romantic love and love-making.

Their message is especially germane today. They remind us that our longing for love in a human relationship is indeed tied to the purpose for which we have come into the world. In sharing the truth about their relationship, they are telling us that romantic relationship is about moving from human to divine love. They experienced the miracle of divine love in their love for each other, and they are offering us a different view of romantic love so that we too can experience the same miracle.

Mary's view of romantic love takes romantic relationship and love-making out of the realm of the profane and into the realm of the sacred. A relationship that is experienced as profane invariably leads to a dead end. We become stuck energetically and unable to grow spiritually. On the other hand, when a relationship is experienced as sacred, it becomes aligned with our life purpose, infusing it with new meaning and opening it to unimagined possibilities. This is because, as we embrace the sacredness of the relationship and open our hearts to love, God comes alive within us. And, as Gabriel told Mary, nothing is impossible with God.

In this approach to romantic love, it may appear that lovers could be overly focused on their love for each to the exclusion of others. Most of us are surrounded by family, friends, coworkers, and others. Love is an energy that moves outward and touches others. So the more we are filled with love, the more that love will touch those around us. Moreover, as Mary says, "When you learn to love one other person unconditionally, you can then love others unconditionally." Through romantic love we can learn to love another and then others unconditionally.

There are many paths to God, and not everyone is called to find God through romantic love. As Jesus reminds us, "There is no one right way to get to love. All that matters is love and that you love." However, for those called to romantic love as a spiritual path, being in love with another opens the door to being in love with God. While any relationship in which love is present can bring us closer to God, this occurs in a special way with romantic love. Some of the reasons are discussed in the following section, as Mary and Jesus speak of the role of sexual energy and marriage in bringing two souls joined in love back to God.

PART TWO

Sexual Energy and Sacred Relationship

CHAPTER FOUR

The Sacred Energies of Love-Making

MARY SAYS WE ARE CALLED TO BE pure love and light. We will find it difficult to reach this pinnacle of spiritual attainment if we do not know about the energies that are tightly interwoven with our spiritual destinies. These energies, when understood and used properly, are critical to the experiences through which we will become pure love and light. One of these experiences is love-making. Mary has already told us that love-making was the way she and Joseph came to a oneness with each other, with God, and with their highest truth. Now she tells us how love-making and the energies involved in it have the power to transform lovers in this way. Jesus also speaks of love-making, its energies, and their role for us as spiritual beings.

Mary sees that many souls whom she seeks to help, especially those in the Christian world, do not know about these energies. She wants us to know about them and to use them to heal and transform ourselves and the world. Together with Jesus, she imparts this understanding so that we will know love-making as one of the most powerful means we have to bring light into ourselves and the world. She is also attempting to remedy one of the principal maladies facing people today: the misuse of sexual energy. How we relate to this energy, she tells us, is one of the most important factors shaping the spiritual destiny of each of us and the world.

The Energy Field and Energy Centers

People in cultures throughout the world have long known that the human body is surrounded and permeated by an energy field. This field, sometimes referred to as the aura, consists of the energies of various subtle, or non-physical, bodies. These subtle bodies and their energies, which can be seen by some people, are critical factors in our physical, emotional, mental, and spiritual well-being. Many traditions have incorporated knowledge of these energies into spiritual practices and healing.

One of these subtle bodies is commonly referred to as the energy body. This "body" is the mold for the physical body and provides it with the energy to sustain its functioning on every level. It has seven primary energy centers and many smaller ones. These energy centers, which extend outward like funnels a few inches in front of the physical body, are also called chakras, meaning "wheels of light" in Sanskrit. They are seen as wheels of light when they are open and their energies are spinning. The seven major centers are located in parts of the energy body corresponding to the following parts of the physical body: the base of the spine, just below the navel, the solar plexus, the center of the chest near the heart, the throat, the midpoint of the forehead just above the eyebrows, and the crown of the head.

The energy body and these centers are directly linked to our health. When the energy centers are open and their energies are flowing, we feel stronger and more alive, and our personalities have a greater power and creative force. Persons with an abundance of energy are often experienced as charismatic. When the centers are blocked or their energies depleted, our energy field is diminished. We become weakened and feel physically, mentally, or emotionally drained. We often feel lethargic and lose the "bounce" we may normally have. When this occurs, the energy field is actually decreased in size. The weakening of the energy field can be temporary or chronic. If chronic, it can result in physical disease or emotional or mental imbalances. The energy field and centers are also vitally important to our spiritual well-being and to the attainment of higher levels of spiritual growth and awareness.

Energy, Consciousness, and Spirit

Our energy field is a mirror of our consciousness. Mary says, "What one thinks, what one acts, and what one lives are in one's energy." The energy field thus reflects what we carry mentally and emotionally on conscious and unconscious levels. Our emotions and thoughts are forms of energy that are interwoven into our energy fields. For example, we hold memories of past experiences, whether we are conscious of them or not, in our energy fields.

Much can be learned through "reading" a person's energy field, although few people have the ability to do this. Positive thoughts and emotions are generally reflected in positive flows and vibrant colors of energy, while negative thoughts and emotions are generally reflected in constricted flows and dark shades of energy. This is true even for thoughts and emotions that we may be unaware of. Actually, what we believe we think and feel on a conscious level is often belied by what is reflected in our energy fields. In this regard, the energy field, which has multiple levels, is closely linked to the unconscious mind. For instance, a person can become conscious of a memory and release the emotions associated with it, and this is often reflected in the energy field as a change in the flow or color of energy.

One's level of spiritual attainment is also reflected in the energy field. A person who is spiritually advanced will be surrounded by a field that is expanded and filled with white light or vibrant rainbow hues. This is because spiritual attainment is directly connected to the amount of light we carry. Without an abundance of energy, we cannot contain Spirit within us or live at higher levels of awareness. A person who is highly developed spiritually can enter a room, and the room will be filled with light, lifting everyone in the room to a higher vibration of energy. On the other end of the spiritual spectrum, a person who has chosen to reject the light will often be seen surrounded by dark energies.

Knowledge of these types of energies, and even the ability to see them, need not be viewed as esoteric. We have the innate ability to see these energies, but for most people it is lost because it never was encouraged or developed in childhood. If we were to teach children to use this innate ability, they would not lose it. If more people could see and work with these energies, it would make a significant difference in every area of our lives, including education, religion, medicine, and how we structure our home and work environments. We would be more sensitive to people, activities, and places that bring us more energy, as well as to those that harm us energetically.

Just as our consciousness affects our energy field, the converse is also true: Our energy field affects our consciousness. This is important because what we do and how we do it will impact us energetically, and any ensuing changes of energy will, in turn, affect us physically, emotionally, mentally, or spiritually. Many types of prayer and spiritual practices are based on this principle. They alter the quality and flow of energy and expand the amount of energy we carry, thereby bringing about a change of consciousness. Likewise, something as simple as physical exercise makes us feel differently because it shifts our energy, affecting us not just physically but also in other ways.

Mary and Jesus discuss the energy field and centers and their importance for our spiritual growth. For example, when they speak of opening the heart, they are referring to the energy center located in the center of the chest near to the heart. Similarly, when they speak of seeing through the "eyes of love," they mean seeing through the spiritual eye located in the energy center in the forehead, when the heart center is also open. In many visions, they have shown their energy centers and fields, which are immense and filled with light of incredible beauty.

In a vision, Mary illustrates how the energy centers are connected to each other and to Spirit. She shows her heart, throat, and third-eye centers. A cross is in her heart center, with a violet light in the center of the cross. Deep within the center of the heart, wherein lies the Sacred

Heart, all levels of existence can be seen. Her throat center is filled with an orange and red light. She says to speak the truth and to speak it firmly. The Holy Spirit in the form of a dove is in her third eye. A ribbon of purple and white light connects these three centers and flows down to the energy center at the base of the spine, where there is a tremendous amount of energy.

Identifying the Holy Spirit with the energy of each center, she counsels, "Call upon the Holy Spirit for healing, discernment, guidance, and truth." She also instructs, "Use the combination of the lower and higher chakras to bring about a higher vibration within you." She is telling us that we can bring the Spirit into us through the energy centers, creating a higher vibration within us as we bring together the energy of the different centers. This vibration can then be brought into the heart center to open it more and cleanse it, making way for access to the secret chamber of the heart and the Sacred Heart, depicted in this vision as all levels of existence.

Sexual Energy

The most powerful energy we carry is our sexual energy. This energy corresponds to the energy centers at the base of the spine and just below the navel. These energies are also called the life-force because we use them to create and sustain life. More specifically, the life-force energy is usually identified with the energy center at the base of the spine and sexual energy with the center just below the navel. During intercourse these energies join together, the life-force energy of the lower center moving into the second center and merging with the sexual energy. We therefore refer to them interchangeably as sexual or life-force energies, depending on the context in which they are used.

Sexual energy is a titanic force. When it is used as an expression of love, it fills us with light. However, when it is used apart from love, we harm ourselves and others. In one of several messages in which Jesus speaks of sexual energy, He states:

> This is a force of power and creativity. It should be used only
> for love. If it is used for anything but love, it is destructive.

It is destructive to the doer and the receiver. Each person has this truth deep within their hearts. They know and feel the truth of this powerful force. It is the force that creates and how it is used is up to each individual. If you use it at its highest potential, which is divine love, then you create the world as a heaven, an ideal that is possible through love.

Describing the purpose of this energy, He adds:

The energy itself is not wrong. It is the creative life-force that takes you to higher levels and understanding. It is man who misuses it. But the energy itself is not wrong. It is man who distorts it with thoughts of lust, of sex. Its true purpose is to love, to create, to move beyond.

Jesus tells us that the use of sexual energy must be connected to love in order for us to experience it as the creative and transformative force that it is. This means that we must bring an open heart to sexual intimacy. It is only then that sexual intimacy is love-making and not mere sex, as Mary explains:

The sexual energies must be connected to the heart and love. There is much power within this. Love-making is sacred and holy. When love-making is connected to the heart, the pleasures are far greater than any physical experience.

Mary equates sexual energy not only with the Holy Spirit, but also with the feminine aspect of God. One of the ways that we come to know the feminine side of God, then, is through sexual energy. Identifying sexual energy as spiritual, Mary states:

This is a time for people to develop their spiritual energies, including their sexual energy. Develop it, refine it, and perfect it in the ways you use it. Think about it and speak about it. There is a tremendous power in sexual energy. You call it sexual energy, but it is far greater. It is the female aspect of God. It is bliss and power, and it is to be used with tremendous respect, honor, and dignity. It is not of the genitals and should not be maintained at such a mundane level.

Mary likewise reminds us that the body is a form of energy meant to be a vessel of light. When we experience the body as merely physical, and not as energy, we limit ourselves and what we can attain while in embodiment. Mary explains:

> The body is a form of energy. You have made it into something it is not. On other levels, beings are pure light, and they are formless. Here (referring to the material plane) you have form, and this limits you.

We are meant to use our sexual energy, as Jesus states, to love, create, and move into higher levels of awareness and existence. The proper use of sexual energy allows us to do these things, which is why our understanding of sexual energy and what we do with it greatly influences our spiritual destinies. Underscoring the power of sexual energy, Mary states, "Sexual energy can heal or kill." How sexual energy affects us will hinge largely on whether we have a correct understanding of this energy and whether we choose to use it for the purposes for which it is intended.

In many traditions, this energy is honored as the supreme creative power of the Absolute Being and its role in spiritual evolvement is well-known. In Hinduism, it is called *shakti* or *kundalini*, the latter meaning "coiled serpent." An Eastern sage writes:

> The awakening of the inner Kundalini is the true beginning of the spiritual journey. Just as when She is directed outward, Kundalini enables us to explore the outer world, when her inner aspect is activated, we are able to experience the inner spiritual world. The Scriptures say that as long as the inner Kundalini is sleeping, it doesn't matter how many austerities

we follow, how much yoga we practice, or how many mantras we repeat, we will never realize our identity with the inner Self. We will never know our own divinity, or understand God, or experience the all-pervasiveness of Consciousness. In our present state, we identify ourselves with the body which has a certain size and shape. We are not aware that we are all-pervasive. It is only when the Kundalini is awakened that we become aware of our true nature, of our greatness, of the fact that not only do we belong to God but we are God. If our shakti hasn't been awakened, then even if God were to take a form and appear before us, we wouldn't be able to know Him or experience Him as He truly is.[1]

One of the most accessible ways of awakening this life-transforming energy is love-making, when lovers come together with open hearts and a genuine and passionate commitment to each other and to love.

Love-Making and Orgasm

The energies we feel so strongly in the body are not meant to separate us from God, but to bring us into union with God. Love-making is a vehicle that brings to life in us energies that connect us to God. Mary has spoken of this in her description of love-making as the way she and Joseph became one with each other and with God. In another message, she adds:

> Love-making will bring you closer to God. In the love-making, the physical pleasure and the union are a symbol of something far greater beneath. This understanding of love-making is known by very few. You should know it as a sacred act and as a vehicle of union with each other and with God.

What happens in love-making that brings about this union? During love-making, there is a powerful movement of energy in the energy centers, especially the two lower centers and the heart center, as well as throughout the energy field. In the heat of passion, the energies in the two lower centers begin to spin more rapidly and vibrate more intensely, making of these centers a boiling cauldron of power and light. This causes these energies to expand and multiply as they flow back and forth between the lovers. Some people may feel this as a strong tingling sensation or a heightened sense of pleasure.

The sexual energy then begins to flow upward through the lovers' physical and energy bodies, while the heart centers of the lovers open to the energy of the divine essence each carries within. These energies merge as a single force as they meet in the heart center. Once joined, they move upward into the energy centers in the throat, the center of the forehead, and the crown of the head, as well as into many smaller centers through-out the energy body. This causes all these centers to open more and their energies to vibrate with greater intensity, creating a further expansion of the lovers' energy fields as thousands of what appear to be small, multi-colored molecules of light are created in and around the lovers. These energies move with the lovers and vibrate as light of different colors around them. The lovers experience a growing intensity of energy which builds toward a volcanic explosion of light and love within their physical and energy bodies. The love-making culminates in orgasm, opening the lovers to a cosmic space outside time and beyond form.

The expansion and flow of energy in love-making occur only when love is present. Then it is a spiritual experience. When love is not present, Mary says, it is merely "sex for sex's sake." When love is present, it makes of the experience something we cannot fully comprehend, as Mary tells us:

> It is important to do it with love. It is a spiritual experience. It is not an experience of the flesh. If it is an experience of the flesh, it is having sex for sex's sake. With love, it is far beyond this. You really do not grasp it, just as you really do not grasp God. It is too much to grasp what it really means.

During love-making, and especially at the moment of orgasm, it is as if a veil lifts and the lovers are now in touch with a cosmic love. As the energy of love-making takes the lovers out of their ordinary consciousness, they open to a direct experience of the divine. They feel a heightened sense of physical pleasure, and at the same time their souls experience a state of bliss and freedom beyond the physical. In the orgasm's explosion of love and light, they experience the energy of divine love most intensely.

Thus, in love-making two people come together, open in body, mind, heart, and soul. Intimate in love, they join together and become one. They move together with pleasure toward an ecstatic moment beyond words, thoughts, forms, and separateness. They join with each other, move into a state of bliss, and experience the divine. Love-making is a gift from God through which we can, as Jesus states, love, create, and move beyond. This is because love-making allows us to release the small self and the ordinary mind and experience the true self, the mind of love. Then we let go of all that we think we are and move into something that cannot be grasped through concepts or ideas. In love-making, and especially at the moment of orgasm, we know divine love. For a moment we experience bliss and step into eternity. As we surrender to love, to another, and to God, the seed of the divine within us comes to life, and we have a direct experience of the divine. While still in the flesh, we know and experience God intimately. It is a knowing of the true mind, the intellect of the heart, only through which a direct experience of the divine is possible.

Mary says that few people recognize the real power and purpose of love-making and orgasm:

> So, so many do not recognize the sacred and the divine in love-making and orgasm. How many stop to think for one moment of the miracle that is love-making. To be able to join intimately in love with another is a miracle. To be able to orgasm and be in another state for even a moment, to know God's existence, love, in the orgasm is a miracle. It is a blessing. It is far beyond a physical pleasure. To see or experience love-making and orgasm as a physical pleasure is a limitation of their true nature.

We long for love, union, wholeness. We find in love-making and orgasm a temporary satisfaction of this longing, one that beckons us to a permanent satisfaction. We feel for a moment the fulfillment of our innermost longing and the healing of our deepest wound. We connect with the pure love and light that we desire to become. The experience is temporary only because we have not yet attained the ability to sustain the vibration of pure love. When we do this, we no longer experience for just a moment the miracle of love: We become the miracle.

When we see love-making as a way to experience the divine, it becomes for us a sacred act. What may at first seem like only physical pleasure becomes spiritual as well, as the part of us that is Spirit moves into union with the Great Spirit, with God. Love-making, then, is love joining with love, as the love of the lovers joins with God, the source of all love. This is felt most intensely at the moment of orgasm when the sexual energy and the love energy of the heart are joined. It is a moment when we lose all self-centered reality and move into the reality of Spirit, love, bliss, and freedom.

In love's orgasm, we know that we are divine and can become one with the infinite. We know, too, that we can create life, and not just biological life, out of love. We experience ourselves as more than physical beings and outside our ordinary consciousness. We can feel the truth that lies beneath our thoughts, concepts, and perceptions and beyond the limitations of the physical body. In orgasm, albeit briefly, we encounter the truth of who and what we are.

For love-making and orgasm to reach their highest expression, the sexual energies and the energy of love in the heart must be in a virgin state of purity. This is what we strive for on the spiritual path: to maintain this purity or to recover it if it has been lost. Then we can truly understand what Mary means when she asks:

How many, when they are making love, think: I am pure love.
The other is pure love. Joining with God is pure love. We are
in a miracle, as a miracle, and we can create a miracle.

We can maintain this purity when we see ourselves and the beloved as God and Goddess who are meant to come together in a holy union.

This union brings the lovers into direct contact with what is most true within them. The true self breaks free from the prison of the ego's illusions in the merging of male and female energies, as the love-making is accompanied by the giving of self to the other in a selfless dance of love and light. It is a giving that comes from the heart, while at the same time it opens the heart deeper to love. Free of the ego and the limitations of the mind, love-making lifts the lovers into the miracle of oneness.

Love-making also creates an abundance of energy in the space where the love-making takes place. This space becomes filled with energy created in the love-making and orgasm. This energy often appears as white, blue, pink, violet, gold, or other vibrant colors. While most people do not see this energy, it has a high vibration and can be felt. In fact, the vibration can be as high or higher than that found in high energy places in nature or in sacred shrines. It is another way that love-making brings light into the world. This light can be taken in by the lovers to further expand their energy fields. It can be directed to places in the body where there may be illness or blocked energy. This energy can also be sent, through visualization or similar practices, to other people or places for healing, protection, or other creative purposes, such as making rain in times of drought.

The Fire of Love

The movement and expansion of energy in love-making will probably vary to some degree from couple to couple. What seems to be uniform is the expansion of sexual energy and its upward flow into the heart, and then the movement of the combined energies into the centers above the heart and throughout the physical and energy bodies. Mary shows what this flow of energy looks like when there is no blockage to the flow of energy or damage to the energy centers. In other words, she presents what love-making and its effects are meant to be when it is engaged in as a sacred act and the energies are pure.

She shows the energies of the lower centers spiraling like a fire upward toward the heart. As they move upward, they fill the physical and energy bodies. Reaching the heart center, they merge with the love energy of the heart, which also appears as a fire. These combined energies lift the lovers to a higher level of consciousness and allow them to join together energetically and spiritually. The fire then expands as it fills the upper parts of the lovers' physical and energy bodies and their higher energy centers. It then enters into and passes through the energy center at the crown of the head at which point it joins with the energy of God.

As the fire moves through the lovers' physical and energy bodies, it fills them with light. This light opens and clears, heals and expands the energy fields of both lovers. It is far more than a physical experience and physical pleasure. It is an awesome spiritual experience occurring simultaneously on many levels. We cannot grasp what it means in its entirety because we do not know ourselves fully as spiritual beings. Nevertheless, love-making has the power to heal and transform in ways that we may never have imagined. As Mary describes it:

> It is a fire coming to life through the physical and energy bodies. It goes through you. It opens and clears. It is much greater than the pleasure of the flesh. It is far greater than that. It is really the expansion of the Self, and it is used to clear and heal and join in an extraordinary way.

Love-making experienced in this way leaves no place for clinging to the ego and illusions. They have to be left behind. Then we come to know that in love-making and orgasm we are experiencing God and that God is in us and we are in God. In this state of bliss, God reveals Himself, telling us, "I am in you, and you are in me. We are one." At these moments, we feel a oneness with light, love, power, and creation. We fall into everything and nothing at the same time. The fire burning in the heart of the mystic now burns in our hearts too.

When we come together in love-making, we step out of the ordinary and into the extraordinary. We move into a magical state that we first encountered when we fell in love. Something wonderful comes to life in us and our relationship as we feel the bliss of pure love and want to hold onto it forever. We want to touch and feel this love, just as we want to touch and feel the beloved and be touched and felt by the beloved. In like manner, we desire to touch and feel God and be touched and felt by Him. We want to make love and create over and over again this miracle. For, as Mary says, to know even for a moment God's existence and love in orgasm is a miracle.

Love-making is one of the most direct means that God has given us to know and experience Him while still in the flesh. As such, it is intimately tied to romantic love. Romantic love and love-making are parts of the same whole. When our hearts are open and filled with the power and beauty of sexual energy, our desire for even more love is kindled, burning away all desire for anything but love. This takes us to the final threshold of joining with God forever as we come to desire God above all else and become, as Mary says of Joseph, a lover of love.

This does not happen in isolation from other parts of our lives. We do not live in compartments, and we bring all of who we are to our love-making. If we do not honor love in other areas of our lives, we will not honor it in sexual intimacy. The consciousness we live with invariably will be the consciousness we love with. As explained in subsequent chapters, a heightened consciousness born out of a life centered on God and devoted to love will bring love-making to its highest expression.

Living the Miracle

Sexual energy is so powerful that, through its proper understanding and use, we can transform ourselves and the world. Jesus states in a vision that with the right understanding and use of this energy we can live as He did when He walked the earth. The fusion of sexual energy and the energy of love, when held in a higher consciousness, lifts us out of our ordinary awareness into the energetic vibration of divine love. Then we can turn water into wine, calm the waters, and heal the sick. We can create with this energy all that we need. God has given us this energy so that we can come to know our God-like natures and live the miracle of pure love. Love-making and orgasm are part of God's magic that make us like Him. This is what Mary and Jesus are calling us to, as they teach that sexual energy is a powerful and creative aspect of God and of us as spiritual beings. It is pure consciousness which, when aligned with love, opens the portals to paradise within and around us.

Understanding sexual energy allows us to grasp how love-making and orgasm fit into the spiritual path and why Mary calls them a blessing. She is teaching us about sexual energy because it is necessary to move into higher levels of consciousness and realms of experience beyond the physical. Many of the experiences that we aspire to spiritually, especially direct experiences of the divine, are dependent on the abundance and vibrancy of this sacred force within us. We therefore need to understand its nature and purpose and restore it to its rightful place in our lives.

As we grasp the nature of sexual energy, we will come to know the power of love and light that it makes available to us. With it we can heal our wounds and rise above the darkness of the world. We can love as Jesus showed us, as the ordinary gives way to the extraordinary and the miraculous becomes the norm. We will then know love-making and orgasm as a celebration of divine energy and a way God has given us to become the beauty, grace, and power of divine love.

Love-making is not the only way to bring together sexual energy and the energy of love. There are other ways found in different spiritual traditions. Some people are not called to a path of romantic love or for different reasons may find themselves in a position where they cannot or choose not to experience love-making. As discussed in chapter 8, prayer, meditation, and spiritual practices (see practices in Appendix B) also are ways to open the heart and to move the sexual energy into the heart. While we may choose different ways to experience and use this energy for the sacred purposes for which it was created, it is essential for the spiritual life and union with the divine.

Many people have been misled about sexual intimacy and its place in their lives. Likewise, many people do not understand the spiritual nature and purpose of sexual energy. Mary wants to free us from the distorted views that cause us to squander one of our most precious resources. In the next chapter, she and Jesus explain the consequences of the misuse of the body and sexual energy and how their misuse brings darkness into our lives and world.

CHAPTER FIVE

The Misuse of the Body and Sexual Energy

 MISUSE OF THE BODY AND SEXUAL ENERGY is one of the most serious impediments to our spiritual growth. Understanding the harm resulting from their misuse puts into relief their true purpose and lays bare the damage caused when they are not used for this purpose. We live in a world of both light and darkness, and we have to choose between them as we make our way through life. Mary tells us that one of the principal avenues by which darkness enters the very depths of our souls and attacks our light is through the misuse of the body and sexual energy. One of the simplest yet most beguiling ways to attack people spiritually is to lure them into this misuse.

The widespread misuse of the body and sexual energy in today's world reveals how easily souls can lose their way in the pursuit of "love's urgent longings." It causes detriment on many levels of our being, including levels that few know exist. As we have seen, sexual energy is divine, and its misuse is a desecration of the divine. Mary goes so far as to declare that "the misuse of sexual energy is violating and raping God." Citing the ruinous consequences of the misuse of this energy, Jesus reveals, "More souls are lost to the darkness because of sins of the flesh than for any other reason."

While the misuse of the body and sexual energy is a serious concern, it does not call for judgement or blame of oneself or others. There are few people who have not made mistakes in this area. Mary and Jesus inform us of the misuse of the body and sexual energy not to judge us, but to teach us a different way. They want us to understand the energetic and spiritual consequences of the misuse of the body and sexual energy and its implications for other areas of our lives. This information can help us to be more discriminating in the beliefs and attitudes we adopt about the use of our bodies in sexual intimacy and in our choices about how and with whom we experience our sexual energy.

Mary's Revolution

If we act in ways that bring harm to ourselves and others, we must live with the consequences. If we dim the light and create darkness within ourselves and others by the misuse of energy, we must live with the darkness and its effects. According to Mary, the misuse of the body and sexual energy is one of the principal means through which the darkness works to destroy us as individuals, couples, families, and communities. The extent to which this misuse occurs throughout the world and the harm it does have prompted Mary to speak out strongly against it:

> The way your society and other societies are misusing sexuality and the body is a crime and a sin. It is a poison that is like a cancer spreading. It saddens me to see how innocent children are taken into this and ruined. Remember, I say, such things are poison, poison from the devil, and have nothing to do with love or beauty.

Mary shows in a vision scenes of people involved in what today are considered "ordinary" activities. These scenes include people engaged in sex, lust, and the degrading of the body. Striking a somber note as she decries the misuse of the body, she states:

> Many things which seem so innocent and harmless are the poison of the being of darkness himself. The body is the temple, and you have allowed the devil into you. You are used and then become that which he is.

Mary says that it is not by chance that the misuse of the body and sexual energy and the confusing of love with lust are widely promoted in the media and entertainment industries. When this poison is planted in people, especially at an impressionable age when hearts and minds are still innocent, the experience of what love-making is truly meant to be is often foreclosed, leaving one trapped in a benighted consciousness of loveless sex. The promotion of loveless sex in the media and entertainment industry is an attack on our spiritual essence. This is why Mary and Jesus address this problem in such depth and offer us an alternative in which the body, sexual energy, and love-making are given their rightful place in God's plan for us. This view, together with an understanding of the harm done to ourselves and others by the misuse of the body and sexual energy, provides us with a compelling rationale to examine not only how we personally relate to and experience our sexual energy, but also the reasons why its misuse is so extensively promoted. Urging us to reclaim the power and use of sexual energy for the purpose of our spiritual evolvement, Mary states:

> Each person, man, woman, and child, should know the power that sits within this energy. It is spiritual and sacred and should be known as such. It is an energy that any person on a conscious spiritual path should know and understand. It is not to be misused or used improperly. It is important to help people, particularly the youth, redirect their consciousness around sex and sexual energy. When sexual energy is misused in any way,

shape, or form, it is sexual misconduct, which is against God's law. It is no accident that the media has raped the souls of the youth for a very long time now. It is time for people to reclaim their power and their knowing through sexual energy.

How did Mary and Joseph experience their bodies and sexual energy? Based on what they share about their relationship, they did not misuse them. Their hearts were open to God and each other, and their love-making was pure, creating more love and light within them and bringing them into union with God. Can we draw a line in the sand and refuse to be lured into misuses of the body and sexual energy and instead use them as expressions of love and means to experience the divine, as Mary and Joseph did? This would be a truly revolutionary shift in the cultural and spiritual foundations upon which our lives and world are based.

Mary is calling us to join with her and her Son in making such a shift. When the focus of the body and sexual energy turns from sex and lust to light and love, sexual intimacy will no longer result in experiences that bring pain and conflict, as so often happens, and instead be a genuine source of joy and fulfillment. We will also be more sensitive to and better guarded against the promotion of the misuse of the body and sexual energy. Countless new possibilities will then be open to us, our children, and our children's children, as we learn anew the blessings that the body and sexual energy hold and make them part of our lives.

Energy Blockages and Imprints

The use of sexual energy when love is not present and the heart is not open has many harmful consequences. One is the creation of blockages in the energy centers and field. These blockages diminish the amount and obstruct the flow of energy. This, in turn, has adverse effects on our physical, emotional, mental, and spiritual well-being.

As we have seen, in love-making the energies of the lower centers join with the love energy of the heart. They become one energy, filling us with light that is powerful, creative, and healing. However, when sexual energy is used in the absence of love and the heart is not open, something very different happens. The sexual energy does not ascend from the lower centers into the heart and from there, joined with the energy of love, into other parts of the physical and energy bodies. Instead, it remains stuck in and around the lower centers where it forms what appear to be pockets of dark energy surrounded by membranes. These blockages lower the vibration of energy in the lower energy centers and prevent their energy, which is our life-force, from flowing into the upper centers and throughout our physical and energy bodies.

Mary illustrates this in a vision in which she states that the sexual energy and energy of love are meant to become one energy. She observes that, when these energies do not join as one, they become "broken." She shows broken bubbles of energy, which form the blockages described above. She explains:

> When there are blockages, the force (of the sexual energy) does not become completely what it is meant to be.

These blockages diminish one's energetic force and vitality. As such, they prevent one from growing and awakening spiritually. As discussed in the preceding chapter, in order to move into higher consciousness and maintain it, one's sexual energy must move into and create an expansion of energy in the heart center and throughout the energy body. If this process is impaired, one's spiritual potential becomes compromised in ways that are hard to reverse, as Jesus notes:

> The misuse of sexual energy destroys one's power, and it is hard to recover it once it is lost.

Sexual acts without love also leave imprints on the energy body that, like blockages, obstruct the expansion and flow of energy. These imprints form because sexual acts without love are traumatic for the soul. While such experiences may bring physical pleasure, they leave untouched the soul's longing for love. What the soul experiences is not love, but a betrayal of love. Out of confusion or ignorance, people often turn to sex in search of love and healing. However, the soul's longing for love and need for healing remain unfulfilled. Without love, sex does not provide what the soul desires.

When the life-force cannot move upward, it acts to fuel any already existing blockages and imprints, adding to the congested energies in and around the lower centers. As Mary explains:

> When the heart is not open, the act is not of love. And when there are blockages and imprints, the life-force does not move as it is supposed to move. The life-force ends up fueling the blockages and imprints.

Where love and light are absent, illusion and darkness rein. Sexual acts without love produce imprints of illusions and darkness on our subtle bodies. We need to free ourselves of illusions and darkness, not become more deeply entrapped in them. These imprints also act as a type of negative conditioning around sexual intimacy. Sexual intimacy then becomes associated with loveless sex and not with the beauty and wonder of love.

Acts of loveless sex, moreover, do not bring freedom and bliss. Instead, the resulting illusions and darkness diminish us on every level. They do not create more energy, but dissipate the energy we have. They do not bring passion into our lives, but numbness, boredom, and meaninglessness. Sexual intimacy without love, when engaged in repeatedly, can destroy one's spiritual potential altogether. Jesus states that the misuse of sexual energy can even destroy one's chance to become enlightened. These are high prices to pay for the fleeting pleasures accompanying mere sex.

The soul also experiences in loveless sex a sense of using and being used in relation to another human being. Two people who do not love each other may consent to engage in sex. However, mutual consent does not alter the soul's experience of the act as a trauma and a betrayal of the need for love. In effect, sexual acts without love are a mutual betrayal of each partner's desire for love and healing. A partner will experience the same trauma caused by the betrayal of love and will also be burdened with blockages and imprints. When mutual consent is absent, the betrayal and trauma can be even greater.

Married couples who do not love each other and engage in sex also damage themselves energetically and spiritually. Without the presence of love and open hearts, the couple's sexual experiences will create blockages and imprints, and their souls will carry the trauma of the loveless sex. As discussed more fully in the next chapter, according to Mary, this is one reason couples should marry only out of love.

Blockages and imprints can also be caused by inhibiting or repressing sexual energy. This is often done for psychological or emotional reasons. For example, a person may associate sexual intimacy with fear or pain on the basis of prior experiences and therefore repress sexual energy as a way to avoid desires that could lead to sexual intimacy. One may not be conscious of doing this. In other words, it is intentional, but the intention may lie outside one's awareness. Most people are not aware of their subtle bodies or the effects that their thoughts, emotions, or experiences have on them. Our subtle bodies, however, are very reactive to what we think and feel and the memories we carry from prior experiences.

Blockages and imprints not only produce a loss of energy and create imbalances in our energy fields, but can cause psychological and emotional disturbances and imbalances as well. They also can cause disease in the physical body. When the energy centers are blocked and their energies are not flowing, the physical body, which needs these energies to survive, will be affected and physical illness may result.

Sexual intimacy without love, therefore, is never innocent or harmless. Sexual energy is powerful and should not be trifled with. When used in tandem with love, it fills us with light and brings us closer to God. When used apart from love, it dims our light and destroys us spiritually.

Exchanges of Energies

When sexual intimacy of any type is experienced between two people, exchanges of energies occur between them. It is a mixing or blending of energies in which each partner is left carrying energies from the other. This is particularly true for the energies of the two lower centers. As Mary explains, "Every time you have sex, you pass to the other person, and the other person passes to you, energies at the level of the soul."

When two people are sexually intimate, they take on not only each other's energies, but also the qualities of those energies. This means that each partner carries the other's energetic vibration, including the vibration of the other's thoughts and emotions, which can be positive or negative. For instance, if a person is angry or sad, the vibration of anger or sadness can be transferred to a sexual partner. The degree to which one is affected by a partner's energy is influenced by several factors, including the strength of one's own energy field relative to the partner's and the vibrational intensity of what the partner is carrying.

Sexual partners carry each other's energies for six months or longer. They carry some energies indefinitely unless they are cleared. This means that some energies from prior sexual partners can be carried for the rest of one's life. Mary points out that carrying a partner's energy can be particularly problematic in the ending of a relationship. The energies of the former partner make it difficult to completely sever the relationship, and the bonds may continue to be felt on emotional or psychological levels. She notes:

> It is difficult to break the ties when two people have sex. At the level of the soul, when two people have sex, they carry each other's energies. It is more than you can understand because sex is more than a physical act.

She further explains that the nature of the life-force, love, and sexual energy are such that we should be intimate only with the person we intend to make our life partner:

> It is very important for people to have one partner. It is not because of judgement or a moral judgement. It is because of the nature of the life-force and love and sexual energy. When two people have sex, they carry the other and become the other. This is why you should be intimate only with the person you will make your life partner.

There are circumstances, for example being widowed or divorced, when a commitment to a new partner may be appropriate.

The exchange of energies becomes more complicated when one or both partners have had several prior partners. The energies of prior sexual partners can be transferred to the current partner. This is particularly true of more recent sexual partners. It is also true if a person is having sex with more than one person. The energies of other partners make it difficult to create or maintain an exclusive bond of love between partners.

Persons who are sexually active with multiple partners can suffer an impaired sense of self. As they carry in their energy fields the accumulated energies of their various partners, and possibly even their partners' partners, they can lose touch with who they are. As Mary indicates, when we carry another's energy, we carry part of their consciousness, part of who they are. Thus, persons having sex with multiple partners can inflict serious harm upon themselves with untold consequences for their personalities and lives.

The exchange of energies between partners engaged in sexual acts without love also creates a "bubble" of dark energy around them, establishing yet another bond between them. This bubble forms on an energetic level that most people do not know exists and that many people who see energies often do not see. The partners are linked together by this energetic bubble until the energetic ties between them are released. Thus, each time we have sexual relations with someone, we are creating consequences for ourselves and the other that can last a lifetime.

Exchanges of energies can also cause holes to form in one's energy field. When love is present and the lovers' hearts are open, the mixing or blending of energies is beautiful as love and light are created as part of the love-making. However, when intimate relations occur without love, the exchange of energies can destroy parts of the energy field. While each person is born with different amounts of energy, most people are born with an intact and vibrant aura. The aura is a radiant garment of light which God has given each of us. The holes are like a tearing or ripping apart of this precious gift.

Holes in one's energy field, moreover, make it difficult to hold energy or to replenish it when it has become depleted. Similarly, when we attempt to expand our energy fields, which is necessary in order to grow spiritually, we have difficulty because the energy field is porous and cannot hold the energy. Further, the lack of energy resulting from the holes can make us feel easily fatigued and function at less than our full potential. In addition, the holes limit the energy field's natural capacity to buffer or filter out external energies that we may not want to enter into us. As a result, we can be more susceptible to thoughts, emotions, and energies from people and places around us. In such cases, we can be confused about which thoughts or emotions are ours and which are coming from outside of us.

Holes can also be caused by the use of alcohol and drugs, including some prescription drugs. It is sad to see young people, most of whom have been blessed with beautiful and vibrant auras, to develop holes in them when they begin to have sex and use alcohol or drugs. Once formed, the holes are not easy to close. This is especially true if people do not know that the holes exist, which is usually the case.

It can also happen in the exchange of energies that one of the partners can place negative or dark energy into the other. The person can be doing this consciously or unconsciously. When we have sexual relations, our energy fields are normally open to our partner's energies. At such times, it is easy for one partner to place negative or dark energy into the other. This can be done for different reasons. For example, it can be done to rid oneself of unwanted or intolerable emotions.

When two people are committed to each other in a bond of love, they willingly take on each other's energies in their love-making. Some of the energies may be negative or even dark, but that is part of the commitment we make when we strive to be unconditional in our love and to help each other overcome flaws and weaknesses. We do our best to accept the other person, including what they carry energetically, as we work together to let go of the parts of ourselves that are not of love. At the same time, when love is present, much of the energy exchanged between partners is filled with light. Then the love-making and exchange of energies have the power to clear away any negative and dark energies and to heal and transform the lovers. This is one of the ways love-making heals.

Exchanges of sexual energy can occur between people in different settings and under different circumstances. Passing a stranger in a supermarket or sitting in a business meeting, for instance, can be encounters in which a mutual or one-way exchanges of energy occur. Sexual energy moves out of one person and onto the other. These types of exchanges take place even if one or both parties are unaware of them. Some people elicit these types of exchanges with provocative clothing or behaviors because they want to draw another person's sexual energy to themselves.

Ways of dressing and the use of make-up and jewelry often trigger, intentionally or unintentionally, exchanges of sexual energy. We have to ask ourselves what purpose such exchanges serve and if we really want to participate in them. If we project our sexual energy onto others or let others take our energy, we lose that vital force for the sacred purposes for which it is intended. Likewise, if we go through the day eliciting others' sexual energies, or being open to receiving them, then we have to deal with the vibration, and the consciousness carried by it, of those energies. It is a senseless way of being in the world and can lead to confusion about who we really are and the place of love in our lives.

Sexual Energy in Seduction

Seduction is another way that sexual energy is misused. The seducing person extends his or her sexual energy out from his or her energy field and into another person and, in a sense, "captures" the person, using the energy like a hook. The seducer's energy remains in the other person, who then may confuse what he or she is thinking or feeling about the seducer with genuine feelings of love or attraction. Such experiences, which have nothing to do with love or a genuine attraction based on love, are a dark manipulation of energy.

Sometimes people feel they have fallen in love only to learn later that they had been seduced. The soul's greatest longing is for love. Many people are desperate for love and can be easily deceived as to what love really is. Where there is genuine love, there is no desire to control and manipulate. When two people meet and truly love each other, their hearts open to each other. They may have sexual feelings for each other, but these feelings are tied to the energy of love they feel in their hearts.

We can avoid falling prey to seduction by becoming more sensitive to energy and trusting our feelings about others. At the same time, we can learn to shield ourselves from unwanted sexual advances on an energetic level. This can be done in different ways. For example, you can visualize yourself circled with golden light and make an affirmation, repeated as many times as needed, that no one's energy will come onto you and that your energy will not be taken by anyone. This can be done before you go into settings, such as stores and offices, where such exchanges may occur.

Mary speaks about how people misuse their bodies for seductive purposes. Continuing to point out that people harm themselves when they fail to see sexual energy as sacred, she observes:

> People do not understand the energy, and they do not understand the sacredness around it. People are just harming themselves. The body was meant and is meant to be the temple in which the divine comes to life. But it cannot be the temple if people do no understand its nature. Women misuse their bodies to seduce men. This is a crime. Men misuse their bodies and try to seduce women. This is a crime. It has nothing to do with what the body is intended for.

She then shows different scenes and images depicting distorted views people have about the body and physical beauty. She shows that we are not what we perceive ourselves to be physically and that the body is little more than an outer shell that does not come close to reflecting who and what we are on the level of the soul. In other words, the body is a sort of costume one puts on. When we identify who we are only with our bodies, we are mistaken about our true identities and fail to see what we carry on the non-physical levels of our beings.

The misuse of the body and sexual energy creates darkness where light and love should dwell. Without light and love we will, in body and soul, disintegrate into darkness. We must be willing to defend our light and love and not be pulled into and suffocated by sexual lures. Their presence all around us is not by accident or chance. They are meant to destroy. They are peddled through the media and are what we have come to accept as normal in advertising and entertainment. Their success is reflected in many of the ways we dress, talk, and conduct ourselves.

It is shameless how the entertainment and advertising industries induce young people to dress and act in seductive ways and initiate them into the misuse and manipulation of their bodies and sexual energy. On whose altars are our children being sacrificed? From a young age, they are being taught to misuse their bodies and sexual energies, and they do not know the consequences of what they are learning. They do not know because too often the adults in their lives have become blinded to the consequences, and the children have no one to teach them that what they are learning is wrong and will hurt them. What we are witnessing on individual and societal levels, as Mary points out, is nothing less than the rape of souls—not only our children's, but also our own.

Taking Sexual Energy From Others

Our energy is one of our greatest resources, and some people take it from others. This taking happens on levels and in ways of which most people are unaware, and for the most part it goes unseen. Yet we know these energetic transfers occur because some people have the ability to see them. Jesus warns about the taking of energy in a message in which He also speaks of the use of sexual energy to control others:

> Many women and men use their sexual energy to control and
> have power over others. Women, and some men, use their
> sexual body and sexual self to pull energy from others.

We all know at some level that we need energy to survive and thrive in the world. Some people make it a practice to take energy from others and use it for their own purposes. If we are sensitive to energy, we can feel when energy has been taken from us. Jesus felt a loss of energy when a woman touched his cloak and was healed by the energy that flowed into her.[1] But many people are not sensitive to energy and may only feel tired or irritable after energy has been taken from them. Actually, energy can be taken from any part of one's energy field. Because of the power of sexual energy, it is common for energy to be pulled from the lower energy centers.

The taking of energy occurs when one person extends what looks like a funnel out of their energy field and into another's. The funnel is used to draw out the other's energy. The taking can be done in a matter of a few seconds during a brief encounter or over a longer period of time, such as at a business meeting. It can take place between strangers who happen to be near each other in a public place or between people who know each other and spend time together, such as spouses. It can also take place during intercourse.

It simply is not necessary to take energy from another person. There are abundant sources of energy in and around us. When we feel depleted or otherwise in need of energy, we can use different means to replenish our store of energy and feel well again. Some ways to do this are meditation, visualization, prayer, breathing exercises, physical exercise, and spending time in nature.

There are times when we may choose to give energy to another. When people are ill, they often need energy. If you choose to give energy to someone in need, it is best to draw the energy into yourself from a higher source and then pass it on to the recipient. As healers who work with energy know, you need not deplete your own energy to help others.

We need to be sensitive to energy, our own and others, and use this sensitivity to assess people, situations, and places. As Jesus points out, there are people who will take our energy, and we need to protect ourselves. It is not difficult to protect yourself from such people if you know such people exist and become more sensitive to your own energy and others'. A greater sensitivity, combined with visualization and affirmations such as those mentioned above, will serve us well for purposes of protection. The best protection, however, is the strength of one's own energy field and the intention to keep it inviolate from those who would take or destroy.

Beyond Darkness and Evil

We have seen some of the ways that sexual energy can be misused. We are energetic beings, and most of what we do has consequences for us in terms of our energy. Jesus characterizes the misuse of sexual energy as "dangerous and deadly." It therefore is important to consider how to structure our lives and relationships in ways that protect this vital resource and to use it in ways that bring light and love into ourselves, others, and the world. We can begin by refusing to be misled into believing that we can be sexually intimate with someone whom we do not love and not harm ourselves and the other. We can also reject the standards of misuse set in the media and entertainment industry and encourage others, especially our children, to do the same. And we need to speak out. If indeed we are witnessing the rape of souls, at what point does silence become complicity?

The consequences of the misuse of sexual energy extend far beyond our individual lives. If we destroy our spiritual foundation as individuals, we destroy the spiritual foundation of our marriages, families, communities, and nations. Are we not now witnessing throughout our societies the bitter fruits of the reckless misuse of sexual energy? We underestimate the power of this energy at our own risk. Mary points out that it is so powerful that it can heal or destroy a nation. She also states that no one really understands the true nature of sexual energy:

> This energy must not be misused because it can heal or destroy an entire nation. Not a single person on your planet understands the truth of sexual energy. It is more powerful than anyone can grasp. To misuse one's sexual energy is to destroy oneself. One must not misuse this energy. One must protect it, honor it, keep it virgin, pure.

The misuse of sexual energy does not free us from suffering, but causes more suffering. It draws us away from love and light and keeps us trapped in what Mary describes as "the world of the living dead." Dissipating our life-force, it leaves us without the power to awaken from our illusions and live at higher levels of consciousness. We no longer have the energy to fuel our passions and feel truly alive. Mired in darkness, we are unable to know the truth we carry within. Then we become the pawns of those who would have us dwell in darkness and not in light.

When we misuse the body and sexual energy, we betray our true natures, which are pure love. We also destroy the potential present in a romantic relationship to move from human to divine love. In our misuses of the body and sexual energy, we attack ourselves and the light and love within us. Over time, we become more susceptible to negative thoughts and emotions as we feel the effects of blockages, imprints, and holes in our energy fields, as well as the energies of others that we may carry. We are more prone to fear, anger, or depression, as we become more estranged from love and the fulfillment of our life's purpose. We perpetuate bleak existences within internal prisons of darkness and illusion and become, as Mary has shown in several visions, one of the countless souls staring out from behind prison bars of their own making.

Societies throughout the world have increasingly fallen under the spell of sex and the misuse of sexual energy. At some future time, it may be seen in retrospect that the demise of our civilization was brought about by the widespread misuse of the divine gift of sexual energy. It may also be seen that this misuse was not an accident. We may awaken from our slumber and learn, as Mary tells us, that darkness and evil are causal forces in our lives and world and that we have been tragically blind to them and their ways. As described in this chapter, one of the most effective means to attack people spiritually is to induce them to misuse their sexual energy. One of the most effective ways to attack a culture spiritually is to promote on a broad scale the misuse of sexual energy. Is there any question that the misuse of the body and sexual energy is one of the principal causes for the spiritual malaise of our times?

Problems with the use of the body and sexual energy also may arise when people are taught to associate them with sin and evil. This taints the experience of the body and sexual energy with shame and guilt. It is another means to render us impotent before the power and beauty of sexual energy. God blesses us with this energy, which is a part of Him. Mary is teaching us, through her own example as a lover and through messages about the nature of sexual energy, that we have been mistaught and lost our way in our relation to this vital force.

We have discussed some of the problems associated with the misuse of sexual energy. Other problems, such as unwanted pregnancies, abortions, and sexually transmitted diseases, also leave pain and anguish in their wake and have consequences we fail to see. For example, Mary says that abortion leaves a scar not only on the mother's soul, but also on the souls of the unborn infant and the father. This is true for the father, she explains, even when he does not know about the abortion.

Young people sometimes believe that they can "experiment" sexually with different partners while they are single and later settle down with one partner in marriage. We are learning that they end up harming themselves and others in ways that have enduring consequences as a result of such behavior. Many people, looking back on such sexual experiences, find that they did not bring love or fulfillment. Paradoxically, one of the most powerful forces God has given us to bring the divine into our lives is for many one of the greatest sources of pain and darkness. If this is the case, would we not be well-served to reevaluate our beliefs, attitudes, and behaviors concerning sexual intimacy and the place it has in our lives?

When and with whom we use our sexual energy are two of the most important decisions we make in life. They have direct consequences for us spiritually and profound implications on physical, emotional, and mental levels as well. What we must strive for in relation to our sexual energy is to be chaste, which is to be pure in thought and action. This is the case whether we are sexually active or not. Even for those who choose to be celibate, their sexual energy still needs to be alive, and they need to relate to it in a pure way.

Mary says that many people who are celibate do not know what to do with their sexual energy. This energy, as in love-making, needs to be brought into the heart and the heart needs to be open. There are practices in different spiritual traditions to awaken the sexual energy, move it into the heart, and raise it through the energy center at the crown of the head into union with God. Romantic love and love-making are but one way to do this.

Releasing Ties and Bonds With Past Sexual Partners
It is possible to release the ties and bonds with partners from past sexual experiences. If we do not do this, we continue to carry the energies of former partners and they continue to carry ours, maintaining links that no longer serve any purpose and, in most instances, are harmful to both parties. As such, we are helping ourselves and former partners when we break the ties and bonds with former partners.

Releasing must occur on several levels because the energies are held on several levels. While we may be aware of some of these levels, we are not aware of others. As Mary indicates, exchanges of energies take place on levels of the soul that we do not grasp. Consequently, we have to use different approaches and techniques for releasing the energies on all the levels that we carry them.

The process of release is one in which the ties and bonds with all prior sexual partners are broken. Prior sexual partners include all prior partners with whom we have had intimate sexual relations and not just intercourse. If one believes in past lives, partners from other lifetimes can also be included among prior sexual partners. What is most important is to create a powerful intention to release any ties and bonds we may carry with all prior partners.

One must make an effort to recall each sexual partner and attempt to ascertain the types of ties or bonds that may still exist with them. These may include unresolved emotions, such as anger or hurt, or ties arising from having brought children into the world together. The releasing of these ties and bonds can be done in different ways. Prayer and the invocation of the Holy Spirit and divine beings, together with the sincere intent that all ties and bonds be broken, can be especially effective for releasing prior partners on those levels of which we are unaware. Using visualization to bring light into you to clear the ties and bonds can also be very effective.

As part of the process, it is important to send back to former partners their energy and demand that your energies be returned to you. It is also important that in our hearts we ask that each former partner forgive us and that we forgive them if the relations were without love. The use of sexual energy without love is damaging to both partners and calls for mutual forgiveness. It also is important to ask from the heart that God forgive you and your former partner or partners, knowing that God's love and forgiveness are without condition or limitation. Mary says that, when we ask for forgiveness from the heart, we are forgiven. We are God's children and carry His essence within us. As the story of the prodigal son teaches, God is waiting with open arms for each of us to return home to His love. Former partners would normally not know we are releasing them and demanding that they release us. But the release, as well as the forgiveness, will be effected on the levels they need to be, and former partners will benefit from them even though they may be unaware they have taken place.

There is no single way to structure the process of release. We recommend that one include, in some form, prayer, ritual, or ceremony. You can create your own ritual or ceremony for this purpose. Some Native American wedding ceremonies include such a ritual. Prior to the ceremony, each partner spends time in quiet and prayer and goes through the process of releasing energies from a former partner or partners and asking for forgiveness. A knot is tied in a cord for each of the former partners. During the wedding ceremony, the cord is thrown into a fire and burned, finalizing the release of all former partners. Before and during the ceremony, ancestor spirits are called upon to assist in the process.

The invocation of divine beings, such as Jesus and Mary, is especially helpful. The divine beings, as mentioned above, know the levels on which we carry energies that we may not see, and they can clear them for us. In addition, the burden of past experiences that were not of love may be heavy and facing them may be painful. Divine beings can help to ease the burden and console the pain as we move through the process. The purpose of releasing is not to fall into a place of judgement or blame of oneself or others, but to let go of all that is not love in order to become all that is love. Remorse is a normal response to a realization that one has harmed oneself and others through a lack of love. But the remorse can give way to healing and joy as we move forward with greater understandings and awareness and a renewed commitment to love and light.

CHAPTER SIX

Sacred Marriage

 MARRIAGE IS ONE OF THE MOST important relationships we
have as human beings. At the same time, it is one of the most
complex. Most people, deep within, desire to be whole in relation to another. They long to know and be known, to love and be loved,
by another. Ultimately, they wish to find a partner, another soul, with
whom they can experience the fullness of love. However, in our humanness, we do not find marriage easy. As Mary says, human love has its
beauty, but also its limitations. It poses many challenges and obstacles,
both inner and outer, and we have to work to maintain love in a marriage.
Instead of finding the love they desire, many people find that their marriages run aground, leaving pain and disappointment in their wake.

Mary is saddened by the lack of love she sees in many marriages. She
says that we do not know what marriage is meant to be and that we bring
harm to ourselves in marriages in which there is no love. She wants to
teach us that marriage, like love-making, is an extraordinary gift and that
we can be successful in our marriages in ways we never imagined. Instead

of being a source of pain and disappointment, marriage can bring two souls into oneness with each other and God. She shows this in a vision of two eagles soaring high in the sky. They are surrounded by white and violet light. As they fly near to each other, their light creates a single ball of light around them. Then together they flew higher, directly into the sun, where their light and the light of the sun become one.

What Constitutes a Marriage?

The desire we feel to become one with the beloved is a reflection of the soul's greater longing to become one with the divine. Two souls joining as one occurs in the pureness of their love, in their divinity. The Sacred Heart of each joins together and, at the same time, joins with God. Mary and Jesus tell us that marriage plays an important role in this union of divine love.

What exactly constitutes a marriage? While marriage can take many forms, it exists only when the partners love each other and bring their relationship into union with God. According to Jesus, it is love between the partners and union with God and in God that make a marriage, as Jesus explains in the following message:

> Marrying someone you do not love, from where I stand, is not
> a marriage, is not a union with God or in God. A marriage
> has to be celebrated with God and in God for it to be looked
> upon as a marriage. However, in your world you consider
> (a marriage entered into without love) a marriage.

He states that the purpose of a marriage is to bring one closer to another and into union with God. He says this cannot happen without love and, therefore, without love a marriage does not exist:

> There is only one reason to marry and that is to bring one
> closer to another and to oneness with God. If there is not
> love, this is not possible and therefore not a marriage.

He then describes marriage as "an extraordinary gift," both sacred and holy:

A marriage is a union of two becoming one and joining with God. It is sacred and holy. It is not mundane, routine, or ordinary. It is an extraordinary gift that people fail to see.

The love each partner has for each other, together with the presence of God, seals their relationship and makes their union a marriage in the eyes of God. Marriage, then, is not a legal commitment, although it can be. Rather, it is a commitment that two people make, in heart, mind, body, and soul, to each other, to love, and to God. A relationship sealed in love and consecrated to God is held in the hands of God, affording the union a special protection against the forces inimical to love that would work to destroy it.

Marriage also provides a sacred container for the sexual energy that is vital for the couple to open to the Sacred Heart within and join as one with each other and God. Marriage is not only a commitment of the lovers to hold sacred this energy between them, but also a declaration to others that the bounds of their love will not be violated. Lovers must surround their union with the energies of love so that it will be protected from all that would try to enter and destroy their love. Jesus says that the only other who should be allowed into this sacred union is God.

Mary likens a marriage of love to a fountain, where the lovers form the fountain and their love the water flowing from it. She shows this sacred water filling the lovers and flowing down to their children and filling them as well.

The Great Vehicle to the Divine

Mary addresses the state of marriage in our world and further explains what a marriage is meant to be. Her messages help us to see how far we have strayed in our pursuit of love and how confused we have become in our understanding of marriage. They also call us to examine more closely our marriages and what societies throughout the world, and not just the Christian world, have done to marriage as an institution. Mary's messages on this subject, which are sometimes harsh, are prompted by her great love for us and her desire that we know the limitless possibilities that marriage holds and how we can make them part of our lives.

Romantic love sealed in marriage, according to Mary, is meant to be the principal way for souls to return to God. As such, it is also meant to be the principal way for souls to heal their deepest wound, which is their separation from God, and to fulfill their innermost desire, which is to become one with God. She thus places romantic love sealed in marriage squarely at the center of our spiritual lives and quests.

Mary says that few people experience what a marriage is meant to be. She also points out that many people marry for reasons other than love, calling this as a sin. She explains that to marry someone for reasons other than love is a sin because it goes against God's law, which is love. She does not judge these people, for judging is not her way. She wants us to know not only what marriage is meant to be, but also the harm we do to ourselves when marriage is not serving this purpose. Commenting on marriages entered into without love, she states:

> Many relationships are sin because people marry for the wrong reasons. There is no love in these marriages. People marry for lust or power or greed or convenience or common goals. These are reasons which are sinful. Marriage is meant to bring one into union with God. It is impossible to come into a place of union with God if you are not in a place of love with the person you are with. The reasons that people marry that are not of love — lust, power, greed, convenience, common goals—these marriages are sin and were never meant to be.

To be in a marriage without love seriously impairs and, in some cases, can destroy each partner's opportunity to become love and join with God. The nature of love between two souls and the energies of that love have the power to bring the souls into union with each other and with God. We are literally meant to be borne by the wings of love back to our Creator. This cannot happen without love. One of the reasons, as Mary states below, is that sexual intimacy cannot be what it is meant to be without love. Without an open heart and the presence of love, sexual intimacy remains, at best, at a level of physical pleasure and does not lift the partners into higher consciousness and higher vibrations of energy where they can be healed and transformed.

What does it mean, then, if something so central to our lives as marriage is not serving our ultimate purpose? Or, to pose the question somewhat differently, how can we live a life of truth if the central human relationship in our lives is not based on truth? Jesus says that many people who marry for reasons other than love create "lies on top of lies," hurting themselves and others. We will not realize our highest truth if our lives are based on lies and not on truth.

Sharing the sadness she feels over marriages without love, Mary speaks of the effects of such marriages:

> These kinds of marriages sadden me because a marriage is sacred. That is the way a marriage is meant to be—sacred. What you have created in your world is something other. There are very few marriages in your world that are sacred. Let me say this to you: To be in a marriage in which there is no love is a sin. It is the greatest sin. Marriage is a vehicle to God if it is sacred. If there is no love, there is nothing sacred about it. And all it is meant to be is destroyed, including the love-making.

Expressing again her sadness over loveless marriages, she adds:

> Many marriages are not meant to be. Many marriages are bad. These marriages sadden me greatly. Marriages should be love, and love should take one to the divine and to divine love. The way people in your world view marriage is distorted and is nothing like what it is meant to be.

She next explains what a marriage is intended to be, describing it as a union meant to be the great vehicle by which two souls are lifted into the divine to join as one with God:

> Marriage is a union that is meant to be the great vehicle to the divine. If a marriage is made of love and if a marriage is

sacred, then everything in the marriage and about the marriage becomes divine. This is what the union of two beings coming together in marriage is about. Marriage is supposed to heighten one's awareness, to heighten one's consciousness, and to lift one fully into the divine. The views of relationship in your world are very inaccurate. When a man and a woman come together in marriage, they are meant to join, to become one vehicle, one energy, one being, a wholeness, a completeness in the human way that lifts them up to the divine for complete and real union with God.

She then shows bubbles of light floating upward. In each bubble are two souls joined as one and ascending to God. Emphasizing the importance of romantic love and relationship as a means to join with God, she motions to the souls ascending to God and says:

Understand that this is the most important thing you can ever do. And the most rewarding. To join with God is far greater than everything and anything in your world. Do not put anything before this.

According to Mary, our views about relationship are inaccurate. Two views she specifically mentions relate to our notions of individuality and "codependence." Stressing once again that love is about oneness, she states:

Individual this or individual that is a very self-centered way of viewing the world. There is nothing individual about relationship. You become one in relationship, one in marriage. There are words and terms which are used by you (here she mentions "codependence"). These words are true if one is not healed. But if two come together as one and are joined with God, they are healed. Then there is no such thing as codependence. There is only oneness. There is only union. You hold certain things that are individual, but you become one. One.

Mary is reminding us that love and marriage are about oneness and that in this oneness with another, and not in our individuality, we will encounter the mystical union of lovers with each other and with God. Concepts such as individuality and codependence belong to the ordinary mind and not to the true mind of love. When we know through the true mind, we are beyond such concepts, and even beyond such experiences, as our perceptions of duality and separateness fall away. We see through the eyes of love and know that we are one with all. As Mary points out, mistaken views about relationship can take us in the wrong direction and leave us adrift in a consciousness of separation and duality. She emphasizes repeatedly that love is about oneness and illustrates this in many visions in which she shows herself as one with God, with Jesus, and with Joseph.

Mary compares a marriage without love to being imprisoned. She wants to help souls in loveless marriages whose light is being dimmed or destroyed. She is trying to free us from the suffering and desperation that often accompany such marriages and to guide us back to love. The suffering that arises from such marriages calls, not for judgement, but for compassion, including each partner's compassion for the other.

Making the Right Choice

The longing to join with and become one with another is one of the most salient characteristics of romantic love. But who is this other we passionately desire to join with? And how do we even know there is such a person with whom such union is possible? Moreover, if there is such a person, how do we find him or her? Or, if we feel we have found another soul with whom such a union seems possible, how can we be sure that we are not mistaken about the place this person holds in our lives?

These are not simple questions, and they do not lend themselves to simple answers. The decisions to marry and whom to marry are two of the most important ones we make. They have enduring consequences throughout our lives and beyond. As Mary says, marriage is central to our life purpose. Choices about marriage are influenced by the complexity of who we are and who the other person is. We are physical, emotional, psychological, and spiritual beings. Moreover, each soul carries into the world a vast history that influences the soul's experiences on many levels. The universe is also complex, having many levels and many dimensions which affect us in ways known and unknown.

Regardless of this complexity, if we know who we are at the level of the soul and how and why we came into being, we will find it easier to make the right choices. Moreover, if we learn to trust our intuitions and feelings about relationship and people, and follow the inner knowing of our hearts, we can better avoid the pitfalls along the sometimes perilous pathways we follow in search of love. We can easily find ourselves in a relationship or marriage in which we do not belong if we do not take the time to know ourselves better and if we choose not to listen to and follow our intuitions and feelings. Many people who feel they married the "wrong" person acknowledge that they felt their partner was not right for them before they married. They simply chose not to follow what they felt.

Few people know themselves or their partners well before marriage. Most people do not know what they carry within their personalities from early in life or from past lives. Both Mary and Jesus have spoken of past lives and their influence on relationships. Jesus states that "reincarnation is a way for souls who want to evolve spiritually to evolve spiritually." The most important lessons we have to learn for our spiritual evolvement are often the ones that we did not learn in previous lifetimes, and many of these have to do with love and relationship.[1]

Experiences from early in life and past lives act as conditioning which predisposes us to think, feel, and act in ways that are influenced by these experiences. We respond to situations, especially those eliciting strong emotions, on the basis of unconscious dynamics grounded in these earlier experiences. We often come to know ourselves better as the deeper layers of our personalities emerge in the context of marriage and family life. We then have the opportunity to face and let go of what we carry that is not love, and we can help our partner do the same.

Most of us have parts of our personalities that are not loving and that can undermine the love that we have for another. It is the sacred work, the alchemy of marriage, for partners to strive to purify themselves. God has provided within the marital relationship certain processes to aid in this. These include the divine energies that come alive in us when our hearts are open to another in love-making, which can purify and heal us on many levels. They also include the presence and grace of God. As Gabriel told Mary, nothing is impossible with God.

In order for marriage to bring a couple closer to God, it is important that both partners be fully committed to marriage as a sacred path. Ideally, this should be discussed by partners before they marry. Some couples who marry out of love, but have no sense of the sacredness of the marriage, often find that their marriages run aground. After the marriage has encountered major difficulties, they may turn to God in an effort to save the marriage and their love for each other. They may then come to learn that their love is sacred and that they need God in the center of their life and marriage for it to truly flourish.

The decisions to marry and whom to marry merit prayer, reflection, and a discerning spirit. If we go deep within ourselves, when we still our minds and listen to the wisdom within our hearts, we will receive guidance. There is a part of us that carries a deeper knowing of who we are, what we are searching for, and what we truly need. When we listen to and honor this inner wisdom, we will know whether a partner or relationship is right for us.

The purpose of marriage cannot be met if both partners are not fully committed to love and transformation through the power of love. Marriages can be destructive, as Mary points out, if one or both partners are committed to something other than love. Some people can deceive themselves and others about their true values and intentions. In addition, not all souls come into this world for the same purpose. Jesus points out, "There are beings who come here (to this world) who do not carry love. Their sole purpose is the destruction of love." In choosing a partner for marriage, then, we will be well served to heed St. Paul's admonition:

> Do not be mismatched with unbelievers. For what partnership is there between righteousness and lawlessness? Or what fellowship is there between light and darkness? What

agreement does Christ have with Beliar? Or what does a believer share with an unbeliever? What agreement has the temple of God with idols? For we are the temple of the living God.[2]

A marriage in which one of the partners is not committed to love puts the light of the other partner at risk. It is even worse if one partner is committed to darkness. As St. Paul says, there can be no fellowship between light and darkness. There are people we simply should not marry under any circumstances or for any reason. They are not right for us as a marriage partner, and we are not right for them. The marriage simply will not work no matter how hard we try. We may not know the reasons for this consciously, but we often feel it. Some people have dreams that warn them about marrying certain people.

What we may not know consciously, we know energetically. Our energy fields respond powerfully to love and its absence. When two people who are not in love marry, their energy fields react to each other's in ways that indicate the absence of love. The partners may be confused about what they feel for each other, but their energy fields reflect the truth they know somewhere within.

When people marry someone who is not right for them or for the wrong reasons, they create many problems for themselves and the other person. If love is absent and the marriage is not sacred, we are setting ourselves up for more than just pain and disappointment. As Mary points out, we are jeopardizing our chances to become love and join with God in this lifetime. Jesus says that one should not feel guilty about leaving a marriage entered into without love, but rather should feel remorse about entering into it in the first place. One need not judge oneself or others for such situations. What is important is to forgive oneself and one's partner and find one's way back to love.

"When There Is Not Love"

According to Mary, there are times when it is necessary to leave a marriage. As she notes above, some marriages are not meant to be. Other marriages, she says, are not meant to continue:

To stay in a marriage when there is not love or the possibility of love is being destroyed, this is not the will of God. There are times when beings must leave relationships. These times are when there is not love.

In some cases, it may be hard to know when a marriage should end. Like beginning a marriage, ending a marriage should not be taken lightly, and the decision likewise calls for prayer, reflection, and a discerning spirit. Ending a marriage is invariably a painful process, especially when children are involved. In such decisions we are well served by being open to and guided by the Spirit and the inner knowing of our hearts.

As mentioned above, marriage is not the only path to union with the divine. Some people may have worked hard to make a marriage work and still not found love. If they remain open to love and truly desire to become one with God, God will find a way to come into their hearts and join with them for eternity. Paths to God apart from marriage are common, as seen in the lives of many saints and spiritual masters who never married and who came into union with God. What ultimately matters, as Jesus says, is love and that we love.

A Remarkable Journey

Most souls lost, at some point during their spiritual journeys, the original state of oneness in which they, together with another soul, were "created out of the same breath of God." The Garden of Eden story is about the original state of perfection of two souls in oneness with each other and with God and how it was lost. Adam and Eve chose to leave this state of bliss and freedom and enter into a state of separation and duality by choosing something other than love and God. In their story we find our story. At some point, we too chose something other than love and God. A veil descended over our eyes, blinding us to God and the truth of our divine essence. Our longing to return to this state of perfection is one reason romantic love is charged with such intensity. We have been there before, and we long to return.

Most married couples would consider their marriages successful if they held onto the human love they had for each other when they married.

They would consider it an even greater success if they held onto the magic they felt when they fell in love. Mary is urging us to set our sights on something even higher: moving from human to divine love. If a couple chooses to pursue this goal, marriage can be a remarkable journey. When they fell in love, they felt the spark of divine love. But this was just a beginning. It was not the total transformation that comes when the lovers merge with the Sacred Heart and become pure love, the goal that lovers commit to and strive toward when they embrace marriage as a path to God.

The journey will not be easy or free of problems and conflicts. Few great undertakings are without difficulties. However, if the partners devote themselves and their relationship to love and to God, they are less likely to become mired in the problems and conflicts that tend to drain the life from a relationship or marriage and undermine the partners' love for each other. Mary says that a problem cannot be solved at the level at which it was created. When we move to a higher level of consciousness, problems that otherwise seemed insurmountable at a lower level of consciousness can be worked through. Mary is teaching us how to live at higher levels of consciousness in relationship and marriage. The problems and conflicts will come, but they can be dealt with in ways that do not destroy love. Being at a higher consciousness, sustained by a higher vibration of energy, permits us to see problems and conflicts in a different light and find solutions that otherwise may have eluded us.

For instance, when we are caught in a conflict, we often spin in its energy without anything being resolved. If we take time to pray or meditate and move into a higher consciousness and higher vibration, we may come to see the situation differently. We may discover meanings that we may have missed before and solutions that might not have occurred to us. This is particularly true if we tap into the vibration of love within the heart. Then we can resolve or, at times, rise above the problems and conflicts, as we live in the vibration of love and see through the eyes of love.

We cannot do this, however, simply by virtue of being in love and marrying. We have to strive to reach the place within ourselves, the Sacred Heart, where we will live fully in the consciousness and vibration of love and see through the eyes of love. At that point, the typical problems and conflicts recede in importance and intensity as we live more in tune with the limitless possibilities of love. What Mary is offering us may seem like a bold proposition, but it is not beyond our reach.

Mary enumerates four basic tasks that a couple will have to commit to in order to reach this summit of love. They are the true measures of love and carry with them the tests that all beings who have become one with God have had to pass. According to Mary, the pursuit of these tasks, and not the senseless activities with which most people are occupied, are what makes one's life truly extraordinary. If a couple succeeds in these tasks, Mary says, they will succeed in becoming divine. These tasks, which comprise what might be called the sacred work of romantic love as a spiritual path, are:

- To love God above all else and place God at the center of one's life and relationship.
- To live a holy life.
- To let go of all that is not love.
- To face one's imperfections and flaws and cleanse oneself of them.

Each of the tasks is formidable by itself, and, together, they may seem too demanding of oneself and one's partner. Yet, if we ask ourselves what we truly desire and what our partner truly desires, as well as what our purpose for coming into the world is, these tasks begin to make more sense. They belong to our lives because they are what our lives are really about. If we settle for anything less, we are betraying ourselves, our beloved, and God, the ultimate lover, who is longing to join with us.

Mary urges us to strive for something truly grand and great. To strive to become one with God is the grandest and greatest of all strivings, and to do this with another soul joined in love is, as Jesus says, an "extraordinary gift." God created us together with another soul and invites us to return to Him also joined in oneness with another soul.

This was Mary's way when she walked the earth. Her relationship with Joseph was made sacred by their love for each other and God, and their love was sealed in marriage. Within the sacredness of this bond, they loved God above all else and placed Him at the center of their life and relationship. They lived a holy life. They gave all their heart, mind, body, and soul to each other and to God. They let go of the illusions of this world as they struggled with darkness and evil. In other words, they did in their relationship and marriage what Mary is calling us to do in ours.

Every marriage has a mission and that mission includes, in one form or another, bringing more love into the world. We are living in times of great darkness, and we are being asked to make of our lives a statement of love and truth. This statement must begin in each of our hearts and come alive in the relationships we hold most dear. Mary is telling us that in marriage we have the vehicle we need to step into the miracle of divine love and rise above the darkness of the world. We then can fulfill that part of our mission to bring more love into the world, as we join with another in a sacred journey to God.

PART THREE

The Journey To God

CHAPTER SEVEN

Loving God Above All Else

MARY AND JOSEPH LOVED GOD above all else. They placed God at the center of their lives and relationship, and He was present in them and in their love for each other. God's presence allowed them to see through His eyes, making their love pure and bringing them to oneness with each other, with God, and with their divine essence. As Mary says, pure love is the way of God's love, and we love purely only when we know God intimately and He dwells within us.

When we open ourselves to God, His love grows within us. The spark of divine love, which comes alive in our hearts when we fall in love, merges with the infinitely greater flame of God's love. As the energy of divine love grows within us and our relationship, we come to know God intimately, for this energy is God. Then we find that not only are we are in love with another, but that we are also in love with God. But we cannot reach this point unless we choose to love God above all else and place Him at the center of our life and relationship.

The Ultimate Love and the Ultimate Lover

Mary says that God is the ultimate love and the ultimate lover and urges us to be in love with Him as He is in love with us. While a union of love with another soul will satisfy some of our desires, it will not fulfill our greatest desire or heal our deepest wound. Only union with God will do these things. Thus, Mary tells us:

> It is God you must be in love with, for He is in love with you, desperately seeking and desiring you and wanting you to want Him above all. He is the lover longing for the beloved. He wants you to be longing for Him as the one true love. In your love, you will know the Beloved, know God. In divine love, all is present.

Mary reminds us that God loves us, longs for us, and desires to be one with us, just as deep within we long for God and desire to know Him intimately and be one with Him. As lovers increasingly feel the energy of God within them, their relationship becomes a dance of love not only between them, but also between them and God. For to be in love with God is to feel and know and move with the energy of love. At these times, we encounter that something greater with which we long to merge, as we experience a bliss and freedom that lifts us out of the ordinary into the extraordinary.

We then realize that we do not have to live with our greatest desire unfulfilled and our deepest wound unhealed. Instead, we rediscover our relationship to the divine and recall, as Mary tells us, that it was not God who left us, but we who left God:

> See God, know God, and give all to God. He has never left you and is always with you. It is you who leave God.

As lovers, we are called to open ourselves to the divine and bring God increasingly into our lives and relationship. It is a choice we make. If we choose to love something other than God above all else and to place something other than God at the center of our lives and relationship, we are spurning the ultimate love and the ultimate lover. We are choosing something other than love as our highest value and oneness with God as our supreme goal.

Telling us that we will find all that we desire in God, Mary urges us to give all to God:

> If you give all in mind, body, and soul to our Lord God, you will have no regret. Everything you desire is in God's will and in love. If you give all to God, you become one with God. He is the Beloved and you are the beloved.

She then shows herself as an incredibly beautiful bride, holding Jesus as an infant, and states:

> In order to become one with God, you give yourself to God. You become the spouse of God. You long for nothing. The Divine Child is then born within you, and you see and love only truth. All that you long for and all that you need are in God. If you give all to God, you can actually walk on water.

Jesus was asked during a vision why we long for other things and not for Him. He answered, "It is because of ignorance and arrogance, and both are of the ego." He was then asked if it made Him sad that we do not long for Him, but for other things. He replied:

> It is a desperate sadness I feel because I see the destruction of souls because of the lack of love. Ask me to come into your heart, your mind, your body. Crave me and long for me because this is what I do for you. I long for you and crave for you. It is the longing of the ultimate love and the ultimate lover.

He then said lovers should long for and crave each other and also long for and crave Him so that the lovers can be one with each other and one with Him.

Romantic love as a path to God is a spiritual quest. As with any quest, at the beginning we may be unsure of what we are searching for or where it will lead us. We may believe that we are searching for human love. We may not yet have come to know God or experience Him as a presence in our lives. As a result, we may not know that we are really seeking God, and we may not have any reason to place Him at the center of our life and relationship. Sooner or later, however, we will find that are human love has faltered and that we are lost. Then we may choose to turn to God and invite Him into our life and relationship. For believers and non-believers alike, God continually courts us. As Mary tells us, He has never left us. He patiently waits for us to let go of, in Jesus' words, our ignorance and arrogance and return to Him as the ultimate love and the ultimate lover.

Mary wants us to know that romantic love is about finding our way back to God. She invites us to chart a different course for ourselves and our relationship, one that will carry us home to the love of all loves. However, without a union with God and in God we cannot do this because we do not recognize and accept God and His love as our ultimate destination. We do not see that God is the greatest of all loves and lovers who desires desperately for us to be filled with the fullness of His love. But, if we choose to love God above all else and place Him at the center of our lives and relationship, we will come to know the fruits of romantic love and the limitless possibilities it offers.

Our Need for God

We need God to be present in all areas of our lives, especially in relationship and marriage. A paradox of romantic relationship for many people is that the desire for God lies at the heart of romantic love, but God is often left out of the relationship. If God is not brought into the relationship, the desire to know Him intimately and be one with Him will not be fulfilled. Yet, for most lovers, God does not have a place in their relationship, and the need for His presence to bring romantic love to its highest expression goes unrecognized. Without God, the lovers will find it difficult to sustain the spark of divine love ignited in the initial opening of their hearts to each other. This spark is too easily extinguished by the ill winds of all that is not love in and around them. The relationship runs aground because God is not brought into it and made its center and foundation.

The Gospel parable of the sower and the seed illustrates what can happen to the spark of divine love ignited in our hearts when we fall in love. Jesus tells of a sower who went out to plant. Some seeds fall on the path. There is no soil in which they can take root, and the birds eat them. Other seeds fall on rocky ground where the soil is not rich. The seeds sprout quickly because the soil has no depth, but without sufficient roots the grain is soon withered by the sun. Still other seeds fall among thorns, and they choke the grain as it sprouts. The seeds that fall on good soil, however, flourish and produce in great abundance.[1]

Not unlike the seeds in this parable, the spark of divine love that ignites when we fall in love must contend with the internal and external worlds of the lovers. If these worlds are hospitable to love, if there is good soil in which love can take root and grow, then the lovers will have a better chance of holding onto their love, and their love will have a greater opportunity to produce in abundance. However, if there is little to nurture and sustain love within the lovers and their lives, it will be difficult for their love to survive. God's love provides the rich soil we need as the foundation of the relationship for the love to blossom into its fullness and produce in great abundance.

The wisdom of placing God at the center of a relationship is reflected in Gabriel's message to Mary, "For nothing will be impossible with God." For most of us, relationship poses many challenges and presents many problems. This is because human love, as Mary says, has its beauty but also its limitations, which mainly stem from the fears of the ego and the illusions of the mind. Yet Mary is telling us that with God we can rise above these limitations and experience the divine, allowing romantic love to soar to its greatest heights. The vibration of divine love that fills us when God is present lifts us into a higher consciousness in which we are no longer constrained by the ego and the ordinary mind. If we ask from deep within our hearts for God to be present in us and our relationship, God will respond. As Mary says, "What you ask from deep within your hearts will be granted."

Lovers and False Gods

Jesus tells us, "You must love God above all things and love each other as God." What happens to a relationship when we love something else more than God? To love something more than God is to worship a false god. In several visions, Mary speaks of the worship of false gods, such as money, lust, greed, power, status, or beauty. In one vision, she comments on the meaning of the First Commandment, which reads "You shall have no other gods besides me":

> Do no make money your god. Do not pursue false securities. Do not choose status or prestige. Read the First Commandment. It is not speaking of gods, such as other spirits or enlightened ones. It is talking about the false gods people make, such as money.

Mary repeatedly reminds us that love is the only thing that matters. Yet, as Jesus says, we pursue things other than love out of the ego's ignorance and arrogance. Ignorance in this sense connotes a lack of discernment as to the true nature of something. When we are ignorant about the true nature of an object or an activity, we do not see clearly its true value and its proper place in our lives. Seen through the clouded vision of the ego and the ordinary mind, we give it a meaning apart from its inherent nature and a place in our lives it does not merit. We are confused and act out of that confusion.

We must try to be honest with ourselves about what we love above all else. The answer will tell us what lies at the center of our consciousness and therefore at the center of our lives. In other words, we will find at the center of our consciousness, whether we are aware of it or not, what we love and value the most, and our lives will revolve around it. Most people live in what they love. If we love God above all else, we will live in God. If we love something other than God above all else, we will live in that.

If our highest value is something other than love and God, then we are opening ourselves to problems, and in matters of the heart we are setting ourselves up for failure. We are creating a conflict within ourselves and our relationship between the love we desire and what we value more than love. Whether the false god be money, prestige, worldly success, an activity, or an interest, we will be divided within ourselves. The false god occupying center stage, together with the illusions it engenders, will create the conditions for darkness to enter into our lives and relationship. The darkness will work to diminish or even destroy the love. As Jesus said in the Gospels, "And if a house is divided against itself, that house will not be able to stand."[2]

To love purely and to become one with God calls for a total commitment. As Joseph says about the world of Spirit, if one does not commit all to the path and to love, one can be destroyed. This is equally true of romantic love, especially when it is embraced as a spiritual path. If we do not commit all of ourselves, the love can be destroyed. As lovers, therefore, we must be willing to make a total commitment to each other, to love, and to God. This is one reason a romantic relationship should not be entered into lightly. There is often much more at stake than what initially meets the eye.

If we are not willing to make a total commitment, where do we think the relationship will end up? As Mary succinctly states: "A relationship that is not God-centered leads to disaster." She then tells us why: "A relationship that is not God-centered is darkness." God is light and love. Without light and love as the center of a relationship, darkness will be its center. This, as Mary says, is why a relationship not centered on God leads to disaster.

Mary's statements explain what goes wrong with many relationships and marriages. What do we bring to romantic love if we do not have love as our highest value and God at the center of our lives? We may believe that we desire to love and be loved in a way that is miraculous and that will open us more deeply to the mystery of love. But, far too often, our hearts are not centered on love and we pursue our treasure elsewhere. We may desire love, but in our hearts we are holding onto something other than love, and we do not give ourselves fully to the beloved, to love, or to God. Like the seeds in the parable that do not fall on rich soil, our love will not survive. The romantic relationship will not open us to more love and draw us closer to God.

The Vibration of Money

Mary draws our attention to the dangers that money and the pursuit of what money brings, such as material possessions, affluence, and prestige, pose to love and our relationship to God. Characterizing money as an evil, she warns:

> Beware of money. Money is what holds many people imprisoned in their darkness. Do not hold onto it and do not value it. Do not honor it and do not be seduced by it. When I walked the earth, I had nothing. Yet, I was rich beyond compare. It is not the riches of the world that bring you peace and happiness. These riches bring about division, destruction, greed, and evil. These riches blind you. I had nothing. Yet I had everything.

> Money is an evil. You must have money in your world to live, but it does not have to be that way. Do not buy into the power of money. Be strong in the truth. There is only one thing you truly need, and that is God. And, with God and in God, your every need is taken care of.

When we are "with God and in God," God will take care of our every need, as He did with Mary. So when we put our faith in money rather than God, when we substitute love of money for love of God, money becomes an evil. In today's world, many people's consciousness is centered on money and the pursuit of material wealth. The consciousness of money and material wealth permeates our lives and world on many levels and blinds us to our need for God and God's love for us. And, as in all cases of evil, it is based on a lie. Money and material wealth promise what they cannot deliver. We too often pursue them because we mistakenly believe they will bring peace and happiness. But, as Mary points out, they do not bring peace and happiness, but division, destruction, greed, and evil. She further explains:

> The things people think have made a big difference have not made a big difference. People come home to their big houses

and all their comforts, and they have plenty. But they are not happy, and they do not know God. They still suffer within. The things you have thought would change the world have not. There is no justice, no peace, no hope. It is because God is not at the center of people's lives. They do not know God and do not know love. They are choosing hopeless dreams and illusions. Of all the great power in the world and its brilliance, there is no peace on a micro or macro level. And those who believe they are high and mighty, they are not.

The vibration of money is so low that Mary says it holds many people imprisoned in their darkness. We ignore this warning at our own peril. We are bombarded from every direction with inducements for more money and material possessions, and it is hard for most people not to fall under the spell of the materialism of our world. Like the sexual propaganda in the media and entertainment industry, it is a type of conditioning aimed at controlling people's thoughts and actions. Mary says, "It is no accident that the media use their power to poison the minds of people." She adds, "When you have access to people's minds, you also have access to their hearts."

When we are filled with the vibration of money and worldly riches, especially when it has entered our hearts, we are living at a low level of consciousness and a low vibration of energy. According to Mary, "Money itself has a vibration. When that vibration enters one's consciousness, it reduces one's consciousness and controls it. It maintains one's consciousness at a low level and a low vibration." In contrast, Mary points out, "Love is the highest vibration." She states this in a vision in which she turns to gold and the space around her is filled with golden light. When we are filled with the consciousness of love, we are filled with the vibration of love and, like Mary, turn to gold.

The danger that Mary is warning against is illustrated in a dream in which a man who had recently died at a relatively young age appeared and asked for help. His story while on earth was that of growing up in a middle class family, but becoming rich as an adult. He became the personal assistant to a wealthy philanthropist, who lavished upon him money and expensive gifts. His employer's largesse made the young man wealthy in his own right, and to his credit he was generous with his wealth. The money, however, had an untoward effect on him, which he did not fully recognize until he passed on.

In the dream he explained his predicament. He was in a place that was neither light nor dark, but wished to move to a higher level. However, he could not move higher because the vibration of money had entered his consciousness so deeply during his life on earth that he carried the vibration to the other side. He said that the vibration was very low and so deeply embedded in him that it prevented him from moving to a higher spiritual level. He asked for energy so that he could rid himself of this vibration and move to a higher level.

Mary is sending a strong warning not only about the danger of money, but also about the materialism of our age. She asserts, "The materialism of your world is a rape of the soul." When the vibration of money or the riches of the world penetrates the soul, the soul is raped. Our souls long to be filled with the vibration of love, which brings with it beauty and freedom, not with the vibration of money or material possessions, which brings darkness and illusion.

Many people are not unlike the young man in the dream. The vibration of money and worldly riches has entered deeply into many people's souls, imprisoning them in a low level of consciousness and preventing them from moving higher. Their souls suffer a painful sense of betrayal as their longing for the divine remains unfulfilled. This unmet desire can become a desperate hunger leading to increased attempts to accumulate more material wealth and spill over into other areas of one's life, such as sex, in misguided efforts to find love and healing. When we live with something other than God and love at the center of our lives, we deny the soul the chance to fulfill its greatest desire and to heal its deepest wound.

Mary is also giving us another important message. She is trying to awaken us to the power of love and to the truth that, if we were to truly know God and put our faith totally in God, we could live at a level of consciousness at which money would be unnecessary. The vibration of love is so powerful that our lives and world would be very different. Mary, like her Son before her, is offering us a different way of being in the world, the way of divine love. She is telling us what it would mean if we were really to put our faith in God and were to become one with Him. We could live a heaven on earth. Joseph confirms this in a vision when he says, "That which is miraculous on your plane of existence is common and normal on other planes of existence."

According to Mary, the vibration of money is woven into all aspects of our lives. It has become so normal that we do not feel it and so pervasive that we do not recognize it as part of us. It is difficult not to be infected by it, as if by a virus, even at the deepest levels of the soul. As Jesus points out in the following message, we have lost perspective about what we really need and what is truly important:

> In your world, people live to the extreme and excess. How much does one really need and what is the madness you believe in? How much do you need? You must live simply and not have so much. Having so much gives you more to be distracted about. It is not the things of your world that bring you joy, truth, or comfort. How many cars, televisions, pants, or shoes does one need? And how happy or true are these things? People are obsessed with the things they think are so important. These things are not only material. The list of these things goes on and on. And your world is obsessed with greed: greed for more money, more things, more education, more, more, more.

> How much does one need? With all that people have, how comfortable are they really? You must not follow and live in the norm.... And do not take more than you need. What you do not need, give to someone who does need. But do not think that having these false securities makes you happier, greater, better. Look around you and you see very little truth.

Until we live in a consciousness of love, we will need money and a certain amount of material wealth to provide for ourselves and our families. It is not so much a question of how much, but of the values we live by. If we give all to God and center our lives on love, we will not fail ourselves or our loved ones, as Mary and Joseph's lives bear witness.

For the Sake of the Children

The souls of children, like those of adults, long for love and truth. They need, especially in these times, to be awakened spiritually. To be filled with the vibration of money and material possessions and the consciousness of materialism is death to the soul. Mary says that a mother's role is to spark the light in her children. It is both parents' role to keep this light alive in their children so that it can grow into the all-consuming fire of divine love. Parents cannot do this if they are filled with the vibration of money and their souls are raped by the materialism of the world. We cannot spark the light and nurture it in others if the light within us has been dimmed.

As parents, we often forget what it is that we and our children are here to accomplish. Our actions as parents often mislead our children about what life is about. If we bow before false gods, like money, we are teaching our children to do the same. The more we worship that which in the end proves false, the stronger will its hold be over us and the harder will it be later in life to free ourselves. False values and the actions that flow from them, repeated over and over again, create illusions that run deep in our consciousness, like veins in marble, obscuring the truth of what our lives are about and keeping us separated from what we truly desire. This will be as true for our children as it is for us.

Parents sometimes justify not stepping out of the madness of their lives because they believe they have to provide their children the best opportunities possible. But what are these opportunities if they do not bring children closer to God and love? Jesus addresses the dilemma many parents feel around what their children really need. He says the greatest thing parents can do for their children, greater than anything else, is to become one with Him:

> It is greater than all the money and possessions of the world, greater than education and safety. It is greater than anything you can give them.

To become one with Jesus, of course, is to be pure love and one with God. As Jesus states, "To know me is to know love. To know love is to know God." Are we not betraying our children if we teach them by our words or example to put something other than God and love at the center of their lives? Mary says that parents often teach their children to mistake love for such things as physical beauty, prestige, education, or power. She encourages parents to "teach their children love" and maintains that "the greatest gift you can give your children is truth."

Living the Truth

In order to make something the center of our lives, we must believe it to be the highest truth. If we do not believe it is the highest truth, then it does not merit center stage. Our age is dominated by secular views of the world, and Mary's message that love is the only truth is easily eclipsed by the many false claims of truth that vie for our attention. We are inundated with views of the world presented in the media, entertainment and advertising industries, and educational institutions that leave God in a marginal place or, more often, omit Him altogether. Yet, while our minds may be confused about what is truth, our hearts are not. They know that love is truth. They desire and relentlessly search for it, even in ways that may be misguided. While the mind may be content with the illusions of the world, the heart continues to crave love. But, too often, the heart cannot break free of the illusions of the mind and find its way to love.

If we choose love and God as our truth and place them at the center of our lives, we will draw closer to God. For some it may be the first step toward living a sacred life. At the same time, we will become more adept at recognizing and avoiding the darkness of the world. Living with love and God at the center of our lives and relationship may put us out of step with the times and many people around us. It may exact a high price. But what is the alternative? Living a life of truth may be hard. Yet, as Jesus points out in the following message, the hardship is only temporary and leads to what is eternal. Sharing His experience when He walked the earth, He asks us to reflect on the choice we have before us:

When I lived as a man, I spoke the truth, and I lived the truth. The light was despised by the darkness. I was killed because I spoke the truth. Do not think that to your world living the truth or being the truth is acceptable or comfortable. But, in my world, it is comfortable. It is eternal comfort, eternal peace. In your world it is not. Think about which world you want to live in: your world which is temporary or my world which is permanent. Speak the truth. Live the truth. Fight for the truth. Why would you choose to be carried away with lies and illusions in that which is temporary?

Further sharing His experience of being rejected, even by members of His own family, He speaks of the suffering that is inevitable if one chooses to live truth:

I suffered as a man, as any man would suffer when they are hated and despised by those closest to them. There were members of my own family who did not believe and despised me and the light.

Mary likewise beckons us to a life of truth. "The only truth is love, and that is the truth one should live." If we live this truth, she explains, we can become like God:

There in only one truth and that is the truth of love. If you succeed completely in knowing love, you know God and become like God. You can create miracles because all the power and all the truth and all the knowing is in love and love is God and God is in all things.

What would it mean to structure our lives and relationships around the truth of love? By sharing details of her life, Mary has shown us what such a life was like for her. We only have to recall what she achieved in her life to know what we can achieve in ours. She says, in contrast, that a life without love is not really living:

It is the power of love that allows one to live, and people whose hearts are closed are dead. They are not alive and living. This is what you see everyday. People are lifeless, like robots, programmed to do their daily tasks and work. But it has nothing to do with love. Follow my example when I walked the earth and my example now. I am nothing but heart, nothing but love, pure and divine.

How can we succeed in love and be passionate and free if we live like robots? Mary speaks of another way of living, in which our hearts are open and our lives structured around love and light. She calls it living a holy life and says we are all called to live such a life.

CHAPTER EIGHT

Living a Holy Life

MARY SAYS THAT TO BE HOLY is to be filled with love and that to be filled with love is to be filled with light. To be holy, then, is to be God-like. To do this is within our reach, but we must be willing to step out of the ordinary. This is what Mary calls us to do so that we can make something extraordinary of our lives, as she did with hers. She says that we can do this by living a holy life, telling us, "In the holy life all things are possible, and the miracle of miracles is waiting for you."

What Is a Holy Life?

Mary says that there are several elements that form the foundation of a holy life. The first is loving God above all else, which is discussed in the preceding chapter. The second element is bringing truth into all aspects of one's life and being. Mary says that love is the highest truth, and we will not be filled with love if we are not living the truth of love. Mary thus calls us to:

Weave the truth into everything: into your being, into your thinking, into your speech, into your seeing, into your actions. Weave the truth into all you are and all you do. Remember that the truth is love and about love. If it is not love and breeding love, it is something else. It is of illusion or of darkness. Be and live the truth.

A third element of a holy life is selfless service through which we express our love in action. We also strive to let go of the small self as we act for the benefit of others and not our own. A fourth element, according to Mary, is to be open to Spirit. This means, among other things, being open to the power of Spirit to transform us and every aspect of our lives. It also means to be open to the world of Spirit as it speaks to us and touches our lives. Mary says that the world of Spirit coexists with the material world:

> The world of Spirit is all around you. What you see when you focus on seeing is the world of Spirit, which coexists here with the material world.

Mary identifies four additional elements that we might consider the "active ingredients" of a holy life: prayer, meditation, spiritual practice, and love-making. According to Mary, these four activities have the same thing in common: They all have the power to create light and bring light directly into us and the world. The light they create can lift us to a higher level of consciousness which will allow us to experience and sustain the vibration of love in our hearts and minds. Speaking of the power of these "active ingredients" to do this, Mary explains:

> Pray, meditate, practice, and make love. These four things are very high vibration, and they will help you move into a higher level of consciousness and vibration and to become pure and total love. You must nourish and nurture the seed of truth, the seed of love, within you and make it grow. The way to make it grow is to do these four things and to live the holy life.

These four activities, embraced as part of a holy life, will bring romantic love to its highest expression. The seed of truth that blossoms when we fall in love needs to be nourished and nurtured. We do this, according to Mary, by living a holy life. We thus find that romantic love and the spiritual life are deeply connected. It is when we separate them that we lose the sense of what both romantic love and the spiritual life truly are.

If lovers can bring the seed of truth to fruition in them and their relationship, they will attain what all spiritual seekers strive for. This can be done, Mary says, by making these four activities central to their lives and relationship:

> Prayer, meditation, practice, and love-making are the tools for this path. These are the tools that the mystics, sages, and saints have used to lift themselves into the heart of God.

She thus tells us, "If you pray, meditate, practice, and make love with sacredness, you live the holy life."

Prayer

Prayer comes in many forms and varies among spiritual traditions. Essentially, prayer is a communication with the divine. This communication may include the recitation of sacred words that have the power to connect one with God and beings of light and love. Prayer, especially when it comes from the heart, fills us with light and love. This is also true of the repetition of sacred words, such as in chanting, which creates light in and around us. This light, which is a manifestation of God, has the power to transform us, others, and the world. Speaking of light and prayer, Mary explains:

> Move into the light. The world needs the light only. The great healing comes through bringing God to earth through light and prayer.

The prayer with which Mary is most associated is the rosary. She asks that the rosary be prayed, especially in these times of great transition, for the "awakening, saving, and enlightening of souls." But, she says, the exact words we say in prayer are not important: "The words do not matter as long as they connect you to truth and to love." She adds:

> It is not the words that you pray that matters. It is that you pray from the heart. Prayer serves as a means of communi- cation. The way that you pray or the place that you pray or the words that you pray do not matter. If your words are words of love and sincerity, they are charged with a different energy, which is the energy of a higher communication. Some prayers are charged with that energy because they are said over and over again by different peoples throughout the world. But only prayers that come from the heart and that are said with love are a communication with the above.

On another occasion, she describes prayer coming from the heart as a love song to her and God:

> Prayer is holy when spoken from the heart. It is words of love, a love song to me and to God.

She encourages us to pray to the Holy Spirit, Jesus, and other beings of light. Appearing with Jesus and several saints, she says:

> Every single one of them is holy. Every single one of them is light. Every single one of them is love. Every single one of them gave themselves over to God completely and is pure and one with God. They are here for you. They will help you and guide you. Turn to them in times of need and in times when you think you have no need.

She also reminds us that no prayer goes unanswered:

> Call upon the Holy Spirit and the angels and the saints for your specific needs. No prayer goes unanswered. Every prayer

is answered, but it may not be answered in the way you think it should be answered. Ask the Holy Spirit to guide you to see the answers as they are around you.

She further states that prayer is the most important way for us to love and to share love:

Loving and sharing love come in many ways, and the most important is prayer. Prayer is an action of love, especially when it comes from the heart.

She likewise points out that prayer is the most important way to bring others to God:

I ask you to pray more, to let God come through in your prayer. Let prayer be an important part of your work. Your work is to bring people to God. The most important way to do this is through prayer.

Prayer affects us in many ways, including energetically. For example, it can clear negative energies that build up in one's energy field as a result of negative thoughts. Mary notes this in the following message in which she speaks of the use of short, repetitive prayers, which she uses the term mantra to describe, to shift oneself out of a negative vibration into a positive one:

When one is flooded with thoughts that are not about love, one should immediately begin to pray a mantra. The energy of the mantra goes into the heart so that one's own love and divine love can flow through. Once the heart is open, the entire vibration of a person begins to shift into love. Then loving thoughts can come through. Rather than contemplating negativity or darkness, begin to say a mantra and open the heart and let love flow. Let the love clear the vibration of energy on the energy field which is building with the negative thoughts.

Her prescription for negative thoughts is also applicable for negative emotions and moods. When we are caught in the grip of negative emotions or moods, we often spin into powerful cycles of negativity, creating a negative vibration that fills our energy field and breeds more negativity. Examples of short repetitive prayers are: "Mary, cleanse me with your grace, cleanse me with your love, cleanse me with your light." "Jesus, fill me with your peace, fill me with your love, fill me with your light." The holy name of God found in any tradition can be used in these short prayers.

Meditation

Mary gives great importance to meditation. While she describes prayer as a love song to God, she says meditation is making love with God. Meditation is a term used to describe different types of spiritual practices. Mary uses it to refer to the stilling of the mind and moving beyond thought to a "place" where one experiences God directly.

God, like love, cannot be grasped by the mind or thoughts. Therefore, to join with God, even temporarily, we need to move beyond mind and thought. Meditation allows us to do this. It brings us to a place of pure light, unmediated by thought, in which we experience the divine directly.

For some people meditation comes easily, while for others the stilling of the mind is difficult. In initial stages of learning to meditate, we may not experience the higher states or only experience them briefly. However, as the practice of meditation continues, the periods of being in higher states will last longer. The purpose of both prayer and meditation, Mary explains, is to bring one into higher states of consciousness in which one is connected to the intellect of the heart:

> You must move into the heart and be only in the heart. In prayer and meditation, you expand the wisdom and intellect of the heart. You connect with that vibration and not the lower vibration you carry. The vibration of prayer and of a high level of meditation connect one to a high level of consciousness.

Spiritual Practices
Mary also stresses the use of light in spiritual practices. She uses the term "spiritual practices," or sometimes simply "practice," to refer to the use of visualization to create and expand light within and around oneself. Light, which is the energy of love, carries the consciousness of love, which is the highest consciousness. When we are filled with light, we are filled with this consciousness, as Mary points out:

> Love will bring you to the highest consciousness and the highest level because love is the highest consciousness and the highest level.

In visualization, we use the mind to create and direct light. This may take the form of specific images or it may simply be visualizing light in and around oneself. Mary often recommends seeing oneself filled with and surrounded by violet light, which she associates with the Holy Spirit. Light may also be invoked from higher planes or by calling upon the Holy Spirit or beings of light, such as Mary or Jesus, to fill us with their light. We can then see ourselves filled with and surrounded by violet, gold, pink, or white light.

Visualization need not be complicated. It can be as simple as seeing oneself filled with and surrounded by light or seeing one's energy centers being filled with light. Visualization goes well with prayer. Prayer draws light into us, and this can be enhanced through visualization.

Light created or invoked in spiritual practices can be used for many purposes. We have already seen that it can be used for protection. We can also use it to cleanse ourselves of thoughts, emotions, and other energies that are of a low vibration and do not serve love. These energies keep us engaged in patterns of thinking, feeling, and acting that are not beneficial to ourselves or others. When we clear such energies, we can be more open to Spirit and more connected to love. Spiritual practices can also be used to heal ourselves and others, to create and expand the light in places where we live, work, and pray, and to bring about other positive changes in ourselves, others, and the world.

Like meditation, visualization comes more readily to some people. Some people are more visual than others and can easily create and hold images in their minds. Even if you are not visual in this way, the intent to create light, to bring light into yourself, or to send it to others is effective, even if in your mind's eye you do not see the light or the specific image created. Visualizations for specific purposes are included in Appendixes A and B.

Love-making

Love-making, as discussed previously, creates and expands the light in lovers and opens them to the divine. For couples who share a genuine bond of love and make a full commitment to each other, to love, and to God, love-making can be an integral part of a holy life. Mary points out that the different aspects of a holy life complement each other. For example, she speaks of the relationship between prayer and meditation, on the one hand, and love-making, on the other. Prayer and meditation, she says, can bring one to a higher consciousness. Lovers can then bring this consciousness into their love-making, and it will take their love-making to a higher level. The higher level of consciousness achieved through love-making can then enhance their prayer and meditation. Prayer and meditation thus can be instrumental in bringing lovers and their love-making to higher levels of consciousness where they move beyond the physical pleasure of mere sex. Mary describes the positive effects that prayer and meditation can have on love-making:

> Thus, in love-making you can be connected to the divine. If you are at a lower level of consciousness, you cannot connect with the divine. You have to get to a higher level of consciousness, which lets the divine energy flow into the love-making. It makes the divine energy flow in and around you. If you are at a lower level of consciousness, the love-making creates a dense, heavy energy. But, if you can expand consciousness through prayer and meditation, you can bring the higher level of consciousness to the love-making, and this will allow the divine energy into the love-making.

The Holy Life and the Sacred Heart

Mary says that prayer, meditation, spiritual practices, and love-making are means to open to the Sacred Heart. When we open to the Sacred

Heart and merge with it, according to Mary, we are enlightened. She speaks of this in a vision in which she shows her Sacred Heart, which is often referred to as the Immaculate Heart of Mary, and the Sacred Heart of Jesus. She begins by expressing concern about the lack of understanding among Western religions of light, visualization, and energy as means to connect with God. She then goes on to speak of the Sacred Heart:

> The Catholic Church and other Western religions are blind to the system of energy. People in the West do not have an understanding of the light, visualization, and energy as a way to connect with God. They do not understand what the Sacred Heart really is. The Sacred Heart is the hidden chamber of the heart, which is beyond the depth of the heart chakra. Anyone who wants to experience truth must move into the heart chakra and clear it and then move beyond it, past its depth. One must open the hidden chamber and allow its light and truth to enter. Once a person moves into the Sacred Heart, they are enlightened, awakened, holy. When one is in this place, one is beyond duality. There is no good or bad. There is everything. You become all, and all becomes you. It is the place where God sits within you and God is you. It is the place where you become one with all, and all becomes one with you.

> The Sacred Heart is the intellect of the heart. It is love beyond a concept. It is love beyond everything. It is purity. It is God's totality which sits within every living being and every living creature and thing. When you connect with it, go into it, everything else about you is cleansed. It is stronger than anything, any darkness, any problems. You see the whole of everything. It is what you are. It is where the cosmic flows into you. You have to clear the heart chakra completely, in human and divine love, and then go into the hidden chamber and the Sacred Heart. Then you become God, and God

becomes you. Teach people who do not know about light and visualization. Teach them about it and the light coming into the heart chakra and opening it up.

Then, showing the light of the Sacred Heart as a salmon-colored fire in the heart, she states:

This is what I am. This is what Jesus is. This is what God is. It is everything. It is all dualities in a non-duality. It is the greatest intellect which the small mind does not know. It is knowing. You know all, and all is you—cosmically—and not just on this level, but everywhere.

She next speaks about how to clear the heart chakra and open the hidden chamber of the heart through the combination of prayer, meditation, spiritual practices, and love-making:

Clearing the heart chakra will come through prayer. The vibration of prayer cleanses the energy field. If the prayer is concentrated in a specific area, such as the heart chakra, and you use the prayer to cleanse, then that area is cleansed. Visualization cleanses with light, like a force that clears the imprints that are held deep within. In meditation, the release of the mind opens the heart. Every time you meditate, the heart can open more. The more you meditate, the closer you come to the hidden chamber of the heart. When you get to the hidden chamber, meditation will open the door. For people in relationship where there is pure love, the love-making can deepen the heart. When you go into the Sacred Heart, which is the totality of God, through the love-making, the love-making itself is expanded into God, and God is expanded into the love-making.

Union with the Sacred Heart in love-making is what Mary and Joseph experienced. It is why lovers should strive for a purity of love and recognize the power of love-making to bring them to a direct experience of God. Mary also affirms the importance of human love, even with its limitations. She says that, even though we may not yet be open to the Sacred Heart, when we love from the heart in the human ways in which we know how, we are creating a space within the heart to be filled with the vibration of divine love when the door to its hidden chamber opens.

The Call to a Holy Life

Living a holy life will create the light in lovers to open their hearts to the depths of the Sacred Heart and lift them into the highest level of consciousness. Then they can know themselves and the world in a different way, as they see through the eyes of love and know through the intellect of the heart. Living a holy life allows a couple to bring God increasingly into their lives and relationship. To live a holy life, however, is not easy. The lives of many saints and spiritual masters attest to this. Speaking of the difficulty of living a holy life, Mary points out:

> In order to live the holy life, you must be very strong. So few choose to do it. This makes it difficult because the world around you values other than God. The world around you loves the darkness, and it is easy to be seduced by its many seductions.

Living a holy life may seem too much to ask of ourselves and our lover. Yet, as Mary says, anything less is not really living:

> There is only one way to really live and that is to live the life of God. If you live something other, you are not truly living. To be awake is to live love. Do not fear doing this. You will have no regrets if you live the holy life.

She further states that living a holy life will free us from illusions:

> Men around you try to conquer the world. The only thing they have conquered is one illusion after another that they

have created. Do not continue to live in illusions. Step out of it completely. Do not fear. There is only one way to God. That is by becoming holy and living the holy life. There is no other way. You have to be holy within. You have to be full of love, love for God, love for love.

When we look to Mary and Joseph's life, we see that it did not matter how high the cost. They accepted God's call of love, and Mary urges us to do the same:

Be the truth and live the truth, no matter what others think or do. Remember, there is only but one truth, which is love. The way to get there is to live the holy life. You will lose nothing and gain everything. What you think you have lost is an illusion, for in reality there is no loss ever. Love. Love. Love. This is the truth. Do not doubt me and do not fear. Live the holy life.

Further encouraging us to live a holy life, especially in anticipation of the changes that she says are coming to our world, she adds:

Live the holy life, and you will have no regrets. It is those who are not living the holy life who will have great regrets and who will be devastated the most. Living the holy life is not choosing money and other pursuits. Living the holy life is loving God above all else. There are very few who do this.

Living a Holy Life Day by Day

It takes effort to sustain the vibration of love. Mary notes, for example, that people go to church and receive something that lifts their consciousness. But then they leave church and engage in activities, like watching television or going to malls, that bring their consciousness right back to where it was before they went to church. She says nothing has changed for them and asks why they even bother to go to church if they are going to persist in engaging in activities that keep them at a low vibration of energy and asleep in a world of illusions. In other words, becoming holy is a full-time endeavor.

What we do impacts us energetically. Mary is saying that many activities in which we typically engage keep us at a very low vibration of energy and level of consciousness that does not allow us to feel the presence of God. She encourages us always to hold God in our hearts and minds and center our thoughts, feelings, and actions on Him. She is guiding us to a total transformation of consciousness that we achieve by making every aspect of our lives sacred. She thus urges us to:

> Think with the heart. Think with love. Feel with the heart. Feel with love. Act from the heart. Act with love. Every thought should be a thought about God and of God. Every feeling should be a feeling for God and of God. Every action should be an action for God and of God.

She similarly advises that everything we do should be an act of love and service to God, as well as a giving to God. Specifically addressing daily activities, she enjoins:

> When you work, your work should be a work you are doing for God. So your intention about your work should be for the love of God so that you do your work for the love of God. And your work should only be about bringing yourself and others closer to God. It should be a source of life and a source of love.

> When you play, you must play with the intention of bringing joy and laughter and love to yourself and your soul and ultimately of bringing God to life in you and others. Even when you eat, you eat with the thought, feeling, and action that you eat for the temple He has given you so you can serve Him.

Mary reminds us that we cannot afford to waste time or engage in senseless activities if we are to succeed at becoming pure love:

When you waste time on foolish activities and foolish things, you waste your time to become that much closer to God. If there are things that you must do that are foolish, then you must remember to bring your soul and your heart and your mind to God while in those actions. It is better not to engage in foolish activities because they waste your time and opportunity for union with God.

Specifically addressing television, she asks, "Why would you spend an hour watching television when you could spend that hour communing with God?"

By living a holy life, as it opens us more and more to love, we can change not only ourselves, but the world. Mary affirms repeatedly that only love will make a difference for ourselves, others, and the world. She states in a vision in which she appears with ripples of light flowing from her heart:

There is only one thing that really matters and truly makes a difference and that is love. Every ounce of your being and beingness must vibrate with love. If you want to make a difference in those around you and that around you, if you vibrate your love and become that total love, you can change anything.

We naturally want to hold onto the magic we feel when we fall in love, which is connected to the vibration of love in our hearts. We can maintain that vibration, according to Mary, by living a holy life. There are many forces within and around us that oppose love and keep us trapped in a low vibration of energy. Mary is teaching us not only how to hold onto the spark of the divine that comes to life when we fall in love, but how that spark can grow into the flame of divine love that will transform us, others, and the world. She is showing us the tools we need and guiding us to a way of living that conforms with our innermost desire to know and become love and join with God. She thus tells us:

It is the intellect of the heart you must focus on. Make every thought love. Make every breath love. Be love. This is how you will grow in the intellect of the heart. The more you grow in the intellect of the heart, the more you will step into the pure mind, and the more you will know all things. If your heart is pure and your thoughts are pure, you become pure. If you are pure, you are one with God.

When we accommodate ourselves to what the world has to offer and live in a consciousness that cannot sustain love, we place at risk what is most essential to us and to our purpose for being in the world. Mary reminds us that the things of the world will pass away, but our holiness, the love we carry within us, will be with us forever:

Live a holy life. Live in a holy way. Do not worry about the rest. All things come and go, but your holiness will never pass away.

CHAPTER NINE

Letting Go of All That Is Not Love

WE WILL NOT BE PURE LOVE if we hold onto that which is not love. Most people find it difficult to let go of those aspects of themselves and their lives that are not of love. For many people, letting go may pose one of the greatest obstacles they face on the spiritual path. It may even evoke a deep fear as the ego violently resists relinquishing its long-standing domination. But how can we become pure love if we cling to fears and illusions that are not love? Mary tries to guide us through this transition, helping us to see what letting go of all that is not love really means and why it is necessary.

When we hold onto that which is not love, we perpetuate an inner division between that which is love and that which is not love, limiting ourselves, our love, and our relationship with the beloved. We may feel in our hearts that we are called to give all in love, but we find reasons not to. We may even know that the greater our love, the richer the relationship

will be and the more we will feel God's presence. We may likewise understand that holding onto that which is not love thwarts our own desire to
be whole in the purity of love. Still, we often fear letting go and feel that
we are incapable of giving all.

Mary says that we need not be hostages to fear. She explains that
everything that is not love is an illusion and that, when we let go, we lose
nothing and gain everything. At the same time, we are not asked to do it
alone. The presence of God in our lives and relationships makes possible
what might otherwise seem impossible. Jesus taught this lesson when He
spoke about entering into the Kingdom of Heaven, which is what we do
when we become pure love. When He told His disciples that it is easier for
a camel to pass through the eye of a needle than for a rich person to enter
the Kingdom of God, they were dismayed and asked how then could anyone be saved. He responded, "For mortals it is impossible, but for God
all things are possible."[1]

Living a holy life can create within us the conditions that will allow us to
truly let go. As we bring love and God increasingly into our lives and relationships, fill ourselves with greater light, and live at a higher consciousness, we
will move closer to the point of letting go of all that is not love. We will gain
the faith and courage to pass this test of love and to step fully into the truth
of love where we will find the freedom, joy, and bliss that we desire.

Any relationship provides the opportunity to give all of oneself and to
give from the heart. This is especially true of romantic relationship. It
affords a unique opportunity to give oneself to another unconditionally and
to sacrifice what Mary calls the small self for the greater self of love. If we
are willing to do this, our human love can become divine love. But letting
go of all that is not love must extend to all areas of our lives. It is difficult
to hold onto love in our personal lives if we are not living the truth of love
in other areas of our lives. Thus, we are called to make a total commitment
and, as Mary tells us, this means giving all of ourselves to God.

Giving All to God

As we have seen, Mary gave everything to God. She explains that it is
only when we give up everything that we gain everything and that everything we gain is God:

In order to know God, you must look up to God and into God. You must give everything that is yours, inside and out, to God. You must give up everything to gain everything. If you do not give up everything, you do not gain everything and you do not gain God. Therefore, you do not know God.

Mary says that we all are called to do this:

Give up everything and give yourselves to God. This is true for all people. It is what all people must do.

Giving up everything can be painful, evoking fear and conflict within us. Few people see it as the path to freedom, joy, and bliss. We desire these things, but, faced with the prospect of giving up everything, we question, make excuses, procrastinate. Mary knows this is a struggle for us and offers the following counsel:

To become one with God, you will give up everything and lose everything as you know it. This is painful. This is what you fear. But when you give up everything, you gain everything. Then you will see that there is no separation. Then you will live without separation in total love and total peace. What you are experiencing is the real conflict and battle. It is the battle within you. Here you have to fight to move completely into love and into God.

Reminding us that without God our lives go nowhere but with God we are everything, Mary urges us not to fall prey to fear or ignorance:

If you engage in foolish and senseless activities, you are not giving everything. You must give everything, everything. Fear and ignorance hold one back. Do not be afraid and do not be ignorant. Without God, your life goes into the darkness. Your life goes nowhere and becomes nothing without God. With God you become everything.

She thus exhorts us to sacrifice the small self for the true self and lets us know that we will receive help from above:

> You must sacrifice the small self for the true self of love, of God. Sacrifice the small for the great. You must give all to know God, to be one with God. The angels will help you, will hold you, and will bring you to the Most High.

Expressing her total faith in the power of love, she adds:

> Love is all you need. With love and in love all is possible. With love and in love all needs are taken care of. You must not fear. In love there is no fear. There is all truth and understanding and knowing. With love all things can be conquered.

The fear of letting go runs deep within us. We may feel we might not survive if we lose everything. We may also fear we will be ridiculed by others. The small self works to convince us that letting go will lead to disaster which we should avoid at all costs. It tricks us into believing that the miracle of divine love can never be ours. Mary challenges us to believe otherwise:

> Follow the sacred and the holy. All that you long for and all that you need are in God. If you give all to God, you can actually walk on water.

A World of Illusions

Mary repeatedly states that we live in a world of illusions. She tells us this because she wants us to understand what giving ourselves to love and to God really means for us. She wants us to know that we are prisoners in a world of illusions and that, if we let the illusions go, we will be free. She illustrates this point in a vision in which she appears with her image reflected in a pool of rippling water and explains:

The world you live in is the reflection. It is only a reflection which vanishes in the ripples and has no meaning unless you love. Open your eyes and do not be blinded by the reflection and the lies. Open your eyes to love, to light, to God. If you love everything in your world, remember it means nothing and is nothing. It vanishes once you open your eyes and you know God, love, and light.

In other visions, she graphically depicts what it is for us to be asleep in a world of illusions. In one, she shows things of the world enclosed within a prison cell with bars and says we must step out of the things of the world. At another time, she again presents a prison cell and, lifting up the bars, enjoins:

You must break free from the prison in which you live and the prison all around you. You are not your experiences, and you are not of this world. You must break free.

Yet again, in another vision, she urges:

Do not be imprisoned. Break free. Break out of it. Do not be blinded by it. When I look down upon the earth and its many beings, this is what I see.

She then shows a vast prison with dark cells with bars through which you can hardly see out. At another time, she equates living without love to being imprisoned in darkness:

Those who live without love are in prison. They allow darkness to come in and destroy.

According to Mary, every institution in our world, including educational, religious, business, entertainment, and government, is part of the prison. In a vision in which she presents these institutions within a vast global prison, she passes through the prison bars and rises above the prison itself. She then shows from above what is within the prison below: schools and institutions of higher learning, churches, office complexes, government buildings, malls, theaters, and many other places that are part of our lives and world. Referring to these places and the activities that take place in them, she admonishes:

> You should not engage in this. You should not engage in senseless activities. They take you nowhere and do nothing for anybody. You need to turn to faith and love and light. You need to turn to them completely and know them.

These messages help us to see that, paradoxically, what we fear the most is freedom from the illusions that we carry within us and that we have institutionalized around us. We are imprisoned not only in our illusions, but also in the low vibration of energy that corresponds to them. Mary portrays in several visions what our lives and world look like to her as we live in this low vibration. In one, she presents the earth's people surrounded by a very dense energy and moving lethargically, as if asleep. From our perspective on earth, we believe we move through the world quickly and at a high level of energy. Mary is showing us that, quite to the contrary, we move very slowly and at a vibration of energy that is painfully low. Mary warns that it is dangerous to live at the vibration of what she calls "the world, the worldly, and the worldly minded":

> The world, the worldly, and the worldly minded are a poison to consciousness. They are of a vibration that is so low that it does not even allow one to feel the Spirit. It has nothing to do with love, with light, or with God. Everything around you has become so distorted.

At that vibration, Mary points out, "people do not know who they are or why they are." She further warns, "To live in the vibration of the world is deadly to the soul." It is also deadly to romantic love. How can love survive if couples allow their minds and hearts to be filled with the low and deadly vibration of the "world, the worldly, and the worldly minded"?

She thus advises us to rise above the vibration of the world and live in the vibration of love:

> The most important thing is not to try to solve the things going on outside of oneself, but to be in a place of God and love and to give that love so that you create a vibration of love that ripples out and affects others. This is a time to be and develop, which is to become one with one's true essence. It has nothing to do with ideas. It has to do with the experience of love that you will find what you are looking for, in loving God and loving God above all things.

Jesus, likewise, calls us to rise above the world by living in a place of Spirit and love:

> If you, like me, stay in a place of Spirit and love, you rise above the material world and can walk through it seeing the truth of everything.

Mary presents in other visions people's lives and the course of human history as going nowhere. In several visions, she shows people moving slowly in circles and going no place. In another, she appears looking very human, with a globe spinning in each of her eyes. As the globes spin, tears fall from her eyes. She says that the spinning is what the people of the earth do and that the course of human history moves in endless cycles leading nowhere. Foreshadowing the changes that will befall the world, she shows parts of each globe beginning to crack and crumble and other parts turning red and brown. She concludes the vision by saying, as she has on many other occasions, that many changes are coming.

In a vision on the following day, she reiterates the same message that people's lives and the world are going nowhere. She first appears gliding back and forth monotonously on a wire. She then appears with a spinning globe of the earth and observes that, when she looks down upon the earth, she sees constant spinning and things going back and forth endlessly, but without any change. Identifying the cause of this as the lack of love, she exclaims with tears again falling from her eyes, "My tears will wash away the sins of the world if the people of the world let love be their guide."

Mary weeps because she sees her children caught in webs of illusions and darkness. In many messages, she says that we are living "in desperate times" and that she is "desperately" trying to awaken us. It our choice to remain asleep in illusions or awaken to truth. Her efforts, she says, are often in vain as her pleas fall on deaf ears. We cling to our illusions and are so accustomed to our dark prisons that we refuse the opportunity to step into the light of freedom, regardless of how bleak and wearisome our lives may be. Speaking of her sorrow over the state of the world and its people, she laments:

> I sprinkle light in the world. But the light only goes into those who want it. The people in your world are blind and this is why I cry.

At another time, she decries what she describes as the utter sense-lessness of people trying to fit into a world or live a life without God. Appearing with an amorphous black object in front of her, she states:

> From my view, fitting into anything that is other than God looks like this to me. It is nothing. Do not be pulled into anything that is not God. Do not waste time on anything that is not God. There is little time, and do not waste it on things that are of no meaning.

She then adds:

> You can see some of what I see, and it breaks your heart. Imagine what I see and what it does to my heart. The state of your world is in disaster. You think you move so quickly and know so much. Most of what you do has no meaning and most of what you do is the work of something other than God and the light. It is illusion. If you think you are losing everything, then think again because you are losing

nothing and you are gaining everything. You run in circles, chasing nothing. You must stop the madness. Your world is inside a tiny little bubble. It knows not God.

Expressing her sorrow over people's denial of God, she again laments:

> I am saddened by the denial of God by His people. What kind of person knows God, and still, at the same time, denies and continues to love other than God.

Mary is trying to help us understand what the world is really like and how easily we become caught in its illusions and confuse them with truth. It is difficult to become love if we do not recognize what stands opposed to love. Mary's messages, while stark and sobering, are meant to guide us to an understanding of the grim reality that we have made of our lives and world. In these messages, she offers us the key to unlock the door to our self-created prisons. The path to freedom, from human to divine love, is letting go of the illusions and opening to the Sacred Heart. Human love is interwoven with illusions about ourselves and others. In divine love, we rise above these illusions. It is then that our love is pure.

The Mind of Illusion and the Mind of Love

Mary tells us that our longing for truth and freedom will not be fulfilled if we rely on the ordinary mind. Yet reliance on it as our primary way of knowing goes largely unchallenged in today's world. It therefore is important to understand how the ordinary mind bars us from truth and freedom and how the mind of love opens us to them.[2]

In several visions, Mary explains the nature of the ordinary mind. Her words are especially germane today in that we devote so much time and energy to educating and living in the ordinary mind and so little to educating and living in the heart. Distinguishing the ordinary mind from the mind of love, she elaborates on the nature of both:

> The mind of a person is a great distraction. It chatters and thinks its own will. Its perceptions, beliefs, and ideas are just

that. They are limited to the individual, and they are not true. There is but one truth, and that is the truth of God's highest expression, which is love. Love's mind sits in the heart when open. It is the highest of all intellects and is the only truth.

If you see through your own eyes, then what you see comes through your own mind. Then what you see is self-centered and not real. Your mind is a great distraction from love and truth. Although you believe you need your mind to function, this is not completely true. The only mind you really need is the mind of love, the mind of the heart. It is connected to God and is God, and with God and in God there is no need. You see, love is the only way. If you want to know all things, if you want to understand all things, simply love, and you will see the mind and the truth that are real.

You do not realize how much time and energy are wasted in mindless chatter that you create. It is worthless. It goes nowhere and does nothing. The only thing that truly creates is love. Mindless chatter destroys and keeps you from love. The mind is only of the surface. The heart and love are eternal, real, and true. They are beneath the madness, and one must dig to find them. It is a treasure in which all things are possible. Listen only to your heart. Do not listen to your mind. Your mind will distract you and convince you of things other than love. See through the eyes of love and the eyes of God only. You must constantly and consciously do this.

Remember, the mind is a major distraction. Remember, there is another way to know and to know what is true, and that is the only way that is real. That is through the heart and through love. Be it, think it, feel it, see it, act it, live it. It is the greatest beauty. It is miraculous, magical, delightful. And it is real.

Urging us to free ourselves from the ordinary mind, which she also refers to as the small mind, Mary calls us to be the mind of love:

> It is by becoming pure in heart and pure in love that one becomes awake, that one knows that they are all and all is they and that they are beyond anything that is perceived. Do not be tangled in the web of illusions that have imprisoned everything and everyone around you. Do not be imprisoned by illusions and the small mind. Be the true mind and the true intellect, which are beyond one's own limitations and limited mind.

Mary relates stepping out of the ordinary mind and into the mind of love with living a holy life. Reminding us that most people are not yet awakened spiritually, she advises:

> Remember, you live in a world where so few are awake. The mindless chatter, the emotions, and the stories are all illusions. They are nothing. It is all of the mind. So why take it into you and make it yours. Simply love. Be the truth and live the truth, no matter what others think and do. Remember, there is only one truth. This is love. The way to get there is to live the holy life. You will lose nothing and gain everything. What you think you have lost is an illusion, for in reality there is no loss ever.

The implications of what Mary is saying are far-reaching. One of the principal reasons we are not awakened spiritually is because we choose to live within the ordinary mind and its illusions. Mary explains, "You are what your thoughts are." She similarly asserts:

> What you perceive is what you become. It is your reality. But it is not truth. There is only one truth and that is love.

We make what we perceive through the illusions of the ordinary mind our reality. Then we define ourselves, others, and the world in terms of that reality. The deeper we entangle ourselves in these illusions, the further we are from truth and freedom. As Mary makes clear, virtually all the institutions with which we interact, their goals, their rationals, and their ways of operating, are based on the ordinary mind and its layer upon layer of illusions. She is trying to awaken us to the fact that we are trapped in multiple tiers of illusions, both within and outside of ourselves, that blind us to who we truly are:

> The nature of who you are you do not understand. You only see a fragment of what is.

Mary says that the illusions of the mind are real, but they are not truth. She thus identifies the thoughts and beliefs of the mind as dangerous. They have a reality, and we create our lives and world based on them. But they are not love, and therefore they are not truth. This helps us to understand the nature of external events as well. Mary states, "Everything you see happening around you, whether it be personal or not, is a reflection of what is within." To the extent that external events in our lives and world flow from the illusions of our ordinary minds, they are no truer than the illusions. She thus admonishes:

> Do not be tangled in beliefs, but be in the truth, the knowing that is in the heart. Beliefs are of the mind, the ego, and are dangerous. They cause conflict and suffering. Be in the heart, which is the place of true knowing and truth.

She similarly cautions:

> The way people perceive is not truth. This is why thoughts and beliefs are dangerous. It is because thoughts and beliefs are perceived and are not truth. Your thoughts and beliefs create energies. Your thoughts create energies. Your beliefs create stronger energies. Your thoughts and beliefs create wars, conflicts, disasters because they are energies that are not truth and they are out of balance.

Mary also tells us that what we take into our minds affects us in ways in which we are often unaware. For example, she has said that access to the mind allows access to the heart. Thus, the battle for the mind is also the battle for the heart. The life of the mind in today's world, mediated largely by popular culture and the rationalism underlying much of modern education, does not lead to truth. Rather, Mary warns, the mind is used by the darkness to keep us from truth:

> The things of darkness attack the mind and keep the mind from truth. This is why it is important to melt away the mind. The mind takes you on journeys that are false, that are illusions, and that oftentimes are more than dark.

What we take into our minds should guide us to the truth of the heart, not obscure it. Yet, we fill our minds with the illusions of the world that are deadly to the heart. As Mary states, "The truth of the world is lies. They have nothing to do with God." She thus advises:

> Be careful about thoughts. Thoughts are not love. They come from a different faculty. Love is above thoughts and all things.

Mary is telling us that we cannot "fix" what is wrong with ourselves and the world through the ordinary mind. It is only when we step out of the mind and into the heart, and let the vibration of love melt away the illusions of the mind, that we will find what we are searching for. Then we will come to another way of knowing based not on seeing through the lens of the ordinary mind, but through the eyes of love.

Seeing Through the Eyes of Love

When we open to the Sacred Heart, we see through what Mary calls "the eyes of love" or "the eyes of God." She thus encourages us to:

> See out of the eyes of love. All this seems like a mystery to you. But really it is no mystery at all. It is the true reality, the reality of God.

According to Mary, to see through the eyes of love is to see through the spiritual eye. She distinguishes the spiritual eye from what she calls the "linear eye," which is the way of seeing linked to the ordinary mind. Alerting us to the dangers of seeing in this way, she instructs:

> You must see through the spiritual eye because seeing with the linear eye will blind you and allow the darkness to hold you back. You must see with the spiritual eye because it is the eye that will serve you, and it is the eye that sees the truth.

In several visions, Mary identifies the spiritual eye with the energy center in the center of the forehead just above the eyebrows. This center, or "third eye," is a faculty of spiritual perception which is known in mystical traditions as a higher way of knowing. In one vision, she appears with her spiritual eye open and filled with light and shows two smaller centers to each side of it. As she touches each center, she says, "Father, Son, and Holy Ghost." At another time, she appears with her spiritual eye very open and simply states: "See through the third eye."

Seeing through the spiritual eye must be connected to love in order for it to bring the highest level of knowing. It is possible for the spiritual eye to be open, but not the heart center. This allows for spiritual perception, but at a lower level. Jesus makes this point in a vision in which He shows His spiritual eye opening and instructs:

> You must open up your third eye. The way to do this is to bring love into it and with visualization with love. You want to see through the spiritual eye of love. If you see through the third eye with less than love, then what you are seeing are lower levels of truth.

Mary similarly states that seeing through the spiritual eye must be connected to the Sacred Heart. She appears with a veil covering her face except for her third eye, out of which flow light and the Sacred Heart. Pointing to her third eye, she advises, "You must know the Sacred Heart and use your wisdom and knowledge from this place."

Seeing through the spiritual eye is not an esoteric practice reserved for the few. Mary says it is meant for everyone. Interestingly, most people are born with the spiritual eye open, but early in life it closes. Although it is closed for most people, it does not have to be. Seeing through the spiritual eye is necessary to ascertain the highest levels of truth. Mary wants all of us to see and know the truth so that we can be free. If we do not see through the spiritual eye, we are blinded spiritually. We may be open spiritually in some ways and have an intuition about spiritual realities, but we do not know these realities directly.

When the spiritual eye is closed and one sees only through the linear eye, one becomes trapped in illusions. As Mary points out, we become what we perceive, and we make that our reality. Thus, we will not be free of illusions until we open the spiritual eye and the heart center and see through them. Then we will not only perceive truth, but become it and make it our reality.

The sexual energy, as discussed in chapter 4, can open the heart and merge with the energy of love. These combined energies can then move into the third eye and open it. This is yet another of the effects of love-making at a higher level of consciousness and the "magic" of the energy centers when they are filled with love and light. Mary is trying to educate us about the energy centers so we can awaken spiritually and live as we are meant to live as children of the light. Visualization exercises for opening the spiritual eye and heart center are included in Appendix A.

A Mystical Way of Knowing
Mary is guiding us to a mystical way of knowing. She says that Jesus taught about the energy centers, light, and knowing through the Sacred Heart and the spiritual eye. It is a way of knowing, she says, that "is connected to God and is God." Describing this way of knowing, she explains:

> It is being one with what is known. A complete intimacy, an intimacy with everything: the mind, nature, air, animals. You are it, and it is you. The only way to really know is this way. You have to empty out the mind and open up the heart. In

the vibration of love, you know all things. You become one with all things. In divine love, pure love, you go into oneness with the other and with God.

This way of knowing is very different than the ways that we have now and that are taught at all levels of formal education. According to what Mary is saying, our focus on the ordinary mind is of limited value. It does not bring us closer to truth, to God, or to the fulfillment of our life purpose. On the contrary, it leads us away from these goals. It is, moreover, a much lower level of knowing than we are capable of. She cites the example of healing to illustrate the practical consequences of knowing through the ordinary mind versus knowing through the heart:

> Your medical doctors spend years of training to learn about the body and technology to help people. They try to create an understanding in this way. In the third eye you have all knowing, and you can heal just by touching because you have all knowing.

She notes that our medical technology and advances are limited and that there are other ways to heal using light, the mind, and the intellect of the heart. Referring to Western medical practices, she comments:

> They can help and for your societies they are advanced. But there are more advanced ways in the use of light, the mind, and the intellect of the heart. In order to know these more advanced ways, you must develop spiritually.[3]

What she says about healing applies to all aspects of our lives. According to Mary, our reliance on the mind is simply misplaced. It excludes the knowing that comes from the intellect of the heart and an understanding of the nature and power of light and energy. We do ourselves and our children a great disservice by educating the mind while failing to develop the intellect of the heart and to teach of light and its many uses. What we are doing, in effect, is obscuring the truth underneath the layers of illusion we call education and misleading our children about the nature of truth and how to find it.

Based on Mary's way of knowing, education, which etymologically derives from the Latin *educere* meaning to lead or draw out from, would primarily consist of connecting with the truth and ways of knowing that are inherent to us. We have within us the knowing of the intellect of the heart. We also have within us a knowing of light because light is our essence. Education would then be a process in which students connect to the highest truth within them and learn to use that truth to heal, create, and transform themselves and the world. Mary is a prime example. She tells us that she could not read or write. But she achieved a level of spiritual attainment that is staggering. If we follow her guidance and example, humankind's endless cycles of going nowhere would mercifully cease, and we could live a heaven on earth. Mary says that the choice is ours: "The way you perceive is your own choice. So you can choose to see through the eyes of love, through the eyes of God."

It is a choice with major consequences. If the world is going to change for the better, we must choose to see differently. Mary explains:

> There will not be peace, hope, justice, and love until the veil is lifted from every being. The veil is over the eyes of the majority. The veil keeps one from peace, hope, justice, and love. It is a choice each soul must make. The thicker the veil, the more darkness one lives in.

As Joseph says, what we consider miraculous on this plane is considered normal on other planes. Mary is inviting us to step into the miraculous and make it our normal way of being. She says that our normal way of being, as things stand now, is to be asleep spiritually and that this is dangerous for us and the world. Thus, there is a sense of urgency in her efforts to guide us into a different way of knowing and being.

We can better understand now what Mary means when she says we do not need money to live in this world. If we were to live in harmony with all that comes from oneness with the Sacred Heart and enjoy an abundance of sexual energy through its proper use, we would be able to create what we need through the use of light, just as Jesus did with the multiplication of loaves and fishes. Money and the present economic system upon which it is based would be unnecessary.

In many messages, Mary tells us that the shift to a way of being based on light and love has begun and that we can choose to be part of it or not. Now our lives are dominated by the illusions of the ordinary mind. Mary says that this has led us nowhere. This point was illustrated in a dream of a vast warehouse filled with endless rows of books. The message conveyed to the dreamer was that none of the countless books contained truth. According to Jesus, we must reevaluate even our notion of progress. He notes that most of what we believe to be progress is just more illusion:

> All the ideas, all the things around you, have not made the world a better place, a place that is healed. Some places appear to be better, but where there is not love, there is not healing. There is not improvement.

Speaking of how we, individually and collectively, get caught in the ebb and flow of illusions, Jesus further clarifies:

> There is only one thing that is true and real and that is love. It is the only thing that is eternal and steady. Everything else comes and goes. Once it comes, you believe it to be so real and so true. You put everything into it. It goes, and then you look back at it, and nothing is there. This is what happens when you live in illusion. People all around have this cause or that cause, this reason or that reason, this way or that way, all of which becomes replaced by another cause, reason, or way. Be only love. Work on emptying the mind. Do not take the mind seriously. Do not take the world seriously because one ignorant person after another you will find. Love the light in all beings, but recognize the truth for what it is. Do not be distracted by stories or events. They come and go. They are not the truth.

Jesus, like Mary, is telling us that letting go of the illusions of the ordinary mind is necessary for freedom. He thus advises:

> Letting go of the mind is letting go of concepts, ideas, per-ceptions, frames of reference, paradigms. Paradigms hold you in, and there are many different paradigms in which one is stuck in one's own mind. Move beyond. Do not analyze, contemplate, and examine everything from every angle. All that comes from the mind, which is not the true mind. The true mind is love, is God, is peace. All it is is love. Simply be love. Then you do not have to understand from the mind. You understand from the true mind the nature of all things, the truth of all things. It is not a concept of the mind.

What Mary and Jesus are saying undermines most of the foundation of modern society, based as it is on rationalism, education of the ordinary mind, and notions of material progress. It is a radical message for a world that is in deep trouble. They are calling us to let go of the old so that they can guide us into the new. As Jesus puts it:

> You must let go and simply be love. Love is the highest and greatest intellect because in love all things are possible and in love and being love you understand the nature of all things.

Romantic Love and Letting Go

Romantic love, then, is also about letting go. It is one way in which our souls try to step out of the world of illusions and to become free by opening to the miracle of divine love. But we too often do not see romantic love in this way and mistakenly believe that we can continue to live a life of illusions and still hold onto the magic of love. Mary is teaching us that this is not possible. To hold onto love and make it grow means that we have to free ourselves of illusions and cultivate the intel-lect of the heart. The alternative is to try to sustain romantic love while living in a prison of illusions and darkness.

Jesus says that when He walked the earth He was a rebel for love. Lovers who truly desire to reach the pinnacle of romantic love must also become rebels for love. At some point along their path toward pure love and oneness with God, they will face the choice of stepping out of the world of illusions, letting go of the things the world values, and giving all to love and to God. Jesus invites us to do just that and walk with Him into the Kingdom:

> The foolishness and distractions of the world around you are illusions. You will be grateful some day for giving up those things you think are important. The truth is none of these things that are valued all around you. The truth is love, and this is God. Put on my shoes, my children, and walk with me into the Kingdom.

What would this be like for any particular couple? The Spirit, as well as divine beings such as Mary and Jesus, will guide couples to shape their lives in the ways they are meant to live on the basis of factors such as innate abilities and gifts, the mission they are called to fulfill, children, and stage of life. If a couple is open to guidance from above and willing to live a holy life, they will find the way that is right for them. What is important is not to give into fear, as Jesus reminds us in a vision in which He removes round pieces of thick glass from in front of his eyes and says:

> Do not fear. Remember, everything is an illusion. It is not the truth. You know this. So do not live in illusion, but in truth, which is walking in my shoes. When you do this completely and fully, you are at peace and in love fully.

Becoming one with God may at times seem complicated. Mary reminds us that it can be much simpler than we think, calling not only lovers, but all people, to:

> Live simply. Pray a lot. Give all to the Lord. And you will be intoxicated in love forever.

CHAPTER TEN

Facing Darkness While Becoming Light

LOVE DOES NOT GO UNCHALLENGED. Both light and darkness exist in our world, and the conflict between them is an unavoidable aspect of our lives. It is of the nature of this conflict, according to Mary, for the darkness to attack love and try to destroy it. The reason for this, she explains, is that "the darkness hates love because love creates more and more light." When we are in love and love is growing in us and our relationship, we are creating light. This does not go unnoticed by the forces that oppose love; and, sooner or later, we will encounter darkness on the path of love.

Some people may find it hard to see the world in terms of light and darkness. Mary tells us that our lives are defined much more than we realize by these forces, pointing out that we are continually faced with choices between light and darkness and, ultimately, with the choice of being light or darkness. Once we understand this, we come to know that we are in a battle, perhaps the most important battle of our lives, and it is a battle for love. We also begin to appreciate better why Mary urges us to understand light in all its many facets and uses. Without understanding the nature of light, how to invoke it, create it, and direct it for protection, healing, and other creative purposes, we are severely handicapped in our efforts to emerge victorious from this battle.

The Reality of Darkness and Evil

In many messages, Mary and Jesus address the reality of darkness and evil in our lives and world. They point out that the problem for many people today is that they encounter darkness and evil all around them, but do not recognize them. They further tell us that darkness and evil have become embedded in our world, institutions, homes, daily activities, and even in our hearts and minds in ways and to degrees that we can hardly imagine.

In many visions, Mary speaks of darkness. For example, she appears with black tears falling from her eyes and states:

> I am crying because the darkness (in your world) is getting thicker. People are believing that things are getting better, but actually they are getting worse. Do not take comfort in the things of the world because there are many hidden agendas.

On another occasion, she again appears crying and explains:

> I am crying because people do not love God and people choose not to love. It pains me to know the darkness in people and in the world.

She similarly observes:

> The world has become heavy. Its vibration is heavy and hard. It is a slow-moving vibration that is on the earth. Nature and beings of light have to fight to keep the light.

As discussed in the previous chapter, Mary maintains that darkness has become part of every aspect of our lives and world. She illustrates the extent of this in a vision in which she appears with a huge cage which holds the earth within it. She shows inside the cage nature, human beings, and man-made systems, such as social and economic systems, and how they function. It could be seen that nature is being destroyed. It could also be seen that all the man-made systems, which are interconnected, have darkness woven into them. The functioning of the man-made systems, moreover, was external and mechanical, holding people entrapped in inhuman ways of living and disconnected from their inner lives and the needs of their souls. While presenting this dismal view of the world, Mary entreats, "You must live outside that cage, even while you are still living in the world." In another vision, she similarly depicts the people of the world imprisoned and admonishes:

> The people in your world are in prison by their false gods, their greed, their lusts, and their sins. You must break away from that before it is too late.

At another time, in an equally somber message, she tells of the extent to which darkness has become part of our lives and world: "Do not live as others live, for they have given into the darkness and darkness is woven into the fabric of every institution."

Mary and Jesus also speak of the existence of the devil and dark beings, telling us that they are part of the world in which we live and that we ignore them at our own peril. Many people today choose not to believe in the existence of a devil and dark beings, holding such a belief to be outmoded. Such people typically ascribe phenomena that used to be associated with the devil and demons to psychological and biological processes affecting human behavior in ways that were unknown prior to the advent of modern science. Mary and Jesus assert that disbelief in the devil and dark beings is simply wrong, maintaining that they exist and actively work to destroy the light in us and the world. Mary and Jesus identify the devil and dark beings as causal factors in many personal events, as well as in many events like war that occur on a larger scale.

Affirming the existence of the devil, dark beings, and the dangers they pose, Mary advises:

> The darkness always exists. Do not let anyone tell you otherwise or fool you. There are demons, there are dark beings, and there are dark realms. Do not be confused about this. The devil is well and alive and taking souls.

It has been said that the devil's greatest victory in modern times is that many people no longer believe in his existence. Jesus addresses this dismissal of the prince of darkness:

> And the devil, do not think he is an illusion. Do not believe those who create half-truths about Satan. He is real and alive and dangerous. Children are killing children, wars are inside homes, and money is your god. Where is there light in this? Where is God in this? For those who do not believe in the devil, they will be pulled into the devil's clutches and devastated. What I am saying is that the devil is real. Some think that the devil is the demons that they carry inside. That is not the devil. The devil is a being of darkness and evil whose existence should be believed. He is as real as I am. Look around you, and you will see his reality everywhere.

Mary decries the devil's influence over people. Appearing with tears in her eyes and with a ring in her nose, she says, "This is the work of the devil." She pulls on the ring, yanking her head forward, and declares: "This is how the devil has his people!" She goes on to state:

> It pains me to see you people on earth welcome the devil into your hearts, your homes, and your lives. Breathe in my life and my love and live a holy life, shedding away all that is evil around you and in you. This is the work that all people must do.

Then, appearing with two halos around her and light rippling off them, she proclaims, "God and light are the only way." On another occasion, she again warns of the devil and his influence:

> Drugs, alcohol, sex, television, your systems of entertainment are not of God. They are the work of the devil. It will all be destroyed. Do not engage in these things at all.

Mary points out that the devil's influence penetrates even into the ways in which we see ourselves and the world, returning once again to the critical theme of perception. She appears and in front of her face is a small, rectangular box, which obstructs her vision. She explains that the devil, like the box, prevents people from seeing all but a very narrow range of phenomena:

> The devil forces people to see through this limited view. Pray continuously in order not to let the devil force you to see through this limited view.

In these and other messages, Mary and Jesus leave no doubt that darkness and the devil exist and are threats to the light and love in us and the world. They do not tell us this to frighten us. Rather, they want us to understand what we have to face on our path to pure love. These realities are inescapable parts of our lives and world, whether we believe in them or not. When we choose not to believe in their existence, when we choose to see in limited ways, we are easily pulled into darkness, often without even knowing it.

Belief in evil and the devil in Christianity, as well as in many other belief systems, has long existed in one form or another. The story of evil runs throughout Christian Scripture, beginning with the Garden of Eden story, through Jesus being tempted by the devil and casting out demons in the Gospels, to the final triumph of light over darkness in the Book of Revelations. Many other spiritual and religious traditions also believe in the reality of darkness and dark beings. Accordingly, Mary and Jesus are not telling us anything new, but confirming what has been known throughout the ages. It is symptomatic of our times that they have to remind us of the existence of these realities and the dangers they pose.

What is new in their messages is their assertion that darkness in the world has reached critical levels and, as a result, the earth and its people are in historically unprecedented danger.[1] These messages are sounding a clarion call to awaken us to what is happening to us and our world. This call is for all of us, including those who are striving to find love and wholeness in relationship and marriage. As individuals, couples, families, and communities, we have critical choices to make between light and love or darkness and evil and how we structure our lives and relationships around these choices. If we do not accept the existence of darkness and the devil, if we hold onto the naive view that evil does not exist or is only an aberration of the mind, we will not see the ways and extent that darkness and the devil are active forces in our lives and world. Without an awareness of the conflict between light and darkness in and around us, we will more readily make choices that take us into darkness and away from the light and the goal of becoming pure love.

We cannot, moreover, be in a vibration of love if we are participating in the things of the world that are dark and of the devil. The darkness woven into our lives and institutions holds us at a low level of energy and consciousness. Mary speaks of this in the visions discussed in the preceding chapter, in which she shows the people of the world imprisoned in illusions and moving slowly and at a low vibration of energy. She is concerned because it is increasingly difficult for us to hold onto the light in a world that she describes as "grim and bleak." Yet few people recognize the darkness and see that the world is not as it appears, as she states in yet another warning of the perils posed by the darkness to our lives and world:

> The world is not as it appears to be. There are layers upon layers upon layers. Most people do not even see the first layers. Blind are the people of the earth. Blind. This is no accident. The dark forces have worked hard to create the webs and layers of illusion, making people into slaves of darkness. Ignorant as people are, they believe the charade they are

playing, a dangerous and deadly game to play. For a soul it is death to be ignorant. Open your eyes and keep them open.

Mary also wants us to know that, despite the darkness and dark beings in our world, we can still become love and light and return to God. She thus points out:

> Although this plane (referring to the earth) has the destruction, darkness, and dark beings, it does not mean that there is not light and love. The beauty is that souls come here and find their way back to who they are.

We are not alone in our struggle with darkness. Mary reminds us that she is always present to help us: "Know that I am always with you and with those who want me with them." This is also true of other beings of light and love. We only have to call upon them, and they will come to our aid. But it is up to us to choose to step out of the darkness and refuse to be trapped in the limited view of ourselves and the world through which the devil forces many people to see.

Light and Darkness on the Path of Love

Facing darkness is a part of any spiritual path, including the path of romantic love if a couple chooses to embrace it as a path to God. Lovers must understand this if their love for each other is to survive and grow. All the great spiritual traditions teach that love is at the heart of the spiritual quest and that the ascent to the heights of love is both difficult and demanding. Yet it is easy to underestimate the power of darkness in ourselves and the world, particularly in the early stages of a romantic relationship when we are captivated by the beauty, joy, and magic that has come alive in us. Many couples who love each other deeply suffer greatly because they fail to recognize and understand the forces in and around them that work against their love.

When we open to love and the light grows within us, the darkness begins to take notice. This is usually not the case when we are not open to love or awakened spiritually. The darkness leaves us in our slumber, which itself is a form of darkness. Noting that the darkness appears when the light begins to grow in us, Mary explains what we must do in order to be free of darkness:

> When one begins to know and see the light, the darkness appears. When one becomes the light, the darkness disappears. In order to make the darkness disappear, you must know the light. To know the light, you must let go of your illusions, perceptions, ideas, senseless activities, and mindless chatter and become one with God. Only then you will know complete and total truth.

At another time, she speaks of the interplay between light and darkness and how light dissolves darkness:

> The light makes the darkness visible. After a period of time, when one begins to face one's darkness, the light in one can grow, and the light can make the darkness diminish and dissolve completely. This is because the light is not just one's own light. The light is the other Light as well.

Inner Purification

Our souls, and not just the world, are the battlegrounds between light and darkness, with our souls as the prize. It is a battle we can win only by facing the darkness within us and letting it go. Such a process of inner purification is a part of the sacred work necessary to become pure love and light. We cannot become pure love and light if we carry within us darkness, which Mary sometimes refers to as impurities. As she points out:

> It is very important to get rid of impurities because impurities destroy the light. You must work on dissolving impurities completely within you so that you become pure light.

What are these impurities? They are, for the most part, conscious and unconscious thoughts and emotions that are not of love and obscure the pure light and love that is our essence. They carry a low vibration of energy and dispose us to feel, think, and act in ways that are contrary to love and harmful to ourselves and others. Mary sometimes refers to these impurities and their effects as sin, stating that "sin is not loving God and living His way and living His word." God's way and word are love, and therefore sin is what we do when we do not love.

The Honorable Tenzin Gyatso, the fourteenth Dalai Lama, describes inner impurities as our real enemies. Commenting on a Tibetan Buddhist text by Santideva, he writes:

> Sãntideva explains that delusions such as hatred, anger, attachment, and jealousy, which reside within our minds, are our true enemies…He states that these enemies do not have physical bodies with legs and arms, nor do they hold weapons in their hands; instead, they reside in our minds and afflict us from within. They control us from within and bind us to them as their slaves. Normally, however, we do not realize that these delusions are our enemies, and so we never confront or challenge them. Since we do not challenge the delusions, they reside unthreatened within our mind and continue to inflict harm on us at will.[2]

The Dalai Lama further comments that, if unaddressed, our inner impurities can bring us serious harm:

> When anger or attachment dominates the mind, a person becomes almost crazed, and I am certain that no one wishes to be crazy. Under their power we commit all kind of acts—often having far-reaching and destructive consequences. A person gripped by such states of mind and emotion is like a blind person, who cannot see where he is going. Yet we neglect to challenge these negative thoughts and emotions, which lead to near insanity. On the contrary, we often nurture and reinforce them! By doing so we are, in fact, making ourselves prey to their destructive power. When you reflect

along these lines, you will realize that our true enemy is not outside of ourselves.[3]

Mary says that, while the impurities may be expressed in different ways, they have their basis in fear. According to Mary, fear is the opposite of love and drives the ego more than anything else. She points out, moreover, that our inner impurities are exploited by evil outside of us to create more evil. Thus, the more we overcome fear and purify ourselves of our inner darkness, the less vulnerable we are to evil on any level. Speaking of fear and impurities and their relationship to evil, she explains:

> Fear and impurities are one and the same thing. Impurities are fear; fear are impurities. They are the opposite of love and light. They are the darkness within. They are manifested in action all around. Evil takes hold of these impurities and breeds evil.

It is the nature of darkness to destroy the light, and outer darkness uses our inner impurities to destroy the light within us. Thus, until we become pure light, we will experience a conflict between light and darkness. We have the choice to engage in this conflict consciously or see it manifest in our lives in unconscious ways, for which we usually try to avoid responsibility. If we engage in the conflict and succeed in the process of inner purification, then the outer darkness cannot touch us, as Mary explains in the following message:

> Remember, everybody has goodness and is light deep within. But many have chosen to work for and become the darkness. One must be cautious with the darkness because the darkness engulfs the light many times. It is only when one becomes pure light in all ways and on every level that one is not affected by darkness. So, before that comes, one must be cautious and wise.

There are may ways to do the work of inner purification. The key is in what Mary calls living a holy life. Prayer, meditation, spiritual practices, and love-making create light within us and bring us to higher levels of consciousness and higher vibrations of energy. Mary says that the higher vibrations will dissolve the lower vibrations of the impurities we carry. Thus, according to Mary, the more we live a holy life, the more our human flaws and imperfections fall away.

The Sacred Heart, which carries the vibration of pure love, has the power to dissolve all our impurities. We might call this the alchemy of the Sacred Heart. Alchemists of old searched for what they called the Philosopher's Stone which, when combined with materials of lesser value, would transmute them into gold. The Sacred Heart is the Philosopher's Stone for the transmutation of our inner impurities. When we open to this essence of divine love and merge with it, our impurities are dissolved, and we become the golden light of love. However, in the alchemical process, the light also makes visible the impurities and draws them out of the dark recesses of our inner worlds. During such times, we may feel anything but God-like. This is why, at the beginning of the spiritual journey, we may feel we rank among the "lowliest of saints," aspiring to rise higher, and later feel we are among the "lowliest of sinners" before finally knowing ourselves as we truly are: beings of love and light.

Different traditions use different practices for inner purification. These usually include some form of prayer, meditation, and spiritual practices, as well as ceremony, ritual, sacrament, sacred song, chanting, and invocation of divine beings. It can also be helpful to listen to our dreams, which often show us what we do not want to face in ourselves, as well as to talk to a trusted person about our inner lives or write about them in a diary or journal. Each person must find the approaches that allow them to open their hearts, while at the same time become aware of their inner darkness. Ultimately, the healing that we desire will come through love. According to Mary, we are meant to be perfect, and it is love that brings this perfection:

> The human body and the human mind and heart and soul are made to be perfect. You can be perfect if you are love. People can heal by turning completely to love. In love are the answers and the way for all things.

Facing one's inner darkness is one of the most demanding aspects of a spiritual path, as well as one of the greatest challenges in relationship and marriage. It requires discipline and commitment. As Mary tells us, when we come to know and see the light, the darkness appears. Each partner must rise to the challenge of facing and letting go of all they carry that is not of love. It is a process that can take us through "dark nights of the soul," as we move ever closer to the goal of being pure love.

We sometimes believe the darkness within us is who we are and then we are afraid to face it. We become caught in the illusion of our separateness from God, as we identify with those parts of ourselves that are not love. This can lead us to feel estranged from who and what we truly are. But, as Mary reminds us, in our essence we are so much greater than such narrow views of ourselves:

> Remember, you are not your experiences. You are not your karma. You are not your illusions, your perceptions, your ideas. You are greater than any of that. You are light. You are love. And you are to be one with God.

If the impurities are not who we are, why do we choose to hold onto them? Why don't we simply jettison them and be who and what we truly are? Mary explains that we hold onto them out of fear and that what we fear are just illusions:

> It is because of fear that you choose to hold onto such things. It is because of fear that the world is in the state it is in. Fear is the opposite of love. What you are fearing is all illusion. When you come to the place of being who and what you really are, which is true love, there is no more fear. You see beyond your illusions and blindness. You see how easy it is to be.

At times, we may become discouraged and even feel our efforts to grow in love are pathetic. Jesus counsels that we should never feel this way:

From the eyes of truth, there is not a single being or action that is pathetic. You can say there are beings who are ignorant and fearful and they do things out of ignorance and fear. They are not pathetic. They are growing and learning.

Although facing inner darkness may be an arduous task, we are not in it alone. We also can turn to those persons in our lives who can respond to our darkness and pain with love and compassion. We can likewise turn to beings like Mary, Jesus, and the Buddha, as well as the saints and angels, for strength and healing. Mary also urges us to call upon the light of the Holy Spirit:

Ask the light of the Holy Spirit to cleanse you. Ask the light of the Holy Spirit to wash away your sins. Ask the light of the Holy Spirit to heal you. Ask the light of the Holy Spirit to wash away you impurities. Ask the light of the Holy Spirit to wash away your darkness.

Choosing Light and Love Over Darkness and Evil

At the core of the process of facing and clearing inner darkness is free will. Mary says that "the free will of man is a cosmic law of God." She also says, "All souls can become light if they choose to." Freedom from darkness, then, is ultimately a matter of free will. Thus, the problem lies not only in the existence of darkness and evil, but also in our decisions to hold onto that which is not love, thus perpetuating the choice we made at some point in our soul's journey to be separated from love and God. The free will that made possible that choice also makes possible the choice to return to God. Reminding us that we choose what we want to be, Mary points out:

Every soul is made of love. Every soul chooses what it wants to be. If souls want to be saved, if souls want to know God and to know love, souls must give themselves to God and to love.

On another occasion, Mary appears with a divider in front of her, with darkness to her left and light to her right. Reiterating that it is our choice to become love, she says:

> Everyone who is human has to see themselves with both sides. You must choose to become the love that you are. When you come into the love that you are, there is no longer a division within you between the dark and the light.

She explains that our transgressions from love will be forgiven when we choose love totally:

> All one has to do is choose the light and choose love. One's sins are forgiven when one chooses love completely and totally. There is only one truth and that is the truth of love.

She thus asks, "You can create any reality you choose. Why not choose the highest truth?"

At another time, Mary appears with a door behind her and a series of doors to each side of her. She opens the doors to each side of her, and behind each is a wide path. Then she turns and opens the door behind her, which leads to a narrow path filled with light. She directs, "You choose the path you want to take." Pointing to the door leading to the narrow path, she states, "This one leads to eternal life." She concludes by again pointing out, "Each soul must make his or her choice to turn to God and to turn to love."

Jesus says that no one can save the soul of another and that each soul must want to be saved. Mary similarly clarifies, "Each soul will be saved on his or her own merits." Stressing the importance of free will, she explains that neither she nor Jesus interfere with an individual's choices. While they try to guide us to truth, we are free to accept or reject it. Mary explains:

> You must understand, know, love, and be the truth. The light is more powerful than the darkness, but each soul, equal to

every other soul, must choose his or her own way. We do not interfere with the choice. We only try to wake people so that they can choose truth. As long as people choose other than truth, they will choose, live with, and worship false gods.

It is our choice to remain asleep or to awaken. One reason we choose to remain asleep is that we may not want to face our darkness or take responsibility for our choices of darkness over light. In our states of slumber, without taking responsibility, we too often choose the darkness that is deeply woven into our lives and world. Mary warns us that these choices will leave us separated from God:

> Those who love darkness and the devil more than God will not be saved. Each soul must make his or choice to turn to God and to turn to love. This is a dangerous time. Do not be pulled into things that are not of the light.

Ultimately, the greatest choice we will make is to join with God or not. If we are asleep, we will make this choice outside of our awareness, but still be responsible for it. Mary confirms that we exist on many levels and are responsible for the choices we make on all of them. How many of us would admit that we are choosing to remain separated from God? Yet, we are not one with God, and, as Mary says, God has not left us.

The awareness that we are holding ourselves separate from God often comes when we begin to awaken spiritually and see the nature of the choices we make. But, Mary says, many choose not to become aware:

> There are many who cannot see and who are at lower levels of consciousness and lower states of being. It is that way because they choose it to be that way and because they do not want to love God or to know God. It does not matter what you teach or show those who do not want to know God or love. If they do not want to see, they will not see. It is for each individual soul to choose a higher consciousness and state of being.

What is Salvation?

What does Mary means when she speaks of souls being saved? It is not what many people typically understand as God judging them. Mary explains that what really happens is more like souls taking account of the amount of light and darkness they carry. She shows what she means in a vision of souls being "exposed" in the sense that they are opened and have the ability to see and know every experience they ever had. It is as if their heart centers open, and they clearly see the amount of light and darkness they carry.

In this vision, God, in the form of light, is hovering above each soul. Mary says that God does "judge" each soul, but it is not about meting out rewards and punishment. Rather, those souls with a sufficient vibration of love in their hearts are pulled into the light, into God. Those without a sufficient vibration of love are not. Mary thus says of each soul, "The love they have within them, and only that love, will carry them into the Kingdom." In another vision in which she appears with Jesus, Joseph, and the Holy Spirit, she further clarifies, "Only those who are pure and total love will enter the Kingdom." Accordingly, the choices we make to love or not to love determine the vibration of love in our hearts and whether we join with God.

Mary is telling us that we will have to face ourselves sooner or later before we become one with God. We can avoid this confrontation, but it will only delay the inevitable. In another vision, Mary shares what the experience of facing oneself is like for a soul. What she describes, it seems, probably occurs for most people after they pass over:

> Before each soul goes with God completely, that soul must know and see everything it has ever experienced and that soul must wash away everything. That soul must face itself. That moment is a devastating moment for the mind of a human. It will come and go like a bolt of lightning, and then it will be forgotten. It is the most devastating event that a soul must go through as he or she faces the harm that he or she has done to himself or herself.

Thus, facing one's darkness is inescapable. Mary therefore encourages us to do it and turn to love and God completely:

Every being is going to have to face their own soul. This will be a time of great sorrow for many, as they see the darkness in their souls. See inside you own souls and ask for forgiveness. In your souls turn to love and turn to God completely.

These messages are a sober reminder of the awesome responsibility God has given us in the gift of free will to choose to be one with Him or to reject Him. As Mary reminds us, we carry light and darkness, and it is up to us to choose between them. God does not punish us for the misguided choices we make. We "punish" ourselves as we live with the consequences of those choices that are not of love.

Romantic love and relationship are about many things. We now see that they are also about salvation, for both romantic love and salvation are about becoming pure love. This is why Mary speaks about romantic love: It is meant to be one of the principal paths to salvation. When we are in love and our hearts are open, we experience the vibration of divine love within us, and we are that much closer to being pure love and one with God. This is also the reason Mary speaks of sexual energy. It, too, is central to our salvation. The power of sexual energy can open us to the Sacred Heart and, joined with the this energy of divine love, lift us out of darkness and into union with God.

But, as stated above, love does not go unchallenged. We have to face darkness along the way. The compassion lovers extend to each other as they face the darkness within themselves is a priceless gift that makes their love for each other and their relationship an even greater blessing.

Love and Forgiveness

God knows our darkness and impurities, and He still loves us unconditionally. Our willingness to engage in the battle is what He asks of us. He never abandons us no matter how dark the darkness may seem. Thus, we must remember that God does not judge us and that we must not judge ourselves or others. Reminding us that we can be forgiven for even the darkest acts, Mary states:

Your past is not who you are unless you carry your past as who you are. If one turns from even being a murderer and turns to love and to God, all that the person has done is forgotten and wiped away eternally. Remember, our God is a loving and forgiving God, and all sins can be forgiven if you truly turn to love in your heart. Do not let the sins live in you. Ask to be forgiven from deep in your heart. You will be forgiven and not judged.

Mary likewise points out that love is not about judging oneself or others, stating, "If people judge, they do not know my religion. My religion is of love, of loving unconditionally." She says of those who have chosen darkness and evil, "Not even I judge." Encouraging us to pray for all beings, even those who are dark and evil, she adds, "Be all loving to all beings, but do not love the darkness. For those who are dark and evil, pray for them." She thus reminds us of the need to have compassion for those who struggle with darkness:

When one becomes true love, one must have the greatest compassion for those who are not yet there and love them with gentleness and kindness. Do not judge them, for all of us have walked in those footsteps before.

Jesus similarly speaks against judging others:

Those who judge and those who are self-righteous know me not. They do not understand or know who I am or what I am. Those who judge and are self-righteous are no better than the darkness they are judging. They are dark. Do not be pulled into such things. They are not of love. Fight for truth. Defend truth and love. Walk away from that and those who are darkness. Ask that a blessing be sent to them. Avoid them. But do not judge or see yourselves as better than them. Do not judge or be self-righteous. Those who judge or are self-righteous, no matter how much they pray and how much they do, they do not know me. I am not impressed by their prayers and so-called good deeds when in their hearts they know not love.

Once we face our darkness we can truly know the power of forgiveness. When we face our darkness and the harm we have done to ourselves and others, we can no longer hold onto the ego's ignorance and arrogance. We are humbled, and out of this humility is born true compassion and the recognition of the need for forgiveness for ourselves and others. Mary reminds us that this forgiveness is necessary in order to become pure love and thus advises:

> Ask forgiveness of those whom you have hurt. Ask forgiveness of those whom you have hurt and do not know you have hurt. Forgive those who have hurt you. Forgiveness is necessary to love and be love. It is necessary to enter into the Kingdom.

Warriors in Love

In order to protect love, we must be willing to fight for love. This means that we must be willing to confront and resist the darkness that attempts to encroach upon our lives and relationships. This darkness may come from within us as a result of the fear of the ego and the illusions of the ordinary mind. It may come from the people around us or the things of the world and their impact on us. It may come from spiritual planes, where both light and darkness exist. Not uncommonly, it will come from all these.

Confronted with darkness, regardless of its source, lovers must be willing to fight to protect their love. They must be honest about those parts of themselves that are not of love. They must be vigilant of the people and things of the world that would bring darkness into their lives. They must accept the reality of evil and dark beings and turn to the light and light beings for guidance and protection. Similarly, they must place their relationship in God's hands for His protection.

In many messages, Mary says that lovers must fight for light and love. She shows what she means in visions in which her light dispels darkness or the darkness recedes before the power of her light. She is teaching us that light is more powerful than darkness. Clarifying what it means to fight for the light, she states:

> To fight for the light means to be in a place of complete and total love and to protect that love with love. You shine the light into the darkness so that you transform it and light it. It also makes the darkness known.

In relationship and marriage, we are called to be warriors for love. Lovers can help each other, with love and compassion, to face and let go of inner darkness, while at the same time stand united against outer darkness. Together they can draw the sword, standing back to back, heart to heart, as they defend their light and love through the power of love. There is no higher vibration than love, and the lovers must work to expand love on every level so that are always circled with a shield of golden light. Then the darkness will not be able to breach their circle of love and destroy the light within them or their love for each other. As Mary tells us, it is a battle that will take all of our strength and courage, as we encounter both inner darkness and the darkness of the world around us:

> The enemy is within you and the enemy is outside of you. You must tackle the enemy within. You must take responsibility for the enemy that is within you. And with all your might you must fight to conquer the world and all who are in it. You must fight with all you are.

PART FOUR

Illuminated Hearts

CHAPTER ELEVEN

Love and Suffering

 JUST AS THE DESIRE TO LOVE and be loved is to be human, so too is suffering. In a series of visions, which in some ways are the most remarkable of all the visions, Mary and Jesus share some of their experiences of suffering during their sojourns in this world. Focused on Jesus' crucifixion and the events surrounding it, which were Mary and Jesus' greatest suffering, their messages delineate the reasons we suffer and provide guidance on how to relate to suffering. They also reveal that suffering exists on both human and divine levels and that it is possible to be free of human suffering and still suffer in a divine way.

While love and suffering may appear on the surface to be opposite in nature, Mary and Jesus speak of a deep connection between them. One reason we suffer, they tell us, is that suffering carries the potential to take us out of the ordinary mind and into the mind of love. Mary and Jesus' experiences bear witness to this truth, as they demonstrate the power of love to deepen one's capacity to suffer and the power of suffering to deepen one's capacity to love. Their messages show us the way through the transforming fires of our own suffering, teaching us that suffering need not be an obstacle to spiritual mastery, but part of a greater spiritual unfolding that opens us to truth at its deepest levels. In this regard, they confirm not only that love and suffering are, in fact, closely connected, but that they are the two most profound mysteries we experience as humans.

For some people, fear of suffering deters them from opening spiritually or pursuing a spiritual path. Fear of being hurt may cause us to close our hearts to love, precluding us from truly knowing and becoming love. Similarly, fear of facing truths about ourselves and the world and the suffering such awareness may bring may discourage us from lifting the veil and awakening spiritually. In this regard, it can be painful to see that most of one's views and beliefs about oneself and the world are mere illusions that crumble into dust once they collide with the power and truth of Spirit. In like manner, the suffering we encounter on the spiritual path may cause us to abandon it before we reach our final destination. As we see in Mary and Jesus' accounts of their suffering, the darkness attacks the light, often in brutal ways. The experiences Mary and Jesus share with us stand as testaments to the power of love to endure even the most horrific suffering.

Yet we find in our attempts to understand suffering the same paradox we encounter in our efforts to understand love: We cannot fully comprehend suffering with the ordinary mind, but only with the mind of love. Mary tells us that only when we become pure love will we know what our suffering is truly about. Still, we feel in our humanness the need to understand why we suffer and especially why we suffer when we love. Mary and Jesus' messages respond to this need at a level we can grasp with the ordinary mind and its limitations, as they gently lead us to the portal of the Sacred Heart where we will no longer know suffering through the illusions of the ordinary mind, but through the eyes and mind of love.

These messages on suffering take on a special poignancy in the world of today as humankind stands poised at the threshold of what Mary foresees as the greatest suffering it has ever experienced. She says that no individual or nation will go untouched by the man-made and natural disasters that are occurring and will continue to occur. As seen in the following visions, Mary stood in horror at the foot of the cross as she witnessed the crucifixion of her Son, yet she never turned from love or God. Like Mary, we now stand in horror as we witness the crucifixion of the people of this world and the earth itself. Mary is making known to us that we too must never turn from love or God, no matter how unbearable our suffering may seem. She is forewarning us that, in the times to come, we will be sorely tempted to spurn the light and remain asleep in darkness. Once again, through her words and example, she is showing us the way out of darkness and into the light.

The messages on suffering, for the most part, speak for themselves and therefore are presented with minimal commentary. While some messages touch on the same themes, each stands out in its own richness. They therefore are presented in their entirety, even though some overlap in content. They are organized around four themes in this chapter and the next: the meaning of the cross and Jesus' crucifixion, Mary's suffering, Jesus' suffering, and truth and freedom.

The Meaning of the Cross

The motif of the cross and Jesus' crucifixion appear in many of the visions. In Jesus' crucifixion, arguably the most pivotal event in human history, we encounter the depths of both love and suffering. Yet, as we learn, the crucifixion is more about love than suffering. In several visions, Mary and Jesus emphasize the importance of understanding what the cross signifies. In one vision, in which Mary appears behind a large cross of white light, she states, "There is great truth in the mystery of the cross. Look for it. Understand it." At another time, she appears with a golden-yellow cross and three large flowers, like rare orchids of the same golden-yellow color, around it. Relating the beauty of love to the beauty of the cross, she further states:

> There is great beauty in the cross and great beauty in love.
> Know and understand them.

In several visions, Mary associates the cross with her Immaculate Heart and with seeing through the eyes of love, once again returning to the ever important theme of perception. She tells us that suffering is connected to living with an open heart and seeing as God sees, through the eyes of love. In one of these visions, appearing with a cross in her heart and light streaming from the center of the cross, she instructs:

> See out of the eyes of love. All of this seems like a mystery to you. But really it is no mystery at all. It is the true reality, the reality of God.

In another vision, she appears with many crosses of different sizes. They are of a white and golden light and slanted, with one cross positioned in front of her heart. Relating both love and suffering to seeing through the eyes of love, she counsels, "Remember, always see through the eyes of love."

At another time when she again appears with a cross and speaks of seeing through the spiritual eye, she addresses many people's identification of the cross with suffering and not with love. As she stands behind a cross, with its center directly in front of her third eye, she speaks of the meaning of the cross:

> Do not let the cross and your perception of the cross stop you from seeing. People for years have not understood the meaning of the cross and the mystery of the cross and Jesus Christ. The truth in the cross is love and the power love gives one to achieve that which you call miracles.

She then characterizes the experience of the cross as a way to truth and light:

> My Son was crucified and, in His suffering and crucifixion, showed you (the people of the world) the truth and the light.

Jesus also clarifies that the cross is not only about suffering and that He should not be identified just with His crucifixion. He appears with a white cross in the center of His face, the cross being small and then becoming very large, and explains:

The cross is not only about suffering. When you see the cross, do not think about it just as suffering, but as love and the mysteries of love. You must not identify with me simply as the crucifixion. When people do that, they limit the truth and they limit what is.

In another vision, Jesus identifies the cross as a way to know and become love:

When you understand the cross, you know love. When you know love, you become love.

In several visions, Mary associates the cross with the Holy Spirit. In one vision, the Holy Spirit, in the form of a dove, flies out of Mary's third eye, and behind the dove appears a cross of golden white light. She advises:

Know the cross, understand the cross, and live as Jesus lived. Call upon the Holy Spirit to come into you.

At another time, she appears with a cross in her heart center, with violet light, which she often identifies with the light of the Holy Spirit, flowing from the center of the cross.

The cross represents total transformation of consciousness. This is illustrated in a vision in which Mary relates the cross with the rainbow body. As explained previously, the vivid colors of the rainbow are sometimes seen vibrating in the energy fields of persons who have become pure love. In this vision, Mary appears with countless rainbows floating around her and states:

In truth all things are possible. In God all things are possible. The rainbow is all color and all light.

Then she becomes a cross, while her features remain visible within the cross. She is carrying a cross of rainbow colors on her back. In other words, she is the cross and is bearing the cross. Urging us to know the mystery of light at its highest levels, she enjoins, "Know the rainbow body!" On another occasion, she points to a crucifix, and at that moment a spark of light appears in the crucifix. What looks like a funnel emerges out of the light and suddenly becomes a large door surrounded by a rainbow. As she points to the door, it opens.

At other times, Mary identifies the cross with the sacrifice of the small self for the greater self. In one vision, gazing up at a crucifix and crying, she states:

> This is the time to give up the small self for the greater self. There is not time to be worrying about other things. This is the time to be giving up the small self for the greater self. Even if you are to be crucified in an internal way, that is best right now because giving up the small self feels like you are being crucified. This is the time to do it.

Jesus, also addressing the relationship between the sacrifice of the small self and the crucifixion, speaks of two types of sacrifice:

> There are two types of sacrifice. One is to live in a self-less way, in a way that is not based on self-interest and ego. It is truly living for others. The other is the sacrifice of the small self for the greater self. This is letting go, sacri-ficing everything of the ego and the small self. The prime example of this is the crucifixion. It means even letting go of the body in the form of a brutal death, as I did in the crucifixion. At the same time, it is not losing anything because everything of the ego, the small self, and the body is illusion.

He then comments on the role of the ego and when it is time to let it go:

> The ego is necessary for part of the path. It is necessary because in it are the lessons the soul needs to learn. Once the lessons are learned, the ego can be let go of.

He goes on to speak of persons becoming enlightened, but still not undergoing the total transformation that letting go of the ego, or small self, entails:

> Many people become enlightened, but do not let go of the ego. Many people over the centuries awaken and reach the point of enlightenment. They even develop or receive gifts. Abilities blossom within them. Yet they do not let go of the ego. Often the result is that they misuse their abilities. They use them for the purposes of the ego. If each person who reached enlightenment had really given up the ego, the world would be a different place.

He concludes by stating, "There are many meanings within the cross and many meanings within those meanings."

In the messages discussed below, Mary and Jesus help us to understand some of these meanings. In a rare glimpse of their personal experiences of suffering, they share with us what made it possible for them to bear great suffering and never fall, even for a moment, from the state of pure love.

Mary's Suffering

In several visions, Mary shares her experiences of suffering around the death of Jesus. In one of these visions, which occurred during Lent, she discloses that it was her union with God that allowed her to endure this suffering:

> This time, this season, was a very difficult time and season for me. When I walked the earth, this was a period of time in which I knew that my Son would die. I suffered. The only reason I got through it was my union with God and my love of God and understanding and knowing as God understands and knows.

She then shows herself as part of God the Father's face. Tears are flowing down God's face, giving the impression He is suffering. Responding to this impression, Mary speaks of suffering as God suffers:

God does not suffer in the way you believe suffering is. God intimately knows the experience of suffering. It is not something you are ready to know. I suffered in the human way while I walked the earth. I suffer in a Godly way now.

Mary then raises her head and, with tears rolling down her cheeks, speaks of the suffering humans bring upon themselves:

The world is suffering and is going to suffer because of all that the world and its people have gone through and created.

At another time, she appears in her essence of white light, with thick layers of white light cloaking her like a garment. The face of Jesus is behind her. His face disappears, and Mary is then leaning over a cave. Not very large, it is made of solid rock on the outside, like the surface of an amethyst. The cave seems to be connected to Jesus' crucifixion and perhaps is the place where His body was buried. Mary's body is conformed to the top surface of the cave, with her head leaning over the entrance to the cave. She begins to cry, her tears falling one by one in front of the opening to the cave. She is asked why she is crying and responds, "I suffered and I suffer."

She is then asked how she was able to bear to see her Son crucified. At that moment, the face of God the Father appears directly behind her, and Mary becomes part of His face, as she did in the previous vision. Her entire being is connected to God, with God's face and hers being one. She then talks of her Son's death:

I went through the most horrible thing that a mother could experience. My Son, the Son, the Light of the world, was murdered before my very eyes. And I knew before this happened that it was going to happen. You ask how I could stand this. It is because I was one with God. I was pure, and I came into that life pure. I was one with God at that time. This allowed me to see through the eyes of the Almighty. To understand the true nature of your world, of that world, I suffered. But

I also experienced joy because I could see through the eyes of God. I am one with God and was one with God then. You must understand that suffering is not what you think it is. And the gift that Our Lord Jesus Christ gave to the world is the miracle of knowing that suffering is conquered by love, light, and faith. This does not mean one does not have experiences that cause pain. It means that one understands the nature of suffering and the truth of love.

Then Jesus appears in front of the cave. His hair is long and loose, and He looks like a rebel. He is shielded by light, with only His face visible. Mary and God's face could also be seen, with Mary again leaning over the cave. The face of the devil appears to the left. He turns to Jesus and attacks the light around His face with thousands of small, worm-shaped figures of black energy. Mary then begins to speak of darkness and Jesus' death:

The darkness has always fought to exist and fought to rein. The darkness has taken over your world, and the darkness is what killed my Son. Few want to understand. Few want to know. Few live and follow the truth. This is not the way it has to be. But this is the way it is.

She lifts her body off the cave, faces the devil, and triumphantly states:

I have no fear of him or all his darkness. You must not fear him either.

In another vision, Mary and another woman are standing at the foot of the cross, as Jesus is dying. A deep and endless pain and a deep and endless joy are visible in Mary's eyes. She begins to speak, explaining that we do not become our suffering when we see through the eyes of God:

Everyone must suffer. But you must not be or become the suffering. You must see above it and see through the eyes of God. See through the eyes of truth.

She then looks up at Jesus on the cross. The obvious is reflected in her face: terror and horror at witnessing the murder of her Son. At the same time, she shows her deep connection to God that allowed her to bear the suffering of her Son's death. As she looks up at Jesus, her eyes are also fixed in a static gaze on God the Father. It can be seen clearly that God the Father is fully present with her in her suffering and that she experiences everything through His eyes. She then explains how she was able to endure the suffering, while not becoming it:

> If you rise above the suffering and if you see through the nature of God's eyes, you will not become the suffering. You move into the suffering, while at the same time deepening the suffering. In the eyes of truth, one is not one's suffering.

Seeing in this way, of course, means not seeing through the eyes of illusion. Mary thus instructs, "You must peel away the layers of ignorance that cover your eyes." She then puts on small, round glasses and breaks the center of both lenses, leaving only the frame around each eye. Pointing out the limitations of seeing through one's own eyes and the ordinary mind and not through the eyes of God, she further explains:

> If you see only through your own eyes, your own mind, your own perceptions, you see nothing that is true, and you see ignorance, you believe ignorance, and you are ignorance. Therefore, you believe that you suffer. If you see through clear eyes, you understand the nature of suffering. But suffering is not this or that problem. Suffering is not this or that emotion. Suffering is the way to come closer to God. Suffering must be understood as many things, and it must be seen through the eyes of God.

She points to a nearby crucifix and continues:

This is another kind of suffering because this is the hardest and highest suffering. This is because the darkness hates, rejects, and opposes the light. This is the greatest suffering and the greatest cross one will carry. My Son's death shows you and all His love for God the Father, while at the same time shows you the hate the darkness has for the light and the truth. Love with the greatest love and have no regrets. And there is no need to fear. When you truly love, there is no fear. When you truly love, you are completely free.

Jesus' Suffering

As we have seen, Jesus' suffering was about love. His words describing His suffering, like His mother's, take us deeper into the mysteries of love and suffering and the relationship between them. Jesus was and is pure love, and insight into His suffering helps us to understand both love and suffering. Moreover, as we know His suffering, we know Him. Then, He tells us, we can understand both these mysteries:

> When one knows my suffering, one knows me. One must then come to the understanding of suffering and love.

As we come to know Jesus through His suffering, we come to know that we too are God-like and that, like Jesus, we carry within us the unlimited power of love. Speaking of the need to know Him, He begins to explain the power of love to lift us beyond human suffering:

> I suffered on the cross and suffered in human ways, but the part of me that is not human is love. In love and in the power of love, every good and every miracle can be performed. Every soul that comes from the Kingdom has this capacity in them for they are God-like. So, in order to come back to the Kingdom, you must be only love, and that is knowing me fully, completely, and intimately.

He thus calls us to:

Walk in my shoes. Be as I. Know, see, and understand suffering and love as I do.

At another time, speaking of His great love for us, a love of desire and passion, He appears with a cross and a heart. Illustrating the connection between His Sacred Heart and His suffering, He ignites a beautiful fire of red and blue flames in the heart and creates a crown of thorns above it. Inviting us to enter into His Sacred Heart of love and suffering, He exclaims:

My love for you is an undying love, a love burning with desire and passion. My heart burns with love. I am love, all-encompassing, unconditional love. I suffer and bleed for love. My heart and my love, my desire and my pain, are endless. Enter my heart and know and understand everything as love.

At another time, He appears wearing a crown of thorns and bleeding profusely and comments that, in His suffering, he never turned from love. Referring to the crown of thorns, He affirms that the love born from suffering is far greater than the suffering:

This was my greatest suffering. In all my suffering, I never stopped loving. I never turned to hate or that which I despised. In all my suffering, I still knew and know joy. Inside you is the seed of truth...When the seed of truth blossoms, the rewards are far greater than any suffering.

In another vision in which He again appears wearing a crown of thorns and bleeding, He proclaims, "To suffer and still love is the greatest beauty."

In a vision in which Mary speaks of darkness and suffering, she presents scenes of Her Son's life and the suffering He experienced. The first scene is of Jesus on the cross, His body rising and falling with each fading breath of life. A sense of terror, that something horrible is taking place, fills the air. Mary and another woman are at the foot of the cross, while other people are standing off at a distance. Jesus, while on the cross, is talking to people. Mary shows other scenes when Jesus is speaking to people at other times. In all these scenes, people are saying cruel and vicious things to Him and trying to make a mockery of Him. It is obvious that He had a hard time, both during His life and at the time of His death.

Mary presents other scenes of Jesus' life. In some, He is very cold or very hot. It can be seen that He possesses the ability to bring physical comfort to Himself at these times, yet in most instances He chooses to suffer as any human would suffer under the same conditions. In other words, He has a full human experience and does not alter it by using His power to do things such as warming Himself when He is cold or creating food when He is hungry and without food. Mary then shows Jesus on the cross again. A black coffin, shaped in the lower part like a human body, is located in the vertical part of the cross, with an eye opening into light in the center of the coffin. Jesus states:

> All humans suffer. They suffer in their humanness. But you must die to this suffering in order not to suffer in the soul. You must move into the wisdom and intellect of the heart of love to know the truth. Here there is no suffering. When you move into this, your human suffering becomes something you will move through. You know it is not real because it is of ignorance. It is the plea for love. The more you suffer, the more you are screaming for love and for God. But you do not know this because you are stuck in the ignorance and you are not connected completely to love and to God. When one is connected completely to love and to God, one has the complete understanding of what suffering is and is not. Carry your crosses with honor and dignity. The more you suffer, the deeper you go. The deeper you go, the greater your love. The greater your love, the more you understand.

Then Mary presents other scenes that show Jesus going through human experiences and having human emotions. They also show Him being tested and tried. In many of the scenes, He is being pushed to His limits in dealing with people and His emotions. There are times when He withdraws because He is overwhelmed. These scenes also show Him as strong and hard. He is a rebel, stirring things up and calling people on their "stuff." In yet other scenes, sorcerers and black magicians, people who intentionally use and manipulate energy for purposes of darkness, try to ensnare Him in webs of lies and deceit. At times, He is pulled into them, but He is smarter than these adversaries and always prevails in this type of spiritual combat.

In other scenes, He is gentle and soft, with His great love evident in His way of being and acting. A bright light shines within Him, and everything He thinks and does is out of love. Still, these scenes show that, like Mary and Joseph, He struggled. Commenting on Jesus' struggles, Mary encourages us to be like Him:

> You must be like Jesus Christ. When He struggled, He was all loving to the very end. This allowed Him to be who He was and who He is.

In a different vision, Jesus shows more scenes of His suffering. He prefaces these scenes with the statement that one suffers in one's humanness, yet at the same time is beyond suffering in one's essence:

> To suffer is human. In your humanness you will suffer. I suffered in my humanness. I suffered in every way that you do and you have and more. When you understand the nature of what you are and who you are, human suffering still exists. But within yourself you are not suffering. If you can see the mystery of the cross, if you look into its true meaning, you will understand the nature of suffering. However, human suffering and human joy are the same thing. They are real only within the human understanding. The wounds that are created within one because of an experience that lacks love are suffering that scars the soul, but nonetheless they are human sufferings. In one's essence, one does not suffer.

He then shows Himself being tortured prior to His crucifixion. He is being whipped and beaten with hard, supple branches and what look like leather straps. He is also being spit upon. His tormentors are enjoying torturing Him, while He screams out in pain. The human part of Him does not want to go through this suffering. He has many thoughts pass through His mind, experiencing in human love fears and doubts that anyone would experience under such circumstances. The scene suddenly shifts, and Jesus is flying on a cross of white light, then floating on His back on the center of the cross, with a funnel of light that looks like a chakra arising out of the center of the cross. He states that He brought light and love to the world and laments that many people have chosen ignorance, darkness, and evil:

> I suffered, and I died from that suffering. I came to bring light and love to the world, and I did. People, instead of choosing light and love, have chosen ignorance, darkness, and evil.

In a vision on Good Friday, Mary and Jesus elaborate on the meaning of suffering and what the crucifixion teaches us about both our humanness and our divinity. The vision begins with Mary appearing and saying, "Today is a hard day for me. I suffered a tremendous grief." She then presents a scene with crowds of people in a place filled with noise, fear, gossip, and darkness—all the madness that took place on the day Jesus was crucified. She is asked, as she was when she presented a similar scene on another occasion, how she was able to endure the pain of her Son's death. She responds that, while she knew it was going to happen beforehand, she did not know what the human experience would be like. She then shows the face of Jesus in her heart, and He shows her face in His heart, both being joined as one in Spirit. She states:

> I could feel His pain, and He could feel my pain. Remember, there are levels of suffering. You must know and you must not be mistaken: When you walk in the light and live in the light, you will be the target of darkness and evil. Do not fear it. Be clothed and draped in light.

The scene continues with Jesus on the cross. The day is dreary and overcast, with a darkness that makes the entire day appear as if it were dusk. Jesus is screaming, crying out to God the Father and begging for help because He cannot stand the pain. It is hard for us to grasp the immensity of the pain and suffering He experienced as related in this vision. What Jesus is expressing in His pain and crying out to God for help with is the level of human suffering He experienced as a man. As humans, we cannot escape this level of suffering, which is connected to the illusions of the ordinary mind and the limited reality through which humans see and know. However, Jesus says that a level of truth exists within us and that He experienced the cross on this level. He explains that suffering can bring us to this level of truth where we will know we are not the suffering:

> I was able to suffer that kind of suffering because I know the truth, I was the truth, and I am the truth. When you are the truth, live the truth, and know the truth, you can endure anything. No single person goes without suffering. It is rising above the suffering and moving through it while you are above it which allows you to be truth and takes you into truth. It allows you to see you are not your suffering, you are something greater.

He goes on to talk about seeing through the eyes of love, a higher knowing, and a greater wisdom. He then speaks about the darkness present on the day He died, which was not just the darkness on the physical plane as described above. It was also the darkness that opposes the light and opposed Him. It is because of this darkness, He explains, that many people who love the light are crucified:

> The darkness was very thick that day. The darkness rejected and continues to reject the light. When one turns to the light, one is very often rejected. People are often crucified when they love the light. They are crucified in many different ways.

He then urges us to love with a child's innocence, but not to be naive, similar to His instruction to His disciples in the Gospels that they be innocent as doves, but wise as serpents:

> You must carry the innocence of the child. In their innocence they love. You must be like that. But, at the same time, you must be sharp, wise, and aware.

Then Mary returns to the theme of what Jesus' death signifies, as she elaborates on the meaning of suffering and its power to transform and open us to the truth of who we are:

> It (the crucifixion) must be seen in its totality. Jesus' crucifixion has many meanings, both about darkness and destruction and about truth. Jesus was teaching you that you are not just the flesh and not just human. He came to show you that you are like Him. But you reject Him and you reject love and, there-fore, fail to realize that you are like Him. He was in despair because He was a man and experienced everything a man expe-riences. But He was the Son of God, and you are the sons and daughters of God. He knew truth and therefore experienced on two levels. He showed you that, even though you suffer, you can become love. And, when you see through the eyes of God, you can see through the illusions of the world.

> Jesus could have escaped His suffering at any moment. But He did not because God the Father wanted to show you and teach you. There are other ways He could have taught you, but darkness is part of the picture and has to be overcome. Thus, He had to show you how to overcome the darkness. He gave you a gift. He could have escaped His suffering, but he didn't so that you could learn.

> Basically, you are no different than Jesus. You just don't perceive the truth. You perceive your illusions. But you do not understand

the nature of suffering or love. In the crucifixion, in the death and resurrection, Jesus showed you the possibilities that dwell within you. They are endless because love is endless. You do not grasp what truth and love and God really are. Jesus showed you all this. Everything is in His life, crucifixion, death, and resurrection. It is all right there. The gift in suffering is that there is a place where the depth of suffering and the depth of love become one and the same. There is no difference when you open up to the reality that is. But you are so blocked and blinded that you do not see it.

Really understand the passion, not in the way it is written, but in the way it is experienced. In that experience, you will know the truth. When you know the truth, you are draped in light. It does not matter what comes. It cannot harm you, and it cannot kill you. There is no such thing as death. There is the death of the body, but you do not die. You are changing forms. You die (physically) because of the limitations you have placed on yourselves. Your bodies could live on. But you do not understand the potential, the reality. You do not understand who you are. You suffer and everything tragic and the crosses that come your way are because you do not know you are sons and daughters of God. You have lost your understanding. It is a process of lifting off the veil that separates you from truth. The darkness plays on this, keeps you blinded, because you have chosen ignorance and illusion. The darkness does not have to fight, but the light does because you have chosen illusions.

In the crucifixion, the darkness has rejected the light, but this does not stop Jesus. He suffers because of the darkness and sin, but He rises above it. When you are love, you rise above it. You are far greater than anything on this earth. The illusions you create trap you because you believe them. The key is to shift yourself into being love and then you shift your perception. You become God and see through the eyes of God. You are sons and daughters of God.

See this as a process. See and know the experience, not what is in writing. The suffering gives you the opportunity to become who you are. This life is a lesson. God does not punish. You punish yourselves because you choose to live in ignorance. You have to die to everything inside and outside of yourself because everything you have created is illusion. It is a perceived reality based on your illusions... You cannot hold onto anything because everything you see is limited. The reality of everything is too vast. You cannot hold it in the human (ordinary) mind. The human mind is too limited.

In the same vision, Jesus also mentions the need to develop what He calls an "awareness of truth." It is this awareness that allowed Him to rise above His human suffering:

You must hold in your consciousness continuously this other awareness. This other awareness is the awareness of truth. So, while you suffer and have human experiences, you are in this other awareness. You recognize the illusion of your experience. You know the illusion, and you know the truth.

How do we develop this other awareness? Mary says it is through living a holy life, especially through prayer, meditation, spiritual practices, and love-making. These activities, as she points out, fill us with light, take us to a higher consciousness and frequency of energy, and open us to the Sacred Heart of pure love within us, where we become the truth of who we are. Being in this truth is the other awareness Jesus is talking about. Jesus adds that part of developing this other awareness is offering all one's experiences, both good and bad, to God and to Him. So we can offer them our most joyful and most painful experiences. Reminding us to call upon Him continuously, He advises:

Call me throughout the day, good and bad alike. Here there is no good or bad. So, for me, what you offer me is the same.

This other awareness can help us to "carry our crosses with honor and dignity" and not become the suffering. Then, it is the Holy Spirit who carries the cross, as Jesus states in a vision in which He appears crying tears of blood. As each tear flows down His face, He draws it into His heart and states, "Your tears and your pain must go back into your heart and into love. Only then will you be free." He then shows a large bird, like a blue bird, flying and exclaims:

With love all things are possible. If you love as I, you will be able to fly. In the power of love, everything is. In love, there is no fear, no need. If you see through the eyes of love, you see through truth and you know everything. With love, to carry the cross of the world is nothing because you see that the truth is love and not the suffering.

He makes an opening into His world, with a crucifix at the top of the opening, and counsels:

Do not fear. Trust in me. I would not mislead you or misguide you. I will only care for you and love you. It is the Holy Spirit which carries the cross.

Two points of clarification are in order. First, God did not crucify Jesus, nor does He crucify us with our suffering. As Mary points out, "Man crucifies man. God does not have anything to do with it." Second, Jesus says that He suffered in His humanness. This does not imply that He is not also divine. He states that He is God and man in a vision in which He comes off a cross and appears as pure white light. Affirming that we too are God and man, He asserts: "I am a man and I am God. You are man and you are God. If you see through the center, you will be like me."

CHAPTER TWELVE

Truth and Freedom

MARY AND JESUS TELL US we will be free when we know and become the truth, which is pure love. They also teach us that much of our suffering derives from the illusions of the ordinary mind and the darkness they engender. They once again make the distinction between truth and illusion and remind us that we have the choice to live in one or the other. When we choose to live in illusion, we suffer from the conditions we create through the illusions. When we choose to live in truth, we rise above the illusions and gain the freedom that comes from knowing who we are. They tell us that we will still suffer, but the suffering will be different because we will know that we are not the suffering. We will know that we are pure love, and the knowing will not be of the mind, but of the heart. This is what Jesus experienced on the cross. He suffered in a human way, but at the same time He was beyond human suffering.

Beyond Human Suffering

Jesus teaches of freedom from suffering in visions in which He is on the cross, but beyond the suffering of the cross. He speaks of this when He appears on a cross of light, with a doorway of light behind Him, and identifies different kinds of suffering. He says that, when one is in truth and love, one can suffer and still be in an ecstatic state of being because one is God and love. This is how Mary endured her suffering at the foot of the cross and how Jesus endured His suffering on the cross. Jesus explains:

> There are many kinds of suffering. There is the suffering that one causes oneself, and there is the suffering the darkness and the devil create. There is the suffering that comes along with following the light and becoming the light. This suffering is a true suffering. It is the only suffering one must do. When one suffers in this way, one suffers side by side with truth, in truth, with love, and in love. When one is in truth and in love, one is in an ecstatic state of being. One knows God intimately. One is God. One is love. Do not push away your suffering, but move deeper into it. Do not push away the ecstatic experiences, but move deeper into them. Soon you will see there is no difference. You will experience both as they are and know that there is no difference.

As seen in visions discussed previously, Jesus often represents freedom by showing Himself flying, especially flying while on a cross. For example, in one vision He appears on a cross, with His physical features clearly visible. His body dissolves into what seem like thousands of tiny molecules of light, as He transforms into His essence of pure light. He then comes off the cross and flies like a dove, with the cross trailing behind Him. As He soars, He explains that suffering is no longer necessary when one knows and lives the truth. He reiterates the need to choose between truth and illusion, stating that truth is the only way to freedom:

One's suffering takes one deeper into the depths. But one's suffering is unnecessary if one truly knows and lives the truth. But because one knows the truth does not mean that suffering does not exist. I am the great example of that. I was crucified because I lived and loved and spoke the truth. Those who are not in the truth despise the truth and fear it. You must not fear it. The truth is the only thing that will set you free, and the truth is love. You cannot live in truth and illusion at the same time. You must choose one or the other.

In a vision on the following day, He again identifies truth as the key to freedom. He is flying on a cross, first appearing as a dove and then an eagle, and states:

I am showing myself in these forms to show you the freedom of flight. In truth there is freedom, and only in truth will you find freedom. Illusions chain you.

He then shows a gate and a huge fence. Gazing upward, as if looking up to God, He urges, "Use the truth to break free."

He is then back on the cross as the scene changes to His crucifixion, similar to a vision described in the preceding chapter. Mary and another woman are standing at the foot of the cross. Other people are standing off a little way. People are heard talking, gossiping, crying, and making judgements about Jesus. It was as if this din of voices is what Jesus heard while He was dying on the cross. At the same time, He is above it all. This is represented by a change to a scene that looks very Native American, and Jesus again appears in the form of a bird while still in His body. His arms are extended to each side, and above Him is the head of an eagle. Jesus talks about love and fear, affirming that the truth of His message is love and not fear:

There is only one truth and that is the truth of love. One must give oneself completely to love. Love is not fear, and fear is not love. There are many who have written about me, who have seen me, who have known me, and who have heard me. They all speak of this through the lens of their own perception. Many of the great books written about me are not of truth. They are not about me. They are distorted writings. There is one truth, and that is the truth of love. And that is who and what I am. I came to bring light and love and nothing more. I was crucified because of fear. Fear is not love, and love is not fear. Many people have written about me through their own perceptions. Many of these writings carried fear. If they cause fear or if they cause separation, they are not about love, and they are not about me.

The next day He again appears flying and speaks of the freedom from suffering that truth brings:

To know and be the truth is not to suffer. It is suffering on the level of illusion and ignorance that one feels, but it is not on the level of truth. Come and be free in me and with me. Those who join with God become free. They are love and truth. They see and know all things. They are not ignorant, fearful, blind, or in illusions. They are free.

The following day He once again appears flying on a cross of light and urges, "Be free! Fly! Fly!" He then shows Himself as He looked when He was on the earth. His hair is brown, long, and wavy, with golden highlights in it. He is wearing a headpiece, which fits around his head like a band. His eyes are very hazel, and you can see deep into them. He has a long face, with a fine nose and a narrow chin. He is very handsome. Then, demonstrating that truth and the vibration of love are the same, He is on the cross again, and His body and face begin to break up, becoming golden light. He is in His body, but His consciousness is not of the body. He is in another consciousness, another awareness. Describing Himself as a rebel for love and truth, He repeats that freedom from suffering comes from being in truth and not illusion:

This is how one does not suffer: by being in truth. I am truth, and love is truth. Sometimes my words were words that were harsh because sometimes speaking the truth requires that. But it was always for love and truth. Many saw me as a rebel, and I was a rebel for love and truth. Be the truth, speak the truth, and live the truth. This is not buying into the surface. Every person has their drama everywhere across the world. It is the surface that is the drama. The surface has nothing to do with truth. It is their illusions. Do not get caught or tangled in your dramas or anyone else's. Live the truth and be compassionate for those who are ignorant.

Two days later Jesus once more appears flying on a cross and says, "Follow me into the center of the cross." The center of the cross opens, and light descends from above. Referring to the center of the cross and the light, He states, "Here you will find what you are looking for." At another time, He appears with what looks like a multi-tiered starburst glowing behind his head, giving the appearance of a giant halo. He explains, "If one does not become one's suffering and turn to the darkness, one can fly."

Mary makes the same point about freedom and truth when she appears flying in a giant parachute. Holding the ropes and steering, she states that we must rise above all that is not truth:

> Be like me. Keep above everything that is around you. Keep your feet off the ground. Be above it. Sometimes the wind will come and try to blow you away, or a storm will come and rain you out. If you are strong enough, you can keep above it. You can get through it.

Then, in a lighthearted vein, God the Father and Jesus, also in parachutes, join her. In their essence and free, they are flying about and having a ball. At the same time, they are desperately trying to help us to be like them. It is clearly seen that, out of their love and compassion for us, they experience some suffering. But, in their essence, they are free and above the storm.

In a different vision, Jesus speaks of how suffering can bring one to God, truth, and love:

> Every person you know, every person you don't know, suffers. They suffer in many ways as you do. Suffering is of the nature of the mind. Suffering takes one into the depths of oneself and reminds one to call out for help. When people are not suffering, many do not think of God. They think they are in charge and own the world and created it. It is through suffering that the opportunity sits to know God, to know truth, to know love. Side by side they sit, suffering and love. Love is the truth. Love is all that is real. Love is the only thing that lasts. Everything around you is impermanent. If one seeks to control it, manipulate it, own it, be in charge of it, be ruled by it, one is in illusion and one is in suffering. Beneath the mind is the true mind. It is clear. It is peaceful. It is love.

He then shows the space of the true mind within His heart, vibrating and alive with energy, and adds:

> It is not possible for man to understand the nature of suffering until man understands his true nature, which is love. If you know love, you know truth and you know suffering. I suffered as a man, but never became the suffering. I was a man and experienced as a man, but always lived the truth.

He next explains how to relate to suffering, noting that there is beauty in both love and suffering:

> When you suffer, you must be. You must not react or speak. You must be. In being, the truth will come forth, and you will see and know just what the suffering brings. The suffering is as beautiful as love because in it you see the possibility. If you see as all others suffer and if you see the truth as all

others are, you will know, see, and find great beauty. There are different kinds of suffering, and I suffer now to see how people reject me and other beings who are one in truth and in love. Your suffering can free you if you see the truth in suffering.

Distinguishing the knowing that comes from truth and the knowing that comes from illusions, He goes on to speak of how we can be free of suffering yet still suffer. He links this seeming paradox to the way of knowing that comes from being one with God:

If you become the truth, you step outside of suffering, yet still suffer. But you become one with God and, therefore, know all. The way your world believes to know is not knowing at all. It is only understanding illusions and ideas, which has nothing to do with knowing. In knowing truth, you know all things. You know everything. With this, there is no need to try to understand politics, the mind, institutions, economics, great minds, ideas. To have that kind of understanding, one understands illusions and believes illusions and believes illusions to be truth and tries to resolve the problems of illusions. If people choose to know, there is no need to understand illusions. One knows all. People suffer because they know not truth.

In another vision, He urges us to let go of the suffering that comes from the small self by letting go of the small self:

You must let go of the small self and the small suffering. The small self and the small suffering are of all the things you see around you. The small suffering is created by the small self. It is suffering because it is not of God. You must fight the small self and the small suffering. Do not worry about the outcome of this situation or that. Do not worry about the things that are worldly. Do not spend time worrying.

Spend each moment loving. For every moment you spend worrying, you are in the small self.

Then He speaks of what He calls true suffering and our love becoming as great as this suffering, as He urges us once again to be pure love:

There is a greater suffering. It is the suffering of knowing that God is not in the hearts and minds of people, that love is not present. This is the true suffering. It is not of the mind and the small self. The true suffering is the suffering of knowing love is absent. Do not fear this suffering because if you love and become love, as much as you suffer and as great as your suffering is, your love will be. Put your troubles and your worries into my hands. For every moment you waste trying to solve your worries could be moments you spend loving. Love is what changes and heals all things. If you spend your time and your energy in becoming love and being love, you can heal someone with a thought. You can touch someone and change them. You can touch someone and heal them. You can walk through an experience and shift it. So your goals and your desires should be on becoming love.

Mary similarly states that love is what will change the conditions that cause people to suffer in human ways:

There is suffering on the surface, and this suffering is to be human. The suffering of the world would change if man changed, if man turned to love and turned away from illusions. This is not the case. So man will suffer. But beneath the suffering and beneath the surface is truth. This sits in every human being. The truth can be experienced by man and during his lifetime. If truth is experienced, then one is at peace because one sees the truth and one sees beyond the illusions and beyond the suffering.

She notes that this truth is found in what Tibetan Buddhism calls the "pure mind," equating Christ consciousness with Buddha consciousness. This mind, she says, allows one to be love and not illusions and suffering. She then adds:

> It is the mind of love that connects you to God, which allows you to see and allows you to be love and not your illusions and not the suffering of the world.

She then describes the relationship between love and suffering:

> There is another suffering, a higher suffering. Suffering creates an opening in you. It forces a depth. When one is in love, the love fills up the opening. The suffering will exist and, at the same time, so too will the love. This allows one to see the true nature of love and suffering. It is simple. Be love.

The suffering deepens the love, but one does not hold the suffering. One holds the love. The suffering is temporary, while the love is eternal. Mary sums up the relationship between love and suffering in a vision in which she again speaks of her suffering and the cross she carries as the mother of souls who know not love:

> I too suffer, and I too carry a cross. It is because I am the Great Mother wanting to save my children. The cross I carry is greater than any cross you could possibly understand because the state of your world is horrible. If you think your own children cause you grief, you cannot begin to understand what I go through and the cross I carry. When my Son was on the cross, I too carried the cross and was crucified. The greater you suffer, the deeper you know. The greater you suffer, the greater you love. The greater you love, the greater you suffer. The deeper you love, the deeper you suffer. At one point, your suffering and your love become all the same thing.

At another time, Mary speaks of finding peace in union with Jesus. She and Jesus appear and join together as one, with each still discernible as an individual. They then separate, with Jesus dressed in white and Mary dressed in a bride's gown. As they join together again in the oneness of love, Mary explains that we will find peace, even in the midst of our suffering, when we become one with Jesus, which is to be pure love:

> Every man, woman, and child must marry our Lord Jesus Christ. He must be their beloved. This is where, in your heart and mind, you will have total peace and love. This does not mean one does not suffer what he needs to suffer. But one feels peace even in the suffering.

Jesus' Request

Jesus instructed that the following request be included in this book: that one million people invite Him into their hearts and pray every day at the same time for one year from deep in their hearts for Him to dwell within their hearts. He said that, if He were to dwell within the hearts of one million people, He could bring enough light into the world to turn around the current world situation. He is reaching out not only to Christians, but to people throughout the world. He is appealing to people everywhere to become pure love. We pass this request on to the reader. As Jesus tells us, it would take only a small fraction of the world's population to turn to love completely in order for the present disastrous course of the world and its people to be reversed. This is because, as Mary notes, "Love is the most powerful thing, and with love all things are possible."

At the same time, what Jesus is telling us about the spiritual state of people throughout the world cannot be overlooked. Out of a world population of over six billion people, less than one million live with a purity of love in their hearts and in oneness with God. One of the more surprising statements Mary made in the visions is that she, Jesus, and others who were critical to their mission suffered so much, yet so few people understand what the suffering was about:

All the suffering was meant to show you (the people of the world) the way. Sometimes it seems it was done for nothing because so few people understand.

The messages in this and the preceding chapter give us a glimpse of what Mary, Jesus, and others sacrificed and the suffering they endured. What they accomplished established the foundation for humankind to turn to the light and for the earth to become once again a place of light. Unfortunately, as Mary and Jesus state in their messages, most people chose the darkness. Some of the reasons for this are discussed in the next chapter, as Mary and Jesus speak of the failure of religions to teach the total truth and guide people into the light.

CHAPTER THIRTEEN

The Truth of the Goddess

 WE CAN NOW BETTER APPRECIATE who and what Mary is. She is the Divine Mother and Cosmic Goddess who comes in different forms to bring love, compassion, and wisdom to people throughout the world. She wants us to know her truth so that we will know ours. Much of her truth has not been known, especially in the Christian world. In a series of messages, she and Jesus augment what is known about her and reaffirm the truth Jesus brought to the world two thousand years ago. In these messages, they relate that the Catholic Church, the institution with which Mary has been identified over the past two thousand years, as well as other religions, have failed to bring people to truth.

Their assertions about the Catholic Church in particular and religions in general are strong medicine, and some may find them hard to swallow. But these messages need to be heard. They are part of a larger story

Mary is revealing at this time. The world is changing in ways few people comprehend, and she is trying to prepare us for this transformation. It will lead, she says, to a new world and way of being in which love and light will rein. She will no longer allow her children to be lied to or misled. The changes to our lives and world will not be easy, and without the truth many souls will not survive. She will not permit any institution, religious or secular, to prevent her from bringing truth to those who want to receive it.

The Many Faces of Mary

Mary tells us that she is the feminine side of God and is coming as the feminine side of God. She is the Goddess who has incarnated in different lifetimes and has appeared in different forms throughout the ages. As she states, "I am the Goddess of light, of love, of peace, and of happiness." In several visions, she speaks of her appearances and the ways in which she speaks to those people to whom she appears. While each form in which she presents herself reveals an aspect of who and what she is, no single one reveals the totality. We are mistaken, she says, if we believe that the truth of who and what she is can be contained in any one form in which she appears or in any one message or series of messages.

She says, for example, that she comes to some people and speaks the language of the Catholic Church. This is not surprising in view of the great devotion the Church faithful have for her. Yet, she reminds us that she is more than this. Speaking of her messages to Catholic audiences, she explains:

> These people understand the language through which I speak
> to them around the language of the Church. This is my way
> of reaching them. They make a mistake in thinking this is all
> of who I am.

She similarly notes that what she reveals of herself in the visions that are the subject of this book is not all of who she is either. She thus cautions, "You would make the same mistake in thinking that what I show to you is all I am."

She points out that she gives different information to different people on the basis of various factors. One factor she mentions is how their minds work. For example, she would not present information to someone who could not grasp it. As we have seen, some of her messages are complex, reflecting our complexity as human beings and that of our world. She has said many times that the world is not as it appears and that she is trying to help us understand things not visible to the "linear eye." Similarly, she would not present information to someone for whom it would cause a crisis of faith they could not resolve. At the same time, her messages to different people are often meant to achieve different ends. It is not surprising, then, that her messages to visionaries address different topics and contain a rich diversity of both language and content.

After all, the Queen of the Universe can say what she wants to whomever she wants and present herself in whatever ways she wants. While the Catholic Church has preserved a devotion to Mary, in many critical areas, as we have seen, it has distorted her truth. Many of Mary's assertions about the Church are nothing less than a scathing indictment of much of what the Church has done and taught over the past two thousand years. Now that she is revealing her truth, the Church is in no position to stand in opposition. It has long since abandoned any moral high ground it may have occupied. As we have seen, those who deny her truth deny their own as well.

On several occasions, Mary has presented herself with different faces and in different forms in the same vision, illustrating that who and what she is cannot be captured by any one of them or, for that matter, all of them together. In a vision in which she appears with many different faces, she says, "I am not the faces." At another time, noting that she and God come to people in different ways, she relates:

> I appear to people in many ways that touch that unique individual. Around the world, God comes to people in many ways that people will relate to and understand Him. Just as I present myself with many faces, so does God.

In another vision, she first appears surrounded by a golden light. Her hair is loose and alive, cascading down to her waist. She then appears with dark skin and hair and with a different face. Next she shows herself as a light-skinned woman with blue eyes and blonde hair, followed by an image of herself with brown hair and brown eyes, and finally with red hair and green eyes. Each time her hair is long, wild, and vibrating with energy. She concludes these appearances by simply stating, "I am the Queen of Light."

Later in the same vision she again presents herself in different ways. She first appears as a Sun Goddess, with light pouring over her right side and creating a wall of light. She then appears as Our Lady of Guadalupe, followed by eight other forms in which she has appeared in other visions, with her last appearance being of Our Lady of Light as depicted in a painting of Our Lady of Light that was displayed for many years in a chapel in Santa Fe, New Mexico. In another vision, draped in a peach-colored light, she clarifies that she is not the colors of light with which she appears. A violet-colored halo surrounds her, with a beautiful turquoise light encircling the peach and violet light. Again commenting on the similarity between how she and God present themselves, she states:

> Note the colors. Realize the colors are not what I am. It is the light what I am. I present myself in many different ways, and the light can appear to many people in many different ways. This is the same when one sees God. There is not just one way to see Him. Each person sees Him through their uniqueness, and the way He relates to them is their unique relationship.

At another time, she adds, "When I present myself to people, I appear in the way in which people will be most comfortable, including dress."

On another occasion in which she again presents herself in different forms, both young and old, she further clarifies, "I appear to people in many ways. What I look like does not matter because what I look like is not who I am." Summing up her statements about the ways in which she appears, she concludes, "I am everywhere. I come in many forms and ways, but I am the same me."

Mary has come in many visions as a Native American or in Native American dress. On these occasions, she speaks very highly of what she calls the "native ways" and the importance of knowing them and making them part of our lives. For example, she appears in a vision as an Indian princess, with rays of golden light, like a sunburst similar to the light that appears around her as Our Lady of Guadalupe, surrounding her. She counsels, "You must know the native ways, the native ways of the land and the native ways of the Spirit." At another time, she appears with a turquoise color, but in her essence of pure light, and instructs, "Bring the native ways into your lives. Live the holy life and live where everything is sacred and everything that is done is sacred." In another message, she observes that native peoples had much intelligence of a higher source and that they were seers, knowers, and dreamers. She says we must turn to these ways to guide us.

One of the native knowings of which she speaks relates to the sun. In many of the visions, including those in which she comes as Our Lady of Guadalupe, she appears with the sun. In one apparition, the sun, with rays of light beaming outward, surrounds her. God is seen behind the sun, fueling it with His light. Mary elucidates about the sun:

> The light of the sun is the energy of God. The sun gives you light and without light you could not exist. It is the light of God and the heat of the Spirit. The cultures who worshiped the sun were not wrong about the sun.

In other visions, she identifies herself with different figures worshiped as divine in different parts of the world. She discloses, for instance, that she was incarnated as the woman who later became worshiped as the Hindu Goddess Lakshmi.[1] She says that she is also the Goddess Isis, worshiped in Egypt and throughout the Mediterranean for thousands of years. She likewise reveals that she is the White Buffalo Woman who appeared to Native Americans and gave them special teachings, including instructions on the use of ceremonies for specific purposes. In several visions, she appears as a white buffalo or accompanied by a white buffalo. At these times, she announces that it is the time of the white buffalo, referring to the Native American prophecy that great changes will come to the earth and her people when the White Buffalo Woman returns.

Mary is the Divine Mother and Cosmic Goddess. Yet, she tells us she also is a soul created with Joseph out of the same breath of God and that she is no different than us. The enormity of her spiritual attainment is far beyond what we can grasp. This is part of the great mystery of who and what Mary is. It also reflects the power of the Almighty, who has described Mary as "the love of all my loves." From what she reveals about herself, we can only conclude that God has exalted her to such a level that she occupies a status in relation to Him unlike any other soul. The key to understanding Mary's unique status, singular and unparalleled among all souls, may be found in Jesus' words about His mother:

> My mother is the greatest of all souls. In God's eyes, she is His favorite. She is the most powerful. She is more powerful than me. Continue to develop, crave, and want a relationship to us. Do not fear the things of the world because they have no meaning. Everything of the world passes. Therefore, do not put your faith in the things of the world. Put your faith and your energy in me and my mother. This is where you will find satisfaction, bliss, peace everlasting.

Today Mary is appearing throughout the world in many different ways to reach as many people as possible with her message of love. She is reaffirming information she has given in the past, as well as imparting new information meant to prepare us for the times in which we are living and the changes that are upon us. Some of these messages, as we have seen, present a much broader understanding of her than many people have had. She says that she is coming to teach the world who she is.

Mary and the Catholic Church
Mary has had a special relationship with the Catholic Church. The Catholic Church, and especially the Church faithful, have maintained a

deep devotion and reverence for her. So it is not without great sorrow that she tells us that her Church lost its way and has misled her people. Some people may be offended by Mary's statements about the Church, while others will recognize their truth. As difficult as these messages may be for some to accept, Mary wants the truth to be known. This is not a time in our history where we can afford to evade the truth or for the truth to remain hidden. We may not want to hear what Mary has to say. Yet we must remember that she sees us as a people lost in a world of illusion and darkness and that she is desperately trying to guide us back to truth and love:

> Like any mother, I have become weary. I have spoken to my children for hundreds of years, and now the time has come for my words and the truth to be heard. My children have become a people of greed, of money, of destruction, of lust, a people without heart and soul. The time has come for my children to hear my words, as I have become weary and the load has become heavy. I weep daily for the sins of the world.

In these times of great turmoil and transition, truth is at a premium, and what we allow into our minds will find its way into our hearts. Truth can free our hearts, just as lies can poison them. Mary's statements, moreover, are not limited to Catholicism. It would be nice if there were just one villain at whom we can point a finger. But the culpability for the present state of our world is widespread. She thus speaks about the failure of religions generally, reminding us repeatedly that God is about love and not religion or dogma.

Mary asserts that the Catholic Church knows the truth about her and her Son, but is concealing it:

> The Church knows the truth. The Church knows of my power. The Church is hiding the message of Jesus Christ and the truth of all truths. I am love, and my Church should be teaching love. Love is not a form of control. Love is free. Love is

alive. Love is peace. Love is all beauty. Love is all-encompassing. Love is truth. Love is light. Love is purity. Love is God. Love is not power. Love is not greed. Love is not lust. Love is not deceit. Love is not lies. Love is not darkness. I am love. I am one with God, and God is one with me. I am one with Christ, and Christ is one with me. I am one with Joseph, and Joseph is one with me.

She further asserts:

> The Church tried to conceal the truth because of power and control and because I am a woman. Jesus and I are one. He is my Son; I am His mother. We are one. People know the truth in their souls and that is why they have such a distaste (for the Church). They know the truth is not being spoken.

In another vision, she appears with a veil covering her head and states:

> I am the Queen of Heaven. I am the Queen of Light. People choose to take away my face and the face of my Son. They choose not to know the truth, to cover up the truth, and to destroy the truth.

She then speaks of the Church's corruption as she addresses a television program on Jesus and the Holy Land in which He was erroneously portrayed as a political activist:

> It is no accident that the media uses their power to poison the minds of people. It is no accident the timing of the program. It is being used to keep people from seeing the truth. My Son's mission was not to be a political man or even to create a Church. My Son's mission was to bring love, light, and truth to all people. Long ago the Church became corrupt. It is greed, lust, and power that destroyed the words

and truth of my Son. He came with a higher knowledge and a higher wisdom and the highest truth, wanting to share and bring them to everyone. Many things have been twisted and misused and are misleading the people. I will no longer have my Church misleading people.

Jesus appears in the same vision and responds to the false claims made in the TV program that his mission was primarily political:

Know that I am love. My purpose, my mission, my being is love. Know that every word I said came from love and from God. Do not be mistaken. In love, what one thinks is impossible is possible. The program lied about who I am. It is the work of the devil. I did and do perform miracles.

Addressing the limited worldview reflected in comments made by some scholars interviewed on the program, He adds, "Remember, there are other worlds, other realities. It is the ignorant who choose to believe otherwise." He also decries what has been made of the places in the Holy Land where He lived and taught that were shown on the program:

Do you see what my people did? They made museums out of the places where I was. They make money off of my memory. This is not what I was about. I am not about money, power, or glory. I am about love.

Then, speaking of His mother and the claim made on the program that He only had a small band of followers, He relates:

She knew the truth, as did many. They (referring to the people who produced the TV program) have taken away the magic of that time. They have forgotten the power of love. This is why your world has become so dark. Follow me. I will not mislead you. My way is love and truth and peace. It is eternal. Their way is limited, dark, and empty. Come with me.

Jesus' Teachings and His Relationship with Mary Magdalene

In several messages, Mary states that Jesus wrote down his teaching and that these writings are still in existence. Jesus was literate and knew Scripture well. It therefore is not surprising that He wrote down His teachings. Mary asserts that Jesus did this and that His writings are being hidden:

> The Church has misused its power to control the people and to mislead them. The Church has many goods, but men have chosen to create lies of their own will. In those lies they have misrepresented our Lord God. There are tablets which are hidden in Rome. They are the writings of Jesus and speak the total truth.

She further declares:

> The writings of my Son will be rediscovered, and the truth of God is in those writings. They are hidden because of power and corruption. But the truth shall be known. There will be talk about the disbelief in those writings, but they are true. They contain the truth of God and of love and the exact instructions on how to join with God. They include (spiritual) practices, meditation, and prayer. They are words that speak directly to the soul. These writings speak of rein-carnation, karma, light, and darkness.

In another vision, Mary appears in white and golden light and holding a large, black book containing what she says are the real teachings of Jesus. She states, "In my churches, the word of Christ and the way of Christ are not being taught." Then, crying black tears and referring to the book in her hands, she continues:

> This book is in existence and is the Word of God. It speaks the truth of love. My Church has led many people in the wrong direction.

In another vision, she holds the same book and again declares, "It is the real teachings and the real Bible. It is the real truth." During another appearance, she has the book in her hands and begins to sing in another language. Then, clasping the book to her heart, she exclaims: "This Bible is the real truth! It is the Bible that speaks of love." At another time, she once again appears holding the same book and, opening it, proclaims:

> This word will become the Word. This word is the Word of the Lord. This word is the Word of love. This word is the Word of truth. This word is the Word of God.

Jesus, in a vision in which He refers to His writings, confirms that some of His teachings are not known. He specifically mentions his teachings on light, energy, the power of what we have been calling the ordinary mind, and the power of the true mind:

> I suffered and the people of the world do not appreciate what I came to do. They had my writings and my teachings, and my people do not know the truth. They do not know about light, energy, the power of the mind, and the power of the true mind. They do not understand, and they have chosen ignorance, darkness, and evil. People do not understand the message and the truth. You are in the time of great change, and I will walk the earth again.[2]

In another vision, He reveals that He taught about the energy centers and that these teachings are also being hidden by the Church:

> The Catholic Church has hidden the truth about the energy centers. In my time, I taught about them.

Speaking of the power and purpose of sexual energy, He further states:

> The Church knew this and, like with so many other things, the Church has misused and distorted truth and reality. There are writings about energy, about life, and about truth.[3]

Mary likewise speaks about the distortion of the truth about sexual energy, which she says is a part of God, by the Church throughout most of its history. Any distortion of the truth about sexual energy by an institution as influential as the Catholic Church is serious. As Mary explains, sexual energy is necessary to join with God. Hiding or destroying the truth about sexual energy has the effect of undermining people's capacity to fulfill their purpose in life by becoming one with God. Jesus came to teach us how to be like Him in this world and not just in the next. He came to show us that we too could have the power to transform water into wine, walk on water, heal the sick, calm the waters, and multiply loaves and fishes. All this is possible through love and the mastery of light and energy, including sexual energy.

It is not possible, however, without understanding the nature and use of sexual energy as the most powerful force that we carry within us. Eliminating such a central part of Jesus' teachings is tantamount to destroying them as a whole. No matter how devoted people may be, they cannot rise to the highest levels of consciousness and become like Jesus unless they allow the fullness of this energy to come alive within them and transform them. What makes the concealment of Jesus' teachings all the more egregious is that it was done with the express purpose of destroying the power of His teachings and mission and to hold people in bondage to darkness. As Jesus states, the Church's concealment of the truth about sexual energy was intended to prevent people from becoming who they are:

> The Church tried to contain the sexual force in people, and it became distorted so that members of the Church could keep people from becoming who they are. And what the Church has done is block this energy and teach that this energy is wrong.

Mary refers to the impact of this when speaking about a group of Catholic nuns living under the vow of celibacy. While acknowledging their deep devotion and noting that it does not go unrecognized, she mourns their denial of their sexual energy:

They do not understand what it means to be virgin. To be a virgin and not know your sexual power and your life-force is to not know God. If this power is misused in any way, through over use or under use, if it is not held as sacred in mind, heart, and action, it is to deny God.

They have denied a tremendous part of God. This is a pity that my Church has done this to my people... They know not this truth. They have been taught incorrectly, and they choose to stay in the place of not knowing through fear of their own sexuality. Few know how to use their sexual energy when they are being celibate.

Mary has said that not only did Jesus teach about the energy centers, light, and the role of sexual energy to bring souls to higher levels of consciousness and ultimately into union with God. She has also said that Jesus and Mary Magdalene were lovers. Jesus and Mary Magdalene, according to Mary, "experienced the fullness of a relationship between a man and a woman." The portrayal of Mary Magdalene in the Gospels is incorrect. She was not only Jesus' lover, but probably one of His most advanced disciples. Jesus says that many of the women around Him understood His teachings about light, energy, and the energy centers. It is possible that Jesus did not give all His disciples the same teachings. It was His teachings on subjects such as light and energy, which His mother, Mary Magdalene, and other women knew well, that were hidden.

In all of this, the power of women, as well as the feminine principle which exists most powerfully in sexual energy, were negated. The feminine is necessary for the full experience of the divine. This is true for women and men alike. It was true for Jesus when He walked the earth. He needed the power of His sexual energy to be fully alive in Him so that He could attain the highest levels of Spirit and fulfill His mission. The power of the feminine is carried by women in a special way. The reasons for this relate to how a woman naturally holds and experiences her sexual energy. Mary speaks of the importance of a woman for a man's spiritual evolvement in a message about Jesus and Mary Magdalene's relationship. Referring to the spiritual role their love-making played, she states:

> A man needs a woman to obtain the highest spiritual goal while in human form. Men do not understand what women are about, and most women do not understand what women are about. There is a difference between the energies of the female and the male. The woman is power. Without an understanding of what love-making, sex, and relationship really are, people fail themselves.

Like Mary and Joseph, Mary Magdalene and Jesus were lovers who shared a special mission together. It is no wonder, then, that Mary Magdalene was at the foot of the cross when Jesus died and that Jesus appeared first to her after His resurrection. The concealment of the truth of their love for each other is yet another tragic loss to the world.

These messages tell us that the Church betrayed its people in a terrible way. It knew of the nature and purpose of sexual energy and its unique role in bringing souls into union with God. Jesus taught about this, and these teaching are included in His writings hidden by the Church. The Church's misrepresentation of Mary as a perpetual virgin is part of this betrayal. This teaching provided a false model of feminine virtue and purity that served, for most of the past two thousand years, to negate the power of sexual energy, love-making, and the feminine as means to develop spiritually and to bring people to union with God. Likewise, Jesus' relationship with Mary Magdalene and the role of their love and love-making in His spiritual attainment were concealed.

The Church, instead of teaching that sexual energy is the light of God and the most powerful energy we have to bring us to the fulfillment of our life purpose, made sexual energy into something dark, rendering this miraculous part of God an impediment to reaching God. As mentioned previously, one of the most effective ways to attack a person spiritually is to destroy a person's sexual energy. This is done in many ways. It is done by disassociating sexual energy from spirituality and thus promoting directly or indirectly its misuse. It is also done by tainting sexuality with shame or guilt and thereby fostering its repression.

The full import of the Church's duplicity cannot be overstated. Instead of sexual energy and sexual intimacy being associated with light, love, and God, they became disconnected from God and their intended purpose and associated with sin and evil, opening the door for darkness to enter where light should rein. As Jesus said, more souls are lost to the darkness because of the misuse of the body and sexual energy than for any other reason. This is a direct consequence of the Church's distortion and concealment of the truth about sexual energy and the relationship of Mary and Joseph, as well as its subversion of Jesus' teachings and writings about light and energy and the truth of His relationship with Mary Magdalene. We have to ask ourselves who is the real whore: Mary Magdalene or the Catholic Church?

The Last Fatima Message

According to Mary, another truth the Church concealed is the last of the messages that she gave to Lucia, one of the three young visionaries to whom she appeared at Fatima, Portugal in 1917. In 2000, the Church released what it represented to be the final message to Lucia. It claimed that this message was about the failed assassination attempt against Pope John Paul II. Shortly after the Church made this announcement, Mary stated in a vision:

> The Church is lying and hiding the truth of my messages. This saddens me. The truth in the last message to Lucia revealed the darkness, the devastation, with dates, of what is to come. I am telling my people these truths because my Church is lying.

Mary instructed Lucia that this message, which is about the apocalyptic changes we are presently experiencing and the end of the world as we know it, be revealed in 1960. Lucia, the only one of the three visionaries to survive past childhood, became a nun living under the rule of the Church, and the Church had the power to reveal the final message or conceal it. If the correct message had been revealed in 1960, as Mary enjoined, the world, and not just the Christian world, would have had the opportunity to alter its course and very likely would not find itself at the precipice of disaster where it is today. Once again Mary tells us that the Church betrayed its people. She further states:

> Lucia knows the truth of the things that will come. She also knows about the Church and dark beings in the Church destroying. All this was written down by Lucia.

The fate of the final message to Lucia is instructive as to the obstacles Mary faces within the Church in having the truth be known. If she had chosen a priest or nun to reveal that she and Joseph were lovers and Jesus had siblings, that sexual energy is an aspect of God and necessary to become one with God, that Jesus' teachings and writings have been subverted and hidden, and that Jesus and Mary Magdalene were lovers, this person would have been silenced by the Church, as Lucia, who is still alive, has been effectively silenced in regard to the final Fatima message. Alternatively, such person would be subject to censure and excommunication by the Church. Mary could not expect someone formally bound by the rule of the Church to be the carrier of these messages.

While Mary strongly decries the Church's corruption and its subversion of truth, she does it out of love and compassion. As she says, a mother sometimes has to be firm. It should also be kept in mind that she has not revealed the details of how and when the Church turned away from the truth and how Jesus' teachings and writings, as well as the truth of her relationship with Joseph, were successfully concealed. That is a story that is yet to be told. Elements within the Church are obviously responsible, but this does not mean that everyone associated with Catholicism is at fault. In this regard, we should remember that, throughout the Church's history, many people within the Church, including its hierarchy, were deeply devoted and some attained high levels of spiritual mastery. The Church honors many of them as saints, and Mary urges us to call upon them to help us in our needs.

One of the great souls in today's Church is His Holiness Pope John Paul II, whom Mary has referred to endearingly in the visions as "my son."

She has spoken about the dark forces and beings surrounding him. Few people, including few within the Church, know the obstacles that this courageous being has had to face and the darkness with which he has had to contend within the Church itself. This is another story yet to be told.

Beyond Religion to Love

Relatively few people have attained the level of spiritual attainment that Jesus and other spiritual masters taught about. Many of their teachings have been formalized into religions. Jesus tells us that today, out of a world population of over six billion, there are not even one million people who have attained the level of spiritual mastery that Jesus and other masters taught. This failure, together with the level of darkness in the world as described by Mary and Jesus, explains why Mary speaks not only of the demise of Catholic Church, but of all religions. In times of great darkness, only the light will prevail. If an institution is not filled with light, it will not survive the darkness. She thus prophesies:

> All religions are going to crumble. There is going to be one religion left, and that is the religion of love. All the truth of all religions will be brought together, and the things that separate will be dissolved. Religion is created by men. Religion can lead men to God. The truths that the masters brought to earth are truths to help individuals grow. They were not meant to set up structures that create duality. All of the churches and institutions are going to crumble. People fighting wars over religion is not about God.

It therefore should not come as a surprise that, according to Mary, very few people today will come to oneness with God through religion. She says people need to turn, instead, to spirituality and to prayer, meditation, spiritual practices, and, where appropriate, love-making in order to bring them into union with the divine. She notes that there is great beauty and many devoted people in the Church. She has spoken, for instance, of the value of the sacraments. Yet, as devoted as people may be, they cannot find their way to God without the right understanding of how to accomplish this. The Church has not taught this, and it is doubtful it will change course. Those who may feel adrift without the Church to guide them can turn to Mary and other divine beings. They will not mislead you.

When Mary says that there will be one religion and that the truth of all religions will be brought together, she is not referring to the creation of a single religious institution purporting to incorporate all religious truth. She will not allow her children to be further deceived and misled. Rather, she is talking about the birth of the consciousness of love and of God, through her intervention as well as that of her Son and other beings of light. This new consciousness will render unnecessary institutional religion altogether. We will witness the fulfillment of what Jesus and our Divine Mother came to accomplish two thousand years ago. As Mary states:

> For those who do not love everybody, it is as if they were walking empty-hearted. They have no love, and they know love not. This is a time to become one people in truth, one people in love, one people in God. It is those who love everybody who will know, see, and be the truth, which is God, and God is love. You must be kind and loving to all people, all beings, regardless of their religion, their race, their status.

Mary says it is now imperative, in this time of encroaching darkness, that we learn to fill ourselves with light and become light. We will not be protected from the darkness without the light. Nor can we become one with God until we are pure light. Mary comes to bring us light, but we have to know how to take it in and what to do with it. This is why she comes as Our Lady of Light and specifically asks that people be taught about light, its use in visualization and related practices, and energy, including sexual energy and its role in love-making. She is, in effect, bringing to us knowledge of things that Jesus taught and wrote about, but were concealed. As stated earlier, much of this knowledge is found in other traditions, but is missing in most Western religions.

Mary, as our Divine Mother, is showing us how to reach a consciousness of love. She is teaching us what her Son taught two thousand years ago. She is preparing her children for the greatest revolution of consciousness the world has ever known, bringing us light and truth and showing us how to become light and truth. She is calling us home.

She is also revealing who and what she is, declaring, "I can no longer be seen as just the Catholic Mary. I must be seen as the Cosmic Goddess of Love and Light." As the Cosmic Goddess, she will no longer be found within institutions or churches. Pointing in a vision to an image of the earth, she says, "This is my church. Pray to me everywhere, and I will come to you." Her way, the way of all the earth, will at last be known:

> The time will come when all will know who I was and who
> I am. The Goddess will be known.

CHAPTER FOURTEEN

The Way of All the Earth

MARY'S WAY IS THE WAY of all the earth. She cannot be contained within any one religion. Nor is her message for any one religion or group. She belongs to everyone, as well as to the earth and all her creatures, and we belong to her. As the Divine Mother, she embraces all peoples in love and her desire to bring them home to truth. She presents herself in many ways, reminding us that we cannot mistake who and what she is for the way in which she appears. Moreover, as we have seen thus far, her teachings are multifaceted, and she is giving them to people of diverse backgrounds and faiths throughout the world.

Mary says she and her Son will bring heaven to this earth, but not before the world as we know it comes to an end. Her role in the transition to a new world and new consciousness is pivotal. She is the Divine

Mother, and the changes will not happen without her. At the same time, we need her love and guidance in order to overcome the darkness that would keep us from joining with her in this new world. She comes for all people and her messages are for all people, showing us the way to become love and enter with her into the light.

The Consciousness of Pure Love

Mary is the consciousness of pure love. To know her is to know love, and to follow her way is to become love and live in the consciousness of love. She has shown us that we can step into this consciousness when we fall in love and open our hearts to another, as she and Joseph did. We heighten this consciousness in our love-making, as we bring the miracle of sexual energy and the magic of the energy centers to life in us. Sexual energy, also known as *kundalini* or *shakti*, cleans and heals us and opens our heart center to the hidden chamber where we come to know the Sacred Heart, our true essence of joy, freedom and bliss. This vital energy, and it matters not what we call it, is the feminine side of God. It is Mary. It is the Holy Spirit. It is the energy of the Divine Mother and Cosmic Goddess permeating all of creation and sustaining everyone and everything. When we honor her, when we feel her and bring her into every aspect of who and what we are, she honors us and brings us to the light and love of God.

Mary and Jesus' messages about sexual energy are meant to restore it to its proper place in God's plan for us to become one with Him. These teachings are intended to bring us into the consciousness of pure love where we will know that we are the same as Mary and Jesus. One by one, as we recognize this feminine power within us, we will transform ourselves and the world into light, creating with Mary the paradise that this earth is meant to be. Sexual energy joined with love is the key to this, dissolving our darkness and illusions and freeing us from the bondage of the ego and the ordinary mind. It clears away the vestiges of the mistakes and misguided ways of our past as it shifts our vibration and lifts us into a higher consciousness. It is the essence of God that allows us to become pure once more. As it opens us to the Sacred Heart, we once again know ourselves as divine.

It is an energy infused with the consciousness of the Virgin Goddess, and it is this consciousness that we become as we move out of the ordinary and into the extraordinary. Not only will it open us to the unfathomable depths of love within us, it will open our spiritual eyes so that we will see through the eyes of God and know as God knows in oneness with all. Then not only will we be transformed, but so too will the world, into the magic of love.

But this will not happen unless we strive to develop and nurture ourselves spiritually. We taste the magic of divine love in romantic love and true love-making, but we will not be able to sustain the vibration of love and remain in the consciousness of love unless we are willing to make a total commitment to ourselves, to our beloved, to love, and to God. Mary thus calls us to make the bond with our beloved "a union with God and in God." In order to do this, we must be willing to put God at the center of our lives and let love be our guide. We have to let go of all that is not love and live holy lives centered around prayer, meditation, spiritual practices and, for those couples who are in a loving relationship, love-making. We also must be willing to serve others in love and weave truth into all we do, as we open more and more to Spirit within us and around us and strive to sacrifice the small self for the greater self of love. At the same time, we must have the courage to face and cleanse ourselves of the darkness we carry and, with our beloved, be warriors for love as we battle darkness on all levels with light and love. It is not a path without suffering. But, as Mary and Jesus explain, the suffering can open us more deeply to love and compassion for ourselves and others and, ultimately, to the truth of who and what we are.

As Mary's life exemplifies, only a total commitment will bring us what we most deeply desire: union with God. It may seem like a high price to pay. Yet, as Mary points out, striving to be one with God is the only thing that makes our lives truly grand and great. All else takes us in circles and keeps us trapped in the illusions that, as Mary states, "man creates and the devil exploits." We have the awesome freedom to choose to become light or darkness, to choose to be one with God or remain separated from Him. No one can make this choice for us. It is ours alone, and God is sending his favorite soul to awaken us to the power we have to become what we choose to be. Mary thus shares with us aspects of her life, her joys and her sorrows, to show us that in our essence we are no different than she and that we too can achieve what is truly grand and great. She is teaching us how to lift the veils of illusions, free ourselves from darkness, and in the most human aspects of our being find our way home to God.

There are many ways to return to God. Romantic love and relationship are one of them. In loving another, in giving oneself totally in heart, mind, body, and soul to the beloved, one can transcend the limitations of human love and attain the bliss and freedom of divine love and oneness with God. In order to become one with God, however, we have to be in love with God. Being in love with another opens us to this divine romance. We can then refrain from the relentless worship of false gods created by the delusions of the ordinary mind and the ego. We can recognize that the devil and dark beings exist, but we need not fear them or fall prey to their tricks. We can live our truth with the help of divine beings, like Mary, and fulfill the purpose for which we have come into this world, as we follow love's urgent longings into the arms of God, the ultimate lover.

Mary's way is not for the few. It is for everyone. Just as falling in love and the beauty and joy of love-making and orgasm are not limited to only a few, but are accessible to us all, so too is the experience of pure love and being one with God. The truth of what Mary has come to teach us can no longer be hidden. The time has come for us to choose light and love once and forever and never look back. The time has come for a new consciousness in which all souls who so choose will join in mystical union with God.

The Time of the Goddess

The people of this planet are nearing the end of a journey and the beginning of a new one. According to Mary, the world as we know it is coming to an end, and we will enter into "a new way of existence, a new way of being, a new way of knowing." She similarly prophesies, "The world is going to experience many changes. There will be a change of consciousness." Announcing the dawn of a new era, she tells us that those who choose love will live in a new world and in a new way:

You are in the end times. You are in the cycle of the sun. You are in the times of greatest change. A new world and way will exist for those who choose love.

At times, Mary calls this new era the Age of the Goddess. At other times, she calls it the Age of God, as she does in the following message in which she says the changes will bring an end to all darkness:

This is the Age of God and the time of great change. A time of destruction of all darkness. A time to repent and ask for forgiveness, to pray, to bow down to our Lord God, to be love, to be in the light. It is a time to give up the old, a time to be.

This new world has been foreseen in many traditions. For example, Mary shows a Mayan calendar with a face in the center and explains:

The face has never been seen in its totality, and it has significant meaning. The face is the face of the new world. The Mayans saw it, but what they wrote was all in code. All that they saw will come to pass.

The calendar has three concentric circles, a small one within a larger one within a larger one. The circles are spinning. They stop and come together to make a whole. Within the whole is a sun, and within the sun is the face Mary first showed. It is the face of the Goddess. Mary continues to explain:

It will be the time of the Goddess. All the things that have been broken will come together in a new way that will allow me to come with all my power.

She further explains that in this new era everything will be recreated, souls will exist at a high level of consciousness, and the world will be as it was meant to be. She sometimes describes this new world as the "New Jerusalem," depicting it in several visions as a city with streets and buildings of gold. At another time, she represents it in a spectacular vision in which all time and no time, as well as the vastness of all that is, can be seen. Many places are visible, but one stands out. It is a place of pure light and love. Referring to it, she says, "If you follow my way, if you follow me, you will come into this."

Mary's way is the way of the Goddess, the way of pure light and love. She says we are in her time, the time of the Goddess:

> It is the time of the Goddess. I am the Cosmic Goddess, the Queen of Heaven and Earth. I am the Queen of the Universe. I am the Queen of Light. I am the Queen of Love. I am the Queen of Peace. I am the Queen of Possibility. I am the Queen of Hope. I am the Mother of all, and I wrap my light and love around all. It is those who love with an open heart who recognize and receive me. But I come for all. It is one simple thing I come to bring, and this is love. My Son and I are one. We have never been separated. We will never be separated. We will always be one.

Speaking of her role at this turning point in human history, she adds:

> I am the light of the world, and I am trying to guide the world into the light. There will be a new world where I will be known and loved as the Queen of Light.

She then shows herself above a city of light, with her light raining down upon it. She reminds us that we have to choose to become the light, stating, "This city is the city of my Son, and not all will be there." Jesus appears in the same vision, and His image and Mary's fade in and out, with one and then the other being dominant. He similarly states:

> I am only love and want only love. All will change, and those who do not want love will not be with me. I am of the Father. I am the King.

Mary repeats that we are living in a time of decision and that only those who choose to be light and love will enter the Kingdom with her and Jesus, stating, "Each soul, each individual, must make up his or her own mind." At another time, she adds, "I am the light of the world. It will be the time of the Goddess. Only those worthy of the Kingdom will be in it."

The Divine Mother wants all her children to be with her in this new world of light. This is why her messages are so urgent and her pleas so forceful. She informs us, "If I do not come, the earth and its people will be destroyed by darkness." But, she laments, many do not respond to her calls or heed her warnings:

> You are a people who have lost all truth. It is a time for you
> to hear and know the words of truth. I come in desperation,
> pleading and begging my children to come home. But they
> love not truth.

Her desire for us to join with her in light and love is the reason her vibration is entering the planet in such a powerful way now. She is coming with all the force and power of God to help us. Her vibration is everywhere, for she holds us and the earth within her divine womb. She tells us we must take her vibration into us. Referring to the changes that are happening, she explains why we must do this:

> The heart of every person is opening to a new depth. The
> people who are open to the spiritual and believe in the spir-
> itual will be filled with my energy.

She is pouring out her love, light, and wisdom, preparing us for the transition to the consciousness of pure love. Stressing the need to hold onto the vibration of love, she states:

> The vibration of love and knowing God and knowing me is
> what will bring about a balance on this earth. Never let go of
> that vibration. I will always be with you.

But, as she says, we have to be willing to hear and accept the truth she is bringing us. She reminds us there is a divine order, as she shows what looks like a platform of light upon which she, Jesus, Joseph, saints, and other beings of light are standing. God is above them on a throne, with rays of light flowing out of Him and into the beings standing below. Mary says that we must give ourselves over to this divine order.

This new world, this city of gold, the New Jerusalem, will be one in which souls live in the highest ideals of love. Mary says that the conflict between light and darkness on this plane will cease and that there will be no place for darkness in this new world. She promises one thousand years of light, during which the feminine side of God will rein. She foretells:

> My people will live in grace, beauty, joy, bliss, and love. These are only words that limit the truth, but the truth is what they will be.

Such a paradise may be hard to imagine. It may seem out of our reach. Well, Mary is divine love, and she says that with love all things are possible. So, if we turn to her and to love, it is possible for us to join with her in this paradise of love. This is why God created us. Mary wants us to know Him as she knows Him. She wants us to be one with Him as she is one with Him. She wants us to be the fruits of His love as she is the fruit of His love.

This paradise is our birthright, our home, and Mary is calling us back to it. If we take a moment to think of the most powerful experience of love we have ever had and multiply it a million times, we would still not grasp the magnificence of this world that Mary is guiding us to. It is what the saints and masters of all traditions have come to know. It is the highest knowing where miracles and experiences, like bilocation, healing with light and touch, telepathic communication, clairvoyance, and much more, will be the norm. We will be on an endless adventure of love with each other and with God. This is what Mary means when she says we are meant to live a heaven on earth. This is what Jesus came to teach us. Mary knew it then, and she knows it now. This time the truth will not be subverted. The Goddess is bringing the truth to those who want it.

Mary does not want to lose even one of her children to the darkness. This is why she is imparting the understanding we need to open our hearts and become pure love. It is only in the consciousness of pure love that we will be at a vibration that will allow us to be in the vibration of this new world. This is what Mary's way is about. As she reiterates, "To reach the level of pure consciousness is to merge with God." She says that this cannot happen unless people develop their sexual energy and use it in tandem with love, which is the reason she is bringing us the truth about sexual energy and calling for a revolution of consciousness around it. As she says, she is coming with the force and power of God. This force and power is of the same nature as our sexual energy. The proper relationship to this energy, therefore, will be indispensable as we move further into the changes Mary is prophesying. Jesus explains the reason for this: "The sexual energy itself is going to become a different vibration and move into something more cosmic."

The energy of Jesus' mother, the *shakti* of the Cosmic Goddess, as it enters our world with all the force and power of God, will transform our sexual energy into a more powerful cosmic force. Those whose hearts are open and who live with an abundance of sexual energy will be lifted into the Sacred Heart by the sheer magnitude of their own sexual energy combined with the energy of the Goddess. Thus, it is more imperative now than ever before to let go of the things and ways of the world, open our hearts to love, and live in harmony and balance with the force of God within us. It is a time to risk all in order to gain all. Mary has shown us how to become holy, to be filled with love and light. Anything less is to continue to live in madness at a time when we can least afford to do so.

In a vision, Mary equates this pure consciousness with the seed of truth within us and says, "For all beings to know the seed of truth, they must know that they are what I am." We are the same energy, the same force, the same love as Mary. We are within her, and she is within us, as she tells us when she appears with different colors—violets, pinks, peaches, and golds—and states:

I am your breath. If you live with my breath and in my breath, you see the beauty and greatness of the world, and you let go of your own ideas and see God's divine plan.

She then shows individual consciousness expanding into an all-embracing oneness of cosmic consciousness and the individual self no longer having any need. She reminds us once again that she is like us and we are like her and that we too are the Virgin Goddess, one in light, love, and purity with all.

The transition to this new world and way of being will not be easy. Mary says that it will be a time of trial and tragedy, destruction and devastation. She tells us, though, that we need not fear and that she and God will not abandon those who turn to them:

Know that I am always with you and with all who want me with them. This is not a time to doubt. It is a time to become stronger in faith and in love. God knows what He is doing and will not forsake His lovers and followers.

Mary comes to guide us to the Sacred Heart, the pure light and love which is our divine essence. It is where we will find refuge in the difficult times that will bring an end to darkness and give birth to an Age of Light. We will not find safety or comfort in the things of the world, Mary says, but only in God. She is leading us, with her words and her example, to the sacred place within us where we will not only find God, but be one with Him for eternity:

The only place you will find refuge is in the heart of God. You will find the heart of God in your own heart. Do not fear or doubt. Follow my example when I walked the earth and my example now. I am nothing but heart, nothing but love, pure and divine.

Appendix A

Visualizations for Purification, Healing, and Protection

The following visualizations and spiritual practices, as well as those in Appendix B, are transmissions from the heart of Mary, the Queen of Light. They can be used with other Divine Beings from ANY tradition, since all is God. Using sacred imagination and sacred meditation, the power of these visualizations can transform your being and consciousness at all levels.

These visualizations and spiritual practices can be done anywhere and at any time. They will help you to purify your energy field, your heart, your mind, and your body and to protect them from negative and dark energies, spirits, beings, thoughts, and emotions. Energizing and healing, they are important to our spiritual paths in order for us to be filled with light and become holy. We can use them to help ourselves and others to become who we are.

Most of the visualizations are best done in a seated position. Sit comfortably, if possible in a meditative posture. Ask Mary to be present in the ways with which you are comfortable in speaking to her. If you are not sure how to speak to her, you can say something like, "Mary, please enter this space. Come with all your grace, beauty, wisdom, and light. Be with me, guide me, and protect me." Sit and feel her divine presence. Then proceed with the visualizations that are needed at a given time. If no specific color of light is indicated in the visualization, use the color of light that first comes to you. This will be the color that is most helpful for the purpose of the specific visualization you are doing. Always give thanks at the end of the practice, as gratitude is a form of love that grows into more love.

There are several beginning practices included as an introduction to understanding the power of Mary and the power of visualization, when used together, to heal and transform. All the practices are meant for GOODNESS ONLY. ENJOY and INJOY.

Practice #1
This practice is meant to increase your energy. See and feel yourself in body, mind, emotion, and spirit. Then imagine yourself at a peak time of your life, when you were in balance and filled with power and energy. See a color of light associated with this experience. Bring this light to life in the form of an image within you and hold it for a few minutes. Now call Mary and see her present with you. Visualize her energy entering your heart and expanding in

power within every part of you, mentally, physically, emotionally, and spiritually. Then see her energy all around you. Breathe in this power, experiencing the sensation of being energized. Record the sensation throughout your entire being.

Practice #2

As you are walking, jogging, swimming, or exercising, see Mary surrounded by light above you. Call her name, repeating "Hail Mary, Hail Mary, Hail Mary." As you call her name, feel your energy expanding into hers, and her energy expanding into yours. See her energy as a vibrating light that invigorates your body, mind and soul, bringing health and harmony to all levels of your being.

Practice #3

Sit quietly. See Mary above you. Visualize a white fire coming from her heart and hands into your heart and hands. See this fire filling you and burning off all the stress and problems from the day and from your life. See yourself becoming this white fire: all powerful, all energy, all loving. Sit with this knowing and become it.

Practice #4

This visualization is very basic, but very powerful. Sit quietly and invoke Mary. Feel her presence and see her in your mind's eye. Melt into the qualities you associate with her. Now see your body being filled with a light coming directly from her. Command the light to enter you from the crown of your head. See the light filling up your physical body, from your toes to your head. Then see the light coming out the crown of your head and spilling, like a fountain, around you and creating a cocoon of light surrounding you. See the light vibrating with a greater and greater intensity as it purifies and protects you. Ask the light to vibrate in your mind, your heart, your physical body, your energy body, your emotional body, and your spiritual body. Sit quietly with and in this energy.

Practice #5

This is a wonderful visualization for the heart. Ask Mary to enter your heart and visualize her there. As she is present within your heart, see and know her divine energy and light. Ask her to reveal to you your source of power. When she does, see her and your source of power dissolving all that holds you back and blocks you from living from the heart. Sit until you feel and see that your body, mind, heart, and soul are purified with the energy of divine love. You will feel exactly what you need to feel at the time.

Practice #6

This is a healing visualization. Call the Divine Mother in whatever form or name is most intimate to you. Ask her to energize and heal your weakened or ill body, mind, heart, or spirit. See the healing light coming from her hands and into you. Feel and see her touching every part of your body, mind, heart, and spirit. Feel her endless love and compassion healing and energizing you on all levels. Enjoy the touch of her hands, as the love and light of our compassionate Mother enters into you and heals you. Take as much time as you need for this and, when finished, thank her for the energy and healing.

Practice #7

Visualize Mary standing in front of you. Look at her energy centers (the seven major ones). See the color red filling her first energy center at the base of her spine. Moving upward, see her other energy centers filled with the other colors of the rainbow: orange in the energy center just below the navel, yellow in the energy center in the center of the belly, green in the heart center, blue in the throat center, indigo in the third eye, and violet in the center at the top of the head. Then visualize these same centers within you. See flowing from each of Mary's centers into yours a brilliant ball of fiery light of the same rainbow color as the center from which it comes. Each ball is charged with an energy vibrating with great intensity. Visualize the balls moving into the corresponding energy centers within you and clearing away any blockages, imprints, patterns, addictions, pain, or fear that you may be carrying. Then see Mary surrounded by the colors of the rainbow. Feel yourself merging with her in a rainbow-colored light of wisdom, love and truth.

Practice #8

Imagine Mary above you, with her hands above the crown of your head. Flowing from her hands is a brilliant, vibrating violet light. Direct this light into your entire body, mind, heart, and spirit. As the light flows in you, feel the power of Mary's energy and ask to be purified, healed, and protected. Sit quietly as this violet light becomes a part of you and you become it. This is a simple, yet powerful practice that purifies, energizes, and protects all levels of your being.

Practice #9

Visualize yourself within a vessel. See Mary standing above the vessel and filling it with a powerful light that looks like a shower of fire. Feel this light surrounding and entering into you. Ask the light to cleanse, clear, and purify all thoughts, emotions, and anything else that keeps you from love. Ask that this light cleanse you of all negativity, inner and outer. Do this practice nine times very quickly. Feel and see yourself clean and pure in body, mind, heart, and soul.

Practice #10

Visualize the Divine Mother or any other Divine Being before you. See this Divine Being entering your heart. Now see a violet light flowing from the heart of the Divine Being, circling over your head, down your back, around your feet, and back into the heart, surrounding you with a beautiful cocoon of loving, violet light. Ask this light to protect you from darkness, evil, harm, and tragedy on every level. You can do this for protection of your loved ones also.

Practice #11

Call upon our Mother Mary and ask her to create a violet-blue cross in front of you. Now see this cross emitting violet-blue light around you continuously, day and night, on all levels. See this powerful cosmic energy creating an impenetrable shield of protection around you. Ask your favorite warrior of light to protect you and your loved ones.

Practice #12

Visualize Mary above your home. Ask her to create a pyramid of light around your home and to fill up the space within the pyramid with pure white light. At the same time, you visualize a pyramid filled with light around your home. This will create a protective field in and around your home and a balanced energy within it. This visualization can be done for communities, states, countries, and the planet. You can also invoke angels of light for their help.

Practice #13

If you are entering into a place or situation where you expect to encounter negativity or dark energies, ask Mary to create a rectangle of light in front of you, extending from the base of your body to the crown of your head. This will shield your energy centers from negative and dark energies. Ask Mary and the light to protect you and prevent negativity and darkness from entering you on any level.

Practice #14

Visualize Mary and an army of Light angels around you. See Mary wrapping her mantle as a blanket of soothing, comforting, and protecting light around you. See this cover of light wrapped around you as many times as you need. Feel Mary's protection, power, and compassion entering you.

Practice #15

Visualize Mary as a cosmic being, enfolding and filling you with a cosmic light. See this cosmic light entering your energy centers at the base, heart, and brows. As it enters you, feel her unconditional love penetrate your entire being, bringing you protection, love, and knowing on a cosmic level.

Appendix B

Visualizations Using Sexual Energy

These visualizations are with the use of sexual energy. They are powerful and intended only for those persons on a serious spiritual quest, with or without a partner. (God or a Divine Being can be used in visualizations where a partner is not present.) They should be done with an open heart and with an understanding that the purpose of the practices is to grow in love. Ask Mary to be present before you begin any of these practices. A word of caution and a warning: If you are suffering from ill health, a head injury, heart problems, or a mental disorder, or are in a generally weak condition, mentally or physically, DO NOT DO THESE VISUALIZATIONS. They could prove to be dangerous to your health.

Practice #1
A very basic way to begin to cultivate the creative/sexual energy within is to sit in a meditative posture and visualize a fire at the base of the body. See and feel the fire heating up. Then see it moving into the belly area, where you imagine there is an internal cauldron. Fill up the cauldron with this powerful light. When the cauldron is filled, move the energy into the heart, joining it with the energy of love. Then "blast" these combined energies into the space of Spirit within you, wherever you imagine this to be. Repeat this nine times.

Practice #2
We have in us "gateways into God." These gateways are located in many areas. For our purposes, we will concentrate on the gateways in the area of the belly, in the cauldron mentioned above. See yourself having eight openings into the cosmic universe of light forming a concentric circle a few inches from the center of your belly. Visualize an endless light and wind entering into this area from Above and from within you. See this light and wind as a sort of merging of cosmic energies taking place in the cauldron. Feel the force of this merging as an orgasmic sensation throughout your body. Be in it as long as you can and see orgasmic light melting into you on all levels of your being. Enjoy.

Practice #3
Another very simple visualization is to bring the energy created in love-making into an area of the body that has a specific need or to send it to a person, place,

or situation for a specific purpose. For example, it can be sent to a person or situation for peace or to the angels for their use. You can also bring the energy created in love-making back into the body so that no energy "leaks out." In other words, after lovemaking, rather than "zoning out" or getting up to eat, together with your partner, gather the energy and direct it through the mind and thought. Use it as you see fit, but be aware: it IS alive and very powerful.

Practice #4

Visualize your sexual energy, either during love-making or in a meditation. See this energy at the base of the spine. Move it up the channel of the spine, using your breath. Seeing it as God, have it flow up to your heart center and then into your brow center. When it gets to the brow center, hold it there for nine seconds. See the energy as a rainbow of colored light raining into your body and transforming you into the power and wisdom of the sexual, vital, and spiritual energies. Feel yourself beyond your body and beyond duality. Do this nine times. This can be done immediately after orgasm.

Practice #5

Another practice that is very powerful is to visualize that you are on fire sexually and see the fire turning into a cosmic bliss. It takes form at your base, like a coiled serpent which is on fire. On the right side of the base of the spine, it rises and turns into a red flaming serpent. On the left side, it rises and turns into a white flaming serpent. The two serpents begin to dance, creating figure eights up the spine as they move into the heart. As this energy enters the heart, see its power opening up the secret chamber of the heart, the place of your divine essence. The energy of the flaming serpents merges with the salmon-colored divine essence of the Sacred Heart and suddenly you melt into nothingness, into emptiness, into cosmic, eternal bliss. You are enlightened as this energy transforms you forever.

Practice #6

During love-making, see your heat and inner light expanding and encoding all of your being. Use whatever image comes to you. Do this in a natural way as a part of love-making. The spiritual goal of love-making is not the orgasm. It is the generating of its blissful energy so that you energetically transform into bliss. This is the energy from which life is created and miracles are performed.

Practice #7

Another very beautiful and powerful visualization that can be done with your partner is for both of you to visualize yourselves joined in love. See your energy centers joined by fibers of light which create a figure eight between them. See you and your partner melting into each other on every level: physical, mental, emotional, and spiritual. As you do this, see yourselves becoming one and entering into God. Be in this state for as long as possible.

Practice #8

This visualization is to release all negative imprints and blockages around sex and past sexual experiences. Many people carry negative attitudes toward sex and the effects of experiences of loveless sex in the form of negative imprints and blockages in their energy fields and energy centers. Ask for Mary to be present and to help you as you clear them. Visualize any negative imprints or blockages you may be carrying. Now visualize a powerful violet light dissolving them and healing and cleansing you. Then see your sexual energy and energy centers as pure and as sources of pure light within you. Affirm that you will use your sexual energy only as an expression of love.

Practice #9

This practice is to release all ties and bonds with former sexual partners. Begin by invoking Mary or another Divine Being or Beings and creating within yourself a strong intent to release all former sexual partners. Still your mind and visualize the ties and bonds that may exist with each former sexual partner. Then using a violet light, or another color of light you may choose, see the light severing and dissolving the ties and bonds. Ask the Divine Being to sever and dissolve all ties and bonds that may exist on levels of which you may not be aware. Next demand that all your energies that former partners are carrying be returned to you and return all their energies that you are carrying to them. Let go of them, send them on their way, and regain you self!

Notes

Introduction

1. Ronald Rolheiser, *The Holy Longing: The Search for a Christian Spirituality* (New York: Doubleday, 1999), pp. 6-7.
2. For readers primarily interested in learning more about Mary, the chapters can be read in the following order: 2, 3, 11, 12, 13 ,1, 4, 5, 6, 7, 8, 9, 10, 14.
3. John Mini, *The Aztec Virgin: The Secret Mystical Tradition of Our Lady of Guadalupe* (Sausalito, CA: Trans-Hyperborean Institute of Science, 2000), p. 148.

Chapter 1

1. The heart center is an energy center located near the physical heart in the mid-portion of the chest. References to the "heart" are not to the physical heart, but to this energy center. The heart center and other energy centers are discussed more fully in subsequent chapters.
2. "The Dark Night of the Soul," in *The Collected Works of St. John of the Cross*, trans. by Kieran Kavanaugh, OCD, and Otilio Rodriguez, OCD (Washington, DC: ICS Publications, 1989), p. 113.
3. The terms "mind' and "ordinary mind" are used interchangeably throughout the book in contradistinction to what will be referred to as the "true mind" or the "mind of love."

Chapter 2

1. Luke 1:37 (Biblical references are to the New Revised Standard Version).
2. Luke 1:38.

Chapter 4

1. Swami Muktananda, *Kundalini: The Secret of Life* (South Fallsburg, New York: SYDA Foundation, 1979), p. 7.

Chapter 5

1. Luke 8: 43-48.

Chapter 6

1. Mary states that reincarnation is one among many of Jesus' teachings that is not found in the Gospels. The topic of Jesus' teachings excluded from the Gospels is discussed in Chapter 13.
2. 2 Corinthians 6:14-16.

Chapter 7
1. Mark 4:3-20.
2. Mark 3:25.

Chapter 9
1. Matt 19:26.
2. Mary is not referring to the brain when she speaks of the ordinary mind. In a vision, she shows the mind as an energy within, but separate from, the brain. The mind is seen imprisoned by thoughts, concepts, and ideas, while the brain is seen congested by their energies.
3. Mary has commented on the strengths and weaknesses of Western medicine in several visions. She says that some of its practices are advanced and help people, while others harm people. She specifically mentions that many drugs, although not all, harm people. The greatest problem in Western medicine, she says, is its failure to recognize the importance of light and energy in healing.

Chapter 10
1. Jesus stated in a vision that the earth was not always a place of darkness. He described it as once being "a place of light with good possibilities."
2. Tenzin Gyatso, The Fourteenth Dalai Lama, *The World of Tibetan Buddhism: An Overview of Its Philosophy and Practice,* trans. by Geshe Thupten Jinpa (Boston: Wisdom Publications, 1995), p. 67.
3. Ibid., p. 70.

Chapter 13
1. This was one of Mary's incarnations. Another was her lifetime as the mother of Jesus. She disclosed that she has incarnated several times. While she has not identified her other lifetimes, she has said that her lifetime as the mother of Jesus was her last incarnation.
2. In many visions, Jesus and Mary have said that we are living in the "end times" and that Jesus will walk the earth again. While they seldom give time frames for events that they foretell, Mary has said about the transition to the new world that "all will be said and done by the year 2012." This means that Jesus' Second Coming will occur at some point before 2012.
3. Despite the distortions and omissions in the Gospels, neither Mary nor Jesus has ever indicated that people not read the Bible. Mary has stated that it contains many truths and can be an important part of one's spiritual path.

Leah Stewart's short stories have appeared in *The Kenyon Review* and other publications. A former associate editor of *Doubletake* magazine, she lives outside of Chapel Hill, North Carolina. This is her first novel.

Praise for *Body of A Girl*

"Sleek . . . a searing psychological portrait of a woman who must become someone else before she can understand herself."
—*US Weekly*

"Fascinating."
—*Los Angeles Times*

"It's hard to believe that this is a first novel; harder still to believe that Leah Stewart is only twenty-five years old. *Body of a Girl* is a smart, sexy literary page-turner, a fully imagined and stunning portrait of two young women's lives and loves. The secret at its heart will astonish you."
—A. Manette Ansay, author of *Sister* and *Midnight Champagne*

"*Body of a Girl* isn't your usual tale of reporter-turns-sleuth to get the story. Olivia gets a story all right, but it's not the one she expects."
—*Chicago Tribune*

"[A] remarkable debut . . . the beginning of a special career of notable novels."
—*The Philadelphia Inquirer*

"The best crime novels recognize that the most important question in life is not 'whodunit?' *Body of a Girl* is one of those. The best crime writers take readers someplace they are reluctant to go. Leah Stewart does that. *Body of a Girl* is a wonderful debut, spare and lyrical. It's full of subtle menace, like a measured walk down a dimly lit alley."
—Stephen White, bestselling author of *Cold Case*

"With this taut, tense thriller Stewart debuts auspiciously."
—*Kirkus Reviews* (starred)

"Like Susanna Moore's *In the Cut*, *Body of a Girl* follows its protagonist into the darkest corners of her psyche. Tautly written, emotionally astute, Leah Stewart's impressive debut disturbs and compels in equal measure."
—Claire Messud, author of *The Last Life*

"A compelling read. . . . Stewart evokes the way we measure death by the number of words we afford it in newspapers and the danger of seeking humanity and truth in the sad, tormented lives of strangers."
—Salon.com

"Leah Stewart has written a compelling novel—a *thoughtful* thriller and page-turner—about the rewards and perils of empathy in a culture dominated by drugs, sex, and violence. The story follows its heroine all the way down to the depths, and in its wonderfully plotted, and very readable way, it has a great deal to tell us about crimes that are merely reported, and crimes that are lived."
—Charles Baxter, author of *Believers* and *Shadow Play*

"*Body of a Girl* is simply a good read, the kind of book you find yourself cutting things short to come home to."
—*Raleigh News-Observer*

"This isn't John Grisham's Memphis; it's way more dangerous. In crafting a psychological thriller about fear and identity, Leah Stewart mates the breakneck pacing of Sue Grafton and the creepy depth of Laura Kasischke. *Body of a Girl* flies by and catches you up; all you can do is hang on for the ride."
—Stewart O'Nan, author of *A Prayer for the Dying* and *A World Away*

Body of a Girl

Leah Stewart

PENGUIN BOOKS

PENGUIN BOOKS
Published by the Penguin Group
Penguin Putnam Inc., 375 Hudson Street,
New York, New York 10014, U.S.A.
Penguin Books Ltd, 27 Wrights Lane,
London W8 5TZ, England
Penguin Books Australia Ltd, Ringwood,
Victoria, Australia
Penguin Books Canada Ltd, 10 Alcorn Avenue,
Toronto, Ontario, Canada M4V 3B2
Penguin Books (N.Z.) Ltd, 182–190 Wairau Road,
Auckland 10, New Zealand

Penguin Books Ltd, Registered Offices:
Harmondsworth, Middlesex, England

First published in the United States of America by Viking Penguin,
a member of Penguin Putnam Inc., 2000
Published in Penguin Books 2001

1 3 5 7 9 10 8 6 4 2

PUBLISHER'S NOTE
This is a work of fiction. Names, characters, places, and incidents either are the
product of the author's imagination or are used fictitiously, and any resemblance
to actual persons, living or dead, events, or locales is entirely coincidental.

THE LIBRARY OF CONGRESS HAS CATALOGED THE HARDCOVER EDITION AS FOLLOWS:
Stewart, Leah, date.
Body of a girl / Leah Stewart.
p. cm.
ISBN 0-670-89164-9 (hc.)
ISBN 0 14 10.0199 2 (pbk.)
I. Women journalists—Tennessee—Memphis—Fiction.
2. Memphis (Tenn.)—Fiction.   I. Title.
PS3569. T465258 B64   2000
813'.54—dc21   99–055518

Printed in the United States of America
Set in New Caledonia
Designed by Betty Lew

For Matt

Acknowledgments

Thanks to my agent, Gordon Kato, and my editor, Carolyn Carlson, for their good advice and faith in this book.

For counsel on everything from police procedure to Memphis geography, thanks to Zack McMillin, Steve Hall, Cletus Oliver, and Dr. Wendy Gunther. I couldn't have written this book without Angie Craig.

Many thanks to my teachers, A. Manette Ansay, Charles Baxter, and Nicholas Delbanco. I am grateful for the support of Wyatt Prunty, Cheri Peters, and the staff of the Sewanee Writers' Conference, and also to Norma Diala at the Harvard Graduate School of Education, for giving me a job while I wrote this book.

For love and encouragement, thanks go to my family, particularly Susan and Skip Francies, Cameron Stewart, Gordon Stewart, and Julie Finch. I am also grateful to my friends and readers Carolyn Ebbitt, Caroline Kim, Surrena Goldsmith, Leigh Anne Couch, Terry Joffe, Shivika Asthana, Nina Reid, and especially my coach, Elwood Reid.

1

This has been a summer of murders. Memphis is so hot people move like they're wearing something heavier than their skin. I can't help but feel that these things are connected. I can't put this in the stories I write. It's not fact. It's not *true,* in the way we mean true at the newspaper, which is that we got someone else to say it.

There are reporters at this newspaper whose whole job it is to interview zoo workers about new baby animals. One guy wrote a three-part series about how to avoid the lunch rush at the fast-food drive-thru. I'm the one the cops like to show photographs of raped and beaten women, looking at me out of the corner of their eyes to see if I can take it. "Okay," I always say, when I think I've looked at them long enough. "I see." I work the police beat. Murders are my responsibility.

It's cloudy this morning, and so humid I'm sweating just standing still. Here and there patches of light shine through the clouds, as though someone poked holes in my jar so I could breathe. On the ground not three feet from me is the body of a young woman, white, my age. Steam rises from the dirt all around her, and when I look down I can see it coming up between my feet. I'm trying to get it straight in my head, how I'll describe this scene in the paper, how to make it simple, clinical, how to explain that what looked like smoke was only rainwater evaporating in the terrible heat. But all I can think is *My God, my God.*

She is curled up. Her hands are bound in front of her, her wrists wrapped round and round with what looks like white string. Her white T-shirt is patched red with blood. From the waist down she is naked, tire marks slashed across her skin. On one foot she wears a sandal; the other is bare. She is lying among tire tracks in a patch of sandy ground, and around her tufts of wild grass and dandelions push up through the dirt. She knew that car was coming. I would ball myself up like that, trying to disappear.

This is not where I'm supposed to be. Normally I'd arrive at the scene after the crowd had gathered, and I'd stand behind the yellow tape, with the rest of the press, the crying neighbors, the mamas with babies on their hips leaning in to get a look, lucky to catch a glimpse of the body bag when they brought it out. Today I was about to pull into the newspaper parking lot when I heard it over the police scanner—DOA, at the park, less than two miles away. I followed a police cruiser to the site and stopped my car next to it. When I got out, the uniformed cop sauntered over to me and asked me what I thought I was doing. I said I was press and he looked me up and down. "You want to look," he said. "Go ahead and look." He's not supposed to do that, but maybe he thought I would faint and give him a story to tell his buddies. So I kept my face blank, and I walked right up to the dead girl and didn't say a word. The cop watched me, and shrugged, disappointed. "Stay out of the way," he said.

I've learned to stomach the photographs they show me, but now I know it's nothing like being so close you could lean down and touch that dead, dead skin.

I flip open my notebook. This is the first time I haven't had to wait for the cops and the medical examiner to give me a secondhand version of the crime scene. Faced with the real thing, I realize I don't know where to look, what details I'll even be allowed to print. The body lies near the river, not far from the park entrance, where the ticket booths were during the two festivals in May, one for barbecue, one for blues. Whoever dumped the body made no attempt to hide it, or to drag it to the water, only yards away.

Around us, cars arrive, their tires kicking up dust. Doors shut, and the rumble of male voices grows louder. Somebody shouts. I don't even turn my head to look, scrawling words in my notebook.

The feet are small and narrow, with tiny pink toenails.

The exposed legs are slender, with just the hint of muscle beneath the skin. There's a little scab near one ankle, as though she nicked herself shaving.

A white T-shirt is pushed up above the curve of the hips to reveal a pale stomach, the edge of a belly button. On the shirt I can barely make out the letters "MUS." Something about the lettering is familiar, and then I realize why. It's the Beale Street Music Festival T-shirt from last year. I have the same one at home in my closet. I wonder if the shirt is what made her killer think of bringing her here.

Her fingers are clenched, the nails painted the same delicate shade as her toes.

Her head is curled in toward her chest. The hair draped across her ruined face is long and dark, clotted with blood, powdered with dust.

Someone bumps me, passing by, and still I don't look. I barely feel it. It's like we are alone here, the dead girl and me, two sides of a coin.

From the ground in front of her face, steam rises, almost like breath.

I lift my hand to write and see that it's shaking. I watch as though those trembling fingers aren't even mine. The body beyond slips in and out of focus as I wait for my fingers to steady. When they do I grip my pen tightly and write in my notebook: *T-shirt*.

This is just my job.

The crime tape has gone up and detectives are arriving. I know they won't want to see me here. I haven't been on the beat long enough to have the contacts other reporters have, and I don't want to antagonize any of the cops. I take another look at her before I turn away. A few steps from the body, I can't help but look again. I turn around, walking backward. A cop stands over her, obscuring my view. I can still see her bare white legs, her tiny feet.

"Hey," someone calls out. "Get the hell back." I turn and see a cop striding toward me. I think his name is Detective Buchanan. He's young enough to still look a little sick at the sight of the corpse. "What do you think you're doing?"

"I'm sorry," I say. "The tape wasn't up yet. I didn't realize how close I was."

"The body should've given you a clue," he says.

"I'm so sorry," I say again, flashing him a smile, wondering if he's lead detective. "I'll be more careful next time."

He stares at me a second. "Getting to you, isn't it," he says. "You look sick."

"So do you," I say, and he snorts. "Do you have a positive ID?"

"I can't tell you anything," he says. "You know the routine; when the lieutenant gets here, he'll talk to the press."

"Come on," I say. "Give me something. Off the record."

He just shakes his head, and waves me away.

Behind the yellow tape I watch the rest of the press arrive. The TV stations park their vans so close the cops have to squeeze in and out of the scene. People shout. The satellite towers go up, and the reporters line up in front of the tape. The cops stare at us from the other side. It reminds me of the Civil War reenactments my father used to drag me to as a child, the two lines approaching each other, volleying fire. If this were a neighborhood, I'd be canvassing the crowd, looking for somebody who knew the victim, somebody to tell me she'd been fighting with her boyfriend, somebody to tell me she'd heard the boyfriend hit her, she'd heard the dead girl ran around on him. But here there's nothing to do but wait for the lieutenant, watching the cops' backs as they bend and stand, cluster and part. Detective Buchanan passes by again, frowning. I can't remember where I saw him before, which crime it was.

Off to the right I can make out the taller buildings of downtown, the red letters on the roof of the Peabody Hotel. Somewhere past that, the glass panes of the Pyramid are glinting in the sun. Nearby is Beale Street, its strip of garish bars and souvenir shops isolated among warehouses and parking lots, as if it had been constructed as a movie set and allowed to stand. A hill rises on one side of the fair-grounds, dotted with the houses of rich people and local celebrities. I squint at the houses, trying to judge the distance. They're too far away for the residents to have seen anything.

This is my job, to give you all the details right up front, what time it was, where and how it happened, so you can use them to deter-mine whether it could have been you. *I'd never go there alone at night,* you think, putting the paper down beside your cup of coffee after you read the headline and maybe the lead. It's my job to keep you reading past that first paragraph, to make you see it like I do, what it is possible for your body to look like, how easily you could be destroyed.

A cop in uniform stands in front of me, turning his head from side to side. It's his job to keep the media and the curious out of the way. His white hair is damp with sweat, and the skin of his neck droops over the too tight collar of his shirt. He takes a handkerchief from his pocket and mops at his face and neck. Then he says something about a little white girl.

"What?" I say.

"Heard she's a pretty little white girl," he says, leaning toward me.

"It'd be hard to say if she's pretty," I say.

"D'you see her?" He's surprised when I nod. "Are you the one that found her?"

"No," I say. "I just saw her. Do you know who found her?"

My notebook is in my hand, but I keep it closed. If he's going to tell me something, I don't want to scare him off.

He doesn't answer the question. He says, "That'll give you night-mares."

"I don't have nightmares," I say. He looks skeptical, but it's the

truth. Lately I dream in words. My dreams aren't movies, with images and sound. Instead I watch them scroll past like a story typed
out on a computer, like when you play a video game so long that you
still see the figures moving even with your eyes closed.

The cop leans in like he's going to tell me something, then he sees
the notebook in my hand and stops cold. "You a reporter?"

I say yes, wishing I'd kept the notebook in my bag. You never
know what casual comment you might be able to use.

"Big story for you, ain't it," he says. "White girl killed, probably
raped. Not the usual black-on-black killing we get here. This girl's
young. Innocent."

"Nobody's innocent," I say. "There's always something."

He laughs. "That's nice thinking for a little gal like you," he says.
"You sound like a cop."

Here we go again. I say, "We cover a lot of the same territory."
Detective Buchanan comes up behind the cop and says something I
can't hear. The cop nods, then moves a foot to the right and doesn't
speak to me anymore. Now it comes to me where I saw the detective before. He was the officer in charge three weeks ago, when four
men carrying semiautomatic rifles kicked down a couple's door in
the middle of the night, mistaking it for a crack house. They raped
the wife in front of her husband, then shot them both. Their toddler
hid under the bed until the men left, and when the police arrived
they found her sleeping, curled up against her dead father's chest
with her thumb in her mouth. My roommate, Hannah, says, how
can you write about these things?

Verb follows subject, I say. Object follows verb.

Lieutenant Nash keeps taking his jacket off and putting it back on,
torn between his need to look professional and his need for relief
from the unbearable heat. He's a large man, and his round dark face
is shiny with sweat. When he takes off his jacket his white shirt
clings wetly to his back, though I can see that he's wearing an un-

dershirt. I'm right behind him, close enough to touch that back, and around me is the rest of the press. We follow him as he makes his way around the perimeter of the crime scene, all of us looking around for someone who might tell us more, who might tell us something no other reporter knows.

Nash, the official spokesman for this case, has told us nothing I didn't already know. I wrote it down in my notebook anyway: *dead girl, white, mid-20s, no ID yet, no cause of death yet, no suspects yet*. So far I barely have who, what, when, where, and how, let alone why, which is what everybody wants to know anyway, like they want to know why that athlete got AIDS, why the neighbor's husband left her, why that house burned down and all the children in it died. They want to know, what made them choose this girl over another, over me? I find the reasons for them.

"Any idea when you might have an ID?" I ask Nash.

He looks exasperated. "By the end of the day," he says. "We'll call you at the end of the day."

That does me no good. By the end of the day, I'll have no time to track down anyone who might know her, my story will be nothing but her name and no one will read it because they'll have gotten all their information from the evening news. "Thank you," I say, and smile prettily at him. A reporter from Channel 7 jostles against me and I resist the urge to elbow her in her pink-suited side. Instead I drop out of the pack and drift back toward the tape to watch the activity around the body. I can't see anything until they all part to let the body bag through.

I swear I must be feeling faint from the heat. When they bring the body bag out, that plastic shimmers beautifully, like water under the sun.

In the police station, it's always cold, even now in the middle of June. The furniture looks as though it hasn't been replaced since the '70s. Twenty years ago, the chairs were bright orange, and maybe when they were new they made the place look cheerful, but now they're just tacky, part of the general drab-and-dirt atmosphere. The interview room in homicide is white, with files spilling everywhere on the rows of metal desks. I'm sitting on a file, because it was in the chair when I went to sit down, and I couldn't see anywhere on Sergeant Morris's desk to put it.

Morris is saying, "I'm not supposed to tell you anything." On Saturdays he brings in barbecue for everyone, even me, and tells me stories from his decades on the force. Right now he holds a photograph, up and away from me.

"Just give me her name, please," I say, looking at his name tag, which I can't stop reading over and over. I don't know if they call those things they wear name tags. It seems like they should have some more official term, like breastplate. "Please."

"I don't know," he says. "The brass is cracking down."

I look at my watch. "Please, Sergeant. You know I never quote you," I say. "I won't print anything without confirmation. Please. I'm on deadline."

"I hate to think about you on a story like this," he says. "A nice little girl like you."

On the streets all over Memphis, I see cops whose muscles are thick under tight uniforms. They stride in twos or threes down the street like a posse in a Western movie, eyes scanning back and forth, their whole bodies heavy with assurance. I never talk to these cops. My cops are always fat and old and grimly sad. They have thick southern accents and call me "little lady." There are female cops, too. The female cops never talk to me.

Morris fingers some papers on his desk. I lean in closer. He's about to give up the name. I can feel it.

"Had a little girl killed a couple days ago," he says. "Guy shot a revolver in the air, bullet came down, hit her."

I nod. I already wrote that story.

"You know what really bugs me?" he says. "On TV? When they

take a revolver and put a silencer on it." He shakes his head. "A silencer doesn't work on a revolver."

My leg starts to jiggle, impatience slamming through my body. "Sergeant . . . ," I start.

"And bodies?" he says. "They don't float. When you're dead . . ." He mimes a shooting, pointing an imaginary gun at me and jerking it back. "You're dead, you sink to the bottom like a rock. Watch when they shoot somebody on TV. They fall into a swimming pool and they just float like a cork."

"Yes," I say. I've heard all of this before. I know if I listen long enough, he'll have to give me something in return.

"Olivia," Morris says. "Does your mother know what you do for a living?"

"She knows I'm a reporter." I hold my pen ready.

"But does she know what you report? Does she know her little girl is crawling around crime scenes?"

"Do you have an ID?" I say.

"You saw the body?" he asks, and when I nod, he shakes his head. "I don't know why you have to look at things like that."

"The other detectives like to show me homicides," I say. "They get a kick out of it."

"Because you're a girl," he says.

"So how come you don't want me to see them?"

"Because you're a girl," he says, and a slow grin spreads across his face.

"I can't win," I say, and I'm surprised by how grim it comes out sounding when I meant to be joking. "Who was she?" I say. "Tell me about her. I need to know."

He hesitates, shaking the photograph like a sugar packet between two fingers, then finally he gives it to me. It's not the crime scene photo I expected. In the picture, a young woman stands holding a beer in one hand, an expression of exaggerated surprise on her face, eyebrows up, mouth open, laughing. A guy in a baseball cap is kissing her cheek. She has shiny dark hair that falls to her shoulders, green eyes, a large mouth. It takes me a moment to understand that this is the girl whose crumpled body I stood over this morning.

Morris tells me that her friends reported her missing this morning, after looking for her since late Saturday night, when she didn't show up to meet them. Neighbors saw her car parked out in front of the apartment building, instead of around back in the lot, so the cops think she must have run in to get something, and somebody got her when she came back out. She worked in the outpatient clinic at the Madison Medical Center. Her name was Allison Avery.

I'm looking for something in her face, some detail, that will tell me who she was. She laughs up at me. She could be any girl who went to my college, any girl I pass between stores at the mall.

Morris reaches out to take the picture back. "Good luck," he says.

"Can I keep this?" I ask, holding on to the picture.

"No," he says. "But I'll let you make a photocopy." He looks from the photo in my hand to my face. "You look a little like her," he says. "Same hair color. Same shape to the face." In the air he traces the curve of my cheek.

"She was prettier," I say. I drop the picture on his desk. He doesn't contradict me, just picks the photo up and stares at it. "What about the car?" I say.

Morris shakes his head. "Haven't found it yet."

"You got any thoughts on this?"

He frowns.

"Point me in the right direction," I say.

He sighs, hunched over his desk. "How long you been doing this? Months?"

"Three," I say.

He nods. "Long enough to know," he says. "Nine times out of ten, girl dead like this, it had something to do with sex. You know that. She turned him down, slept around on him, whatever. If it's a stranger, maybe he raped her and got carried away, or scared she'd identify him after."

"What's your guess here?"

"None of this is for the paper?" He waits for me to nod, then says, "I'd say the way she was found, outside, some stranger grabbed her, drove around trying to figure out what to do with her. Boyfriend kills you, it's usually at home. He shoots you or beats you to death. Now, could be a premeditated thing, or could be she was out someplace with a guy she knew and he brought her there." He hunches down lower, his voice heavy with exhaustion. "You know," he says again. "We're gonna be looking for any boyfriends, any exes, trying to figure out where she was those missing hours between when she left work and when the neighbors saw her car."

This is all he knows. "Thanks," I say. "I really appreciate it."

He stares at the picture, rubbing the back of his neck with one hand. He says, "She was just your age."

Outside the interview room, I sit and make a list in my notebook. *Get family. Go to workplace. Call Peggy. Where's the car? Boyfriend? Cause of death? Call medical examiner. Get milk. Deposit check. Do dishes. Call Mom.* It's not a list I need to make, but it passes the time. I'm hoping to catch the family coming out after they talk to the cops. They're easy to identify because they're always crying. I draw a series of little flowers across the bottom of the page, thinking about the dead girl's body. When I close my eyes it's not the image that I see. It's the words I wrote in my notebook—*T-shirt, string, blood.*

I've been a full-time reporter for three years, and I can't remember half of what I learned in college, but these words are growing in me like weeds. It's been three months since they put me on the police beat. All summer I've had photographs of dead bodies fanned across my desk, buried under stacks of paper until I come across them looking for something else. It's not these pictures that appear in my dreams, but the words I used to describe them.

Again and again I check my watch, every second putting me

closer to deadline. After a long time the flowers on my notebook page have overtaken the list, and I'm thinking this may be a lost cause when a couple walks out clinging to each other. The man has obviously been crying, the woman has the look of someone who's just been slapped, and her cheeks are red, the rest of her face white as paper. I'm certain these are the girl's parents. I stand up slowly. The trick is to make it sound like you're giving them some kind of opportunity, and never, never ask how they feel—that's for television reporters. Refer to the victim in the present tense, say nothing directly about her being dead, ask whether she has a boyfriend, because more often than not it turns out to be him. Be polite. Be apologetic.

"I'm very sorry to bother you," I say, "but I wanted to talk to you about your daughter."

"Are you a reporter?" the woman asks.

"Yes, ma'am." I'm staring at her face. She looks familiar. I can't place her.

"We can't talk to you right now," she says. Her voice breaks, but she doesn't move to find a tissue, or bury her face in her hands or her husband's shoulder. Instead she stares angrily at me, even while tears start down her cheeks. I notice that her husband doesn't comfort her. His eyes never move from her to me, as though as long as he doesn't look at me, I'm not here.

"I know this is difficult," I say. "I'm sorry."

"Difficult?" she says. "What do you know about it?"

It's a conversation I've had so many times I feel like I'm watching it from outside, like something on a television drama. There's only so many ways you can say these things, only so many ways they can respond. *What was she like*, I'll say. *She was our daughter,* they'll say. *We loved her.* Some people are eager to talk, grateful for your desire to listen. Some, like this woman, have to be coaxed.

"Ma'am," I say as gently as I can, "I just want to write about Allison's life."

"If she weren't dead," she says, "you wouldn't give a shit about her life."

They turn their backs on me and walk away. I listen to the sound of their footsteps receding, then I glance at my list and put a line through *Get family*. I rummage through my bag for my car keys. *Go to workplace* is next.

"She's just a nice, nice person," the receptionist at the Madison Medical Center keeps saying. Tears are starting in her eyes. "Just the nicest person in the world." She has also told me that Allison was a nursing tech in the clinic, that she had a big smile and was good with patients. I resist the urge to drum my fingers on her desk.

One thing I know, people hardly ever say anything about someone that couldn't be said about anyone. I don't know if this is because lately the people I talk to are almost always talking about someone who's dead, and therefore immediately becomes a nice girl, a great guy, a loving mother, a generous friend. I'm beginning to think it's because this is how people see each other, as members of these sad generic categories. Allison Avery, Nice Girl.

The receptionist tells me Allison was friends with Angela Schultz, one of the nurses in the clinic. She directs me down the hall to the third door on my right.

"Thank you," I say. "You've been very helpful." She never even asked me who I was. People don't, in general. If you ask them a question, they answer it.

Before I tell her, Angela Schultz doesn't know her friend is dead, and the way her eyes empty and her face drains of color when I say it, I think for a moment her heart has stopped.

Angela is one of the friends who was supposed to meet Allison Saturday night, so from her I learn that Allison had some errands to run after work and then was going home to change and drop off her groceries. She was supposed to be at the Lizard Lounge at nine. I write that down, *Lizard Lounge,* and sit staring at the words. I've been there, with my boyfriend, David.

"How long did you wait before you called her?" I ask Angela.

"Half an hour," she says. "Allison was always late." At midnight, after calling Allison's house, her parents' house, and another friend's house, Angela called the police. That's all she knows, and she's choking as she talks, so it takes me a long time to get her to say it. Angela is another version of the girl I saw in the picture this morning, her hair dark and sleek and pulled back from her face, her features even and unremarkably pretty. She is made up in the manner of a respectable southern girl, light foundation, peach lipstick, muted eyeshadow, and mascara that's now smudged around her wet eyes.

This won't be the last time today I'll bring this news to some unsuspecting friend or relative. It's exhausting, my throat tightening with the grief of someone I don't know, for someone I've never met.

When you're told something terrible about someone you don't know—your cousin says her sister-in-law is dying of cancer—you have a moment of anxiety about what to say. Maybe you've met the woman once, and for a moment you really do feel bad, but in the end you're just going to say, "That's awful," and let some silence pass before you talk about something else. When you're a reporter, you're always talking to strangers who have just had something terrible happen to them. In college, I interviewed a famous journalist for the school paper. "In Vietnam, the rivers were thick with bodies," he said. "Either you had the stomach for it or you didn't."

I have the stomach for it.

If I didn't I couldn't sit here listening to Angela Schultz talk while the image of her friend's dead body rises in front of me, as real as this live woman's face. "That's all I know," she is saying, her hands covering her eyes as she begins to rock back and forth in her chair. "Oh God. Not Allison. Oh God. Oh God." I write in my notebook: *all she knows.* She lifts her face, ghoulish now with black streams of mascara tears, her lipstick half chewed off. "Are you sure it was her? Are you absolutely sure? Did you see the body?"

I hesitate. Then I nod. "It was her. I'm sorry." She wails and drops her head again. The room is a typical examining room, chair, rolling stool, someone's diploma framed on the wall. Altogether sterile, except for a vase of lilies tucked in the corner of the counter, near the sink, and a framed photograph nearby on the wall. I go over for a closer look while behind me Angela's wails quiet into sobs. It's a staff photo. Allison and Angela smile on either side of a tall man in a white lab coat who must be one of the clinic doctors.

I'm glad I've seen these pictures of the dead girl's face, and not the eight-year-old senior yearbook shot they'll probably run on the front page. If you die young, they always pull out those high school pictures. No one really looks like that—the false smile, the cocked head, the hands folded awkwardly against the cheek.

Next to the picture, you'll see my byline. Then the copy. The victim was twenty-four years old. She was a nursing technician from a middle-class family, and she had just moved into her own apartment in Midtown a year ago. Saturday night, she worked late at the office, went to the grocery store for a few things, and drove to her apartment. She was late to meet friends at a Midtown bar, so she parked her car on the street in front of the building, instead of behind the building in the lot. When she came back out, hurrying, maybe checking her watch, someone grabbed her. What happened next is not entirely clear. I'm guessing that they'll tell me someone drove her in her own car to Tom Lee Park, raped her, beat her, and killed her finally by running her over.

Her name was Allison Avery. She was a nice girl.

I turn from the picture. Angela is folded in on herself, not making a sound. I go toward her and let my hand hover over her shoulder, not quite close enough to touch. My voice low, I ask her if Allison was seeing anyone, if she had been on a date lately, if anyone had shown any interest in her.

She shakes her head, not looking up.

"She didn't have a boyfriend?"

Angela lifts her face. She says no with such finality, her eyes so deliberately fixed on mine, I'm certain she is lying.

"There was no one?"

"No," she says again. We stare at each other for a moment. Then she returns her head to her knees. I stand looking at her bent neck, the wisps of hair escaping from her bun. Who could Allison's boyfriend be, that her best friend would keep him a secret, even after death?

A man comes hurrying in, like the answer to a question. I recognize him from the picture on the wall. He steps between us and scoops Angela up into a standing position and into his arms, as easily as lifting a baby. He is startlingly handsome, between thirty-five and forty, with a strong jaw and dark hair lightly touched with gray. He wears a wedding ring. "Is it true?" he asks me.

"I'm afraid so, sir," I say.

Angela shudders and presses her face to his chest. She's going to leave black smudges all over his straw-colored linen jacket. "I'm so sorry," he whispers. "Poor girl." I wonder which of them he means.

When I ask, Dr. Gregerson tells me what I expected, that Allison was a hard worker, a good worker, a nice girl. She used to bring in flowers for the office, unasked, which is, finally, a detail I can use. She liked carnations, because they last a long time, but every once in a while she brought in lilies because, she said, they were too beautiful to resist. "There, in the vase," he says. "Those are hers."

Straightening up, out of his embrace, Angela carefully pulls her loosened hair back into place. Her sobbing has slowed into an occasional hiccup and she seems oddly calm, her eyes glazed over. Over her shoulder I see the doctor noticing the black and tan traces of mascara and foundation on his jacket. I'm staring at his face, eyes narrowed, looking for signs of grief. He brushes at the streaks of makeup, frowning, then catches my eye and drops his hand, embarrassed. After a moment he lifts the same hand and squeezes Angela's shoulder.

"Angela," I say gently, brushing my fingertips lightly against her forearm, "do you have a picture of Allison I could borrow?" I move to indicate the framed photo on the wall, though I'd prefer to have a shot of the girl alone. I open my mouth to give the speech about why we need a picture—personalize the crime, make it visceral—but Angela just nods, reaching numbly for a red purse and extracting a wallet. She flips it open to one of those plastic picture holders and slips a small photo from its casing. She says nothing when she hands it to me. "Thank you so much," I say. I look down, and there it is, the high school yearbook photo, teased hair framing the dead girl's carefully made-up face, some boy's class ring heavy on the hand beneath her chin.

Angela is saying that if I really want to write about Allison I should know she had a secret ambition. She wanted to be a singer in a rock and roll band.

"She's too practical to give up her job for it," Angela says. "She had gigs around here sometimes." When I nod, she goes on. "That was what she really loved. If you saw her up there, you knew right away, the way that big voice came pouring out her little body, it just washed you away. That was her. That was who she was." She tells me Allison's voice made your heart ache—it was the sound of longing, just hanging in the air. It moved you, she says. You couldn't help but cry. And now she's crying too hard to say any more, but that is enough.

It was the truth, what I said to Allison's mother. What you want to write about is someone's life, even if her death is the reason you're writing about her at all. Allison Avery has slipped out of her category, and I come out of what used to be her office scribbling in my notebook, circling *lilies,* underlining *rock & roll,* crossing out *nice girl, nice girl, nice girl,* all down the page.

2

My next stop is Allison's apartment building. It's a tall wide building, fairly new. I park my car in front of it, just like she did, and stand in the parking lot trying to imagine what it would feel like to have a stranger grab me from behind, whether I would scream, or freeze, or elbow him in the groin like the heroine in an action movie. Everything seems clear and sharp in the bright sunlight. The front of the girl's building is perfectly landscaped and it's impossible to imagine anything bad happening here.

Inside, I stand outside the door to her apartment, listening for sounds that would indicate the police were still inside. Nothing. Maybe they've already been and gone. It's just a white door like all the others on the hall. Slowly, I try the doorknob. Locked. Below the brass apartment number Allison hung a drawing of the New York skyline, sketched in bright streaks of pink and purple on a deep black background. With my finger I trace the brass 13, a good number for a girl with such terrible luck.

The building is quiet and my footsteps make no noise on the beige carpet in the hall. I rap briskly on the doors around Allison's. Two apartments down, I hear someone coming to the door. It opens partway and a woman peers out at me. "Excuse me, ma'am," I say. "I'm sorry to bother you. I'm from the newspaper, and I wondered if I might ask you a few questions."

The door opens all the way. A short woman with slack brown hair and glasses stands blinking at me. She is so skinny her skin stretches away from her mouth like fabric pulled tight on a frame. "Is this about the girl in thirteen?" she says.

"Allison Avery?" I ask.

She frowns. "I told the police everything I know."

I take a guess. "About the car?"

With an aggrieved sigh, she says, "I saw it out front around ten. Next time I looked it was gone."

"Do you know what time that was, ma'am?"

"Right after the news," she says.

I write that down. "Your window looks out on the front of the building?"

"The bedroom window," she says. "But you can't come in."

"That's fine, ma'am," I say. "I just wondered if you might've noticed anyone you didn't recognize out front last night."

"I already told the police I didn't," she says. "How many times do I have to go through this?" She peers at my notebook. "Is this going to go in the paper?"

"Maybe," I say. I get her name—Joan Bracken—and ask her how well she knows the dead girl.

"I've had to go over and ask her to turn her music down." She looks down the hall toward the apartment as though she expects the radio to come blasting on. "I've had to ask her more than once."

I make a sympathetic noise, and she goes on, "Once I asked her to water my plants while I was gone for the week. This was before I knew what she was like. She stole from me. She said she didn't, but I know it was her. She had a key to my apartment!" She shakes her head. "She played innocent, but I'm not a fool."

"I'm sorry to hear about that, ma'am. Can you tell me what she took?"

"A pink angora sweater," she says. "And some shell earrings. They were from the Philippines. My brother sent them to me. He's in the air force."

Looking at what she's wearing now—a long denim skirt, a garish

T-shirt with raised plastic letters spelling out the name of a country singer, and dangling silver earrings in the shape of a knife and fork—I'd have to guess those earrings were not something the girl would bother to steal. "I'm sure they were lovely," I say. "Did you report this to the police?"

She snorts. "Why would they believe me? That pretty girl would have made her big eyes at them and said she didn't do it." The way she says "pretty girl," I can tell she means "slut."

"That's a shame," I say. "It's terrible to be taken advantage of." I give her a sympathetic smile.

She crosses her arms across her chest and narrows her eyes.

"Would you have recognized anyone Allison knew?" I ask. "A boyfriend?"

"There's always boys coming and going from her place," she says. "I saw one of them a couple nights ago. Noticed him because I heard him yelling. I looked out in the hall and saw him kicking her door. Then he left." She sniffs.

I keep my voice even. "What did he look like?"

"Just some boy," she says. "How am I supposed to tell them all apart?"

"Was he tall, short, dark-haired?"

"I don't know. I just looked out for a second. I didn't want him coming after me." She shakes her head while I list the things she might have noticed—clothing, glasses, facial hair. "Facial hair," she repeats, letting her head come to a stop. "He had one of those . . ." She plucks at her chin. "One of those little beards."

"Goatee?"

"Goatee." She nods briskly and puts her hand on the doorknob. "Now, I've told you all I know."

"Thank you, ma'am," I say. "One more thing, if you don't mind. What kind of car did she drive?"

"A blue 1993 Honda Civic." She smiles for the first time. "I know cars," she says, stepping back inside. I say, "Thank you," to her closed door and listen to the deadbolt click into place.

In apartment 17 I find a young blond woman with a Mississippi accent and two small children. Cartoons blare from the television in the living room as she stands at the door shifting the weight of her sleeping baby from hip to hip. Her white T-shirt is marked with green and orange stains, but she wears a perfect coat of pink lipstick. I tell her I'm from the paper, that I was wondering if she knew the woman in apartment 13. She says sure, she knows Allison. Allison baby-sits for her from time to time. She's good with kids. A nice girl.

"You're friends?" I ask, and she nods.

"It's weird, though, you know," she says with a laugh. "She's older than I am, but the way she comes and goes, while I'm home with these two, it makes me feel about a million years old."

"How old are you?"

"Twenty-two," she says.

"You are young," I say, and then a crash sounds from inside the apartment and a loud wail starts up. She looks around as though searching for somewhere to set down the baby.

"Can I hold him for you?" I ask.

"Oh, thanks," she says, thrusting him at me and turning to jog down the hall. He is heavy and hot and moist all over. I hold him up and press my cheek against his warm soft head. "Come on in," the mother shouts from inside. The child's howling goes on and on. The baby only opens and closes his eyes like a dreamer and snuggles into my chest. I pass through a gallery of family photographs into the living room, where the girl is bent over her wailing child, an overturned plant on the floor beside him. "You're okay, you're okay," she is murmuring over and over, stroking his hair. The little boy's cries trail off into sniffs and hiccups and his mother scoops him up and stands. We face each other, arms full of her children.

"He was more scared than hurt," she says. "Weren't you, pumpkin?" The little boy stares at me. I cross my eyes at him and he smiles.

"Two boys," I remark.

"Yes," she says. "And less than a year apart, Lord help me."

I'm trying to imagine that this is my life, my face in a cloud of white tulle in the bridal picture on the wall, my eyes painted to look wide and hopeful, my pink mouth smiling that sweet and eager smile. My arms began to ache from the weight of the baby. I ask her the boys' names—Nathan and Parker—and her own—Lisa—and what her husband does, where she's from, what brought her to Memphis. By the time I bring up Allison again, we're sitting in her living room with Nathan playing on the floor at her feet, two cups of coffee on the table and the baby still in my arms. Though Lisa offered to take him back, she seemed relieved when I said I liked holding him, and to my eyes her whole body looks lighter with no children hanging on. She hasn't spoken to the police, and says she must have been napping when they came by, because, Lord knows, she's always at home. I've told too many people already today that Allison is dead, so I've just said that she's missing. She says again and again, "I do hope they find her. She's a sweet girl."

I ask her if they ever go out together, if she knows any of Allison's friends or boyfriends. She's met Angela, but never any of the boyfriends, and she knows nothing about an angry man outside Allison's door. Joan Bracken, she says, is an old busybody.

"What do you and Allison usually talk about?" I ask.

"Oh, you know, if she should call a boy she hadn't heard from in a couple of days, if it sounded like he liked her. The usual sort of thing. Sex. Whether to, you know." She looks at her children. "It's hard to know what to say. You see where it got me." She laughs.

"You mean Allison is waiting for marriage?"

"I don't know for sure," she says. "I know she goes to church regularly. She's a good girl. I do hope they find her."

"Can you think of anything else that might be important?" I ask her. "Anything about an angry boyfriend?"

She shakes her head. "I never saw anyone angry at her. All the boyfriends, it sounded like they really liked her."

"Do you know her family?"

"I've never met them, no, but I know who her mother is."

I pause. I must have missed something. "Who is she?"

"Oh, you don't know? She runs the children's hospital. Or maybe she doesn't run it, but she's some kind of bigwig there. She was in those ads they ran in the paper, remember?"

"That's right," I say almost to myself. "I knew I recognized her." I jiggle my knee, excited. This gives me a much better chance of making the front page. I make a note to check the paper's library for clips on the mother.

I ask Lisa to call me if she thinks of anything else, and when I leave she waves good-bye to me from the door, baby in her arms, like I'm an old friend who dropped by for a visit. "I hope to see you again," she calls.

"Yes," I say, and for a moment I do feel that we're friends, that I might call her to ask what she thinks of my boyfriend, David, whether he's the one. The feeling is gone by the time I get to the end of the hall.

We're not friends. This is just my usual rhythm, slipping in and out of all these strangers' lives.

The newsroom is like an outsized classroom, long and rectangular, with row upon row of tan metal desks and, at the front of the room, the glass-walled offices of editors. The outside wall is top to bottom windows. I almost never look out. All that's there is the street, and my desk is on the opposite side of the room. In the far corner a cluster of desks forms the features department, a part of the room I rarely enter. I walk to my desk past people leaning into computer screens, vertical lines appearing between their eyes, people murmuring into telephone headsets, fingers flying over keyboards, people spreading today's papers out on their desks, looking for their names. Some people wear suits, some wear short-sleeved shirts and casual pants, depending on what they cover and whether they need to impress anyone. Me, I wear suits to look older. I say hi to one of the metro editors, and he nods, dreadlocks bouncing against the back of his neck. I pass a reporter who sits constantly chewing sunflower seeds, whistling under his breath. I exchange a sympathetic glance with the reporter whose desk is next to his, a chain-smoking nervous woman who covers education and goes everywhere with a fanny pack around her waist. She rolls her eyes and sighs. All of the women in news are either borderline anorexic or plumping up from too much late-night pizza and after-deadline beer. I'm still hovering somewhere in the middle.

At my desk I run a search on Cynthia Avery, the dead girl's mother. I skim a few articles that quote her, many about fundraising, one a feature piece about her, the joys and trials of caring for terribly sick children. I write down one of her quotes. "We do our best to be of comfort to the families. There's nothing harder than losing a child."

I pick up the phone. I don't usually call the family first, because it's easier to hang up than to avoid someone who's at your door. But since the direct approach didn't work at the police station, I dial the number and get the girl's mother on the phone. I never gave her my name, so she doesn't have to know it's me again.

"I'm terribly sorry to bother you, Dr. Avery," I say. "I'm calling because I want to tell the city about your daughter. I understand from talking to her co-workers that she was a very gifted singer."

She makes a choking sound and hangs up.

I count to ten and call back. Often someone much calmer answers the phone the second time. The phone just rings and rings. From his desk next to mine, Evan Fitzpatrick is pretending not to watch me. I've known Evan since we were both summer interns here in college. He is always here when I get here in the morning; he is always here when I leave at night. Once a week or so he brings in clippings from *The New York Times* or *The Boston Globe* that he wants me to read. "This guy really knows his stuff," he'll say. "Look how he works the background information into the lead." I can't call him on Sundays, because he is making his way through three or four

Sunday newspapers and will speak sharply to me on the phone. He is the only reporter I've ever known who writes other reporters fan letters. Evan believes in The Truth; he takes on a story like a mission from God. He never has to stop and wonder what he's doing on someone's doorstep, because he carries the answer around like a cross on a chain—the public's right to know. Evan makes me feel ashamed any time I have doubts, the way my Southern Baptist high school boyfriend made me feel ashamed for not wanting to go to church.

"I hear you're working on the girl's murder," he says when I put the phone down. I pick it up again and dial the weather report. "Phone call," I mouth at him. I don't want to talk about this yet.

"I'll wait." He crosses his arms and stares at me.

I pretend to take notes, then I realize how ridiculous that is, since I haven't said a word into the phone, so I hang up. "What?" I say.

"What's the scoop?"

"Nothing," I say. "They know nothing." Evan loves words like "scoop." When he gets depressed he goes home and watches *All the President's Men*, and it restores his faith. I watched it once with him, and when it was over I said, "But then what happened?"

"What do you mean?" Evan said. "You saw what happened. They got the story."

"Too bad you don't get stories like that all the time," I said. "That story was really important."

"Every story is important to somebody," Evan said.

Now he rummages under his desk, to reappear after a moment with a torn and dirty magazine, cheaply printed on white paper. "Look at this," he says.

I reach for it, but he pulls it back. "Look with your eyes, not with your hands," he says in a schoolboy's taunting voice. "It's a Satanist magazine."

"So?"

"Don't you get it?" he says, paging slowly through the magazine. "I found it in that kid's trash."

"What kid?"

"The one they suspect of killing that ten-year-old in Arkansas. You know about it?"

"Of course I know about it. I wrote the first story, remember?" I glare at him. "So you dug through his trash?"

"It paid off," he says. "This is front page."

"You're frightening me," I say, only half joking.

"Hey," he says. "I have to write something." He seems hurt, and he puts the magazine away and doesn't talk to me anymore.

That's one reason why we're so eager for news, because when it's not there we have to manufacture it, and that's no easy task. When I was still a general assignment reporter, I spent one Sunday afternoon at the Mississippi River Museum asking people why they were there. "We wanted to do something touristy and tacky," one girl said. "It was this or Graceland, and I've been to Graceland before."

"I haven't," her boyfriend said.

"He hasn't," she said. "But I have."

Then I went back to the office and made a story out of this. When I wrote it, it said, essentially, that a few people were at the museum. The headline in the paper said MISSISSIPPI RIVER MUSEUM COULD BE IN TROUBLE; LACKS VISITORS.

Peggy, one of the metro editors, leans over me, both palms flat on my desk. "How's that story coming, kid?" she asks. Peggy is black, with close-cropped hair and a few dark freckles on her cheeks. She is my favorite editor, because she never changes a lead without showing it to me first. She is also the smartest, and so the hardest to fool. I'm leaning toward leaving the girl's parents alone now. I know she won't go for that, and I need her behind this story. For this, I want better than the front of Metro, where local crime goes unless it's particularly sensational.

"Peggy," I begin, leaning forward and lowering my voice, "I think this could go front page."

"Do you now?" She laughs, rocking back a little. "Why's that?"

"Young girl, brutal killing, probably sexual, and she's got promi-nent parents."

"I don't know, kid," Peggy says, pulling a list from her pocket. "We've got competition today. See what else you can come up with."

After she goes I sit, drumming my fingers on the desk. Evan hits me in the back of the head with a balled-up piece of paper.

"What's that for?" I say.

"Front page," he says. "You brazen hussy. What else *can* you come up with?"

I pick up the phone to dial Sergeant Morris. "Listen and learn," I say to Evan as the phone rings. A couple of weeks ago Morris men-tioned that the city was approaching the one-hundredth-murder mark earlier than ever this year. I'm wondering if Allison Avery might have hit it.

"I don't know," Morris says when I ask him. "We did brisk busi-ness over the weekend. Don't know times of death yet."

"But she could be, right?" I say. "She's close."

"She could be," he says. "We're over one hundred now. For all I know, she's the one."

I hang up the phone, writing down: *Allison Avery equals 100.* It may not be the truth, but it's close enough to count.

At Peggy's desk, I say, "She's the hundredth murder victim in the city this year. Earliest we've hit the mark since cops can remember."

"All right," she says, glancing up from her computer screen. "I'll push for it."

"Thanks," I say, turning to go.

"Get the family," she calls after me. "We have to have the family now."

The Averys live in a quiet, middle-class neighborhood of elegant two-story brick houses and two-car garages, each a slight variation on the last. Their lawn is neatly mowed. There's a basketball hoop in the driveway. I stand on the porch and look at the landscaping, low clipped bushes and daffodils. Off to one side, three tall orange lilies sway a little in the breeze.

After I knock on the door, I hear slow footsteps, and then a breathing silence that tells me someone is watching me through the peephole. I try for an expression that is somewhere between a smile and a sad face, and end up, I'm sure, grimacing horribly. A moment passes, and then another, but whoever watches me from the other side of that door doesn't open it. I listen to the footsteps retreat.

I turn to go, feeling all of a sudden tired and heavy with disappointment. Here on the porch it's cool and shaded, and I'm reluctant to step back out into the heat. I lean against the banister, looking out from Allison Avery's porch at the neighborhood where she lived. It's a lot like the neighborhood where I grew up. For a moment I can hear my mother's voice, as though from the house, saying, "Don't go too far. Stay where I can see you." The sun behind me bathes the street in light. A few houses down two small children squabble over a tricycle in the driveway. Over their high angry voices I hear the slap-slap of rapid tennis shoes on pavement, and then a teenage boy comes into view, running hard, right down the middle of the street. I watch him. In a T-shirt and gym shorts, he's running as fast as he can, his long arms and legs all right angles, knees high, feet pounding on asphalt so hard every step must send a jolt through his whole body.

As he reaches the house next door, a red sports car comes flying around the corner, headed right at him. Horn blaring, it swerves wildly just in time to miss him as he jumps aside. The boy takes a few steps after it, jabbing his arm into the air and shouting, "Fuck you." The whooping of teenage voices trails after it down the street. The boy stands for a minute with his hands on his hips, his chest rising and falling rapidly. He shakes his head. "Goddamnit," he shouts. Then he turns and walks back up the street in my direction, head lowered.

When he reaches the end of the Avery's driveway he stops and bends over, hands on his thighs, breathing hard. Then he lifts his head and squints up at the windows on the second floor. I'm watching him watch the house, and I wonder who he is, whether he knew her and has heard what happened. He's an attractive kid, moving with an easy long-limbed grace. After a moment he opens the mailbox and reaches way inside. I take a step toward him, trying to see what he's doing. With the sun in his eyes, he doesn't see me. He straightens up, a pack of cigarettes and a lighter in his hand. Lighting a cigarette, he keeps his eyes trained on the house. He lifts his T-shirt and slides the pack into the waistband of his green gym shorts.

He starts walking toward me up the lawn, looking at the ground and taking deep drags on his cigarette. That's when I realize, he must be her brother, coming home. He's tall, with that unformed skinniness that boys have before their weight catches up with their height, and his hair is the rich brown of good leather, with a touch of curl around his heart-shaped face. His white T-shirt is patched with sweat, clinging to his stomach and chest.

Standing up straight, I walk down the porch steps and out onto the lawn. I don't want to startle him. "Hello," I call out. He stops short and looks up. He squints into the light, trying to make out my face. To him I must look like a dark outline against the sun. I lift my hand and wave as though I know him. He takes a quick step, and then another, his hand reaching out toward me. An expression comes over his face, of hope and astonishment, and he opens his mouth and says, "Allison?"

It is a terrible moment. How badly he must want to believe she's not dead. I take a breath but find myself speechless, and so he goes on for a few seconds thinking I am his sister. He smiles, and his eyes fill up with tears, and he is suddenly so beautiful that I can't even look at him.

I move forward, so that he can see my face. His hand drops to his side, and on his face there is a look of such stricken sorrow, as though I have just broken his heart. It's gone quickly, his mouth smoothed into a thin line and his eyes blank. Turning away, he runs his free hand through his damp hair and takes another drag of his cigarette. Then he looks at me again. "Are you one of my sister's friends?" he asks.

"No, I'm sorry, I'm not," I say, and to my astonishment my voice wavers, like I'm about to burst out crying.

"Who are you then?" he says, his voice all sharp edges.

I consider saying, "I'm at the wrong house," but I'll probably see this boy again, so I tell the truth.

He looks down at the ground. Then he drops his half-smoked cigarette and rubs it out with his toe. Slowly, he lifts his T-shirt and uses the bottom of it to wipe his damp forehead. His flat boy's stomach is bright white in the sun. "Don't you feel bad, coming here like this?" he says, dropping the shirt. "My sister's barely been dead one day."

"I do feel bad, yes," I say. Then I just stand there, my mind turning over possibilities for what to say next. After a minute I realize my mouth is hanging open, so I close it.

"I thought you were one of her friends," he says, looking me up and down. He lets his gaze linger over my breasts, as though trying to unnerve me. He must want revenge for that moment when he thought he had his sister back. "You're young to be a reporter."

"Old enough," I say. I cross my arms over my chest. "I mean, I am a reporter."

"Now I know where I've seen you before. At the Four Corners."

"That's across the street from my apartment."

He nods slowly. "I work there weekends," he says. "I'm a busboy." He looks me in the face now, studying me. "Your hair used to be longer, didn't it? About to here." He reaches out as though to touch my shoulder. "You always order the banana pudding. Once, I told you we were out and you left."

I don't recognize him. I don't know what to say. It's too late to try the "I want to tell the world about your loved one" approach on him. I don't know what's become of my professionalism. Then it clicks into place, how I should be—sympathetic, regretful, even a little ashamed. "Are your parents home?" I ask, gently, watching him take the cigarette pack from the waistband of his shorts.

"They don't want to talk to you." He slides another cigarette out and puts it in his mouth, then offers me the pack. I look at him. The cigarette dangles from his lips as he watches me with hooded eyes, playing the tough kid. I imagine him practicing this look in the mirror.

I shake my head. "I wouldn't want to talk to me either," I say. "I'm sorry about your sister." I start to go past him. He grabs my arm, then quickly drops it.

"Will you put something in the paper?" he asks. He takes the un-lit cigarette from his mouth and jabs it in the air. "Whatever I say?"

"Yes."

"Here it is," he says. "My sister's dead. How do you think I feel?"

By the end of the day I know that the boy's name is Peter and that he is seventeen. I know where he goes to school, where he works, where he lives, and what he looks like. But I don't know how he feels.

The truth is nothing really terrible has ever happened to me, although before I learned to harden myself I was afraid of all kinds of things. I used to believe I would be killed by a serial killer, not someone who would just shoot you, but someone who would torture you and cut you up and scatter your body parts throughout the city. Before that, I was afraid of sharks and alligators, for the same reason, the way they chew you to pieces. Then it was death—just dying, no matter how. I couldn't even let myself think about it without getting a cold burning in my stomach and face. Until I was twenty-two, I had never been to a funeral. Now I've been to the funeral of a baby shot inside her mother's womb, the funeral of a teenager stabbed in an alley, the funerals of all manner of strangers, but I have never been to the funeral of a person I have loved.

Allison's funeral is in three days. It's my job to be there. I put it in the story, what her brother said. Peggy thinks it's a great quote. "I like the steam rising, too," she said. "Nice touch." It's running front page. Headline: CITY CLAIMS 100TH MURDER VICTIM THIS YEAR. Subhead: Daughter of Prominent Doctor Found Dead. Byline: Olivia Dale.

It's 11 P.M. Instead of leaving I'm sitting at my desk watching the second hand make its way around the clock on the wall. The newsroom is almost empty and quiet like it never is during the day, the only sounds the murmur of two editors' voices and the click the clock makes when a minute passes. I just sit here thinking about that boy, Peter. A seventeen-year-old boy hasn't shriveled me up inside like that since I was fourteen and Fred Lamar tried to feel me up on the band bus when he hadn't even kissed me yet. I played the clarinet for seven years. At my school we were called "band fags," and when someone asked me my schedule I said, English, Band, French, with the "band" said so quickly the *a* and the *d* disappeared. My mother wouldn't let me quit. She said, "Some day you'll understand it was good for you." I hate feeling ashamed of something, wishing I could quit. I'd like to live a life where that was never true.

The first edition is on the presses. I get up and go down the hall to the window overlooking the press room. The huge steel machines turn and whirr without stopping. I press my forehead to the glass, darkened by newsprint, and watch the pages fly by. While I watch, it comes back to me, the rush I get from what I do. I've stood here just like this and watched every night I've thought that a story was important, that what I had written meant lives would be changed. This is what I live for through the boredom of highway fatalities and armed robberies and endless hours of pretending to be busy at my desk, waiting for someone to commit a crime. It's like driving alone for hours on a straight Texas highway, just to see the sparkling lights of a city rise over the darkness of the plains.

The front page goes by again and again and again. That's my story there, under that big bold headline, leading off the day's news.

3

On my way out of the building, I say good night to the security guard, a plump older man with the swollen features of an alcoholic. "Be careful out there," he says jovially. I nod, my lips pressed together, gripping my keys tightly in one hand, the points jutting out between my fingers the way I learned in a college self-defense course. The newspaper building is not far from crime-ridden government housing. When the door closes behind me, I start moving as quickly as I can toward my car, which is just outside the dim light thrown by the building's lamps. My footsteps sound on the pavement, and when I'm close enough I bend down to make sure no one is beneath the car. Last month I wrote a story about three women who had their Achilles tendons slashed by a man lying in wait beneath their cars in a mall parking lot. He was never caught.

I open the door, swing my legs in and pull the door shut, locking it. I turn around. I forgot to make sure no one was crouched in the back. I'm alone. I take a deep breath and relax against the seat. The car starts and I shift smoothly into first and glide from the parking lot. There is nothing I'd like better than to go home now, but I'm scheduled to meet a midnight-shift cop named Smiley at the police station for a ride-along. Peggy suggested it as a good way to get to know the cops. "Could be a story in it," she said. "Maybe you'll get lucky."

Officer Smiley is leaning against his patrol car in the parking lot, his arms crossed over his chest. A light-skinned black man, he's the sort of cop who looks like he divides his time between his beat and the weight room, his close-cropped head a solid block on his wide, thick-veined neck. He watches me approach with the slightest movement of his eyes.

"Officer Smiley," I call out when I'm two feet from him. "I'm Olivia Dale." I go toward him with my hand held out.

He waits another beat before easing his body forward off the car and extending his own hand to grip mine. "Ma'am," he says formally.

I laugh. It's involuntary, a quick nervous burst. I'm afraid to look at him again, but when I do, he's smiling, and I suddenly realize how young he is, maybe even younger than I am.

He walks me around to the passenger side and watches me settle in against the warm black vinyl before he shuts the door. He moves around the car with the slow wide-legged walk of the muscular, and when he gets in the car it seems to sag with his weight.

"Thanks for agreeing to this," I say.

"I didn't *agree,*" he says. "I was told."

"Oh," I say. "Well, thanks anyway."

He seems tense as we pull out of the parking lot and negotiate our way out of downtown, both his hands tight on the steering wheel. Then he relaxes back against the seat, dropping one hand to his leg and jerking his neck from side to side in the weight lifter's stretching motion. He hasn't said a word.

"Are you from Memphis?" I ask.

"Orange Mound," he says. "I stay there still. My family's there."

I get him talking about his background, how he left his poor neighborhood to go to college, then decided to come back to the people who raised him and do something for the community. He tells me that he really thinks he can make a difference. I nod, working up a hometown rookie cop angle in my head, just in case I need it.

"What do you think the city should be doing about crime that it's not doing now?" I ask him.

"More cops, number one. I know the mayor wants that, but nobody wants their taxes raised." He shakes his head. "Always the same thing. Nobody wants to pay for you, but everybody thinks you should be there the second they pick up their phone."

"What . . . ," I start. He holds up his hand to stop me and turns up the radio as the dispatcher's mechanical voice recites the code for domestic disturbance. He radios back and I grip the door handle as he swings the car into a U-turn. We hurtle down the street, the siren wailing our battle cry.

The house is enormous and decrepit, one of those grand old Memphis houses with half the windows boarded up, the roof caving in. It's quiet. "Stay here," Smiley says. He shuts the door and leaves me cocooned inside the stifling car. After a moment I push open my door and sit facing out. I watch him knock on the door. "Police," he calls. He leans over, trying to peer in the closest window. Then I see his body stiffen. "Hey," he yells. "Hey." He reaches for his gun and flings himself through the door into the house. A gunshot cracks the air and I am on my feet, running up the lawn. I trip over the first porch step and clamber up on my hands and knees. Inside a woman's voice is rising toward a scream. On the porch I press my face to the window.

Smiley and another man stand facing one another, each with a gun aimed at the other's face. A woman in a pink housedress, her nose dripping blood, stands rocking herself from side to side, moaning. I draw a stick-figure diagram in my notebook so I'll be able to describe this later, the room, the distance between the two men. I draw a squiggle of blood down the stick woman's face.

"Drop it," Smiley says between his teeth. The man looks wildly from side to side. Then he spots my face against the window and his eyes narrow. He raises the gun, and I drop to the floor of the porch as a bullet shatters the window, glass raining down on my back. I hear the woman screaming, and the sounds of a scuffle, and when I rise up gingerly, pieces of glass cascading down my back, the man is on the ground, Smiley's gun pressed to his head, Smiley's foot planted firmly on his back. The woman's throat is convulsing as though she's going to vomit.

"Damn," I say out loud. "I missed it." I pick up my notebook and shake off the glass. There's a smudge of red on the white paper. I look at my hand and see that my finger is bleeding. I pluck a tiny shard of glass from my skin. My heart slams against my chest like it's going to burst on through.

Officer Smiley comes out the front door, pushing the handcuffed man before him. Reciting the man's rights, Smiley looks right through me. The man stares at me as he passes, his face red and pulsing with rage. I just stand there, my notebook slack in my hand, while the woman inside keeps screaming, while Smiley walks the man to the car, puts his hand on his head and gently eases him into the backseat. He moves slowly around the car and reaches in for the radio.

Then I start moving. When I reach Smiley's side, he's putting the radio carefully back into place. "What happened?"

"What happened is you almost got shot," he says.

I wave my hand to dismiss this. "I mean, how'd you get him on the ground?"

"When he turned toward the window, I tackled him and he dropped the gun," he says.

"Why didn't you shoot him?"

"I don't know." He looks up at the house. "Shit," he says. "Can that woman scream."

"What are you going to do about her?"

"They're sending someone," he says absently.

I lean into the car and look at the prisoner through the wire mesh that divides the front seat from the back. He glares at me. "Why did you hit your wife?" I ask him.

He says nothing. A lump of chewing tobacco pushes out his lower lip, making him look like a petulant child.

"Why did you have the gun out?" I ask.

"To kill the bitch," he snarls. He turns his head to the side and spits a brown puddle onto the seat beside him.

I straighten up. Officer Smiley looks at me and shakes his head, as though to say, why did you even ask? I look down at the blood welling out of my finger in a neat little bubble. We stand together in silence until another squad car arrives, listening as the wailing goes on and on, until it just seems like part of the night, the heat, the smell of wet dirt and grass, that agonized, endless sound.

When we get out of the car at the station, Smiley says, "Am I going to see this in the paper?"

"Hero John Smiley," I say, making a headline in the air with my hand.

He laughs. "Don't say that," he says. "I'll get endless shit." He shakes my hand and goes around the car to retrieve his prisoner.

"Thanks," I say. He doesn't hear it, and I don't repeat it. I just turn away and walk back to my car.

When I get home, the house is dark. On my way through the living room I bump against the flimsy coffee table Hannah and I found out on the street and one of the stacks of magazines cascades onto the floor, scattering across a cardboard box with half a pizza still in it. I know if I went in the kitchen I would find a sink full of dirty dishes, a counter dirty with bits of food and the occasional cockroach, and an overflowing trash can surrounded by crumpled paper towels that didn't make it in. The couch is draped with clothes, some mine. I settle down among them and watch the clock on the VCR blink 12:00. I'm working on an angle in my head, thinking I can use this incident as the lead-in to a series about domestic violence in Memphis, or violence against women in general if I tie in today's dead girl. I think of making a list—*get stats, call a shelter*—

but I'm too tired to go digging through my bag for my notebook, or even to turn on the light. It seems like a million years since I stood over that dead body this morning.

I say to myself, *I could have been shot.* No matter how hard I try I can't make myself believe it.

One thing I know, when you read about what happened tonight in the paper, it will never occur to you that I was there.

4

When I open my eyes, my roommate, Hannah, is standing over me. She is wearing a black cardigan over a sleeveless pink cotton sundress that buttons up the front. She looks as though she has no idea what the season is and is trying to allow for all possibilities. "What are you doing here?" she says.

"I live here," I try to say. My tongue feels swollen inside my mouth. I sit up. "Aren't you hot?" We don't have central air, just window units in our bedrooms, and the heat is like another presence in the room. I must have fallen asleep in my clothes, my shirt soaked through and clinging to my skin.

"Why did you sleep on the couch?" Hannah sprawls beside me and turns on the television.

I look down at my rumpled skirt. "I didn't mean to."

"David called like three times last night," she says.

"What did he want?" I put my wet face in my hands and rub it vigorously.

"I don't know," she says. "He's *your* boyfriend." She says this with scorn. Hannah believes in being alone. She thinks no woman enters a relationship with a man without sacrificing something. She's afraid of men who want more than sex from her. When we're out late at night, she'll walk home by herself, because she wants everyone to believe she's afraid of nothing.

"What time is it?" I ask. "Aren't you going to work?"

"Aren't you?" she says. "It's quarter of ten."

"Oh my God." I jump up. "I'm late. Why didn't you wake me?"

"I thought you needed the sleep," Hannah says without looking at me. She is watching a music video; a very young, very undressed girl with frightening wide eyes is looking bewildered in a close-up. Her hair is straight and unwashed. She is so thin that the thrust of her lips seems violent after the deep hollows of her cheeks. "How could anyone find that attractive?" Hannah says. I notice that she doesn't change the channel.

Hannah herself is thin, though not as thin as the video girl. Her cheekbones, her collarbones make elegant lines beneath her skin, pale as soap. She's a green-eyed redhead—another reason she shouldn't be wearing pink—and her hair is a rich red-brown, cut short to her chin and smooth against her face. She dated a guy in college who used to call her "red velvet," which she hated. She is tall and in every way lovely, a fact that she steadfastly refuses to acknowledge. "Did last night go okay?" I say.

"Obviously." She leans her head back to look at me. "Don't I look okay?"

"You know what I mean. What happened to your date?"

"We had a drink, then I sent him home." She makes a face. "He was an eager puppy."

"Did he lick your face?"

"My neck, actually." She shudders. "Let's not talk about it anymore." She turns back to the screen. The video girl rolls over and over on a carpeted floor, her long white legs bony and exposed. I can see what she would look like without her skin, the shape of her skull, the enormous caverns for her eyes. It makes me feel sick. I keep watching. I'm a television junkie. I get sucked in by all those imaginary lives. I become involved in commercials. So even though I'm late for work I stand there until Hannah says, "Sit down. You're looming."

"I can't," I say. "I've got to get ready."

"So go get ready," she says.

"Are you going to want a ride to work?"

"I don't know," she says. "Are you going to hit the curb like last time?"

"Memphis woman kills roommate with couch pillow," I say. "Police say Dale, twenty-five, snapped after third bitchy comment in five minutes."

"Quote this," she says, giving me the finger. But she laughs, and gets up off the couch to give me a quick hug. "Good morning," she says.

My bedroom is strewn with clothes, on the floor beside the open closet, across the unmade bed, hanging out the open drawers of the dresser. This is why David almost never comes here. I stuff jeans and underwear back into the drawers, push them shut with my hip, and find something on the bed to wear.

When I come out of my bedroom Hannah is no longer in the living room, though the television is still blaring. I turn it off and go looking for her, slinging my bag over my shoulder. She's sitting at the kitchen table, her head bent over today's newspaper. I come up behind her and look at the paper over her shoulder. There I am, front-page lead. "I'm leaving," I say. "Do you want a ride?" Hannah is working as a temp; right now she's doing data entry at a hospital near the newspaper.

She doesn't say anything.

"Hannah?" I say. "Do you want a ride?"

"You didn't tell me you were on this story." She says it like an accusation.

"You didn't ask," I say. "Hannah, I've got to go."

She looks up. To my surprise, her eyes are filled with tears. "Olivia," she whispers. "I know this girl."

"Are you serious?" I say. I slide into the seat beside her and grab my notebook out of my bag. "How do you know her?"

She doesn't say anything, staring at me.

"How do you know her?" I repeat.

"What are you doing?" she says. "Do you think you're going to *interview* me? I just said this girl I know is dead, and you take out your notebook?"

I feel a flush creep up my cheeks. "I'm sorry," I say. "I'm sorry." Slowly I open my bag and put the notebook away. I make my voice gentle and say, "How do you know her?"

"I didn't know her well," she says. "I knew who she was. She went to my high school. I probably talked to her twice."

"It's still a shock," I say. I hesitate. Then I ask, "What was she like?"

"She was a high school girl. I don't know. She seemed okay. She was one of those girls who always had a couple of guys following her around."

"Was she the type who invites that? Or couldn't she help it?"

"I don't know," Hannah says. "Should she have helped it?"

I shrug.

"Come on," Hannah says. "Don't tell me you wouldn't be one of those girls if you could." A pink flush mottles her pale throat. "I mean," she says. "Not that you're not."

"I'm not," I say. "And I don't want to be." I turn my gaze from her face to the newspaper and read my lead. *The body of a 24-year-old Memphis woman was found yesterday in Tom Lee Park.*

Hannah sighs. "I can't believe it. That's a pretty nice neighborhood, where she lived."

"Let it be a lesson to you," I say. "Don't walk home alone."

"She wasn't walking two miles home, Olivia," Hannah says. "She was right outside her building. That's why there's no point in living in fear. You can't avoid danger."

"Maybe," I say. "But you don't have to invite it."

"You think I invite it?" She's turned toward me, her eyebrows raised.

I meet her gaze. "Sometimes."

"How did this girl invite it?" She shakes the paper at me, crumpling the girl's smiling face.

"I don't know," I say.

"You . . . don't . . . know."

"That's right." I look at my watch. "I've got to go, Hannah."

"See you later," she says without looking at me.

I push my chair back with a clatter. At the kitchen door I turn to look back at her. She leans forward over the table, her shoulders hunched in tight, running her hands over the newspaper, trying to smooth the creases from the dead girl's face. "I don't know," I say to her back. "Yet."

"The big bad reporter," Hannah says. She doesn't stop what she's doing. "I bet if you keep trying, some day you'll know everything."

On the porch I stand and take a deep breath. No one is visible on our dead-end street of duplexes and small brick houses. Everybody's blinds are down.

Our street opens onto a road with wide lanes and an arching corridor of trees, running alongside Overton Park, where the zoo is, and the art museum. When I had regular working hours, I would go running through the wooded areas, past the museum and the baseball fields and the picnic tables. When the path disappears into the woods it's like you are the only person in the world, the smack of your footsteps and the rush of your breathing the only sounds you hear. Through tall thick trees the sunlight makes dust glitter like gold shavings in the air.

Once I made the mistake of going there close to sundown, and when the light faded the whole place changed. Somewhere near I could hear a car moving far too slowly, and then I heard somebody shout. I started running like someone was chasing me, the blood pounding in my ears, and when I burst out of the woods the families had vanished from the fields and picnic tables, as though they all disappeared the instant the sun went down. I forced myself to walk calmly to the car.

Hannah and I moved to this neighborhood to be safer. We used to live on the third floor of an apartment building on Madison, across the street from a nightclub. We went there sometimes for a drink, and at night we could sit by our windows and watch the people going in and out, drunks stumbling off the curb, girls in high heels leaning against guys, their laughter echoing down the dark street. I was a general assignment reporter, covering south Memphis and DeSoto County, Mississippi. Church ground breakings, programs for inner-city youth, Graceland's battle against Elvis copyright violations. One Saturday, when the cops reporter called in sick, they sent me to the station to go through the day's reports. It wasn't the robberies, the assaults, the murders that shocked me—I had been reading my own paper. I had been hearing it every night on the evening news.

But three women had been raped the night before, one in the alley of the nightclub across the street from where I lived. It had happened at eleven o'clock, while inside the music was still playing and outside the people ambled tipsily down the street. Why hadn't I read about it in the morning paper? From our window, Hannah and I could see the part of that alley where the trash cans were. Then it disappeared into darkness.

Hannah and I knew some of the regulars by sight, and we noticed that one had stopped appearing, a middle-aged blonde with a bad dye job who wore heavy makeup and tight skirts, shirts cut short enough to expose a roll of flesh at her waist. She drank too much and leaned in close to men when she talked so that they could look down her shirt at her heavy white breasts. We thought maybe she was the one. I didn't want it to be a girl like us.

I went into work Monday and looked through a month's worth of papers, trying to find a story or even a brief about a woman being raped. I couldn't find a single one. Next I checked the weekly breakdowns of crime statistics for each Memphis neighborhood, maps that show you what to look out for on your street: car theft, breaking and entering, homicide. There was no statistic for rape, as though the terrible things that happen to women are either too shameful or too commonplace to report. Flushed with indignation, I went to the managing editor and asked him why we never ran rape stories. An hour later he was having a heated conversation with the news editor.

This is how I ended up on the police beat.

This is how I came to find myself sitting down with women like the one I interviewed last week, who was dragged off her front porch on a quiet street by a stranger with a knife. He took her in her own backyard and raped her, and she didn't fight it. She said, "I knew he might have AIDS. I thought, I can die now or I can die later." She is still waiting for her test results.

This is my city. Every morning in Memphis people eat their breakfasts over the list of crimes in the newspaper. Every summer thousands of people gather at Graceland in the terrible heat of mid-August to mourn a man who died twenty years ago. They cry as though it were yesterday.

At my desk, I spend some time on the phone, getting nowhere with the medical examiner's office. I hang up and watch Bishop ambling across the newsroom, hands in his pockets. Bishop is one of those men who always gets called by his last name, so that his first name seems to have nothing to do with him, like most people's middle names. I wouldn't even know his first name if I didn't see it in his by-line every day—it's Martin.

Bishop is white, thirty-seven, with a high forehead and straight black hair that sweeps back from the middle of his head to end just below his chin. He wears John Lennon glasses, and lets his front teeth show all the time. To work he wears khaki pants, sneakers, and short-sleeved plaid button-downs, and he always has a little note-book in the breast pocket of his shirt. He drives a Dodge Colt with no seat belts and a jagged gap where the glove compartment used to be. If you saw him on the street, you might think he was the kind of man who still lives with his mother, but he has his own apartment and a series of girlfriends, mostly career waitresses. His nonnewspaper friends are all martini drinkers who throw a party every other weekend. I've never gone to one. I don't like parties. When I asked Evan about it, he just shook his head and said, "Whew." Bishop kissed me once in the back room of a bar, near the rest rooms and the pay phone. It was a very gentle kiss; he didn't even touch me, just leaned way forward and pressed his lips to mine. "Well . . . ," I began when it was over.

"If you didn't like it, I'm sorry. I won't do it again." He touched my arm so lightly I could only just be sure that he had touched me, and then he went back to the table. The truth was, I did like it. But I was drunk, and that can explain a lot of things.

Now Bishop catches my eye and winks. I wave him over and he comes, whistling between his teeth. "Do you have a source in the ME's office?" I ask him.

He props his hip against my desk. "The streets are crawling with my sources," he says. "Can I help you with something?"

"The girl from yesterday," I say. "I'm not having any luck getting cause of death."

He straightens up, nodding. "I'll be back."

I'm watching him walk away when the phone rings. "Olivia Dale," I say, tucking the phone between my ear and my shoulder.

"Hi," a male voice says. "This is Peter."

There's a beat while I try to think who Peter is. Then I see the front-page spread across my desk and I realize. "Hi, Peter." My voice melts with concern when I ask, "How are you?"

"Um . . . . ," he says, letting his voice trail away. He sounds matter-of-fact when he says, "Have you heard anything more?"

"Not yet," I say cautiously, wondering if he's hinting at something. "I haven't been to the station yet today."

"Okay," he says.

"Have you heard anything more?"

"No," he says. "Nothing." Then he bursts out, "Not a goddamned thing!" His breathing grows labored. I say nothing, giving him a moment to compose himself. When he is silent, I say, "Peter? Did you want to talk about something?"

"I saw your article," he says. "You quoted me. It's strange . . ."

"Yes," I say. "I know." I make my voice low and smooth, like what would be my phone-sex voice if I had one, like I want to wrap this voice around him, soft and warm. "I'd like to be able to say more about your sister." I pause. I don't know what he wants, but as long as he's called I might as well get what I can. "Are you close?"

"Of course," he says. "She's my *sister.*" His voice veers close to the edge of hysteria.

"You're lucky," I say gently. "Not all siblings are close."

"Do you have a sister?"

"Yes," I say, then stop, the word a lie I didn't even know I was going to tell. "I mean, no. I *am* a sister. I have a brother."

"What would he do if something happened to you?" He asks as though he really thinks I know, as though he's seeking a model for his own behavior.

"You mean, how would he feel?"

"No, no. What would he *do?* Would he sit around looking at photo albums, like my mother?" His voice drops to a whisper. "Would he go looking for the guy?"

"No, Peter, definitely not," I say. The fact is, I have no idea what my brother would do. If something happened to me, part of him would probably be saying I brought it on myself, the line of work I'm in too dangerous for a girl. "He would know to leave that to the police."

"So what would he do?" he asks again. Then, almost as if talking to himself, "I don't know what to do with myself."

"I don't know," I say. "I guess he would grieve."

"Yeah," he says. "Yeah." There's a silence. "How?"

"That's different for everyone." I venture, "It might help to talk."

"Yeah, to who. My parents are . . . I don't want to talk to my friends. I don't have a girlfriend."

"You can talk to me." I hold my breath during the silence that follows.

He says, sharply, "You'll just put it in the paper."

"That would depend."

"I'm not stupid," he says.

"Why did you call me, Peter?"

"I don't know," he says. "I shouldn't have." I hear him inhale deeply, probably lighting a cigarette, and a picture comes to me, of him looking up at the second story of his house, hiding the pack in the waistband of his shorts.

"Isn't your mother going to catch you smoking?" I ask.

He laughs bitterly. "She's got other things on her mind." He falls silent for a moment. Then he says, "Gotta go," and abruptly hangs up the phone.

I sit for a moment, looking at the receiver in my hand. "What the hell," I say.

"What?" Evan asks, looking up from his computer.

"I just had the strangest conversation." I hang up the phone. "Brother of the dead girl. Called me, asked if I had a sister, hung up."

Evan shrugs. "Crazy with grief, maybe."

"I guess," I say. "Or just crazy."

"Who's crazy?" Bishops asks, appearing at my desk.

"Nobody," I say. "What did you get?"

He drops a notebook in front of me. *CAR*, it says, in big block letters. *SKULL*.

"What's this mean?" I ask. He has written "jack-o'-lantern" in the middle of the page.

"He said the car crushed her skull like a jack-o'-lantern," Bishop says. "He asked me if I ever smashed them on Halloween."

"Did you?"

"Of course," he says. "All the boys did." I don't tell him how I cried the year the neighborhood boys smashed our jack-o'-lanterns to pieces on the front steps. Every year after that they stayed in the window. My mother never put them outside again.

I page through the rest of his notes while he narrates. They found signs of rape, semen, a few fibers. Under her fingernails they found skin. The physical evidence points to one man, though he may have had accomplices. He or they probably bound her wrists after they took her out of the trunk, after she scratched at least one of them. I read Bishop's notes on the condition of the body. Scrape marks and road burns. Bruises on the lungs and liver. Rupture of the bladder and stomach. Blood in the chest and abdomen. Rib fractures, dozens of them. Pelvic fractures. Tire tracks on the clothes and the skin.

"Looks like a stranger attack to me," Bishop says.

I say, "So they think she was alive when the car came at her."

"They know it," Bishop says. "She was badly beaten. But she was alive."

"I hope she was unconscious." I see it again, her body in fetal position, her hands to her face. I'm certain she was conscious. She heard the sound of the engine approaching, she felt the tires touch her skin, the crushing weight.

"That's the best you can hope for," Bishop says. "What an awful way to go."

I slide the photocopy of her face out from under today's newspaper on my desk. She's laughing. The boy is kissing her cheek. "Why her?" I say, tapping my pen on her face. "Why this girl?"

"She was there." Bishop shrugs. "Sometimes there is no reason. Just the wrong place at the wrong time."

"Even that's a reason," I say. "Isn't it?"

"I don't know," he says. "That's the kind of thinking that can make you crazy."

"Not having a reason makes me crazy," I say. "Fate, and all that. That makes me crazy. There is no fate. One action leads to another. There's always some reason, no matter how small. There's some reason this girl died. There has to be."

"Jesus," Bishop says. "Don't think about it, okay? You can't think about stuff like that. Some people are bad, and one of them saw this girl and took her and killed her. It's a terrible, random thing. The important thing for you now is to keep it in the paper so the police feel pressure to catch the guy who did it." He leans in and looks at the picture. "Look at her," he says. "She looks so normal."

The phone rings. I reach for it, and Bishop touches me on the shoulder and goes back to his desk. I watch him walk away, his lips moving like he's singing. "Olivia Dale," I say into the phone.

"Hey, it's Hannah." She sounds friendly, as though she's forgotten or forgiven our earlier exchange.

"Hey you," I say. I push the picture of the dead girl away. "What's up?"

"You know that guy Carl? With the weird goatee?"

"I don't."

"You know, he came to that party we had in January. He's a friend of Kathleen's. Somebody dared him to eat a whole bag of potato chips in three minutes and he did it, remember?"

"Oh yeah," I say. "Are you going out with him or something?"

"God, no," she says. "But he called me. He knew that Allison girl. I guess he went to my high school, too, though I've been racking my brain and I can't remember him from there. He saw your story in the paper."

"Did you say goatee?" I ask, paging through my notebook.

"What?" she says. "Yeah. He's got a goatee."

I'm looking at my notes from Joan Bracken. *Guy kicking door. Goatee.* "What's his last name?" I say. "Can you tell me anything else about him?"

"I've got his number," Hannah says. "That's all I know."

She gives me the number, and I thank her and tell her I'll call her later. There's a silence. I say, "Hannah? Are you there?"

After a moment she says, "It's scary, isn't it."

"What?" I say, tapping my pen on the paper where I've written Carl's number.

Hannah says, "How close she was to being one of us."

❧

Carl Fitzner lives in one of those monolithic apartment buildings that look like something out of a science fiction movie, floor upon floor of identical modern kitchenettes, thin gray wall-to-wall carpeting, and the musty scent of too many residents, not enough vacuuming. He lives on the lowest level. When he opens the door he smiles at me with tentative hope, as though I'm his blind date, and invites me in. His small, high windows look out at the ground and his neighbors' feet.

Carl is tall and plump; his face has a soft roundedness that gives him an air of bashful naïveté, despite his trendy all-black outfit and goatee. He seems nervous, and we stand awkwardly in his living room for a moment before he asks me to sit. The couch is 1970s brown velour and when I sit on it a puff of dust rises around me. Carl blushes and excuses himself, returning a moment later with a towel, which he drapes over the cushion beside me like a man laying his cloak over a puddle. I thank him and slide over onto the towel. Carl shuffles his feet on the carpet and asks me if I'd like something to drink, then disappears into the kitchen. I hear him washing glasses in there. He must not get many guests.

He returns with two glasses of water and sits on the edge of the armchair next to the couch. I warm up by making small talk about his acting ambitions, his part-time job as stage manager at the Black Horse Theater Company, people we know in common, like Kathleen, whom he knows from acting class and Hannah knows from her gym. "When I saw your name in the paper, I remembered you from your party," he says. He speaks slowly, as though everything he says has to pass through a layer of cotton in his brain, and I wonder if he's still in shock. "I called Kathleen and she gave me Hannah's number. Hannah's a nice girl." I nod, and he says, "Did you ever meet Allison?"

"Not that I remember, unless you brought her to that party," I say. "Did you?"

He shakes his head. "I came with Kathleen."

I'm relieved to hear it. I wouldn't want to know I'd shaken the hand I saw clenched, bound tight with stained white string. "So," I say. "How do you know Allison?"

"Our mothers were good friends," he says.

"Were?"

"My mother died when I was in sixth grade."

"I'm sorry," I say gently.

Carl shrugs and looks down into his water, swirling the ice cubes in the glass. He seems embarrassed to have revealed this information. He says, "Allison's mother helped me through it."

"So you and Allison grew up together?"

"We were close as kids. And then in high school we went out a couple of times, to a dance or two."

"You must have been very fond of her," I say.

He smiles wistfully. "For years I had this huge crush on her, you know? I mean, she was beautiful. You can't even imagine how beautiful."

"I've seen pictures."

"You would have had to see her in person. She practically glowed. It sounds silly, I know. But it's true."

"But you were never a couple?"

He shakes his head.

I touch him gently on the knee. "Did you want to be?"

He laughs and sighs at once. "Of course. She was always saying, 'Too bad I can't fall in love with a nice boy like you, Carl.'" He blinks, then tilts his head and drains his water glass.

I wait for him a moment, knowing that if I don't fill the silence he will.

"I loved her," he says finally, rolling his glass between his palms. "But I was only her friend."

I feel sorry for him, his lonely apartment, his motherless childhood, the way his voice cracked over the words "loved" and "only."

It's hard to picture him screaming in a hallway, kicking the dead girl's door.

I smile at him. "So you were still close friends in high school?"

"We hung out with different people, but I was over at her house a lot. We went out a couple times, like I said."

"What was she like then? Was she a cheerleader?"

"No." He looks at me oddly. I can't help it. I picture her in a short skirt, with pompoms.

He says, "She ran more with the arty crowd. You know, theater and the school paper and such. She was in the choir. She never cared for sports."

"I'm sorry to have to ask this, Carl," I say. "Was she ever into any kind of risky behavior? Drugs? Anything like that?"

"She smoked marijuana sometimes." Then he catches himself. "Please don't put that in the paper."

"Off the record," I say. "This is all off the record. I'm just trying to get a feel for what she was like, who she might have known . . ."

"I don't think anyone she knew could have done this to her."

"You'd be surprised," I say. "The killer is often a boyfriend. Or an ex-boyfriend."

"Maybe," he says. "Maybe."

"Do you know of anyone who could have been angry with her? Anyone she might have rejected?"

"She went out with a lot of guys. I don't know of one in particular who . . ." His voice trails off. He becomes very still, watching me, as though it's just occurred to him I might not be his friend.

"When was the last time you saw her?" I ask.

"A few days before it happened."

"At her apartment?"

He nods.

"And you didn't have a fight, then?"

He nods, shakes his head, then is still again, looking as if he doesn't know what to do next. He asks me if I mind if he smokes and then he takes out rolling papers and a pouch of tobacco and starts trying to roll a cigarette. "We didn't have a fight," he says. "We never fought." He licks his finger, gets bits of tobacco stuck to it, licks it again, and then sits there trying to pick tobacco off his tongue, grimacing. The rolling paper falls open and tobacco leaks out.

"Here," I say, and I roll the cigarette smooth and hand it to him. "I ask because a neighbor saw a man with a goatee leaving Allison's apartment."

"Lots of people have goatees," he says, fingering his chin.

On the coffee table is one of those fat silver Zippo lighters that people carry to draw attention to themselves. I pick it up and lean in to light the cigarette for him, putting us eye to eye over the unnecessarily large flame. "The neighbor says he seemed angry. That he kicked the door." Carl looks away. "Thanks," he says.

I watch him take a drag. He's working very hard to appear relaxed. "Must have been somebody else," he says. "Wasn't me. Definitely wasn't me."

"Any idea who it could have been?" I try to say this without sarcasm.

"Well," he says slowly. He studies the cigarette in his hand. "Allison knew a lot of people. And she did like to live dangerously." He looks up and laughs nervously. "I don't mean she had a secret life as a stripper or anything."

"What do you mean?" I ask, picking up my pen.

"She drove a little too fast, drank too much, ran with a fast crowd."

I write it down: *drank too much*.

"Some of the fellows she dated," he says. "And that Angela." He says her name like my mother says "pimple."

"What about her?" I ask, trying to picture the smooth-cheeked girl in the doctor's office. All I can see is her white coat, her ringed hand clutching at a tissue.

"She's no angel," he says. "Despite the name."

I press my lips together against the urge to laugh. In my notebook

I write: *Angela no angel?* "Do you know if either of them ever stole anything?" I'm thinking of Joan Bracken, her sweater and earrings.

Carl frowns. "I remember Angela stole from a teacher's purse once. Allison probably did it too, when we were kids. The thing about Angela, she had a boyfriend in high school, liked to play with knives. I heard he was into some unsavory business." He hesitates, then leans forward and whispers, "S and M." He doesn't need my questions anymore. He settles back in his chair and keeps talking. "He was in my gym class, and once I saw him with his shirt off. Long marks, all down his back, like whip scars."

I'm beginning to notice a habit he has of smacking his lips, like he's imagining something savory in his mouth. I sound interested, respectful, when I ask, "And Angela?"

"She dated him, didn't she? You wouldn't know it now, but she was a big-haired heavy metal chick in school, painted her fingernails black and hung out in the parking lot smoking cigarettes during lunch. When we were fourteen, Angela was at a party where this kid died from snorting butane."

"What about Allison?"

"She seemed like a normal girl," Carl says, putting the emphasis on "seemed." "But she was Angela's best friend, wasn't she?"

He goes on to tell me his low opinion of the rest of the people Allison knew. He tells me Allison wore her necklines too low, her skirts too high, laughed too loud at the jokes that boys told, spent too much time in the backseats of cars. Insinuation settles on my skin like a layer of dust. Some of it could be true, so I just keep nodding and taking notes.

"You talk like you think Allison brought it on herself."

He lets out a breath like I punched him in the stomach. "That's not what I'm saying," he splutters. He stabs out his cigarette and stares at the ashtray. Then he holds up his hands, palms facing me. "All I'm telling you," he says, "she was no Goody Two-shoes. She ran with a wild crowd. If you ask for trouble, you get trouble, right? Right?"

I don't say anything. For a moment I'm sorry to have turned him inside out, the lonely young man who laid a towel on the couch for me, and found this. This is what they all end up giving me, the bitterness, the hate, what lies underneath.

He stares at me, his defensive expression crumpling into sorrow. "You look a little like her," he says, and his eyes fill up with tears.

Sitting in my car with the windows rolled up and the doors locked I watch the light dim around the crime scene. There's no breeze and the yellow police tape is still. One end has already pulled loose from a tree, trailing on the ground. I'm smoking one of David's cigarettes, and the smoke floats in the hot thick air inside the car.

Allison Avery and I were born in the same year. I grew up like her, in a white middle-class neighborhood of two-car garages and driveway basketball hoops, with two parents and a brother, though mine is three years older and we are not close. It's surprising that, like me, she was on the school paper and in theater, that our paths didn't diverge as early as I would have thought. Before I talked to Carl, I thought Allison Avery was like the girls in my high school that you didn't have to know well to know. These girls started bleaching their hair and wearing bikinis to the swimming pool at twelve. They joined the cheerleading squad and dated football players and were voted to the Homecoming Court. They called their fathers "Daddy" and were rumored to give blow jobs at parties and drove around in red cars with big cups of orange juice topped off with their fathers' vodka. I still think Allison Avery had something in common with those girls. They looked at you and held your gaze and you knew they never thought about the consequences, even getting caught another kind of thrill. I wanted, briefly, to be like them.

I had a friend named Lydia who, despite her wealthy family, had a penchant for shoplifting. She taught me to boost makeup from the drugstore, and to jimmy her parents' liquor cabinet open and replace the vodka we drank with water. When I was thirteen, we got silly drunk and painted our faces with our stolen makeup and fell giggling off the bed. We got caught. My mother cried. I never did it again. One day I noticed Lydia had become one of those girls, her hair as shiny as a model's. After that we passed each other in the hall without saying hello, both of us embarrassed we had ever been friends. For me there have always been consequences.

If I had grown up with Allison, I think there would have been that same moment, when we averted our eyes from each other as we passed, less than a foot apart. I don't know what would have caused it. There is something that she did that I didn't, and because of that, she is dead. I am alive.

When I press the unlock button the click reverberates, and I step quickly out of the car, drop my cigarette on the ground and rub it out with the toe of my shoe. Even out here the air is so dense and wet it's like breathing liquid.

Hands in my pockets, I take a slow walk around the perimeter of the yellow tape. The place has the postapocalyptic stillness that comes when something terrible has been and gone, as though even the air has slowed like a passing car to survey the damage. I've grown familiar with these places—the rubble of a burned house, the lonely stretches of highway littered with bent metal and broken glass—places most people go by as though in slow motion, craning their heads backward for another look at what, thank God, didn't happen to them. Like tourists on a boat ride, they pass safely through the wreckage of someone else's life.

Me, I stop and take notes.

The dirt all around here is crisscrossed with tire marks—some of them made by my car, some of them made by hers. It's impossible to tell now which is which, until her tracks split off from mine, the cops', the other reporters', and veer into that cordoned-off space. There they swerve over a blood-darkened patch of dirt and pass out again, heading off, away from here, the place where Allison died.

5

The Lizard Lounge, where Angela was waiting for Allison the night she died, is the main venue in the city for small bands. I pull into the parking lot, late to meet David. The building is square and windowless, with Lizard Lounge spelled out in green neon script below a giant lizard with pulsing yellow eyes. Before I go in I stand for a moment in the hot parking lot, watching the eyes blink on and off. I hate meeting David at clubs. It's always too loud to talk, and he's only interested in the music. I don't know why he insists I come. About tonight, he said, "This band could take off, I'm not talking just local, and I think they're going to sign with us. You gotta come." David is an A&R man for a small Memphis label. He and his friends sit around smoking joints and cigarettes and talking about Stax and Big Star and seeing Al Green preach at the Full Gospel Tabernacle. Memphis, they say, will rise again. "Memphis is the pop culture Bethlehem," David likes to say, waving his beer bottle in the air. "Elvis may have been born in Mississippi, but *Memphis*," and here he leans back in his chair, tilting so far on two legs that I always think he will fall, "Memphis is the birthplace of the King."

When I walk in the bar, the music hits me in the chest, the girl singer's baby-doll voice rising like a scream. I give my money to the bored bouncer, and while he checks my license I read the band names scrawled in red marker on a bulletin board. The Barnacles. Guys and Dolls. The bouncer hands me my ID back, taking a long suspicious look at my face. "It's really me," I say, and he waves his hand to indicate that I can go past him into the bar.

For a moment I see nothing but dark figures bobbing in unison, smoke hanging in the air from their heads to the ceiling, and I think that if Allison Avery had walked into this room on time Saturday night she would still be breathing now. I wonder if we've ever been here on the same night, bumped against each other in the crowd.

I can't even see the band over all the people, just the face and hair of the bass player, a tiny severed head bobbing in time to the beat. Then I see David, back by the bar, leaning against a stool with one foot on the rung. I stop, watching him. It's one of those moments when the world swings around and a person you've had in your bed looks like no one you've ever seen before. I'm looking at a man, back by the bar, tall and unremarkably attractive, tufts of his brown hair sticking up like he's been running his fingers through it. His hands are large and thick-veined, the fingers long and graceful. He wears a T-shirt and jeans over a lean muscled body just starting to get softer.

He's not smoking, but by the way his knee jiggles I can see he's itching for a cigarette. I think, *That's why he's stood his hair on end,* and then he's David again, my boyfriend of nearly six years.

"Good timing," he shouts when I reach his side. "They just went on."

"Sorry I'm late," I shout back.

"What?" He removes an earplug from one ear.

"Sorry I'm *late.*"

"That's okay," he shouts. "I didn't notice."

"You didn't notice?"

"You're always working," he says. "I expect you to be late." He gestures behind him at the bar, eyebrows raised, to ask if I want a drink and when I shake my head he asks me if I'm sure. Then he turns and orders himself a beer. While he's waiting he points across the bar and shouts, "Hannah's here." I follow his gaze. At first all I can see is a swarm of bobbing, oblivious faces, and then a girl with a frozen grin that pulls her lips back so far it looks painful. She steps aside, and I see my roommate on a tall stool, leaning her elbows on the counter that runs behind her along the wall. She is not so much sitting as propped, one long leg dangling off the front edge of the stool so that her foot hovers inches from the ground. The other foot rests on the rung. A man is standing beside her, talking and gesturing, and though she nods at something he is saying, her eyes are focused on the stage, and her head is tilted away from him. Her red hair slides forward across her face. Even in a resting position, something about Hannah always suggests motion.

"I think that guy's in love," David says, his voice lower now, his lips inches from my ear. "Poor bastard." David himself used to have a crush on Hannah. I listened to him talk about it for six months before he turned his attention to me.

I watch as the man leans in close to Hannah, touching her lightly on the knee. He says something in her ear, and she turns to look at him, raising her eyebrows. She shakes her head slowly, and then he says something that makes her laugh. Whatever the question was, though, the answer is still no, and after a moment he walks away, across the bar to the bathroom. Hannah spots me then, lifting her hand in a wave. She slides forward off her stool and disappears into the crowd.

I lean back against David's warm chest. Over my head he watches the band I can't see and I watch the crowd, trying to picture the dead girl among them, laughing with a beer in her hand as a boy gazes at her, desire in his eyes. On my tiptoes I tilt my head back and say David's name over and over until he hears me and takes the earplug from one of his ears. "Do you know a girl named Allison Avery?" I shout up at him.

He frowns. "Who?"

"Allison," I say, enunciating each syllable, "Avery."

He shakes his head. "Doesn't sound familiar. Why?"

"She wanted to be a singer," I shout. "Just thought you might have heard of her." He keeps shaking his head. "Can you ask around? Maybe someone you know knows her."

"Sure," he says. "Remind me." Then he puts the earplug back in and turns his attention to the stage. The crowd parts enough so that for a moment I can see the girl up there singing, thrusting her pelvis at the microphone like a female Elvis. Then she disappears again behind the bobbing heads before me, and I come down from my tiptoes and see Hannah stepping out of the crowd. She never looks like she's pushing people aside. They part for her, like curtains on a stage. "Here she comes," David says in my ear with amusement, "Miss America." Then he raises his voice and says, "Did you make a conquest?"

Hannah rolls her eyes. "He asked me to do coke with him," she says. "I took a rain check." Then she turns to me and touches my arm. "You look tired," she says. "Hard day?"

"The usual," I say. "You're not going to, are you?"

"Do coke? No. I don't like it. It makes me feel like my heart's jumping on a trampoline. Besides," she says, grinning, "I'm already really stoned. Why taint a perfectly good downer with an upper?"

"You've done coke before?" I've known Hannah for seven years, lived with her for five, and yet she still manages to have secrets.

"A couple of times." She waves a hand vaguely. "Did you talk to that Carl guy?" she asks, and when I nod, she says, "Creepy, isn't he?"

"He had a thing for the dead girl," I say. "Classic stalker. Like that guy Hardwick in college that used to follow you home."

She shudders. "Remember when you saw his room?"

"That was awful," I say. A friend of mine lived on Hardwick's hall, and once when I was passing by I happened to glance in through his open doorway. The room was a shrine to Hannah, pictures of her all over his walls. Some of them he'd cut from the school paper or yearbook. Several were snapshots, like he'd been lurking behind bushes, snapping her picture as she laughed, or searched through her backpack, or sat talking over lunch, gesturing with her spoon. It was frightening and sad, and the worst part about it was, I was jealous. I stood there looking at Hannah, every expression of hers captured. The girl in the pictures was my friend, and yet she wasn't, because I'd never looked at her this way before, as an obsession, a symbol of unattainable perfection. She was so beautiful and remote. I couldn't help but feel it, the terrible strength of his longing for her, and I was jealous. I don't know what part of it I wanted, to long, or to be longed for.

I look at David. His eyes are on the stage.

When the set is over, and the bouncers turn on the lights, David says, "Come meet the band." I trail after him across the dance floor, through the dispersing kids looking dazed in the sudden brightness. David pushes the door to the dressing room open, and I see him framed there, walking toward one of the guys with his hand out to shake, saying, "Great set, great set." I stop and let the door swing closed. I stand with my hands in my pockets and watch two girls bump into each other, then scream, "Oh my Gawd," and dive into a frenzied hug. If I went in there, David would after a moment introduce me, and they would all say how nice it was to meet me and maybe shake my hand, and then I would stand there trying to look interested while they talked about the acoustics, and how the mix sounded, and how David thinks next time they should open with a different song. And tonight I know what I would be doing while I pretended to listen to the baby-doll singer's opinion on crowd reaction, because it's what I can't stop myself from doing when I look at every careless girl in this place.

I would be picturing her dead.

When David finally comes out I'm leaning with my eyes half closed against the wall, and he doesn't see me. He walks past me and stands looking for me, turning his head from side to side. He's muttering something under his breath, but I can't make it out. Then the singer emerges from the room, wearing a tight tank top, a miniskirt, and thigh-high boots, her bleached blond hair moussed into disarray on top of her head. She goes up behind my boyfriend and touches his arm. He turns, smiling. She stands on her tiptoes, her hand on his shoulder while she talks to him, cocking her head ever so slightly to the right. He listens intently, nodding, and then finally she stops talking and he says something back, gesturing toward the stage with his hand. She stands so close to him I can barely see through the space between them.

Finally she takes a step away from him, walking backward, and says so I can hear it, "So I'll see you later?" He nods, and she turns to go back into the dressing room. Watching her go, David spots me. Her eyes glance over me without seeing me and she disappears through the door.

David strides over, grabs my hand and shakes it a little. "Where did you go?" he says. "Do you know how embarrassing that was? I said, 'And this is my girlfriend,' and turned around and you weren't there."

"I wasn't in the mood," I say.

He stares at me. "You weren't in the mood," he repeats slowly, then he turns away from me, shaking his head. Across the bar, the same man is talking to Hannah. I catch her eye and she smiles. "Do you want a ride home?" I mouth.

She shakes her head. "I'm going to walk," she says, her voice traveling the nearly empty room.

I go over to her. "You can't walk," I say. "It's the middle of the night."

"I'll be fine, Olivia."

"Let us give you a ride. It's not safe."

She sighs. "I want to walk," she says. "I'm going now. So I'll see you tomorrow, okay?" She turns to the guy, who has been watching this exchange with wide eyes, and tells him that it was nice to meet him, and then she says good-bye to David and walks out the door. I watch her go, and I wonder if Allison Avery had that easy grace, if she took her pretty body and marched it down the streets at night.

I leave the guy standing there without a word and go to David's side. "Let's go," I say. "I want to follow her."

"She's fine, Olivia," he says.

"It's too far for her to walk."

"She walked here, didn't she?"

"I'm serious, David," I say. "It's not safe."

He sighs. "All right. Let's go."

In our two cars we go after Hannah, and when I come alongside her I roll down my window and ask her to get in. "Go away," she says, not looking at me, still walking. "Or I'll call the police." I glance in my rearview mirror and see the guy from the bar running as fast as he can down the sidewalk toward Hannah. When he catches her he grabs her arm and holds her there, breathing hard. "Are you all right?" he says, casting a suspicious glance at me. "Are these guys following you?"

Hannah laughs, the sound echoing down the quiet street. David must have had enough, because he honks his horn twice and pulls a fast U-turn. When he passes me, I see him leaning out his window waving for me to follow. I take another look at Hannah, and she, too, is waving for me to go. I swing my car around and go after him. I watch Hannah in the rearview mirror until I can't see her anymore, striding up the sidewalk like she couldn't be safer while that guy does his best to put his arm around her waist.

David lives on Mud Island. I follow him down Third past a series of dark and empty parking lots, my headlights shining on the white signs advertising $5 All Day. The cars bump over the trolley line to the Auction Street Bridge, and we are out of downtown, over the river and onto the island. We turn into David's neighborhood and pass down streets lined with houses that remind me of childhood beach vacations, the temporary homes I remember seeing squinty-eyed through the car window at night as we pulled, finally, into town. David's taillights disappear ahead of me as I slow down, looking at the houses. The buildings look lightweight, wood painted in pale yellow, the windows angled and huge, and inside ceiling fans, spider plants with their tangled shoots dangling from the hanging pots. I can't help but feel that here life isn't quite real, as though no one ever has to vacuum, the dusting and the polishing and the washing done with precision by unseen maids.

When I pull into David's driveway, he's letting his dog, Lou, out of the house. The dog stands on his hind legs, his tongue reaching for David's face, and the two of them do an awkward circular dance. Finally the dog sprawls on the ground, and David sits on the front steps. He doesn't look at me as I approach. He's rubbing Lou's stomach vigorously, one of the dog's legs flapping helplessly in the air. I sit down beside him on the steps. He takes a cigarette from a pack and lights it.

"Thought you were quitting."

"I'm working up to it," he says irritably, still annoyed with me. I lean back on my elbows. My body is heavy with exhaustion, but my mind is jumping and the music has left a high ringing in my ears.

A young redheaded woman strolls by with a large white dog. David waves, and Lou lifts his heavy head, ruffs softly, and then returns to sleeping, his barrel chest heaving as though he's just run a mile. "It must be nice to feel that safe," I say.

"This is a good neighborhood," David says. I close my eyes and open them again. The woman has passed on. The street has the cheerful misty look that comes from bright artificial lights at night, and sometimes a breeze shifts the air that sits wet and heavy on my skin.

David is quietly singing "Every Little Thing She Does Is Magic" by The Police. It's his favorite song. I know a great many facts about David: his favorite songs, his fear of heights, his statistics: twenty-seven, six feet three, and 190 pounds, give or take one or two. Hair: brown, that shade that tells you he was blond as a child. Eyes: gray. I can remember the first time I was close enough to notice that they weren't blue, as I had thought, but gray, and how that made him

seem unusual, intriguing, mysterious. I can't remember how it felt
to think those things about him.

"You know her?" I say.

"Hmmmm?"

"That girl who just walked past."

"The redhead? I don't know her name. I just run into her sometimes when I'm out walking Lou. Lou really likes Petra."

"Who's Petra?"

"Her dog," he says. "That big white dog." A firefly blinks, inches
from David's face. "You know," he says, "that was the first time I'd
been to a club in at least three weeks."

"That's not like you," I say. When I first knew David, he was constantly searching for new and better fake IDs, not because he
wanted to drink, like most of our friends, but because he wanted to
go see bands. After a good show, he'd come back and tell me that he
thought this band had something, his face shining, as breathless
with excitement as if he were in the band himself. "Someday I'm going to discover someone, Olivia," he'd say. "Someone big."

"I don't know," he says now. "If I know a band is good, that's one
thing. But I haven't got time to waste on crap anymore."

"What about all those lectures you gave me?" I say. "'You have to
take a chance, Olivia. You never know what you might find.'"

"Yeah, well," he says. "I get tired of coming home with my ears
ringing and smoke in my clothes. Too many bands confuse loud with
good, you know?" Lou rolls over on his back, paws flopping in the
air, and David leans forward to rub his stomach hard. "I came home
from work today and took Lou out in the yard, and the bastard ran
off," he says. He thumps Lou. "You bastard."

The dog is part hound, and so stubborn and half stupid, chasing
anything that moves. Every now and then I come in the room and
find the two of them in a frenzy of love, Lou pinning David to the
carpet, vigorously licking his face with his washcloth of a tongue.
Lou and I don't really get along. "I left him out in the yard and went

to the bathroom," David says. "When I came back he'd run off. I had to walk two blocks over before I found him."

"Why did you leave him in the yard?" I say. "Didn't you know he'd run off?"

"I thought he'd be okay." David shrugs, nudging the dog with his foot. "Goddamn dog," he says, grinning. "You goddamn dog."

We are silent. I'm waiting to see if he's going to ask me what I did today. David doesn't like it that I'm on the police beat. He was happier when I still wrote stories about senior citizen swimming meets and small town arguments over zoning.

"Stupid dog," he says, tugging on Lou's ear. Watching him, I find myself wrestling with an urge to provoke him.

"David," I say slowly. "You remember me asking if you knew Allison Avery?"

He nods.

"I was asking because I stood over her dead body yesterday morning. I was this close," I say. I slide a couple feet away from him and reach my arm out to touch his knee. "This close. Somebody picked her up, raped her, ran her over with her car, and left the body." He winces, lifting his cigarette to his mouth. "The rest of the day I spent talking to the people she knew, her friends, her family, and watching them cry. Some of them didn't even know before I told them what had happened to her. Last night I watched a cop stop a man from shooting his wife." I tap his knee with my finger, trying to decide how much to tell him about that man, the gun he pointed at me through the window.

He drops his cigarette and rubs it out with his foot. Then he reaches his arm around my shoulders and slides me back up against him. "I don't like to think about you around guns," he says quietly. "It scares me."

I say, "What did *you* do today? You dealt with the pretty girl singer from Guys and Dolls. You probably went out to lunch and talked about what you think of their guitar sound."

David stiffens, dropping his arm. "Well, maybe tomorrow I can arrange for some corpses at the office," he says. "Maybe then my job will be as important as yours." He picks up the pack and grabs another cigarette.

"That's not what I'm saying."

"Oh?" He lights the cigarette. "What are you saying?"

"Forget it," I say. "I'm sorry I brought it up."

Lou raises his head and looks at us, his eyebrows dancing up and down with worry. "It's okay, boy," David says, his voice low, soothing. I think about a postcard David sent me one summer, when he was on vacation with his friends. Every sentence ended with an exclamation point. The beach is gorgeous! We went swimming! I miss you! Only the "Love, David" went without one.

"I had a bad day," I say. "Let's not fight."

David nods, bringing his cigarette to his lips. I put my hand on his thigh and play imaginary piano keys. "Für Elise," the right-hand part, which is all I remember from five years of lessons. The red-headed woman walks by with her dog again, on her way home.

A radio is playing in the house across the street. By the look on David's face I can tell he's trying to hear what the song is. "Okay," he says absently. Then he smiles. He recognizes the song. He starts to play the drum part on my leg. I close my eyes and let my irritation go. The warm air wraps around me like a blanket and David's fingers dance up and down my thigh. I try to imagine us, like this forever, but I can't make it seem real.

The dog's chest rises and falls with his heavy breathing. David sings a melody without words. A breeze slips across my face. Then I say I'm going to bed.

"Okay," David says, "I'll be there in a second." I kiss him on the cheek, stand up, and go inside, where it's cool, and everything David owns is neat in its proper place.

6

There is nothing more important in this city than crime. It's always there, running its current through your body, like the high electric hum of computers and fluorescent lights.

There can't be anyone in this city who doesn't know that Allison Avery is dead, who doesn't know the way she died. It led the morning news on every channel again today. They picked up on my hundredth-victim line, showed the spot where flowers and candles and scribbled prayers now cover up the bloodstains on the ground. You all know, *this is the modern world and its dangers,* and you touch your own skulls, thinking how fragile they must be, no matter how solid they might feel beneath your hands.

I'm sitting at a round table with seven men in jackets and ties, poking powdered eggs with a fork. I'm listening to them trade stories—who was shot in what neighborhood, which stores have been robbed. This is the Concerned Citizens for a Better Memphis breakfast, where the mayor comes to address the problems that concern them, which is to say he comes to talk about crime. Waiters quietly refill our water glasses as the mayor takes his napkin from his lap and stands to approach the podium. A hush falls over the room. I reach for my notebook.

The mayor is a good-looking man, tall and strong-featured, his skin a deep, rich brown, and as he steps up to the podium I note how nicely his silver-gray suit hangs on his shoulders. When he begins to speak his voice rolls out over the room like a flag unfurling. "Ladies and gentlemen, thank you for coming here today." He takes his time, scanning the room, and for a moment his eyes rest on my face. He smiles as though he knows me, and automatically I smile back. "Let me begin by saying that I know you all love this city as much as I do, and that, loving it, you are in pain every day over the dangers that threaten it."

Dangers, I write down idly. He goes on to push his plans for revitalizing the downtown, for annexing parts of Shelby County, and then he comes to the budget, and from the budget to increasing the police force, which brings us back around to crime.

He says, leaning in close, "There is no more fundamental concern than our safety and the safety of our children. I won't stand up here and say that it won't cost money. But I want you to know that money won't be wasted. We're going to make Memphis a safer city. We are going to look the criminals in the eye, and say to them with a unified voice, 'We will fight back.'" He pauses for applause, which bursts forth as though everyone here has simply been waiting for the chance.

"You all read in the paper the terrible story about a young lady brutally killed in one of our public parks, already the hundredth murder victim in our city this year. A promising young person, daughter of an esteemed physician, working in medical care. Who knows how many lives she might herself have saved if she had been allowed to live? We've all seen too many of these stories, about people from all walks of life, young and old, black and white. We must refuse to let those deaths be in vain. We will let the tragedy of that young woman's murder drive us to strike back at those who took her life, who have taken so many of our city's young lives."

He looks at me again as he says this. I can feel his eyes on me as I copy down his words in my notebook, and I wonder if he knows that Allison Avery is mine.

❧

Afterward I wait patiently while the mayor shakes hands, and smiles, and thanks people. I page through my notes, wanting to ask for details, how many new officers, and where.

"Mayor," I say when it's my turn, "I'm Olivia Dale, from the newspaper."

"Yes, Miss Dale," he says, taking my hand. "I've been seeing your byline. You've done a fine job with that poor young woman's death. A terrible, tragic story."

"Thank you," I say, feeling a flush rise in my cheeks.

Another man approaches, and the mayor turns toward him, still holding my hand. "Charles Franklin," he greets him. "I want you to meet Olivia Dale, the young woman who has had the sorrowful task of writing about Miss Avery's death." He passes my hand to Charles Franklin, who squeezes it and says, "A tragedy. A young, innocent life cut down like that."

As the mayor turns away, Charles Franklin goes on to tell me about a story he thinks I should write, an inner-city program run by a reformed drug dealer now looking to give kids a place to go after school. I make a note of it, thinking I'll pass it on to Neighbors, and then I look around for the mayor. He's in the center of a cluster of people, with more waiting outside the circle. I give up. I'll call his office for the details.

Heading for the door, I see a man walking purposefully toward me, his hand extended. He looks at me as though he knows me, but I can't place him. I keep a smile fixed on my face, searching my mind for his name. "Miss Dale," he says when he reaches me, taking my hand. His voice is deep, his grip firm.

"Hello," I say, trying to keep the uncertainty out of my voice. "How are you?"

"I'm well, thank you," he says. He pauses, letting go of my hand. "I'm the Reverend James Freeland. You and I met last year, at the ground breaking for my new church."

"I remember," I say, relieved. I drove around in a panic for half an hour before I found the place and climbed out of my car. The rain was coming down so hard the ink ran down the pages of my notebook when I tried to take notes. All the congregation in their Sunday clothes stood huddled together under umbrellas singing "To God Be the Glory" while the women's heels sank into the mud. "Is the church finished?"

"Not yet, not yet," he says. He rocks back on his heels, as though to physically change the course of our conversation. "You know I am the president of Concerned Citizens for a Better Memphis."

"Yes," I say, though I didn't.

"As the mayor says, one of the biggest concerns for the people of this city is crime, as you yourself are well aware. I appreciated very much the article you wrote about our church, and I believe you would be interested in a meeting we're having tomorrow night."

"Reverend, I'm not sure . . . ," I start.

"Miss Dale," he says gently, looking into my eyes. "Are you or are you not concerned about crime in this city?"

"I am," I say.

"Because I believe it is just as important to write about what the people are doing to fight back as it is to write about the times when we lose."

"All right," I say. "I'll be there. But, Reverend," I call after him as he turns to go, "if a crime does occur, I'm afraid I'll have to miss the meeting."

"Then we will hope one does not," he says.

At the police station, the first news I hear is that a dog carried a woman's head onto a playground in a poor black neighborhood and dropped it at the feet of two children. "If it rains, it pours," Peggy says with a sigh when I call to tell her I'm going to the crime scene.

Driving down Vance, I pass old hotels turned into low-income housing and enormous, abandoned houses with their paint faded or flaked off, shards of glass where there should be windows. All these old Memphis houses, coming down slow, crumbling into dust. Two black women in sundresses sit on one of the porches, too hot even to fan themselves, watching their children splash in a wading pool in the yard. If I traveled the other way down Vance, I would come to the part of Midtown near the Annesdale Historic District, where rich white people sip iced tea on their wraparound porches, sitting on swings beneath the green profusion of hanging plants.

Turning into the housing projects, I hear on the scanner that the police have found the woman's body in a nearby Dumpster. This time, I know I won't get close enough to see anything, and I'm not sorry.

Each building here is like an outsized brick with doors and windows, and the whole place is just brick after dull red brick, kids sitting on the tiny porches, riding old bikes over patches of dead grass and dirt, down streets lined with beat-up and ancient cars. Getting out of the car, I see that the area around the small playground is crowded with the cops and the curious. The nearby fertilizer refinery fills the air with the smell of chemicals and manure.

I spot a cluster of people and head over to see a circle surrounding two children, a young woman standing behind them with a protective arm around each. "I'm from the paper, ma'am," I say to the woman. "Are these the children?" She nods. I ask if she's the mother—yes—and if she minds my asking them a few questions. It would be so helpful, I say, and would only take a minute of their time. She nods.

I squat in front of them. The little boy is wearing a bright yellow windbreaker and clutching a toy car close to his chest. The girl twists the bottom of her striped shirt round and round in her hands. "Can you tell me what happened?" I ask.

The smaller child is shaking and can't even look at me. He looks guilty and frightened, his eyes screwed shut as if he's flinching from punishment. His sister says, "It was bleeding," in an awed voice. "The Tuckers' dog had it in his mouth."

"What did you think when you saw it?" I ask her. She looks at me, chewing on her lip. "I know what it's like," I tell her as an image comes to me of a head rolling over blacktop, dark hair flying. "I've seen things, too."

She nods, and her face clears a little. We understand each other. "I thought it was a joke," she says. "But it was a real head." She shakes her own head. "Poor lady. Now she's dead."

"Did you know the lady?" I ask.

She nods. Her mother says, "She's from this neighborhood. Her name's Bernadette Smith." She points to a woman standing silent and expressionless inside the moving crowd. "That's her sister Janice."

The little boy suddenly bursts out, "I touched it." His voice trembles on the edge of hysteria. "I touched her *face.*" He wails, and his mother bends to scoop him up. I can imagine it, the way his little voice shook when he said he wasn't scared to touch it, the way his nervous laughter erupted into screams when he pushed his fingertips against that skin and felt it give.

"He didn't know," the little girl says. "We didn't think it was real." She wraps a protective hand around her brother's ankle. "It's okay," she says, turning her face up to his. "You didn't know." He shudders against his mother's shoulder.

The mother says, "We have got to get out of this neighborhood." I don't know if she's talking to me, her children, or herself. She hugs her little boy close. How frightening it must be to have these horrors thrust upon you. At least I choose to see the things I see.

The little girl looks at me calmly, waiting for me to say something.

"Is there anything else you can tell me?" I ask her.

She thinks for a minute. She says, "I've seen a lot of bad things. That was the worst thing I've ever seen."

Bernadette Smith's sister Janice stands with her hands in the pockets of her jeans, staring so hard at something that I involuntarily turn to follow her gaze. There's nothing to see but the street, the playground, the crowd kept back by the yellow police tape. "Ma'am," I say. "I'm terribly sorry about your loss. Would you mind if I asked a question or two about your sister?"

"Go ahead," she says.

"Do you have any idea who could have done this?"

Slowly she moves her eyes to my face, then looks away again. She shrugs. "My sister was a prostitute," she says. "She was a junkie and a prostitute, and she'd been on the streets about ten years now. I'm the one raising her kid and holding down a job. I don't know who killed her, somebody she fucked, somebody she owed money. The way she lived, something bad was bound to happen. Just a matter of when."

I write that down: *just a matter of when*. Watching the woman's face, I wonder at what point her life diverged from her sister's, so that her sister is dead, and she is alive. I ask, "What made her become a prostitute?"

Inside her pockets, Janice Smith's hands ball into fists. "Bernadette made a lot of bad choices," she says. "Ever since we were kids. I feel sorry for those two." She gestures toward the two children with her head. "Having to see that. Probably see it in their dreams."

"Did Bernadette work for someone?" I ask. "A pimp? A boyfriend? Anyone she would've been fighting with?"

"Bernadette had a lot of boyfriends," she says, putting a sneer into the word. "There's nothing I can tell you." She moves her eyes back to my face. "It was just a matter of when," she says again. "Just a matter of when."

As I walk away I turn my head to take another look. The area just inside the crime tape is thick with cops, two of them laughing together, one slapping the other on the shoulder. Passersby stop and turn their path toward the crowd, their mouths slowly coming open, shaping the words "what happened, what's going on." Felicia Fitzgerald from Channel 2 is speaking into a microphone, her brow carefully furrowed with concern as she glances down at some notes in her hand, out of view of the camera. In the midst of the crowd, unmoving, stand the mother, holding her children close, and Janice Smith, her body drawn up tight and her face hard, absorbing yet another blow.

Back in the newsroom I read my notes over and over, trying to find a quote I can use. Finally I settle on the things the little girl said, on the mother saying she had to get out of that neighborhood, on Janice Smith saying she felt sorry for the children. I add in the statement from the cops. Then I sit typing in "just a matter of when" and deleting it, once, twice, three times. Finally I leave it in and send the story to Peggy.

Later Peggy comes to my desk to ask me to edit the story to a one-inch news brief. I cut it bare. Body found. Known prostitute. Police investigating. One short paragraph is all this death is worth.

In the afternoon I write an obituary and spend some time on the phone with the highway patrol, checking fatalities. Two teenagers died last night in a drunk-driving accident. I hate to write 18 or 19 after a dead person's name. When I look at the obits, I scan them for ages. On good days everyone who died was over sixty. If the dead person is under fifty, I'll skim the obit, and if she's my age, I'll slow down and read it word for word, looking for cause of death, relieved if it says "after a long illness." Those deaths are expected and couldn't have been prevented by one less drink at the dinner table, one turn of the steering wheel.

Allison Avery's picture is propped up against my computer. The boy kisses her cheek, the beer bottle tilts in her hand. I watch her as though she's going to kiss that boy, to finish that beer, to wink at me, shape her lips around my name. Somewhere there must be a picture of me from college, looking just like this, half-drunk and flushed with giddy joy. I page through my notes and make a list. *Pretty. Hard worker. Singer. Thief. Slut. Sweet. Young. Churchgoer.*

Pothead. Drunk. Tease. I wonder what pulls these things together to make a person, if it's only skin and bone.

One page is blank except for what her brother, Peter, first said to me. I add that to the list. *Dead.*

I call Angela Schultz and ask if I can come talk to her. I tell her I've spoken to Carl Fitzner and would like to get her version of some things.

After a long pause, she says, "All right. I guess I'd better set the record straight."

Angela's apartment is sun-bright and spacious, with the walls muted shades of green and peach, and shiny hardwood floors. The carefully hung pictures, the plants, the curtains, all make me think of how little Hannah and I have done to our apartment, how temporary it still looks. We have crates stacked in the kitchen, box springs and mattresses on the floor in our bedrooms, a dead plant on the porch in a cheap plastic pot.

It's true that Angela Schultz, at home, is not the same demure girl I saw at the doctor's office. Her hair is down, falling past her breasts in a dark smooth stream. She's wearing jeans and a clingy V-neck T-shirt, her feet bare, with red toenails. I can't picture her the way Carl does, snorting butane, cracking a whip. If those things are true, I'll see it in her. What you are always bubbles up eventually, a dead body rising to the surface of a lake.

"That little shit," Angela says after I tell her a few of Carl's opinions. Then she tells me that Carl was infatuated with Allison, that she turned him down and he soured. He left a poem tacked to her door about how he used to want to cradle her like a kitten but now he could see she was no soft kitten but a vituperative snake who had bitten him and run hot poison through his veins.

"Something like that," she says, sighing. "He's not normal. Even all these years after high school, he still followed her around. He would turn up at her gigs, at places where he knew we hung out. She was much nicer about it than I would have been." She doesn't look angry anymore. Her eyes well up. I pretend not to notice, writing in my notebook: *vituperative snake.* I think of Carl's tongue, the way he darted it out, picked the tobacco off it. I write down: *not normal,* and underline it twice.

Whips? Angela says. Knives? She hauls out pictures of herself in tight jeans in high school and shows me that she painted her fingernails black. She asks, "So what?," turning the thick pages of her photo album. "Didn't you wear too much makeup in high school?" she demands. "Didn't you?"

"Of course." The truth is I can't remember when I stopped. It doesn't matter, because nothing wins a source's trust like sympathy. I have looked into a murderer's eyes and said, "I understand." It's nothing to pretend I coated my face with foundation and blue eyeshadow until I was twenty, that that could be me in the pictures, wearing jeans as tight as skin.

The front of Angela's album is decorated with cut-out felt letters spelling her initials, the name of her high school, and the year of her graduation. She tells me she decorated matching albums for herself and Allison. Purple and white, she says, running her fingers over the felt like it's braille, were their high school colors. Allison is in some of the pictures, her hair like an explosion, permed into curls, her lashes thick with mascara. There are pictures of her with boys, with beer bottles in her hands, and in one it looks as though the white object between her fingers is a joint. In another Allison is on a stage in a high school gym, leaning into a microphone with a band behind her. "You can't really see, but that's me on the drums," Angela says. "I was terrible. Allison said, 'Angela, honey, your talents lie elsewhere.' She knew how to tell you the truth without making you feel you'd been criticized."

"Is that a joint?" I ask, pointing at the photo.

"Yeah, I think so," Angela says, leaning in close.

"So Carl wasn't lying about some things," I say.

"Of course not," she says. "Allison gave great parties when her parents were out of town. We knew how to have a good time."

"And when you got older?"

She sighs. "Look, I'm sure some people would describe her as a little wild. But a lot of them would be Bible beaters like my mother."

"Mine too," I say, and she smiles.

"Allison wasn't like Carl says," she says. "She did what she wanted, that's all."

She shows me a picture of the two of them standing together in flowered dresses, squinting into the sun, arms wrapped around each other's waist. "We were just normal girls," Angela says, "me and Allison."

"What about your boyfriend?" I ask. "The whip scars?"

"Truth is, his daddy beat him. If he said it was S and M, it's because that sounded better to him than telling people his daddy whipped him in the basement when he got drunk." She shows me a picture of a slim dark-haired boy in a heavy metal T-shirt and sunglasses, a cigarette in his hand, a smile pulling at his lips. "He wanted to seem tough," Angela says, "but he was just a poor scared boy." She shuts the photo album. "People have secrets," she says sadly. "They're just not always the ones you think."

"I believe you," I say.

She leans forward and touches my knee. "Men like Carl," she says, "they have a way of making you feel dirty just for being a woman. You know what I mean?" She watches my face seriously while I nod. Then she smiles. "I'm sorry," she says. "I never offered you a drink."

Although I said it to win her over, I do believe her, because our opinions of others are built on details, Angela's felt-lettered photo album versus Carl's Zippo lighter. It's true that I left Carl feeling like he had revealed himself as the kind of man who believes a rape victim in a low-cut shirt deserved what she got.

It's also true that if I see a woman walking down the street with her breasts bouncing out the top of her shirt, I think *slut,* just like he does.

I am watching Angela's face. She cries a little, I hand her a tissue, she grows angry, I shake my head with her in disgust, she wanders into her philosophies, I murmur agreeably. I prompt. I've stopped taking notes, but I'm listening to everything she says, and the whole time I'm thinking, *Why does she trust me? I never said I wouldn't put any of this in the paper.*

According to the surveys, no one likes a reporter. No one is supposed to want to talk to me. The secret I know is that almost everyone does. They're on their guard at first, until they realize what they have in me. I'm a rare thing, a listener so interested she writes down their rambling sentences word for word. It starts slowly, with the facts. Once they get started they can't stop. One revelation tumbles after another. Because they want to be heard, they want to explain themselves, they want to be famous, because seeing their opinion in print makes it fact. And because I listen they think I am their friend.

Often they don't remember what they've said. Some of them read their words in the paper and call my editor screaming that I've gotten it all wrong. One woman insisted on coming in to hear the tape of her interview. We sat in an editor's office and listened together as her voice recited each and every word I'd put in the paper. Still she didn't believe it. "But that's not what I meant," she insisted. She pointed at me. "She knew that wasn't what I meant."

Whatever I knew or didn't, it doesn't matter what she meant. I reported what she said.

Angela says that she took Allison to an abortion clinic when they were sixteen. "I talked her into it," she says, her eyes fixed on my face. "I said she was too young. And if I hadn't . . ." She chokes up, presses her hand to her mouth. "If I hadn't, maybe she would have had it. And now, she'll never have any."

"You couldn't have known," I say. I reach over the coffee table and squeeze her hand. She squeezes back and holds on. I think of the girls I knew in high school who got pregnant. Some of them kept coming to school until they were too big to fit in the desks, and then you'd see them working at McDonald's or the 7-Eleven. The wealthier ones disappeared for a few days and returned with stories about visiting an aunt in the city. One girl left town halfway through the school year. When she was back at school in the fall she joined the cheerleading squad, as though she wanted the whole school to see her in those short skirts, shaking her pom-poms in the air. She was on the JV squad. Varsity wouldn't have her.

"I'm just glad her mother doesn't know," Angela says. "She'd be thinking there was a piece of Allison she could've kept." I remember how my own mother shook her head over those girls, said they were all careless and sinners, and some of them murderers. I never knew how she knew about them. I didn't tell her.

Angela dissolves again into gasps and sniffles. Her hand is hot and moist and my shoulder begins to ache but I hold my position. "What's her mother like?"

"I hate to say this now," she says. "But the truth is I never liked her. She looked at Allison like she wanted something from her. I always thought she was jealous of me, that she thought I wasn't good enough for Allison."

"And Peter?"

"Peter's a great kid," she says. "He idolizes Allison. You know how some younger kids, it's almost like they have a crush on their older siblings? He's like that. She's a good big sister. She takes care of him, looks out for him. Once, before he got his license, she let him drive their mother's car and he hit a parked car, did some damage. Allison took the blame. She had to pay the deductible, and she wouldn't let Peter help, said it was her fault for letting him drive." She squeezes my hand. "That's what she was like. Those things Carl told you, that's not what she was about at all."

She lets go of my hand to reach for a tissue, and I sit back, resisting the urge to rub my shoulder. "What about Allison's boyfriend?" I ask. "What's he like?"

"I already told you," she says sharply. "No boyfriend." Her hands hide her face. I don't ask again. "I'm just crying all the time," she says in a small voice. "I can't make it stop." She looks at me and I notice that her eyes are enormous and green, and that she has again blinked wet mascara onto her skin. If Hannah had just been killed, I wonder if I would still put on my makeup.

"Is it because I miss her?" she asks me, voice trembling. "Or because I'm afraid?"

"Both," I say. "It's only natural. You're grieving." I reach for her hand again.

"What happened to her, it could've been me. It could still be me." Her hand is still beneath mine, and she is not crying now. She says, "It could be you. You even . . ." She stops without saying "look a little like her," watching my face. Her voice is suddenly so firm, so cold, I lift my hand from hers and put it back in my lap. "You know that, don't you?"

Across from me on the sofa is a girl like any number of girls, pink-cheeked with blush and emotion, smooth and painted and smart enough without being too smart and pretty even in her grief. Across from her she sees a woman her age, wearing no makeup but lipstick, hair cut short, businesslike in a skirt and tailored shirt, a closed notebook beside her on the couch. We've been sitting here comfortably, talking like friends, but now as she stares at me my head whirls with the thought that neither of us has any idea what lies beneath the skin.

Then her eyes tear up again, and she puts her face in her hands. "She didn't deserve to die this way," she sobs. I watch her, my discomfort fading. I know exactly who Angela Schultz is. I could take a few details and put her in the paper for anyone to see, captured in a sentence like a moth beneath a glass.

At the door, I turn and hug her. She sags against me like her own weight is unbearable. Her body in my arms is everywhere soft, her breasts against me, the cotton of her shirt beneath my hands. She takes a trembling breath. "Thank you for listening," she says.

"You're welcome," I say. I don't say "It's what I do." "Please call me if you need to talk. Not for a story or anything. Just if you need to talk."

She pulls back, but keeps one hand on my upper arm. "Listen," she says, "I need to go over to Allison's and get some things before her mother clears it out. Would you come with me? I can't bear to go alone."

This is how easy it is. A few tissues, one hug, and this girl opens up her life and asks me in. I like her. I feel sorry for her. We could be friends, although I'm using her. If it's hard for me to tell the difference, she can't be expected to. I think about asking her why she's asking me, if she's sure, if she wouldn't rather take another friend of Allison's instead of me, a reporter.

When I joined my college paper, the news editor told me the best way to get an answer someone doesn't want to give is to close your notebook, exchange pleasantries, and then, as an aside, ask the question you really wanted to ask. Off guard, because you're standing, and smiling, and your notebook is tucked away inside your bag, the person answers. You say thank you, go out in the hall, and write it down. I think about telling her that just because I don't have my notebook out doesn't mean I'm not taking notes.

"Of course I will," I say. "When?" We make plans to meet at the building Monday morning, and she says she'll see me later. "By the way," I say, turning at the door, "who was the father?" I'm imagining a lean-muscled football player, or a dark troubled boy like the one in Angela's picture.

She looks at me blankly.

"When Allison got pregnant."

"Oh." She gives a short, bitter laugh. "I think it was her boyfriend at the time. Tommy."

I hesitate. "You *think*?"

She shrugs. "Allison was never exactly faithful. She sort of . . . scooped people up."

"Even Carl?"

"Oh, Carl. I think she went out with him once, kissed him maybe." Watching my face, she says, "You have to understand. She was special. Everyone wanted to be around her. It was like she was buzzing with something."

"Sex?"

She frowns, taking it as a criticism of her dead friend. "More than that. It was like, she wanted to *touch* everybody. Not just physically." She shakes her head. "I can't say it right." Lifting her eyes to the ceiling, she says slowly, "It was like she wanted to touch the whole world."

We stand in silence. I think, *and this death is what finally made her famous,* though I know that what this girl is talking about is not exactly fame. Then Angela drops her gaze to mine. She presses something into my hand and closes the door. I'm left standing in the hall, the picture of Allison I had been forming blurred once again, like a home movie that keeps slipping out of focus. I look down to see what she's given me. It's the photo of her and Allison in flowered dresses, their arms around each other, smiling into the sun.

I come back to twenty messages on my voice mail, three of them hang-ups, one a man who says, "Oh," in a surprised voice and then breathes heavily into the phone until the beep cuts him off, sixteen of them women telling me they know who killed Allison Avery, every one of them with the same rushed, anxious inflection in her voice.

I spend a couple of hours calling them back, all of these women giving up their fathers, their boyfriends, their ex-husbands as the murderer, their voices sharp with bitterness and fear. He hits me, they say. He hit my mother. He broke my leg. He drinks too much.

He's a thief, he's a liar, he's a drug addict. He tied me up and raped me, one woman says, and then breaks down, sobbing quietly into the phone.

I take down the names they give me. One name I recognize, though it takes me a few minutes to remember why. He's dead. His body turned up on a golf course almost three months ago, and still his daughter tells me with conviction that three days ago he raped and killed a young girl. "I know it," she says tightly. "I just know it."

I don't think any of these women know what happened to Allison Avery. All they can tell me is what has happened to themselves.

After I hang up with the last woman, I rest my forehead on my desk and close my eyes. I keep thinking about things Carl Fitzner said to me. When he told me about Allison's fast crowd, her low-cut shirts, her short skirts, he meant the same thing Janice Smith meant. Just a matter of when.

The phone rings right by my ear, making me jump. "Olivia Dale," I say into the receiver, my voice sharp, annoyed.

There's a silence. Then, "It's Peter Avery."

I sit up straight. "Hello, Peter. What can I do for you?"

"Do you know anything?" He sounds businesslike, abrupt, not the lost boy from yesterday.

"There's been no news," I say carefully. "Have you talked to the police?"

"Why bother," he says bitterly. Then he lapses into silence. I wait it out. After a moment he says, "My mother asked me to call you. She's going to offer a reward."

I reach for my notebook. *For information leading to an arrest in the murder of.* "How much?"

"Ten thousand."

"That's a lot," I say before I think.

"Yes," he says slowly, scornfully. "It is."

I'm picturing a headline: VICTIM'S FRIENDS, RELATIVES SAY SHE 'DIDN'T DESERVE TO DIE THIS WAY,' or something better, depending on what the mother says. Subhead: Distraught parents offer reward. "Peter," I say. "I can run this information, but it would help if I could speak to your parents. A personal appeal is always—"

"No," he cuts me off. "They're not ready. My mother is . . . my mother is very private."

I consider pushing it further. "All right," I say finally. "When they are ready, I want you to know I'd do it right."

"You'll be the one they call, don't worry," he says. "We don't want to deal with television."

"Okay," I say, letting it go. I soften my voice. "How are you?"

He swallows hard. "I don't know."

"You don't know?" I say gently.

"I've gone running a lot, and I, uh . . . I just . . ." He trails off, then says, his voice very small, "I don't know."

"How are your parents?"

"My mother just sits in Allison's room. I tell her that I'm going outside and she says, 'Please don't leave,' and it's like she thinks if I step outside the house . . . but she's not talking to me. She's not talking to my father. She's just sitting on the edge of the bed. This morning I walked by there and she was curled up around Allison's pillow. Not crying. Her feet were hanging off the end of the bed." He swallows again and stops talking.

I wonder if, lying there with her knees to her chest, the mother knew she was mimicking her daughter's death pose.

"You have a brother, right?" Peter asks me. "Are you close?"

"Not really, no."

"How come?"

"My family's very religious," I say. "I'm not."

"What's your mother like?"

For a moment, I'm at a loss. Then I say, "She's nice. She does a lot of charity work."

"Charity work?" he says, and I think I hear in his voice that I should be able to say more than that about my own mother. "Do you see her much?"

I find myself telling him about the last time I saw my mother, for dinner at my brother's house. How they asked me about my job, and I answered with the truth. How my brother, Rob, took me aside afterward and hissed at me through his teeth, saying I wasn't to talk about such things in front of his kids and for God's sake didn't I know it wasn't normal? How my mother said she couldn't understand why I had to intrude on other people's tragedies, though I know she scours the papers for them. How all my life she has read to me about the carjackers who would box me in on a dark road, the men who would drag me from my car at stoplights, the rapists who would come upon me walking alone through the park and force me into the bushes.

"She doesn't have to read me those stories anymore. Now I write them."

"Now I am one of those stories," the boy on the phone says. "Or my sister is."

I wince. "Oh God, I'm sorry. How thoughtless of me."

"That's okay." There's another silence. Then he says, abruptly, "I think you're a good person."

Tears spring into my eyes. *How odd,* I think, blinking them away. "Thank you."

"I have to go," he says. "I'll talk to you again."

"I hope so," I say.

I hang up the phone and sit for a little while, staring at the wall. Then I pull his sister's picture closer to me. I trace the curve of her face with the end of my pen. *Who are you?* I think. *Tell me.* Some superstitious impulse makes me close my eyes and wait for the answer. The only voice inside my head is my own.

"Olivia?"

I open my eyes. Evan is looking at me, his head cocked quizzically. He says, "Me and Bishop are going to get a drink. Want to come?"

The M&O is Bishop's favorite hangout, close and dark, with a pool table in the back and city politicians and eccentrics caricatured in bright colors on the walls and the ceiling. We come here after work two or three times a week to have a beer or two and ease into going home. Bishop likes to ask questions—what's the most pain you've ever been in, what's the craziest thing you've done for love—and after Evan and I tell our stories, he looks into his beer mug like it's a crystal ball until one of us asks him the same question. Then, no matter how good our stories were, he tops them.

Tonight, Bishop buys a pitcher of beer and says, "What's the worst story you've ever had to write?"

"How do you mean, worst?" I say. "I can tell you the stupidest story I ever had to write."

Bishop nods at me, filling my mug.

"When Charles and Di first hit the rocks," I say, "I was working for the Nashville paper, and they asked me to call marriage counselors and ask them if the marriage could be saved."

"You're kidding," Evan says.

"I called one guy, who was horrified by the question, and wouldn't talk to me. I was so embarrassed, I lied to my editor and said I had called seven people and none of them would talk to me. She said, 'You'd think people would have more of a sense of humor,' but she didn't make me do the story."

"Okay," Bishop says, unimpressed. He nods at Evan. "What's yours?"

"It would have to be one of those man-on-the-street stories," Evan says. He acts it out. "Excuse me, sir, what do you think about the situation in Bosnia?" Then he says, in a redneck drawl, "Kill 'em all, let God sort 'em out."

"Ah," Bishop says. He takes a swig of his beer, sets it down slowly, and gazes deeply into it.

"Okay, I give," I say. "What's yours?"

"Well, my children," he says. "You may recall that kid who got killed in DeSoto County. Yours truly was assigned to go talk to the parents, never an enviable task. When the photog and I got to the parents' house, the lawn was packed with reporters, photographers, TV cameras, everything. And the father was standing there, drinking a beer, wearing a T-shirt." He forms a square with his hands, like a director sizing up a shot. "Now picture this," he says. "The shirt has a bottle of Jack Daniel's on it, and there's this hand wrapped around the neck of the bottle. Across the top it said 'Jack-off Daniel's.' And everybody's snapping this guy's picture."

Evan roars, slapping the table. "You're shitting me," he says.

"You're changing the rules," I say. "What's that got to do with the worst story you had to write?"

"That was a pretty bad case," he says. "That murder." I can see him withdrawing into himself—his head down, his shoulders pulled in.

"If that's what you mean," I say, "the story I just wrote is the worst. The dead girl." I reach in my pocket and find the picture Angela gave me. "Let me show you guys something." I put the photo on the table. They lean in close to see.

"Is one of them her?" Evan asks.

"Yeah," Bishop answers for me. "The one on the left." Then he looks at me. "What about it?"

"Look at her," I say, and obediently they fix their gazes on her face. "You don't think I look like her, do you?"

"Why?" Evan says.

"People keep telling me I do," I say. "I don't believe it."

Bishop sits back in his chair. "Hate to tell you, but they're right," he says. "There's a slight resemblance."

Evan is nodding, looking from the picture to my face and back again. "Definitely," he says. "Around the eyes."

"Sergeant Morris said it was the shape of my face," I say. "You guys wouldn't have noticed if I hadn't asked."

"I noticed earlier," Bishop says.

"And you didn't say anything?"

"I don't say everything I think," he says, turning his gaze back to his beer mug.

"Forget it," I say, reaching for the picture and slipping it back in my pocket. "It's no big deal." Then I reach for the pitcher and top off our mugs.

Bishop appraises us. He says, "How about this: What's the farthest you've ever gone for a story?"

"Into a Dumpster," Evan says, and laughs. "I ruined my shoes."

"Did you find anything?" I ask.

"I showed you," he says. "That witchcraft magazine." He lifts his glass and says, "Front page!" We clink our glasses against his.

Bishop nods at me. "Come back to me," I say. "I have to think. You answer."

Bishop tells us about the time he was trying to get a quote from a state senator suspected of tax fraud. While he's talking, I signal the waitress and order a bourbon, straight up. I watch her walk across the bar and bring the drink back, the little glass in the center of her large round tray.

Bishop tells us he followed the guy to a four-star restaurant, where he had his terrible car valet-parked, borrowed a jacket and tie from the maître d', and sat down to a five-course meal, keeping his eye on the senator while he ate his Cornish game hen. When the senator got up to go to the bathroom, Bishop followed. He sallied up to the urinal next to his. "So we're standing there pissing, right," Bishop says, "and I zip up and turn to the guy, who's still going, and I stick out my hand to shake and say, 'Hello, Senator, I'm Martin Bishop from the paper. What can you tell me about the charges made against you?'"

"What did he do?" Evan says.

"He shook my hand," Bishop says. Evan bursts out laughing. "I guess it was a reflex," Bishop says.

"I hope you washed your hands," I say.

"Of course," Bishop says. "With soap and hot water."

"Did he give you a quote?" Evan asks.

"He said, 'They're absolutely false, son. I'm guilty of nothing. Now pardon me while I zip my pants.'"

"You're making that up," I say.

Bishop holds his hands in the air, palms out. "Would I do such a thing?" He nods at me. "Now you."

"I'm thinking, I'm thinking," I say.

"Time's up," Evan says.

"I don't know," I say. "I don't think I've done it yet."

The waitress passes by and leans down to pick up my glass. "You want another, honey?" she says.

"Sure," I say. "Why not." Evan raises his eyebrows at me. "What?" I say.

"You drank that fast," he says.

"I'm a reporter," I say. "I'm supposed to drink hard." When the waitress brings my drink, I pick it up and throw it back in one motion. It burns going down but I don't flinch. I smile at Evan and turn the glass upside down on the table. He shakes his head. Bishop laughs. "Go easy, cowgirl." He winks at me. Then he says, "Why did you become a reporter?" and looks from one to the other of us before he fixes his eyes on Evan.

"Because I wanted to be like Woodward and Bernstein in *All the President's Men,*" Evan says. "I wanted to be the person who found the truth and made sure others were held accountable for their actions. It sounds silly . . ." He trails off.

"Go on," Bishop says.

"I felt like I had a mission."

Bishop nods and turns to me. "Why did you become a reporter?"

I spin my empty glass on the table. "The same reasons as Evan."

Bishop smiles and shakes his head. "Why did you become a reporter?"

"I just told you."

"If you ask a cop why he became a cop, what do you think he'll say?"

"Because he wanted to protect and serve," I say, looking around for the waitress.

"And why do you think he really became a cop?"

"Power. A gun at his side and a siren so that he could go flying past everybody else on the road."

"Right," Bishop says.

"That's not fair," Evan protests. "Some cops do want to protect and serve."

Bishop ignores him, keeping his eyes on me. "Why did you become a reporter?"

"Why don't you ask Evan again?" I say, signaling the waitress to bring me one more drink.

"Evan told the truth," he says. "I want to know what about you makes you do this job. Are you curious? Are you a thrill seeker? Do you find it easier to examine others' lives than to live your own? Why did you become a reporter?"

I look hard at him. "I just did." Sometimes it doesn't feel like something I chose. It's just what I became, the way I grew a few inches every year until I was five feet two.

"It's never that simple and you know it," Bishop says. "You'd never take that answer from someone you were interviewing."

The other day I said to Sergeant Morris, "I need to know," and he didn't ask me why. It never occurs to anyone to ask me why. That's my job. "Okay, how about this," I say. "My mother says I always wanted to watch people. She says I would cry if someone held me so that I couldn't see the rest of the room."

"So you were born for it?" Bishop asks me, turning the words over in his mouth like they taste bad.

"I guess," I say. "Why did *you* become a reporter?"

"I'm curious," he says. "I'm a thrill seeker. I find it easier to examine others' lives than to live my own." He grins at me and lifts his glass as though in a toast. "Don't worry," he says gently. "I've been at this longer than you."

I have another drink while they make their way through the pitcher. When the beer is gone, Evan says it's time to go. "One more drink," I say. "Come on."

He stands up. "You've had enough," he says. "I'll drive you home."

"No thanks," I say. "I want another." I turn to Bishop and smile. "Bishop? One more drink?"

"Can't turn down a lady," he says, deepening his southern accent. "I'll have a whiskey."

Evan leaves, saying again that I shouldn't drive home. Bishop and I sit and order drinks and he tells me stories, some of them terrible, all of them funny. He imitates a drunk who was arrested taking pot-shots at neighborhood pets in the street, weaving a little as he sights down an imaginary gun, loading on the accent as he calls, "Here, kitty, kitty, kitty." He tells the "Jack-off Daniel's" story again.

"That's terrible," I say, over and over, laughing helplessly. "That's terrible."

"Let me tell you, kid," Bishop says. "That's not the half of it."

There is nothing Bishop doesn't know about this city. Everywhere he goes he sees a story he wrote.

If I go to the music festival next May, I'll watch crowds of people walk right over the spot where that car crushed Allison Avery's skull. I'll watch them: the dreadlocked white kids in hemp necklaces, the cowboys in tight Wranglers and sharp-pointed boots, the middle-aged couples in denim jackets, the frat boys in khakis and baseball caps, the girls with too much makeup, breasts swelling out of tank tops. The guys squeezing the girls' butts, the people huddling under umbrellas as their feet sink into the mud, the enormous bouncers glaring with their backs to the stage, the screaming women, grabbing at the air when Al Green throws down a rose. Plastic beer cups and candy wrappers will litter the ground, churned to mud by the rain and the thousands of moving feet. There will be no sign it ever happened. But I'll know. I'll know exactly where.

I have to call Hannah to come pick me up. "You're wasted," she says accusingly as soon as I get in the car. "You're not walking straight."

"Well, hello to you too," I say. This is a bad drunk. When I finally get in my bed, I'm going to have to keep one foot on the ground to stop the room from spinning. We pull over three times so I can lean out the door to vomit.

Our neighbor Denise's car is blocking the driveway, so Hannah drops me in front of our duplex and goes to find a parking place on the street . . . I'm on my hands and knees at the edge of the curb, my whole body swaying. I get up and go to sit in a dignified manner on the front steps.

I wake up. There are steps beneath my back, and the porch light shines right in my eyes. I turn my head from side to side and see that my arms are spread out above my head. I lift my head a little and look down. My legs are spread as wide as my arms, and my skirt is hiked up around my waist. I can see my underwear. Blue stripes. I hear footsteps. "Hannah?" I call out, but no one answers, and when I raise my head again, a man is just passing me. He turns to look at me, and the thought of what I must look like hits me so hard I almost feel sober. "Hey," he says. "Are you okay?"

"I'm fine," I say. I sit up and yank my skirt down.

He takes a step toward me. "I'm fine," I say again, but my voice wobbles, and he takes another step toward me and starts to reach out his hand. I squawk, and he jerks his hand back. "Go away," I shout.

He takes a step backward, hesitating. He is not tall, but thick and powerful through the shoulders, his features indistinct in the darkness beyond the porch. The porch light flickers. My thighs, pressed together, are sticky with sweat. No one else is on the street. When I turn my head I see nothing but darkness, houses where everyone sleeps behind locked doors.

I stare at him. He stares at me. If he moves in my direction I'll scream. "What do you want?" I say. My voice comes out terrified.

I think I see him smile, a ferocious appraising smile, and panic bubbles up in my throat. "Look, miss," he says. "I'm just being nice. I'm just a Good Samaritan." His voice drips with scorn. "Take a look at yourself, why don't you. Ask yourself what *you* want. You're the one sprawled out half-naked on the street." Then he rotates on his heel and stalks away.

I bite my fingers to stop my hands from shaking. I was passed out on the front porch, arms and legs out, spread out like a starfish just waiting to be slipped in someone's pocket. "Where are you, Hannah," I say. "Where are you, where are you."

Then I'm halfway across the porch, half falling, half leaning on Hannah. "Did I pass out again?"

"Yes," Hannah says.

"Where are we going?"

"To bed."

"Hannah," I say. "I feel awful."

"Okay," she says, propping me against the wall so she can unlock the front door. She looks at me. "You're going to have a bad headache."

In my bedroom, she eases me onto the bed and goes out of the room. When I close my eyes I see red, blood red. Everything spins together like clothes in a drier, the dead girl, the man on the street, my messy room. Hannah is standing there. I prop myself up on one elbow and catch her wrist with my other hand. "You have to be careful," I tell her. "The world is filled with danger." I shake her arm. "Promise me you'll be careful."

"You're just drunk." She extracts her wrist from my grasp.

"Oh. Okay." I lie back down. My throat fills with the urge to cry. "A lump of sorrow," I say, stupidly, trying not to weep.

"Open your mouth," Hannah says. She puts two aspirin on my tongue and hands me a glass of water.

Then it is so quiet I think Hannah has gone until I feel her taking off my shoes. She comes to the head of the bed and holds out my contact case. "Here," she says. "Pop them out." The small effort of sitting up makes me nauseous.

"This is going to be really bad," I say.

"When I drove by, after I dropped you off, you were spread-eagled on the front steps, right under the light. It was like you were in a spotlight," Hannah says. "It scared me. I ran home. What if you had passed out like that, on the street outside the bar?"

"I was sitting up properly," I lie. "I was careful."

"You were passed out, Olivia," she says. "After all those lectures you've given me. All that talk about inviting it. You idiot."

"I don't want to talk about it anymore, okay? Please?"

Hannah slips my earrings out of my ears. She says nothing. I know she won't say anything tomorrow, and if I'm lucky I won't even remember just how bad and scared and stupid I feel right now. Hannah runs her hand across my hair. She shuts out the light.

7

Tiny black and white kittens live underneath the porch of the house next door. One day I spent an hour trying to entice them closer by waving a stick, clicking my tongue. One came within inches of me before bounding away. It was sunny, the kind of sunny when patches of grass seem spotlit, and the hairs on my arm were golden in the light. Across the street a man and his two daughters were washing their car, and the light bounced off the car and off the water that pooled in the street. The houses here are all the same, one brick level, hunkered down low to the ground. I don't know any of my neighbors. I wanted to follow those kittens onto their own lawn but I didn't want their owner to come out and yell at me.

I don't see the kittens now. I'm sitting on our front porch drinking a glass of water. The sun beats down like noon, though it's only 8:30. Today is Allison Avery's funeral, and I am so hungover I can barely stand. I can't stop picturing myself, sprawled here like a dead thing, like a careless, stupid girl. This morning I pulled off my clothes before the mirror, searching my body for signs that someone had touched me, that someone else had pulled up my skirt. There was nothing, only the red marks my own fingers left where I pressed them hard against my skin.

My body feels like it's trying to turn itself inside out. If I call in sick they'll think I don't want to go to the funeral. I'll get assigned a new beat, or even fired. I'll be known as the one who didn't have the stomach, for alcohol, for blood, for death.

So I have to get up now, and go stand in the shower, and try to keep from vomiting when I bend over to shave my legs. I have to put on a black dress and find my notebook and have Hannah take me to my car, because the funeral is this morning and I have to be there. I have to get up now.

I have to go.

At funerals I try to stay away from the immediate family, and in that way try to make a bad thing better. I don't care what Peggy says about quotes. I get what I get. At first it looks like I'm going to get nothing, because when I try to walk into the funeral home, an undertaker comes up on quiet feet and asks me to leave. So I wait, leaning against my car in the hot parking lot, trying not to throw up. I flip open my notebook and scan my notes. *Drank too much,* it says across the top of one page. I shut the notebook. When everyone emerges, blinking into the sunlight, I follow them, over the arch of the Dudley Street Bridge, under the intricate wrought iron sign for the Elmwood Cemetery.

I once wrote a story about this cemetery and the eighty thousand corpses I called "inhabitants" in the paper. Annie Cook, a madam who opened her bordello to the sick during the yellow fever epidemic in 1878. Robert Church, the city's first black millionaire. Dorothea Henry Winston, daughter of Patrick Henry. Fifteen hundred yellow fever victims tumbled together in mass graves called No Man's Land. This is a beautiful place, bursting with greenery, and narrow winding roads take you past ornate statues of angels and the dead. As I get out of the car, through the damp still air comes the sound of a bell.

At the graveside, I see the brother, Peter, with his parents, two people of whom I can only say: moderate height, dressed in black. It's not a good day for black, my dress clinging to my skin. The newspaper photographer, Bryce, snaps a picture and the father shoots an angry look in his direction. I keep my distance from Bryce, standing on the other side of the crowd. I fan my face with my hand. My stomach lurches.

I don't know how I'm going to write this story, because I can't keep my mind on anything. I keep reaching down to smooth my black skirt, as though I'm going to walk up to someone asking for a quote and discover it hiked up around my waist. I snap to attention after a few minutes, and I don't remember what I've been thinking about. I scan the crowd. Peter's mouth is set in a straight thin line, his eyes fixed on some point in the distance. The mother has an almost identical expression on her tight face. The father's shoulders shake as he reaches in his pocket for a handkerchief. Angela is demure in a tailored black dress. Her hair is up, tendrils sticking to the back of her wet neck. With her head bowed she stares resolutely into the grave, lifting her hand from time to time to wipe her eyes with a crumpled tissue. She seems to have learned a lesson—no mascara runs down her cheeks.

Carl stands right behind Allison's mother. The material of his jacket strains as he raises an arm to squeeze the mother's shoulder. He leaves his hand there a moment and she reciprocates, holding his thick fingers in her own slender ones. He sees me and gives me one of his tentative smiles. I lift my hand in a greeting, then look away. Toward the back is the dead girl's neighbor, the young woman from Mississippi, without her children. She is openly weeping, her hands cupped around her face. The only other face I recognize is the doctor's. A pretty blond woman leans against him, her features arranged in an expression of polite sorrow.

Near the grave of Allison Avery stands a tall stone angel with spread wings, her face a picture of heavenly rapture, her eyes uplifted. This is a tribute to Mattie Stephenson, a girl who came to Memphis after her fiancé married another and broke her heart. I remember her story. The audiotape guide I rented at the cemetery office said she "gave her life" nursing victims of the yellow fever epi-

demic. Imagine a time when so many people died in this city that
bodies were piled in the streets, so numerous that no one could
identify their faces before they were hauled away. I doubt it was
possible, then, to care when one more person died.

There will be no statue, no angel, to mark Allison Avery's grave,
just a plain granite block engraved with her name, the dates of birth
and death, the words "Beloved Daughter." People who come here
won't notice the headstone, except perhaps to note the shortness of
her life. She won't be mentioned on the next audiotape, though like
Mattie Stephenson she was young, and this city took her life. What
could they say Allison Avery gave her life for?

I manage to stand for fifteen more minutes before a wave of nausea hits me so hard I feel like I might faint. As fast as I can I walk
away, trying to step lightly on the gravel path, and then when I can't
go any farther I duck behind a bush and throw up. I'm on my hands
and knees on the ground, beside the flat tablet engraved with the
score to "Dixie." After I stop shaking I crawl backward, retreating
from the mess I've just made, and put my head down on the ground
between my elbows.

"Miss?" a woman's voice says from behind me. I turn my head a
little and catch a glimpse of an older woman in church clothes. "Are
you all right?"

"Fine," I whisper. She hesitates for a moment before she walks
away, leaving me alone, she thinks, with my grief.

I don't see Peter when the burial is over, so I go looking for him,
walking off between the headstones. I'm holding on to my bag with
both hands like it can keep me standing up straight.

I turn a corner, and there he is, lying lengthwise on a bench with
his feet still on the ground, as though he had been sitting but
couldn't support his own weight anymore. His open black jacket
hangs off either side of the bench; his white shirt is untucked and
pushed up, his hands resting on his bare stomach. He hasn't seen

me, and I watch as his fingers explore the bottom of his rib cage, pushing on the bone as though he's surprised to find something that substantial inside his own body. He lifts his hand to his face and runs a finger around an eye socket.

When he sees me, he turns his head and frowns, his hands going quickly to pull down his shirt. "What do you want?" he says. "Leave me alone." He wants to sound angry and dismissive but his voice cracks over the words. He closes his eyes, the simplest way to make me disappear. This seems to happen very slowly—I can see his eyelashes tremble—and then he starts to cry.

"Oh," I say, and approach him, taking his hand. His hand doesn't move so I close it in both of mine and rub his fingers as though to warm them, though they're as hot as my own. My face is so close to his I can feel his breath. He opens his eyes, squinting up at me. "You're that reporter," he says, trying to steady his voice. "What are you doing here?"

"I was sent here," I say. I wonder if he thinks the photographer is right behind me, ready to snap this picture, if he thinks I'm already writing the caption—"Boy, 17, mourns his sister's murder. The killer is still at large." And then I can't stop writing captions in my head—"Peter Avery, 17, brother to the dead girl." "Brother, 17, lets reporter hold his hand." I picture this photograph in the paper—me, all in black, crouched over his body, shadowing his face. I sit on the far edge of the bench, still holding his hand. His whole body shudders. Then there is a whispering sound, and after a moment I realize that it's him, saying something under his breath. "Oh God," he says, "oh God oh God oh God," until it's not even like words anymore, just breath, just painful breathing. I am not good at this. Questions cluster in my throat. *Who's the boyfriend? When's your mother going to talk to me?* It would be heartless to ask these things now. I think, *Win his trust.* I consider touching his soft cheek, splotched red with crying. If I were another sort of person, I would take him in my arms but I just hold his hand until he stops crying, with a deep breath that he holds for a long time.

He sits up and says, "I've got to find my parents." He's still holding my hand, and in this moment I realize that he is holding it, it's not just me hanging on.

I squeeze his hand again and he gives me a terrible smile. "It's just me now, you know," he says. He's not crying anymore, but I can see the film of water balanced on the skin that rims his eyes. Then he stands, taking his hand from mine, and pulls himself up tall. He tucks his shirt back in, straightens his jacket, and rubs his eyes hard. "Do I look like I've been crying?" he says, turning to show me his face. His nose is red, his eyes pink and watery.

"No," I lie.

"Good," he says. He nods once, sharply. I watch him walk away.

For a long time I sit there with one hand pressed to my wretched stomach, the other flat on the bench where the stone is still warm from his body. I don't know what it's going to say underneath my by-line in tomorrow's paper. All I can picture is a big blank space, two columns of nothing under my name.

It takes me all afternoon to write the funeral story, fifteen inches I would normally pound out in less than an hour. My mind feels as wrung out as my body. When I'm finally done I send it to Peggy and leave, telling her I don't feel well. I'm halfway to David's house before I remember the Reverend James Freeland's anticrime meeting. "I'm not going," I say out loud, even as I'm turning the car around.

Half an hour later I am sitting in the basement of the Brighter Day Baptist Church. One of the long fluorescent lights flickers—brighter, dimmer—above my head while the Reverend James Freeland describes "why we're all here tonight." I'm not sure why I'm here tonight, as this story is probably destined for the weekly Neighbors section unless somebody with a gun shows up to mug us all right now.

I shift in my metal folding chair, slowly unsticking one thigh, then the other, knowing from experience they'll just get stuck again. I glance up at the reverend's face, heavy with sincerity, and back down at my feet tapping lightly on the slick gray floor. The long tables, the low ceiling, and the metal and plastic decor, the lingering smells of cooked meat and disinfectant—I could be sixteen again, sitting in a prayer circle at my parents' church, head bowed, looking at my pink flowered dress, my hands in my lap. Here is the church, here is the steeple, open the doors . . .

". . . Olivia Dale," the reverend booms out. I jerk my head up to see everyone half turned and smiling in my direction. "I want y'all to tell her how the crime in this city has touched your lives and your neighborhoods, and how we're going to fight back. We're going to send out a message today."

Of the twenty people in this room, all but four are women, one a young man who looks to be about my age. He's slouched low in his chair, his arms crossed over his chest, and doesn't turn his face toward me. Everyone else looks at me expectantly. I lift my hand in a tiny wave. "Hi," I say. "Thank you so much for asking me here. I just want to listen, and then if it's all right I'll ask you some questions at the end."

Clothes rustle and chairs creak as they turn their attention back to the front. One woman keeps her eyes trained on me. She is a heavy dark-skinned woman with darker shadows under her eyes. I smile and nod at her. She nods back, but does not smile. Then slowly she turns herself back around.

They talk for a while about the drugs infiltrating their quiet, middle-class neighborhood, where many of them have lived for twenty years or more. A sixty-something woman named Katie Mae Olson remembers sleeping on her porch without a worry. Someone else describes hearing gunshots in the distance, seeing people she's certain are drug dealers pacing on corners, watching strange cars prowl her street. "We've got to unite," she says. "We've got to give them someone to answer to."

"Amen," the reverend says. "When I see a strange car I walk past it so they know I'm watching. They'll get the picture they're not wanted and leave. It's a prime fact," he says, leaning forward in his chair, "if we sit back and do nothing, our quiet community can change overnight."

I take notes while they talk about the need for increased police presence in South Memphis, about long waits for officers to respond to 911 calls. I make a note to myself: *check average response time.* Someone mentions the possibility of a petition calling for increased manpower. One man talks about starting a Neighborhood Watch.

Then the heavyset woman pushes up onto her feet. "My daughter Tamara was eighteen years old when somebody shot her dead on the sidewalk near our house," she says. "Eighteen." She grips the back of the chair for support, though when she speaks her voice is slow and even. "The police came, but they never found out a thing, and the monster who did that to my baby is still out there. That was last year, a year ago May fourteenth. You think anybody cares about that now? There's been a hundred murders since."

I copy her words into my notebook, thinking it's probably closer to 130, 140, thinking *this is good, I'll probably use this.* I write down: *Check stats. Get her name.*

"Nobody cares," she says. "Nobody's got the time to care."

A murmur goes up of "we care" and "we love you." She turns her head toward me, her eyes trained on my face. "And that white girl," she says. For a moment I think she means me, and I work to keep her gaze, resisting the urge to sink down in my chair. "She's all over the front page. When my Tamara died, not one reporter came to ask me anything. Not one. What's the difference between Tamara and that girl but that she's white? Both young. Both gone. Both dead and gone."

I drop my eyes to my notebook. I write it down: *nobody cares.*

Katie Mae Olson has risen from her chair to put her arm around the woman. "We care about your Tamara," she says, her voice rising with indignation, "and we're going to fight. This used to be a nice place to raise your children, and we're going to make it that way again. We're not going to stand for crime anymore." She turns to me. "You put that in the paper," she says. "We're tired. And we're not going to stand it. Not anymore."

They all turn to me now, so I ask, "Do you think you can make this neighborhood as safe as it used to be?"

"I hope so," Reverend Freeland says. "Residents used to be able to sleep out in their backyards at night without fear of some maniac running and raping and cutting somebody's throat. I don't know that we'll ever again be able to sleep in our homes and not worry about whether or not we've locked our doors."

Katie Mae Olson tightens her grip on Tamara's mother, who sags a little against her. "I'm sixty-eight years old, and I've lived in this city all my life," she says. "I'll tell you one thing, it's not what it used to be." She looks around the room, taking in the upturned faces of her neighbors. "But I'll live here till I die, and I'm damned if I'll give up until then. This is my city." Her voice rises as she leans toward me. "You tell everybody that. This is my city too."

I write that down and circle it. I can already tell her quote will be my last graf. It's the perfect way to end.

I'm walking through the dark parking lot toward my car, the fat yellow moon hanging low in the sky. I can feel the humidity settling into my hair, the temperature probably only ten degrees lower than it was before sunset. When I get home I'm going to strip naked and stand in front of the air conditioner until it goes away, the stickiness in my hair, between my breasts, at the backs of my knees.

Somewhere behind me a man calls out, "Hey." Without stopping, I glance back over my shoulder. The young man from inside is walking toward me, one hand lifted in my direction. "Hey, wait," he calls out again. I turn to face him, taking a couple of steps backward. He ducks his head and jogs toward me.

"Thanks," he says when he comes to a stop in front of me. He exhales hard. I say nothing, waiting for him to speak. He extends his hand, and I take it. It's warm and dry. "I'm Russell Freeland," he says.

"Olivia Dale," I say automatically.

The corners of his mouth lift a little. "I know," he says. "I was inside." He lets go of my damp hand and wipes his palm on his jeans. Then he sees me watching him and stops.

"Are you related?" I say, nodding toward the church behind me.

He turns to look back at the church. "Yeah," he says. "He's my dad."

I wait for a moment. He just stands, rubbing his fingers hard on the back of his neck. "Okay," I say, the heat making me impatient, "nice to meet you."

"Wait, please," he says. He shifts from foot to foot. "I need to talk to you."

Over his shoulder I see the church door start to open. A man's voice calls, "Russell?"

His body tenses, as though bracing for a punch to the gut. "It's my dad," he says. His voice goes low, urgent. "I've got to talk to you. Can we meet somewhere?"

"What's this about?"

"Allison Avery," he says, taking a step back.

"Allison . . . ," I repeat. Without thinking, I put my hand in my bag, searching for my notebook. "What about her?"

"I know her," he says. He presses his lips together and blinks rapidly. He takes another step back.

I put my hand on his forearm to stop him. "Do you have something to tell me?"

"Russell?" his father calls again. "You out there?"

"Coming," he yells. Then to me he says, "I've got to go. Can I talk to you?"

"Give me your number, tell me how to reach you."

"I'll call you," he says. He spins on one foot and starts jogging back toward the church.

"When?" I call after him. He doesn't answer. I stand and watch as he reaches his father, who puts his arm around his shoulders and leads him back inside the church. The heavy door eases shut behind them.

I let myself into David's house with the key he leaves inside the mailbox. Lou greets me at the door, woofing mightily and rearing up on his hind legs. I shout no at him until he drops to all fours, and then I pat him once or twice and he licks my hand. "Where's your daddy?" I ask him, wiping my hand on my pants. He lets his tongue dangle out, looking up at me with his droopy eyes.

I like being at David's when he's not home. Lou follows on my heels as I wander from room to room, looking in cabinets. Everything is in order. I open a drawer and run my hand over his neatly folded boxers. A white T-shirt lying on the bed has the scent of him still.

On his desk is a shoe box labeled "Demo Tapes," with two neat rows of cassettes in plastic cases. He's even alphabetized them. I run my finger up to the As, and there it is. Allison Avery. He told me he'd never heard of her. I pull the tape out and stand for a moment with it in my hand.

I put the tape in my pocket and start searching his desk, going through drawers, rifling through stacks of papers, looking for something else marked with her name. Lou paws at my leg. "What do you want?" I ask him. He cocks his head. Then I look at what I've done to the desk. The drawers are all open. The papers are splashed across the desktop. Some tapes have fallen to the floor.

Hurrying now, because he might come home at any minute, I start cleaning up the mess I've made, shutting the drawers and stacking the papers. The phone rings, and I pick it up, thinking it might be David.

"Hey," Hannah says. "I thought you might be there."

"Didn't I tell you I would be?"

"What are you doing?"

"Cleaning up some papers I knocked over," I say. I step back and look at the desk. It looks neat and organized, and I don't think he'll notice I touched it. I take the tape with her name on it out of my pocket and look at it again. He gets a lot of these tapes. He probably just forgot her name.

"Why so quiet?" Hannah says.

"You know the dead girl?" I say. "I found one of her demo tapes on David's desk."

"Creepy," Hannah says. "Did you listen to it?"

"Not yet. I wonder why he didn't tell me he had it."

"Did you ask him?"

"I asked him if he knew her. He said no."

"He probably forgot," Hannah says. She pauses. "Unless of course, he's the murderer."

"That's not funny, Hannah."

"Oh come on," she says. "It is, too. Jesus, you're paranoid."

"What do you mean?"

"How many years have you been with this boy?" Hannah says. "Don't you think he would have told you if he remembered the girl's name?"

"She was very pretty. Maybe he had an affair with her and he doesn't want to tell me," I say, only half joking. I turn the tape over in my hand. "Maybe I don't know him as well as I think."

"He tells you he loves you, right?" she says. "What else do you want?" She laughs. She thinks that's funny.

"I want everything," I say.

"I don't think you do," she says.

For a moment I say nothing. I listen to her breathing. "What are you doing now?" I ask.

"Listening to Denise have sex. It's so loud today."

Denise lives in the other half of our duplex, which does not have thick walls. We know a lot about her life considering how rarely we actually talk to her, because she lives it at a very high volume. She has a crazy boyfriend, who, she screams, does *not* treat her *right*. From time to time, judging from the sounds she makes, he treats her very right.

Hannah wants to know if I'm spending the night here, and I tell her yes, that I'll see her after work tomorrow. We hang up the phone. I turn on a TV movie, and Lou flops down at my feet. He keeps his eyes trained on my face, his anxious eyebrows dancing. On the television, a man searches frantically for the woman he loves. She's been in an accident. She lies in her hospital bed, doing nothing but breathing, and he waits all night for her eyes to open. In the morning they tell him to go home and get some sleep, and when he gets home he can't be strong anymore and he just sinks to the floor and cries.

So what I want to know is, if David came home and I wasn't there, if I were dead, missing, lying in the hospital, unconscious, beyond the reach of anything he could do, what would he do? Would he sink to the floor, slide down the wall to his knees, would his breathing turn jagged, gasping, would he make any sound, would he sob, cry out, would he hold his hands out in front of him like this man, down on his knees, his hands spread, impotent, powerless, in love? Or would he hang up his jacket and go to bed, and come visit me in the hospital early in the morning, bringing flowers? Would it be tulips, because they're my favorite, or roses, because they're his?

A hand brushes against my thigh. I sit bolt upright in the armchair, blinking. It's dark. "Allison," I say. My outstretched fingers touch skin.

"Who?" David says. He is leaning over me, smiling with gentle amusement.

"Oh." I sink back into the chair. "What's going on?"

David settles on the arm and strokes my hair back from my face. "You were sleeping." He holds something up. "What's this?"

It takes me a moment to understand, as though I'm translating from a dimly understood language into my own. I want to ask David, "Who *are* you?"

"It's a tape," I say.

He laughs softly, his fingers still in my hair. "I know. Why were you sleeping with it? You had it clutched in your hand."

"I was looking at your demo tapes. This tape, it's Allison Avery."

"So? Who's that?"

"Jesus, David, don't you listen to me? Don't you read my stories? It's the dead girl. The one I asked you about."

"Don't shout, Olivia," he says evenly. "I haven't had time to read the paper lately. I didn't remember her name."

"Did you listen to it?"

He shakes his head. "I just brought that box home from work yesterday. She must have sent it to me right before she died."

He pushes up off the chair and goes in the direction of the stereo. I close my eyes. In a moment Allison Avery's voice fills the room.

"How old was this girl?" David asks, whispering so his own voice won't drown out the sound of hers.

I tell him she was twenty-four. I know why he asked. It's not the voice of a girl. If I didn't know better I'd imagine a much older woman, someone who's known twenty years of loss and heartbreak.

"Gorgeous voice," David says in the space before the next song begins. "What a waste."

"Would you have called her?" I ask.

"Definitely."

We listen in silence, her voice with us like a ghost in the room.

Neither of us moves to pop the tape out when it's over, listening without speaking to the whirring of empty ribbon through the speakers. David turns off the stereo and finally it's quiet. Then he comes back to me, and I'm surprised to see that his eyes are filled with tears. "It's terrible," he says.

I don't say anything. "What happened to her?" he says.

"I told you. Somebody grabbed her outside her apartment. They beat her, raped her, killed her."

David shakes his head like he can't believe it.

"I told you this before," I say.

He reaches for me and pulls me into a hug. "Now it seems real," he says, his breath warm against my ear. He tightens his arms around me.

I close my eyes. I stood over her body in the dirt. It always seemed real to me.

"I love you," he whispers.

I want to say it back but I don't. How can I, when I know he's only saying it because he's imagining me dead?

David is beside me when I wake up in the morning before the alarm goes off. I put a hand on his cheek, soft from sleeping. He sighs when I kiss him and then opens his eyes and smiles. "Good morning," he says.

"We'll see," I say.

We make love without kissing. No matter how long or tightly I hold him, he is never close enough. He gets out of bed and goes to shower. I lie there, sweating, stupid with desire.

8

At my desk, I read my story about the funeral over a cup of coffee. From the story, someone who wasn't there could learn what the minister said about faith and comfort, what expressions the family members wore, what flower—a lily—the mother carried. My lead begins, "Like the lily her mother laid on her coffin, Allison Avery was . . ." I skip ahead, already embarrassed by something I wrote only yesterday, its slick sentimentality. I quoted Allison's employer saying how much she will be missed, Angela saying what a wonderful friend she was, and some Avery cousin saying the family has faith in the police to bring about a swift resolution to the case. Someone who wasn't there wouldn't know how hot it was in the sun-baked black clothes we wore, how quiet it was in the moments after the minister stopped speaking, how that boy's hand felt inside my own. Next to the copy is a photo of Allison's mother, leaning forward with the flower in her hand. Her husband stands behind her, his head bowed. Half of Peter's body appears at one edge. Some careless person cropped out the rest.

I put down the paper and check the phone book for James Freeland. There are two J. Freelands. I call the first number and a querulous old woman complains that she's never heard of Russell Freeland. When I call the second, I get a machine. A girl's voice recites the phone number but no names. I hang up before the beep. If you leave a message, you can't call back.

I check my E-mail. One from Bishop. "I'm bored already," it says. "Any news on your dead girl?" I write back, tell him I'm shit out of luck with the cops and not sure what to do next. A few minutes later he appears at my desk. "Let's take a ride to the station," he says. "I'll try one of my guys for you."

As we pass a cheap motel on the way, Bishop says, "Guy killed his wife there."

"Oh yeah?" I turn to watch it go past. "How?"

"Strangled her."

"See that corner?" I say, pointing. "That's where that professor got busted picking up a twelve-year-old prostitute."

Bishop says, "What happened to him?"

"Still teaching literature to freshmen," I say, and laugh.

At the police station I sit on a bench and wait while Bishop goes into homicide. After a few minutes Sergeant Morris comes out. I stand up.

"Got nothing to tell you," Morris says as soon as he sees me. He walks toward the water fountain, and I trail after.

"Does that mean there's nothing going on, or there's nothing you can tell me?"

"Can't really answer that, can I?" he says. "Just write the same thing: police still following up leads." He bends over the water fountain. I can't tell how old he is. He looks as old as sixty to me, but police work seems like the type of thing that could age you early.

"Come on," I say. "How many times can I write that story?"

"I read your piece on the funeral," he says, wiping water from his mouth. "You're holding off on this one, aren't you. No quotes from the immediate family."

"Give me something," I say. "Anything."

He holds his hands out toward me. "I got nothing, Olivia. Nothing. Now I'm going in the bathroom, so quit following me, okay, sweetie?"

"Will you let me know . . ."

He cuts me off. "You just keep asking," he says. "Sooner or later I'll have something to tell."

I go back down the hall and take my place on the bench again. A woman sits next to me, hitting the bench hard. She's about fifty, white, with gray-blond hair to her shoulders and a face creased as crumpled paper. She's wearing green polyester pants, a yellow shirt tucked into them. A worn and enormous purse balances on her lap. She clutches white-knuckled at the handles.

I ask her how she is, and when she says not too good I tell her I'm sorry and ask her what's wrong. To her it seems like I'm just being polite.

"It's my brother," she says. "The cops called him in for an interview."

I tell her I know how that is and watch her twist her wedding band round and round her finger.

"He's not even a suspect," she sighs. "I hope not, anyway. He's got a history."

"He's got a record?"

She pops open her purse, searching through it for something. Bottles of medication rattle. She pulls one out, empties a pink pill into her hand and swallows it without water, tossing her head back. Then she says, "He's a sexual predator. They're talking to him about that girl."

"What girl?"

"That one got raped and killed at the park," she says. "Don't you read the papers?"

"Do you think your brother's involved?"

"He's no killer," she says.

"But he's a rapist?" I look hard at her. Her face is set, nothing in it to show what her brother is to her, except maybe those deep lines in her skin.

She starts rummaging through her purse again. "He is what he is. Nothing you can do."

I watch her going through her purse, looking for something in it to tell me how it is to live this woman's life. I see crumpled tissue, lipstick, a wallet bulging with change, a comb full of gray-blond hairs. She pulls out a roll of mints and offers me one. I take it. My mouth is dry. I get up and go to the bathroom, where I stand inside a stall and write down everything the woman said. When I get back to the bench, she's gone.

After a while Bishop comes back out, shaking his head, and says, "Let's go home," and by the head shake he means he got nothing from his source, and by home he means back to the paper. When we get in the car he throws his notebook in my lap and I see that he's written *"Nada"* across the page and circled it. It's funny how you get in the habit of writing down everything, even when it's nothing. In the car I tell him what I wrote down: that the police are interviewing blind, groping in the dark, that that woman's brother, he is what he is.

"That's more than I got," he says. "At least we know something."

I know something. I know what it says in my notebook: *nothing you can do.*

On the drive back I write the word *"nada"* over and over down the side of the page. "How can I get something in the paper on this?" I ask Bishop.

Bishop shrugs. "Not much to say, is there," he says.

"I want to keep it out there. What do you think it would take to sell Peggy on it?"

"Get confirmation they've got no leads, that they're interviewing," he says. "Maybe call the family. Get some quotes from them."

"They've been uncooperative," I say.

"Get them to cooperate." He glances at me. "That's your job."

Back at the newsroom, I call the Averys' house. The machine picks up. "This is Olivia Dale from the newspaper," I say. "I know you don't want to talk to me, but I want to write a story about Allison, what she was like. I need to keep this in the news. You don't want people to forget about it. The police . . ."

"Hello," a woman's voice says. Then a squeal of feedback comes through the phone. "Hold on," she says, and then she goes to turn off the machine.

"Okay," she says when she picks it back up. "I'll talk to you."

"Now?" I can't believe my luck. I wasn't even expecting her to answer the phone.

"You can come to my house at three," she says. Then she hangs up.

Evan is watching me. "She said yes?"

I nod.

"That's great."

"It's incredible," I say. "A few days ago this woman thought I was the devil incarnate."

"People change their minds," Evan says.

"Or maybe now there's something she wants printed."

"Jesus, Olivia." Evan shakes his head, grinning. "You have such a suspicious nature. She's probably just ready to talk about the girl."

"I'm going at three," I say. I look at my watch. It's quarter to twelve.

"What are you doing now?" Evan says. "I was going to go for a drive. Want to come?"

Evan likes to take these tours of the city, because, he says, it reminds him where he is. In his car we pull out of the parking lot onto Beale, driving past low-income housing and into the commercial area. Slowly we cruise past the bars. Without the crowds milling about and the darkness to make their neon signs bright, they lose their garish charm. It's so much quieter here in the day, the whole street just waiting for night to begin.

We drive down the bluff and stop at Wolf River Harbor. This is where the riverboats dock, and the tourists board for their slow trips down the Mississippi. From here down to the water the street is made of uneven cobblestones. Evan turns off the car, and the heat rushes in. I roll down my window, though it doesn't help. Evan's brought me here before. He likes to sit and watch the river go by.

Out on the water in front of us are the boats, a floating restaurant, and Mud Island, where David lives. To the south is the Arkansas-Tennessee bridge, which I last remember crossing two months ago, when that ten-year-old got killed, though I must have been over it since. To the north is the Hernando DeSoto bridge, which is big and new and shaped like an M. At night they light it with a multitude of tiny white bulbs. Their reflections shimmer in the moving water below.

When the river's high these cobblestones, and the south end of Mud Island, are underwater, and then the river rushes along so fast and hard whole trees uproot and go with it. Even now if you look at the water you can see how quickly the current's moving, fast enough to suck a body under before you could blink. We sit and watch what look like little whirlpools forming, the water whipping itself into circles. An enormous branch floats by. "Look at it go," Evan says softly. "Fast as you please."

Then he shifts in his seat like he's coming out of some kind of trance and says in a louder voice, "When we canoed in there—I told you about that, right?—I looked up and there was a tree coming right at us. We were both going along with the current. It was just going a lot faster than we were."

"What did you do?" I watch the branch spin slowly to the right, then back again.

Evan laughs. "We got out of the way quick." He turns his gaze back to the river. "Whoosh," he says.

I look past him and out his window to the left. Going that way on Riverside you come to Tom Lee Park, where Allison died.

"You hungry?" Evan asks. He reaches in the backseat for a paper bag and pulls out two cheese sandwiches and a little carton of chocolate milk. He pops the milk open ceremoniously and hands it to me. I laugh. "I love you, Evan," I say.

"I know," he says, unwrapping the sandwiches. "But you can never have me."

Evan is gay, but I am one of the few people who knows that. It's not easy to be a gay man in Memphis, Tennessee, and even harder in small-town South Carolina, where Evan is from. His parents are starting to wonder when he's going to meet that nice girl they're hoping for, but homosexuality is so far from their realm of experience that it never crosses their mind that Evan is gay. I think that his sister Kate suspects. She came up to visit and when he was out of the room she said, "Evan certainly is *outgoing*, isn't he."

Sometimes I think about Evan's parents, how they must believe they know exactly who he is, and all the time they have no idea what really happens in his life.

"Don't hog that milk," Evan says, handing me a sandwich.

I ring the Averys' doorbell promptly at three. There's a long silence. I listen for footsteps and hear nothing. Then I lean forward to ring the bell again and Cynthia Avery opens the door. I jump like a startled cat. She is taller than I am, wearing a sleeveless white shirt tucked into black linen pants. Her hair is the shade of bleached blond I particularly associate with upper-class southern women. She squints into the sunlight, her gaze fixed on a point somewhere above my head. "Come in," she says, and then she turns and walks slowly down the hall.

I follow, closing the door with great care behind me. This is a woman who would turn and frown—a slow half turn, a quizzical frown—if I let the door bang shut. I step as quietly as I can on the tile floor. The living room is all done in white—thick white carpet, white couch with some sort of shiny pattern barely visible in it. I stand until she tells me to have a seat, and then I perch on the edge of an embroidered white armchair. There's a kind of insanity to this room, so single-minded, all of these white things so clean. Cynthia Avery eases down onto the couch and lets her head fall back like she's getting her hair washed at the salon. Over the fireplace are two enormous framed photos of Peter and Allison. Allison is wearing white.

Speaking to the ceiling, their mother says, "Peter told me you talked to him at the funeral. And then I saw in the paper that you didn't quote him or say anything about it. So that's why I'm talking to you. Because if this has to be done I want it done in the best possible way."

"I understand."

Abruptly, she stands. Without a glance in my direction she glides from the room. I wait. I'm not sure where to turn my eyes. I feel as though I should let my gaze linger respectfully on the floor, as if she were in the room, trying not to let me see her cry. When she comes back, there is no trace of tears on her face, and she says nothing about her sudden departure. She walks right up to me, so that I have to turn my face up to hers like a child. She reaches down to lift my hand from my lap, pressing it between both of hers. "This is *your* story," she says. "I'm not going to talk to anyone from television. When they ask, I'll tell them I'm only talking to you."

I nod.

"I wouldn't even talk to you, but they tell me keeping it in the papers means public interest, means pressure on the police. It may help ensure that my daughter's killer is caught."

I nod again. This is usually my speech. She's stealing my lines.

"That's your responsibility, as a journalist. It's my responsibility to help you." Her face looms even larger as she says, "Together, we'll make sure no one gives up on this."

Her grip on my hand tightens, her eyes fixed on mine, until I say, "Yes, we will." My voice comes out smaller than I meant it to. Finally she drops my hand and goes back to her own chair. I sit up straight, swallowing. I feel as though I've pledged allegiance to the memory of Allison Avery, as though her mother and I have signed a pact. It makes me wonder why she thinks we need one.

"I'm going to turn on the tape recorder now," I say. "This is so I can be sure and get what you say right."

Dr. Avery waves her hand in assent.

"I'd like to know more about Allison," I say. "What was she like?"

"She was . . ." She pauses, and then suddenly lifts her head and looks me in the face. I hold her gaze, and we sit staring at one another. Everything about this woman is careful, the hair-sprayed perfection of her blond chin-length hair, the muted blush applied precisely to the apples of her cheeks, the way her gold locket nestles into the hollow of her throat, circled with the faintest lines of age. She is the type of person who puts layers between what she means and what she says, the way she puts layers of makeup between her face and the world.

I blink first. She lays one slender hand over the other in her lap. "She was perfect," she says. She presses her lips together. When I don't say anything, she raises her eyebrows to prompt me.

"Perfect?" I say.

"Look at her," she says. I turn my head obediently toward the photo of the dead girl. She looks about seventeen, her cheeks soft and lightly powdered. Wearing a short-sleeved white dress with lace across the bodice, she sits with her body at an angle, her face turned back over her shoulder to look at the camera, her eyes lifted up, one hand curved over the other in her lap. Her nails are painted a pale pink, her dark hair curled into loose ringlets over her shoulders. Her pink shiny lips curve in a faint smile. When I look at her, the perfect stillness of her face, her hands, the line of her body, I know she could have held that pose for hours, like a mannequin. "Look at that sweet face," her mother says dreamily. "Look at that sweet smile."

To me, that smile is sly, those eyes hide a laugh bubbling up inside. Her mother says, "I couldn't have asked for a better girl."

"I'm told she was a gifted singer," I say.

She lifts a hand to push her hair behind an ear and then responds as though I'd asked another question. "I remember when we took her to her first movie—*Dumbo*, I think it was. She cried and cried when Dumbo was taken from his mother. She was always like that—she really felt for people. She used to get teary-eyed at those UNICEF commercials. Or the ones, you know, where the son has been away and he comes home unexpectedly, and the mother is so happy to see him, and then they make coffee together." She plucks at her pants with one hand and flicks her fingers, ridding herself of lint. "I used to laugh at her," she says quietly. "But once, I remember, we were watching the news, and the pope was visiting America and a very large crowd had come to see him. He got all choked up, and then so did I, and Allison looked like she was about to cry, too, and then we just burst out laughing, that we were both sitting there with tears in our eyes. We're not even Catholic." She turns her head toward the picture again. "She had a sensitive soul."

Allison Avery, Perfect Doll. I let a moment pass before I ask, "And her singing?"

"She had a lovely voice. She sang in the church choir," her mother says. "But she didn't want to sing professionally. She wanted to follow in my footsteps."

I know this isn't true. I'm not sure if she knows it. "Is that why Allison worked in health care?"

She nods. "I wanted her to go to medical school right away, but she wanted a break from school first. She said she had a lot of time ahead of her." As she says this, her voice breaks for the first time, and she presses a finger against the bottom of her eye.

When she recovers, we talk about Allison's friends. She tells me Carl is a sweet boy who had been a good friend to Allison. She hesitates when I ask her about Angela, just enough to let her displeasure show, and then she says that Angela is a nice enough girl but perhaps not the best influence on her daughter. She won't elaborate. When I press her, she just waves her hand to indicate the usual teenage highjinks, things I should already know.

I flip through my notes, then remember to ask about Russell Freeland. "Russell Freeland," she says slowly. "Yes, I think he and my daughter were friends in college. I met him only once or twice." She leans forward. Her eyes narrow, her mouth tightens, and then she seems to think better of whatever she was going to say. She smiles. "Why do you ask?" she says pleasantly. "Have you spoken with him?"

"I met him. He mentioned that he knew your daughter."

She nods slowly. "Why do you ask about him?"

"I'm interested in all your daughter's friends."

"But why him, in particular?" Irritation sharpens her voice. "He must have said something to you that made him worth asking about. What was it?"

I frown, pretending to think. She's the one making me think he's important.

"What did he say to you?" She stretches over the coffee table to lay her cool hand on my arm. "Tell me dear. Is he the one who . . ."

"Is he the one who what, ma'am?"

She shakes her head, drawing herself up tall. "What did he say to you?"

"I don't really recall," I say. I can keep secrets, too, small as mine are. We sit for a moment in brittle silence. I'm formulating another question when she says, "I don't believe in capital punishment, but I want whoever did it to die. When they catch them, I want them to die. Do you know what they did to her?"

"Yes," I say. I know exactly what they did.

"I wish I didn't know," she says. "I can't stop . . ." She shakes her head. "I can't stop thinking about it."

"Will you feel any better once they catch them?"

"I don't know," she says. "I hope so. It's terrible to feel like I do now. I don't know what could be worse. It just doesn't . . ." She shakes her head again, and reaches forward to pluck a white tissue from the white box on the coffee table and wipe her eyes. "It doesn't make any sense, what they did to her. There's no reason, there's no . . . my God. There's just no reason."

Against my will my own eyes are filling. I start blinking furiously. "How is Peter doing?" I ask her.

"Peter?" she says. "I hear him crying at night sometimes. I stand outside his door. I don't know whether to go in or not. Last night I went in, and he cried in my lap, like he hasn't since he was a baby. He cried until he wasn't even making tears anymore." She stops, and looks at me sharply, like she's just remembered who she's talking to. It's a look I'm familiar with. "Please don't put that in the paper."

"I won't."

"It's paralyzing," she says. "All this sadness."

"I'm so sorry," I say. I write it down: *all this sadness.*

Typing up my notes in the newsroom, I think that Cynthia Avery told me only what she meant to tell me, that she knew what she was going to reveal before I even walked in the door. I see her again, the way she smiled sadly and pressed my hand when she said good-bye, the way she thanked me for being so circumspect and said I was different, I wasn't like most reporters, and that that was why she had chosen me. It makes me angry to remember that I was gratified.

I write the story the way she wanted it, the tale of a tenderhearted young woman brutally killed, leaving her mother to drown in grief, praying for the police to do their job. Lucky for me it's a slow news day. Peggy's not too thrilled about it, but the story runs.

After work, I go to the Four Corners for dinner. Peter's not there. I sit alone at a table by the window and order banana pudding from a slim, rosy-cheeked blonde. When she brings it over, I ask her if she knows Peter.

She nods, rocking back and forth on her heels. "Isn't it awful about his sister?" she says. "Poor Pete. He's a sweetie."

"Did you know his sister?"

She shakes her head, then leans in and lowers her voice. "From the way Pete talks it sounds like she was a wild one," she says. She straightens up, and speaks at a normal volume. "It's terrible, isn't it?"

"Yes," I say. "It is terrible."

She nods, looking down at her hands. Then she lifts her head and smiles. "Can I get you anything else right now?" When I shake my head she says, "Enjoy your dinner," and walks away, swinging her arms.

I stare at the plate, my appetite gone. I see Allison Avery in her mother's picture again, her perfect smile, her gently clasped hands. I see her hands the way I first saw them, rigid and bloody, grasping at the air.

9

Saturday morning I wake up slow, sweating and heavy as a dead thing in my bed. My arm is so numb from lying on it all night that in the first groggy moments I think that limb beneath me isn't mine. I reach a hand out for David and find only bedsheet, damp to the touch. I open my eyes. The first thing I see is the dead girl's face, grinning at me from the bedside table, where I must have propped it last night. I swipe at it with my hand and it flutters to the top of a pile of papers and notebooks on the floor. It lands faceup, still grinning. Sitting up, I rub my numb arm until sensation returns with a painful tingling. "Hannah?" I call. "Are you up?"

She appears at the doorway to my room in shorts and a jogging bra, her hair held back with a barrette, her face red and shiny. "Am I up?" she repeats. "I just ran five miles." She flops down across the bottom of my bed and pulls her knee toward her forehead, stretching. "I tried to wake you," she says. "You mumbled something and rolled over."

"What did I say?"

She lets one leg drop to the bed and grabs the other one. "I think it was *nada*," she says. "*Nada, nada, nada.*"

For some reason, I'm relieved. "Bishop wrote that in my notebook."

"Still seeing words in your dreams?" she says. "That's so weird."

I put on my glasses. "Did you bring in the paper?"

"In the kitchen." Suddenly she jumps up and stands, legs apart, her hands in loose fists at her sides. "I'll race you."

I fling back the covers and she dashes out of the room and ahead of me down the hall, her laughter trailing behind her.

In the kitchen I make coffee while she reads the arts section. "That guy Carl," she says, rustling the pages. "He works for Black Horse Theater, right? They've got an ad in here. They're doing Macbeth."

"Let me see that." She hands me the page.

"There's a performance this afternoon," I say. "Let's go." She raises her eyebrows. "Seriously, let's go."

"Why not," she says.

The Black Horse Theater Company is located on top of a pizza place. To get to it, we climb metal fire-escape stairs up the side of the building. The stairs tremble beneath us and I cling to the railing. Inside it's dark and the smell of fresh dough mingles with dust and disinfectant. A cheerful girl wearing stage makeup sells us our tickets, hand-printed on white paper. "Can I ask how you heard about us?" she says, handing us programs.

"We know Carl Fitzner." I watch her face for reaction. Her lips shade an "oh." "You're in luck," she says. "Carl's in the play today. Bob's out with the flu."

"Was Carl his understudy?" I ask.

"Not exactly," she says. "Carl just always knows everyone's lines, even mine." She laughs. "I think if I were sick he'd put on a dress and go on for me."

"Shakespeare plays started that way, after all," Hannah says. The girl looks at her blankly. "With men in drag," Hannah says. The girl nods as though she still doesn't understand, turning away toward an older couple behind us. "What are we doing here again?" Hannah asks me as we make our way to our seats.

"Research," I say, searching for Carl's name in the program. I find it on the back, beneath the lighting guy and the costume designer. Hannah takes what I said as a joke and laughs.

An older man passes by, heading up the aisle, then turns back and stops beside me. "Excuse me, young lady," he says. "Have we met?"

I look up at his face. He's smiling hopefully at me, laugh lines around his eyes. "Yes, hello, sir," I say, rising to my feet. "I'm Olivia Dale." I offer him my hand.

He takes it, squeezing it in one hand and giving it a grandfatherly pat with the other. "I knew I recognized you. How did we meet? Are you a friend of my granddaughter's?"

"Yes, sir," I say. "Please tell her hello."

"I will." He pats my hand again. "So nice to see you."

"You too, sir," I say, and when he lets go of my hand I sit back down. He smiles at Hannah, who is watching him with open curiosity, and then moves up the aisle.

"Nice man," Hannah says. "Who's his granddaughter? Do I know her?"

"No idea. Never met her," I say. "He's a city councilman. I did a story on him two years ago."

"Why didn't you just tell him that?"

"Because the story was not flattering," I say. "He got caught with a hooker."

"That cute old man?" she says, astonished.

"Yes, ma'am," I say. "The very same."

"Jesus," Hannah says. She cranes her head to look back at the old man, as though now she'll see a lustful old goat in boxer shorts instead of the sweet grandfather who was there just moments before. She turns back to me and shakes her head. I have to laugh at her openmouthed astonishment. "Damn," she says. "It makes me wonder what my own grandfather is up to."

It's not long before the lights dim and then come up on the three witches. Macbeth himself strides out of the wings. It takes a moment before I recognize Carl. Most of the actors are absurdly bad, intoning their lines without the slightest idea of what they mean.

Carl is the exception. He doesn't even look the same. He seems taller, thinner, his jaw set, his mouth firm. When he turns murderous, I look at his face and believe he's capable of anything. Maybe the sad and lonely man I met the other day was only another role.

After the play, we hang around until Carl emerges from backstage to receive praise. His cheeks are flushed, his eyes lighting restlessly on one face, then another. We wait behind four or five other people to congratulate him on his performance. He catches my eye over another woman's shoulder and grins at me, all his teeth showing. I smile back, just as though we were friends.

"Carl, that was wonderful," Hannah says when we reach him, patting his arm. I nod. He puts one hand on each of our shoulders. "Thank you for coming," he says. Through my shirt I feel the warm dampness of his palm. It makes me feel dirty, dirty and hot. I resist the urge to step away. Lined with black, his eyes seem huge. His lips are chapped and shiny. There's a smudge of tan foundation in his goatee.

"We enjoyed it," Hannah says. "You were great."

"Thanks," he says again, nodding and nodding. "Thanks a lot." He squeezes my shoulder. I try to relax the muscles beneath his hand, to imagine what it would be like to want this boy to touch me. He looks into my face and I smile and lower my eyes. "You really were great," I say. He lifts his hand from Hannah's shoulder and wipes his mouth with the back of it, leaving pink streaks across his skin. The hand on my shoulder stays.

"Listen," he says. "What are you girls doing now? I've got an evening performance, too. I was going to grab a bite to eat first. Do you want to come?"

Hannah looks at me. I nod. "Sure," she says, and I say okay. Carl squeezes my shoulder again before he finally lifts his hand. I can't resist the urge to brush off my shoulder, as though to wipe his fingerprints away.

❧

We go to The Pie Lady, a restaurant run by a woman who started selling pies to raise funds for her daughter, paralyzed by a robber's bullet to the head when she was only eighteen. Glory Hallelujah is her most famous pie. As I step into the restaurant, Carl touches the small of my back. I move away, then force myself to turn and smile at him. There's no one in the place except the Pie Lady herself, on a stool behind the counter. As Carl speaks to her, Hannah whispers, "Are you flirting with him?"

I shrug, studying the pies inside the glass case. Hannah raises her eyebrows.

Carl turns to us. "The lunch buffet is over, but she says she'll fix us something."

"What would you girls like?" she asks, showing us to a table. "I could do fish sandwiches or maybe fried chicken."

Hannah and I order the fish, Carl the chicken, and the Pie Lady wipes her hands on her apron and bustles off into the kitchen. I've interviewed her before. I don't think she remembers me, and yet I know so much about her. "So you really thought I was good," Carl says after she's gone.

"Of course," I say. "You were the best one onstage."

He smiles at me, then his expression grows serious. "How's your story going?" he says. "Have they found out anything?" He picks up his knife. I watch him turn it over and over in his hands.

"About Allison?" I say, just to see his face when he hears her name. He keeps his eyes on the knife in his hand and nods. "I haven't learned much. Just that her mother thought she was perfect."

"She was," Carl says. "In a way." He sets the knife down and sighs. "For her mother, she was perfect."

"And for you?"

He turns his eyes to me. "She wasn't perfect," he says. "But I loved her for a long time anyway." He holds my gaze, his eyes filling with tears. "I wish she could have seen me in the play today," he says, his voice trembling over the last words. For a moment I believe that his heart is breaking. Then I remember what a good actor he is. "I'm sorry," I say. "I'm doing my best to find out what happened." I reach out and squeeze his fingers and he smiles gratefully at me. "I'm glad you were there," he says.

For the rest of the meal I am quiet, watching him as he rips the chicken off the bone. He's laughing, telling Hannah a story about a set that fell over, eating the Glory Hallelujah pie he ordered. I shake my head when he offers me a bite of pears and crumb topping, holding his fork toward my mouth. Across from me is a set of untouched silverware, an empty chair. I imagine that Allison Avery sits in that chair, her dark hair falling forward across her shoulders. She looks right at me and smiles, that mischievous, mysterious smile. Hold my gaze, that smile says. I dare you.

As we get up to go, Hannah slips off to use the bathroom. Carl and I stand in the doorway. I pick up a matchbook and open and close it, reading some of the articles the Pie Lady has taped to the wall. I don't see mine. Carl's sucking on a mint and playing with his fat silver lighter, turning it over and over in his fingers, opening it to watch the flame catch and then closing it again. I'm rocking back and forth on my heels, staring at the ceiling, because every time I look at him I discover that he's looking at me. I glance his way again and find his eyes on my face. "Listen," Carl says. "I was wondering if you'd maybe like to go out some time, um, you know."

I start to tell him that I have a boyfriend. I can feel the color rising in my cheeks. He's watching me, and now his eyes are big and sad. The motherless boy. "Sure," I say. I'll gamble that he has something more to tell me. "Give me a call."

Hannah comes back and says, "Ready?"

"Bye now," the Pie Lady calls.

❖

Five hours later I'm crammed inside a crowd, so stoned I can't tell whether I'm swaying or standing still. David brought me to this club to hear some new band, because, he says, "there's a good buzz on them." Every relationship I've had has been a course in something. My high school boyfriend was an expert on the Bible. I fell asleep trying to read Deuteronomy. He also tried to teach me how to sing—from the *diaphragm,* from the *diaphragm*—but my voice always came croaking out my throat. When David and I first started dating he went through my CD collection and separated them into two shelves. "This is the cool shelf," he said. "These are . . . not so good."

"Not so good" meant Elton John, Lynyrd Skynryd, much of the country I'd collected as a college freshman. I resented his condescension then. But I just can't help it, I don't listen to those CDs anymore. I'm embarrassed to admit I ever owned them. He's right. They're not good. Everything changes when you know what you're looking for.

Right now I'm looking at David, wondering how long I can stare at him before he'll glance my way. He is standing perfectly still, his arms crossed over his chest, his neck craned to watch the band onstage. The club is a long and narrow room with the stage at the front and the bar and tables at the back. Around us, kids in tight T-shirts are dancing, moving by inches, shoulders against shoulders, hips against hips, a hand brushing the side of a breast. Their faces are the faces of addicts and zealots, glazed and ecstatic. A tall boy dances wildly beside me, his head down, his dark hair flinging sweat. He throws himself in my direction and I fall hard against David. I turn back toward the boy, my fist raised, and David grabs the back of my shirt. The boy flails off in the other direction. The crowd parts and then re-forms, absorbing him. David asks me if I'm all right and squeezes my shoulder. "Maybe we should sit," I say to him.

"I want to stand," he says.

"Well, I'm going to go sit."

"Okay." He keeps his eyes on the singer. "I'll come find you in a little while."

I stand there for a minute, looking at his profile, the clean strong lines of his jaw, his perfect nose. "I might go out with this guy Carl some time," I say. He can't hear me over the music so I lean in close and repeat it in his ear.

"You mean like a date?"

"Not exactly," I say. "He's a source. He might think it's a date."

"I don't know if I like that, Olivia," he says. He's staring at me now, frowning. "I don't like that at all."

"It wouldn't really be a date," I say. "I wouldn't kiss him or anything."

He makes an incredulous face. "What's going on with you? You've never needed to date your sources before."

"It's not a date," I say. "Really." He's still staring at me. "Don't worry," I say. I lean in and brush his lips with mine. He looks at me hard. I want him to pull me close, to tilt back my head with a kiss. "All right," he says. "You be careful." He turns his attention back to the band.

"I wish we had gone to a movie," I say.

"I wanted to hear this band," he says irritably. "You can see a movie anytime. I thought you were going to go sit."

I can't find a table so I just lean against the bar. The bartender comes over and I order a beer that I don't want, though it's cold and feels good going down my throat. This is what I love about being stoned—the pleasure of small physical sensations, liquid on your dry throat, air in your lungs, lips pressed against your lips. Someone leans in beside me to signal the bartender. His arm is warm against my shoulder. His thigh brushes my hip.

Evan told me that he was once in a "grope room" in a gay club in New York. The lights are out, and the room is filled with men, and they just touch each other, and sometimes one man will take his clothes off, and a crowd will gather around him. I can imagine the freedom of it—no faces, no expectations, just body to body. Skin to skin. Evan kissed one man and left. It was too much for him, he said. Too anonymous. Too animal.

When Evan told me this I recognized it as a fantasy I had as an adolescent, before I had ever been kissed, when my whole idea of sex came from novels I hid under my bed when my mother came in the room. Now it seems like a strange fantasy for a young girl to have. Because women are supposed to want intimacy. Women are supposed to want love. Anonymous sex is supposed to be the province of men.

"Excuse me," the man next to me says. "Did I bump you?"

"It's okay," I say.

"You like this band?"

"Never heard them before," I say. The man props himself on the bar like he's going to stay and talk awhile. All I want is for him to go away as soon as possible. Look at me, thinking about anonymous sex, and then as soon as any possibility arises I'm as nervous as a cat in a car. If Allison Avery were the one leaning against this bar, I imagine she would cock her head and smile as automatically as I turn my face away.

"I think they're pretty good," the man says.

I tilt my head in his direction and try a smile. I can feel how awk-ward it looks, my lips stretched over my teeth. He smiles back un-certainly, then turns toward the bartender, who hands him his change. The man lifts his beer in my direction. "See you," he says, and walks away. I put my hand to my mouth.

Over the bobbing heads of the crowd I can just see the faces of the band, three men and one woman frowning seriously into their microphones. The bass is so loud I can feel it in my breastbone like a second painful heartbeat, and the smoke from a hundred ciga-rettes settles into my hair, my clothes, my skin.

The line of people in front of me parts to let a jostling group through. "Let's get out of here," one of them says. She doesn't look more than sixteen, in tight black pants and a tank top, her blond hair grazing her bare shoulders. "I'm bored," she whines. "This place is lame." Her friends, all male, ignore her, so drunk they're weaving on their feet, laughing with wide-open mouths. "Y'all," she says, drawing the word out into two long syllables. One of the guys turns to her. He looks about my age, and he's sweating profusely, his face red and his eyes huge and wild. I recognize him. He's the one who slammed into me earlier. Now he scoops the girl up into a dancing position and whirls her around, his laughter loud and manic. She's insisting he let her go. Instead he hugs her tighter and tighter while her voice rises toward a scream. The other boys laugh, except for one. He stands, staring at the floor, rolling a bottle of beer between his palms. He lifts his head, and I see that he is Peter.

I look away before my eyes meet his. The girl's voice rises and rises, louder than the band. The guy spinning her seems lost in the motion, his forearms flexed with the effort of holding her tight. I go toward them. "Hey," I call out. "Hey, put her down." The guy stops spinning, glaring at me over the girl's shoulder. For a moment I could swear his eyes are whirling in his head, like pinwheels. "Let me go, Steve," the girl says. "Please."

"No problem," he says. He loosens his grip and the girl slides down his body until her feet touch the floor. "Who the fuck are you?" he says to me.

I ignore him, touching the girl on the arm. "Are you all right?" She glances at me, then looks away. "Fine," she mutters. "I'm fine."

"She's fine," Peter says, stepping forward. "Everybody's fine." The bottle falls from his hand to the floor. He stares at me, his lovely face flushed. "Are you following me?"

"You know this girl, Pete?" Steve says. He's looking at me as though he'd like to hit me.

"We've met," he says. "I don't *know* her." He looks at me again, that appraising gaze. "She's a friend of Allison's," he says suddenly, his eyes on my face. "But I don't like her." I raise my eyebrows and say nothing. He's beginning to make me angry.

At the mention of her name the rest of the group falls silent. I wonder if they're the "fast crowd" Carl told me about. Only the girl looks young enough to be a friend of Peter's.

"We were all friends of Allison's," one of the guys says quietly. He wears a concert T-shirt and army pants, and he looks stoned, his eyes small and red. He lifts a hand as though to touch Peter's back, but lets it fall away before it reaches him.

"That's right," Peter says under his breath. "That's right."

"Let's go, Pete," the girl says. She lays a hand on his arm, but he shakes it off with a quick, impatient movement. "Go ahead," he says. She hesitates, uncertain, and then she turns and disappears into the crowd. The guys follow her, the one who last spoke offering me his hand to shake before he goes. His palm is sweaty and hot.

Peter stays a moment, still looking at me. I meet his gaze. "You know what?" I say. "You're an asshole."

He doesn't laugh, or call me a bitch, or any of the things I expect. Instead he blanches, his eyes going wide, as though I've hurt his feelings. "I'm sorry," he whispers, his face a map of confusion. He stands there, weaving on his feet, and presses both hands to his forehead. Poor kid. He looks sick, and like the girl, he's much too young to be here. Then he drops his hands and takes a few steps toward me. In the half-light I can barely make out his features. "Olivia." He smiles grimly. "I've been reading your stories." He sways, and I put a hand on his arm to steady him.

"What are you doing here anyway?" I say. "How did you get in?"

He reaches into his back pocket, moving with the extreme precision of the very drunk. "You want to card me?" he says, handing me his wallet.

I pull out a driver's license. "Voilà!" he says. "I'm twenty-two." He leans over my shoulder, looking at the license. "He looks like me, don't you think?"

"You're drunk." I hand the wallet back.

"Allison got it for me," he says. "She got me this wallet, too. She said it was time I had a grown-up wallet."

"It's nice."

"Yes," he says. He shakes his head, as though to clear it. "I'm very drunk. It has me worried."

"Why?"

He sighs. All the bravado is gone, and he looks like a child. "You met my mother," he says. "I have to go home sometime."

"Better sober up first then," I say.

He laughs. "That could take a while."

"Where did your friends go?"

"My friends," he repeats. "My *friends*. They're around here some-where." He takes the beer from my hand and drinks. "You're stoned, aren't you?"

"How did you know?"

"Your eyes," he says, gesturing with the beer. "All red and squinty." He grins. The discovery seems to please him. "Are re-porters supposed to be potheads?"

"Are teenagers supposed to hang out in bars?" I take the bottle from his hand. "You should probably go home."

"You're right," he says, turning away from me. "I should find my friends."

"Peter," I say, stepping toward him. He turns, and I touch his arm, lightly, with just my fingertips. "Please be careful." I don't know where that came from, the urgency in my voice.

Peter raises his eyebrows in a question and then smiles. Then he lifts his hand and tousles my hair, as though he were the adult and I the scared and reckless kid.

He disappears into the crowd, and I go back to the bar and climb onto a stool, turned out so that I can watch the room, thinking about that hand in my hair. That boy has a car crash feeling about him. I wonder if he learned it from his sister, how to live your life like a rock and roll song. Everyone but me has a reckless youth to look back on, even my brother, Rob, telling tales of redemption for his church youth group. I've never slept around or danced on tables. I've never jerked my car over the railroad tracks just in time to miss the train. There is nothing I can claim to have survived. I'm just growing older with my same cautious self, like settling into marriage without ever feeling that first wild flush of love.

Next to me a big-breasted girl bounces up and down on her toes, trying to get the bartender's attention. Her breasts jostle against my arm. "Hey," she keeps saying, her voice pitched high. A man leans over and asks me for a light so I pull matches from my pocket and strike one. I love the way that flame appears, something from nothing.

Peter comes weaving back toward me. It seems hours since he left me. I look at my watch. It's been five minutes.

"I can't find my friends," he says. "I think I'm going to be sick."

"Hold on to me," I say. "I'll take you outside." He takes my hand, and I lead him through the crowd to the side door. Faces, confused and laughing, bob before me and disappear. I'm looking for David, but I can't see him. I tighten my grip on Peter's hand. We go through a heavy metal door into the alley, and Peter drops to his knees at the side of the building. I crouch beside him. His head is swaying back and forth. "Fuck, fuck," he mutters. "I'm going to die."

"You'll be okay. What did you drink?"

"Everything," he says.

"I know you feel awful," I say. "Just try to be calm." I put a hand on his back and rub it in small, slow circles. "You'll be okay," I say over and over, I don't know how many times, until the voice saying those words doesn't even seem to be mine. He vomits, more than once, and I try not to pay attention because it makes me nauseous. I'm focused on the circles my palm is making against his back, I'm watching the way the T-shirt wrinkles and smoothes as my hand goes round and round.

After a while I notice he's quiet. "Are you okay?" I ask. "Peter?"

"I don't know," he says. "I don't think I'm going to throw up anymore."

Pulling on his arm I manage to get him to a sitting position. He leans his head back against the wall. His throat is smooth, a perfect curve. I lift my hand and let my fingers brush it. He doesn't seem to notice.

"We need to find your friends," I say. I take my hand away, embarrassed by the impulse that led me to touch him.

"I can't go back in there," he says. "Please don't make me go back in there."

"Stay here," I say. "I'll be back." The metal door is locked from this side, so I go around the club and show my hand, smeared with a blurry stamp, to the skeptical bouncer. He looks from my hand to my face, my hand to my face, before finally stepping aside. Down the dark hall, and the music roars up and hits me in the chest again, the woman singer wailing while the bass drum plays a heavy thudding beat. I push my way between warm sweaty bodies, muttering "Excuse me." A girl's cigarette stings my arm, a fat man steps on my foot, a woman pushes back against me so that I almost fall. I keep pushing and pushing. All of the faces wear the same oblivious expression, shifted by degrees like pictures in a flipbook. I'm not even sure where I've been or where I'm going anymore, like I'm a child lost at the swimming pool without my glasses. Then hands are reaching out and grabbing me. It's David. He lifts me off my feet and then lowers me down so I'm leaning against his chest.

"Hey," he says. "I was just about to come find you."

"I've got to go somewhere," I say, breathing hard against his shirt. "I'll be back in half an hour."

"Where are you going?"

"To give someone a ride home."

"Someone you know?"

"This girl Hannah knows," I say. "Kathleen. She's wasted, so I think I should get her home as quickly as possible." The lie just slips out. I want to correct it, but there's no way to explain why I lied in the first place.

"That's nice of you," he says. "Do you want me to come with you?"

I shake my head.

"Are you okay to drive?"

"Yes, David."

"All right," he says. He pulls me to him and kisses me quickly. His lips are warm. "Be careful." I go back through the crowd with my hand pressed to my mouth. When I push that metal door open I find myself gasping in the air outside.

In the alley, Peter sits with his eyes closed, his legs sprawled out in front of him. I'm relieved that he opens his eyes when I say his name. I don't know how I would've gotten him to the car if he'd passed out. It's hard enough with him conscious. Somehow I get him standing and then I walk behind him with my hands on his waist, steering him toward the parking lot. My palms and his shirt are damp with sweat. "Where are we going?" he says.

"I'm taking you home," I say.

He weaves abruptly to the right, almost falling, almost knocking me down. "Careful," I say.

"I can't go home like this," he says.

"I don't know what else to do with you," I say.

"Allison used to drive me around first. We used to go get coffee." He stops walking, leaning back against me. "I should go get coffee."

I hesitate, bracing myself against his weight, and think of David waiting for me in the club. "Not this time," I say.

"Allison used to drive me around first," he says again.

"I'm not Allison," I say sharply, pushing him to start walking again.

"I know." His voice catches, and I am ashamed. "You'll be okay," I say. "Here's the car." I prop him up against the car and open the door. He gets in, and I go around to the other side. He has his head back at an impossible angle, his eyes closed. "Put on your seat belt," I say.

"I can't," he says. I feel a flash of irritation, and then I look at him and see that tears are slipping out from underneath his lids. I sit for a moment and watch. He turns his head from me and lifts his hand to his face, trying to sniff quietly.

I reach across him and pull the seat belt down past his chest, over his thighs, to snap into place with more force than was probably necessary, my hand brushing against his soft flat stomach, over his long thighs. The sensation lingers on my skin. I shake my hand to get rid of it. His house is less than ten minutes from here. Neither of us speaks on the way.

When we pull into his driveway, he opens his eyes and looks around as though he's never seen this house, this yard before.

"You're home," I say.

He turns toward me, his eyes wide, appealing. "Come in with me," he says. "I don't want to go in there alone."

"You know I can't do that," I say. I hand him a piece of gum. "Just go in, take some aspirin, and go straight to bed."

He opens the car door. "Listen," he says. He's not looking at me. "I'm sorry I was such a prick before."

"It's okay."

He takes a shaky breath. "Can I call you again? At home?"

"What for?" I say. I think of Carl, flipping his lighter, the way I smiled when I told him he could call me. It seems like days ago. I'm so tired, I could curl up and go to sleep right here, where Peter's parents would find me when they came out for their paper in the morning.

"I'm not hitting on you," he says. "Jesus. I guess you think I'm stupid. I probably wouldn't ask you if I weren't drunk. It's just, I miss . . . I feel like I can talk to you."

"Why?"

He shrugs. "You saw me cry."

"How do you know I won't put it in the paper?"

"Why would you say that?" He looks hurt.

"I'm sorry," I say. I take the gum wrapper and write my home number on it. When I hold it out to him, he takes it, and then touches my fingers. I'm looking down at his bent head, the brown curls, the curve of his slender neck. He turns my hand over in his like a palm reader and runs his fingertips over the lines in my skin. Then he raises his head, searching my face. I don't know what he sees there, but something makes him smile. He leans forward. Without thinking I close my eyes, as though I were back in high school and this were the end of a date, sitting in the car outside his parents' house. He kisses me, his lips slightly parted, tugging gently at mine. Then I remember where I am and who I'm with, and I open my eyes and pull away.

With a confident touch he tucks a strand of hair behind my ear, lets his hand run down the side of my neck to my shoulder. Like a well-stroked cat, I want to lean into that hand. Instead I frown at him. I can feel the color rising in my cheeks. "You should go in," I say, trying to make my voice sound firm and adult.

He nods, his expression serious. "Thanks," he says. He squeezes my shoulder gently before letting go. As he gets out of the car he says, "I'll call you," and then he stands in the driveway, his hand lifted, as I back out onto the street. I can see him in my rearview mirror, still watching me, until I turn the corner and he is gone.

When I pull into the club's parking lot, I can see David waiting, his tall figure spotlit beneath the streetlight, his face creased with worry. When he sees me, his mouth relaxes into a smile. He lifts a hand in greeting and starts toward the car.

As we drive back to Mud Island, David says, "I've been thinking about that dead girl. Allison, right?"

"What about her?"

"The tape she sent me," he says. "Do you think her family would be interested in us putting it out? We could even give a portion of the profits to some charity, victims' rights or something. What do you think? Should I talk to them?"

I don't say anything for a moment, asking myself why I want to tell him no. Finally I say, "If you want."

"I just think people would buy it. Pretty girl, tragic story. And that voice. It's a shame to let it go to waste," he says. "Can you give me their number?"

"Sure," I say. "Remind me." I picture him listening over and over to her tape, talking in a low, sympathetic voice to Cynthia Avery, shaking Peter's hand.

"It'd be a good story for you, don't you think?" he asks. "Human interest?"

"Sure," I say, although he should know by now that that's not the kind of story I write. Soon he'll be sitting in that white living room, staring at her perfect picture. Even David, coming under her spell.

10

Monday morning and Angela is late. I pace in front of Allison Avery's building, walking the path the dead girl must have taken from the front door to her car. I stand on the doorstep and look at the street. This is what she saw in the moments before her life turned upside down—trees, thick with summer leaves, grass in need of mowing, a patch of pink and yellow tulips, her car, waiting, only a few feet away. Or maybe she saw none of that, hurrying, her mind on the rest of the evening, searching in her purse for her keys.

A car pulls up and parks, and Angela steps out. She lifts a hand in greeting and bends to retrieve her bag. Then she walks quickly toward me, traveling that same path. She looks demure in a blue linen sundress over a T-shirt, her hair pinned up behind her head. "Sorry I'm late," she says. "Thank you so much for coming." She touches my arm and leads the way inside.

The entryway to the girl's apartment is a jumble of shoes—sandals, running shoes, cowboy boots, elegant black high heels, tall silver boots designed to hug a slender calf. "She likes shoes," Angela says. "She spends half her paycheck on them."

I notice she's using the present tense. She stands staring down at the profusion of sandals, boots, and sneakers. Maybe she imagines that Allison is in her room, taking too long to get ready for a night out, that she'll call out any minute, asking her what shoes she should wear. Or maybe she's picking out the pairs she wants to keep.

"Come on," she says after a minute. She reaches out toward me, and I take her hand and squeeze before letting it go.

"You can do it," I say, and she moves on down the hall, turning on lights. In the living room, cassette tapes and CD cases litter the floor near the stereo. Videotapes are piled on the television. I pick one up. It's labeled: Allison 5, May 9, 1992. The rest of the tapes are labeled, too: Allison 1, Allison 2, up to 11. Angela has wandered into the kitchen. I put the tape in my bag, meaning to ask her about it later. Stacks of magazines cover the coffee table. A half-full coffee cup sits on one stack, with the pink lipstick print of Allison's lower lip visible at the rim. I notice a bottle of moisturizer smashed beneath the table, shards of glass glinting in the yellow stain on the floor. I check the answering machine. The tape is missing. I wonder if the police have taken it.

In the kitchen, pots and Tupperware spill out of cabinets. There's a pile of laundry on the table, more magazines spread across the long counter. Angela is staring into the sink.

I wander over to the refrigerator and open the door. A gallon of skim milk, not even opened. A bottle of diet Coke, a few eggs, a carton of sugar-free strawberry yogurt, half an apple, browning. Not much food for someone who had just gone to the grocery store. Angela says my name. I turn my head; she's staring right at me, a little frown creasing her forehead. I shut the door and go to stand beside her. She says, "There's still food in here," and points at the sink. She looks at me with tears in her eyes. "SpaghettiOs. She never could cook."

Some last meal, I think. I say, "I wondered why there weren't more groceries."

"Did you look in the freezer?" Angela says. "It's probably full of frozen stuff. I used to cook for her sometimes. I should have done that more often."

"Why aren't you two roommates?" I ask. I'm careful to use the present tense, like Angela, although in my own voice I hear the falseness of it, the lie.

"She's too messy," she says with a wave of her hand. "Just look at this room." She turns on the water and uses her hand to scoop the noodles into the garbage disposal. When she switches it on, the dishes on the counter rattle and shake.

I open the freezer. The walls are packed thick with ice. There's an open box of Popsicles, something wrapped in tin foil, a bag of frozen french fries. Nothing else but empty ice cube trays. "I don't think she went to the grocery store," I say.

Angela turns and stares into the freezer. "Where the hell was she then?"

"I don't know. With a guy?"

Angela lowers her head, shoulders tensed, and says nothing. I spot something tucked into a corner of the freezer, behind the ice cube trays, and reach in to find a fat bag of dope. I show it to Angela. "You might want to take this out of here before her mother sees it," I say.

She takes it and turns it over in her hands. "Do you want to smoke some?" she says. "It's good stuff."

It's eight o'clock in the morning, and I have to be at work at ten. "All right," I say.

"There might be rolling papers in that drawer," she says, indicating where with a nod of her head.

I open it and start rummaging through expired coupons, rubber bands, scissors, and tools to find the papers. When I reach for the papers I prick my finger on something. I snatch my hand back, then reach in carefully again. It's a hypodermic needle.

I find a cap for the needle in the drawer and put it on. Angela is standing with her back to me, looking at the photos on the refrigerator. I grab the papers and call her name. When she turns she sees me holding the needle in the air, like my mother used to hold up a lighter when she found one in my brother's drawer.

"What's this?" I ask.

She comes over and takes it from me. "It's a hypodermic needle," she says, handing it back.

"Why would Allison have this?" I set it on the counter and roll it back and forth with one finger.

"I don't know. Maybe she brought it home from work. Maybe her mother left it here." She plucks the papers from my hand. Sitting on a stool at the kitchen counter she begins to roll an expert joint.

"Do you bring needles home?" I ask.

She shakes her head, her eyes fixed on the counter, where her fingers delicately slide each leaf into the crease she's made in the paper.

"Why would Allison do that? Was she diabetic?" I swallow. "She didn't have AIDS."

Angela shoots me a look. "Of course not."

"I pricked my finger on it," I say, sitting on the other stool.

"Even if she had it, you couldn't get it from that. The virus would be dead by now," Angela says. She finishes the joint and pulls matches from her pocket. "I don't know why she had that. I'm sure it's nothing." She lights the joint and takes a drag, then offers it to me.

"Angela," I say, taking the joint from her hand, "was Allison into anything more than dope?"

"Like what? Heroin?" She shakes her head, frowning. "We draw the line at dope. Never even shroomed or dropped acid. I had a friend who dropped acid in college. She said she thought the walls were bleeding. Doesn't sound like any fun to me." She watches me take a drag, a smile playing over her lips. "Allison's a pack rat," she says. "You should see the shit she kept. Clothes she hasn't worn since tenth grade. You saw all those shoes in the hall. I don't know what the needle was for, but I know it wasn't heroin." She leans in close. "I knew everything about her," she says. "You can bet I would've known that."

I hand her the joint. She believes what she's saying, but I might tell someone I knew everything about Hannah, and I didn't know she had ever done cocaine. "Can I ask you something?" I say. "Why did you want me to come with you?"

"I like you, Olivia," she says. She inhales and lets it out slow. "You want to know what she was like."

"Yes," I say. *Was,* she said, the truth slipping through her unwillingness to believe it. "What was she like?"

"She was fun. She was . . . generous. She . . ." She gestures helplessly with the joint, trailing smoke.

"Yes," I say. "But what was she *like?*"

"We were closer than sisters," she says, her eyes watery and bright. "I loved her."

Later I sit on the bed, the needle in my pocket, and watch as Angela rummages through the dead girl's bureau. "I've never seen this before," she says, holding out a pink sweater.

"Can I see that?" I ask.

Angela hands it to me and I check the tag. It's angora, a petite small. Joan Bracken's sweater. "I think this belongs to Joan Bracken," I say.

"Who?"

"The skinny woman down the hall."

"That figures," Angela says. "It's ugly as shit."

Angela says Allison just borrowed the sweater, and keeps saying it, until I've told her three or four times that Joan Bracken said it was stolen. Then she says maybe Allison did it on impulse, maybe she did it to fuck with that anorexic bitch, maybe she didn't do it at all and Joan Bracken is lying. "At any rate," she says, "it doesn't matter now." She takes the sweater from me and stuffs it back in the drawer, then slams the drawer shut and stalks out of the room.

I sit for a few minutes, bouncing on what feels like a brand-new mattress. This apartment has central air, like David's, and I think how nice it would be to sleep on a firm new mattress and wake up cool every morning, instead of glued to the sheets by the sweltering heat. Allison's bedroom is even messier than mine, clothes draped everywhere, an ashtray trailing ash onto the dresser. The trash can beside the bed nearly bursts with her garbage. I lean forward to peer into it. Tissues. A broken eyeshadow, powdering everything around it a glittery bronze. I think of Evan and his front-page Satanist magazine, and gingerly lift away the tissues that form the top layer of trash.

Below I see balled-up notes, an empty toilet paper roll, a box the right size for jewelry. I plunge my hand into the trash, turning over more papers, more soft, damp tissues, the crinkly foil wrapper of a chocolate bar, until my hand meets something sticky and slick. I jump back as though stung. It's a used condom.

In the bathroom I wash my hands five or six times. I don't want to think about what I just touched, the queasy intimacy of it. I wonder if that happens to Evan in his rummaging through people's garbage, if he puts his hands on used tampons, dirty diapers, wet pieces of dental floss that cling to his fingers like cobwebs, and if, when he does, he shrugs it off as part of the job and goes on digging.

I dry my hands on one of Allison's towels. Reaching for the doorknob, I hesitate. I go back and wash my hands again, my fingers turning a faint red from the hot water, and then I wipe them on my shirt. I'm thinking about my options. I could confront Angela with this evidence and ask her again who Allison's lover was. I could take it to the police. Surely they'd want to analyze it, compare whatever they found to the result of the rape kit. To do that, though, I'd have to touch it again. I look at myself in the mirror. I look harried and pale. My mouth is dry from smoking. I put two fingers to the pulse in my neck and feel how quickly my heart is beating.

I go to the door of the bedroom and listen for Angela. I can hear her moving around in the living room, picking things up and setting them down, talking to herself in a low, bewildered murmur. Satisfied that she's not about to catch me rifling the room, I start with the desk by the window.

A "to do" list, dated the day of her death. *Get groceries* is at the top of it, and then a list of other things she'll never do: *Mail demos. Call Grandma. Return videos.* Allison had that curlicue handwriting girls perfect in elementary school. My handwriting used to look like that too, before I grew up.

Underneath the list is a letter from someone at a record company, saying he found her demo tape "promising" and that he would like to hear more. David might have written her a similar letter; his address could be somewhere in her desk, one more possibility for a future of lights and smoke and crowds. In the moments before she died, I wonder if she thought about all these things she would leave unaccomplished, or if the pain and terror drove everything else from her mind.

The top right drawer is a jumble of letters and postcards, birthday cards from Allison's mother—To a Special Daughter. I pick up a postcard of Memphis at night, lights shimmering in the dark river below. I turn it over "Allison," it says, in careful childish print, "I hate the Boy Scouts. Today they made me eat powdered eggs. I miss you. It makes my stomach hurt. Your brother, Peter."

I set that on the desk and keep looking.

A letter from Carl, dated last October. "You are the most precious person to me. Why are you building a wall between us? You say I seem like a completely different person, but you go out of your way to treat me like I'm not the Carl you've always known. Don't shut me out. If you love me like a friend, like you said, then I can handle that. As long as you love me. Please, Allison."

A piece of paper folded into a tiny rectangle with a pull tab, the way we used to fold notes in high school. "PRIVATE!!!," it says. "DO NOT READ." I open it. It's from Angela. "A, I don't know what to do about Bryant. Help. Tell me what to do. A."

Two sentences on the back of a receipt. "Where are you? I'm out looking for you. R."

I look at these letters and notes, spread out across the desk. *I miss you. Tell me what to do. Where are you? Love me. Please.* I imagine them, still writing these letters, putting them in a drawer because there's no one to read them now. All these people adrift without her, like planets that once circled a star.

❧

I take a quick glance in the closet, running my hand down the long row of brightly colored shirts and dresses, silk and cotton and slick polyester. I hold one of her dresses up to myself. The skirt wouldn't even reach halfway down my thighs. The shiny black material gives off a faint odor of smoke and sweat. Strange that I can still smell her, days after she has gone.

Hanging up the dress, I move on to the bureau. I'm hurrying now, thinking Angela's going to wonder what I've been doing in here so long. I open the drawer where Angela found the sweater and run my hands over the cotton and wool and linen jumbled inside. The angora is soft beneath my hand. I shove that drawer closed and open the one above it. Allison Avery was one of those girls who wear matching bra and panty sets. The drawer is a mess of lacy pink and purple and red things. I pick up a black satin bra and put my fist in one of the cups. Then I realize what I'm doing and drop it back in the drawer. I wonder what color set she was wearing the night she died, if the panties the killer kept look like any of these.

What am I going to do with all this, the matching underwear, the letters, the condom, the detritus of this girl's life. I sit on the bed, imagining the girl's mother discovering the bag of dope in the refrigerator, the condom in the trash, confronted with this fact of life none of us can get used to, that everyone we know has a world we can't enter.

I run my hand across the smooth wood of her headboard. Some instinct makes me rise up on my knees to peer down into the space between the headboard and the wall. Sure enough, there's something wedged there. By forcing my arm down until it feels like my shoulder is going to wrench out of the socket, I'm able to reach it, sliding it up the wall until I can hold it in both my hands.

It's a rectangular box, about six inches long, and the lid is painted with a silvery-blue fish. I open it.

A large metal spoon. Another needle. A tiny foil package, which, unwrapped, reveals a white pellet, about the size of an aspirin.

I close the foil back around the pellet. Then I close the lid and stand for a moment weighing the box in my hand.

Angela calls my name. "Coming," I shout back. I wedge the box back into that space and leave it there. When I find Angela in the kitchen, she hands me another joint and leans forward to light it for me.

We are sitting on the floor in the living room, near the stereo. Being stoned makes everything around me look sharp and bright, and I feel I'm coming close to understanding something. Maybe the girl's death had nothing to do with Carl or the condom in that trash can and everything to do with that box and the needle inside my pocket. Maybe she did know the people who killed her. Maybe they sold her drugs. I touch the needle through the fabric of my pants. Right here in my pocket I could have the explanation for everything.

"Listen," Angela says. She pops a tape in the cassette player and hits play. There is a click and a whirring sound, and then a female voice says, "April 24, 1997." Her voice is husky, lightly flavored with a southern accent. I hear an intake of breath, and then she begins to sing, a John Prine song called "The Speed of the Sound of Loneliness." I try to imagine what Angela is feeling right now, as the disembodied voice fills the room. A cough cuts short the last note. "Ah shit," the voice says. There is a loud click, and then the whirring again. Angela removes the tape and holds it in her hand. She strokes the tape with one finger as though the plastic were the dead girl's skin. Then she folds in on herself. Her back shakes with sobs. She barely makes a sound, rapid breathing, a gasp, an almost inaudible moan.

There is not a foot between us but I don't reach to touch her. One thing I know is how to hold myself apart. I know how to absorb another's life until it's as familiar as my own and when the story is over I know how to put that life away with my clip file. What I don't know is how to feel what she feels, the hot unbearable rush of it.

I watch, as always. Then I reach out and pull her to me. With my arms around her I rock us back and forth. Her tears are hot and wet against my neck. "Allison," she says. "Allison."

On the way to work I stop for coffee and a doughnut. I'm taking deep breaths, blowing out hard as though I could expel the dope from my system with the air from my lungs. I'll just spend the morning at my desk until the high wears off.

Walking through the newsroom, I keep telling myself no one knows, no one is staring at me. When I checked my eyes in the rearview mirror they were big as ever and clear of any red. "Good morning," Evan says when I sit at my desk.

"Good morning," I say brightly. "How are you?"

"Tired," he says, and yawns to demonstrate. "I was here late last night finishing up my story."

"Which story?" I pick up today's paper and scan the front page.

"That story," he says, pointing. "Haven't you seen the paper yet?" I read the headline: SUSPECT INVOLVED IN CULT ACTIVITIES, NEIGHBORS SAY. Evan says, "The Satanist kid who killed that ten-year-old. *Allegedly* killed."

I skim the story. A plastic skull in his locker. The witchcraft magazine Evan found in his trash. An upside-down cross a teacher thinks she remembers him wearing on a chain around his neck. "Well," I say. "I guess he did it."

"Are you being sarcastic?" Evan taps his pen on my hand.

"No," I say. "He probably did do it."

"These things add up," he says. "They might seem small, by themselves. But two and two equals four, you know. It always does."

"You don't have to tell me," I say. "I believe it."

After Evan turns back to his computer I pull the needle from my pocket and study it, holding it out of sight beneath my desk. I grab a notebook and write: *Heroin. Where did she get it? Who did she do it with?* I don't imagine she had a solitary habit. Someone had to introduce her to the drug. Someone had to sell it to her. I think of Carl, telling me Allison Avery lived dangerously. There are only so many ways to live dangerously if you're a middle-class girl. I write them down: *1. Sex. 2. Alcohol. 3. Drugs.* "Whatcha got there?" I hear Evan say.

I turn and see him leaning over his desk, peering under mine. "Doing a story on me now?"

He winks. "Better be careful what you put in your trash."

"I've got nothing to hide," I say, curling the needle inside my palm. I don't want him to see it. It's my story, my secret for now.

He sinks back down in his chair. "Seriously, what's in your hand?"

"Nothing," I say. I drop the needle on the floor and hold up my hand, "See?"

He studies my face. His eyes are a warm brown, and he has the long eyelashes mascara is supposed to give you. "What's wrong?" he asks me.

"Nothing." I'm fighting an urge to put two fingers to the pulse in my neck, my heart beating double-time with marijuana and caffeine. "What makes you think something's wrong?"

"I know you, Olivia," he says. "You're not yourself. Is it this story? Is it getting to you?"

I meet his gaze, looking right into those pretty eyes. For a moment I know how good it would feel to curl up inside his arms and let him rock me until I fell asleep, nowhere safer than in his embrace. I look away. "Evan, I'm fine," I say. "Nothing gets to me. I'm one tough bitch, remember?" As I say it, I believe it. A feeling passes through me, almost like elation. I say, "I can handle anything," and grin at him until he smiles back, relieved.

❧

I spend the rest of the morning in the paper's library, looking at clippings on heroin use in the city. The library is shelf upon shelf of boxes filled with envelopes filled with cut-out articles. My fingertips turn black as I go through them. The clippings are flimsy between my fingers, their brittle paper easily torn. I learn that heroin is now so pure it can be snorted or smoked, that the emerging junkie demographic is young, twenty-something hipsters, often from middle- or upper-class backgrounds, that heroin-related arrests in the city are on the rise. I get this last piece of information from an article on crime statistics with my byline above it. I sit staring at the letters spelling out my name. I have no recollection of writing this, no memory of making the phone call to Lieutenant Nash, who's quoted here. I look up at all the shelves of boxes and think how many other stories I must have forgotten, how many facts and opinions have passed through me and out into the world, gone now, as if I had never known them at all.

I put the clipping away and lift another one from its envelope. It's a story by Peggy, about three years old, on drug use among middle-class kids. I skim it. Most of the kids Peggy quoted were using pot and cocaine. There are a few quotes from a junkie named Paula, who says she grew up in a normal family, making A's in math and science, before she found heroin. "Even though it's screwed up my life," she says, "nothing is better than getting high. It's the best feeling in the world."

Carefully I fold the clipping along its creases and put it back in the envelope. I'm having visions of dark houses with bad green carpeting, Allison Avery passed out on the floor. In Peggy's article, Paula says she knows about thirty users. There can't be too many sources for heroin in this city. Maybe Peggy can put me in touch with Paula, with someone who can tell me about what Allison Avery was putting in her veins.

Back in the newsroom, I see Peggy walking in my direction, reading something and frowning. I stop her and ask if I can talk to her about an old story.

She leans in toward me, still frowning. "You've got newsprint all over your face. Hold still." She takes a tissue out of her pocket and wipes the side of my nose. "Hazard of the job," she says, and laughs. Then she turns back to the papers in her hand and starts walking.

"Peggy," I say to her back. "Can I talk to you about this? It's important."

"Catch me later, kid," she says. "I've got a meeting."

When I get back to my desk, I remember the needle and bend down to retrieve it. It's not there. I straighten up so fast I crack my head on the desk, and I'm sitting there cursing, pressing my hand to the bump forming on my head when I notice the needle off to the side, next to my trash can. I must have kicked it over there when I got out of my chair. I take a quick glance around. Evan is gone. Everyone else is on the phone or frowning at their computer screens, fingers flying over the keyboards. I grab the needle and drop it inside my bag.

I call my house to check my messages, wondering if Carl has called, if Peter has called. My head aches. I count four rings and then a woman answers. "Hannah?" I say, though it doesn't sound like her voice. The person hangs up, so I dial again.

"Hello?" the same woman says. Hannah sometimes brings a co-worker home for lunch. I rack my brain for the woman's name.

"Hi, is this Alice?"

"Who?"

"Sorry," I say, thinking that's the wrong name. "Is Hannah there?"

"Who?" she says.

"I must have the wrong number."

"Okay," she says.

I dial again.

"Hello?" It's the same voice.

"Is this 555-5999?"

"Uh . . . hold on," she says. There's a silence. "I don't know. The number's not on the phone. Who are you looking for?"

"Hannah."

"She's not here, but you can come over if you want," the woman says.

"Who is this?" I ask.

"Who is *this*?" she says.

"This is Hannah's roommate."

"Oh shit," the woman says, and drops the phone. I hear her shout something, then there's a crash, followed by a click and a dial tone.

I pick up the phone to call the police, then hang it up again. It occurs to me that our neighbor Denise could be in our side of the house. Or she might have heard something. So I dial her number instead.

"What are you talking about?" she says. "You know I don't have a key. No way was I in your side of the house."

"Have you noticed anything?"

"Everything seems peaceful," she says. "Maybe you dialed the wrong number."

"I know my own number."

"Well maybe the wires got crossed," she says. "These things do happen."

I ask her to call me if she hears anything, and then I hang up. If I call the police and it was just a wrong number I'm going to feel like an idiot, like when I make a doctor's appointment and complain of symptoms and the doctor says, "Can't find anything wrong with you." On the other hand I should know my own number. I dial it again. The answering machine picks up, and I listen to Hannah's voice calmly saying that we're not home. "Hello?" I say after the beep. "If anyone's there you better leave because I'm calling the police. Do you hear me? I'm hanging up and calling the police right now."

I hang up, and stare at the phone. Then I call Hannah.

"It probably *was* Denise, making long-distance calls on our phone or something," Hannah says. "That woman's crazy."

"That makes sense," I say.

"Think about it. Why would a burglar answer the phone? And why would Denise get so snippy about it if it wasn't her? And, if it wasn't her, wouldn't she have heard people breaking in? We can hear her having sex and someone breaking our door down would surely be louder than that. You know what else? She lied—she does have a copy of our key. We traded keys a long time ago in case we ever locked ourselves out."

"I forgot about that," I say.

"Let's check our phone bill for calls to Cookeville."

"Why Cookeville?"

"That's where she's from."

"Who?"

"Denise," Hannah says. "What's the matter with you?"

"I'm a little jumpy," I say. "So you don't think I should call the police?"

"No," Hannah says. "I'm sure it's fine."

I don't want to tell her that I'm scared, that I want to call the police. I don't want to be a child imagining a bogeyman in the closet, screaming at nothing.

Peggy appears at my desk and motions for me to hang up the phone. When I do, she says, "An abandoned building's collapsed downtown. Get on it, kid."

I'm out the door in less than five minutes.

I spend the afternoon studying rubble. The story runs front page, with color art of the building, caved in like something in a war zone. When I get home at six-thirty, all the lights are on, but Hannah's car is not parked anywhere on the street. I sit in the car a few minutes, staring at the front door. It looks untouched. Maybe Denise left the lights on. Just to be sure, I walk around to the back. The storm door is hanging open, but that's nothing unusual—it's broken. I'm feeling silly for even worrying about this now, but when I get closer I can see that the main door is cracked open, and the light picks up broken glass all over the kitchen floor. "Fuck me," I say.

I bang the door open and jump to the side of it like someone in a cop show. I fumble in my bag for something heavy, cursing myself for not thinking of this before I opened the door. I grab and drop a roll of Tums, a pen, and my notebook before I find my makeup bag, heavy with lipstick and bottles of moisturizer. With this in my hand, I swing around the door, crouching low.

Glass is all over the floor. The window on the kitchen door has been shattered and the lock is smashed. I step on a cockroach. It crunches horribly and I gasp, then clamp my hand over my mouth. Giant moths are flitting insanely around the kitchen light. It looks like a camping trip in here. I drop the bag on the table and grab an empty champagne bottle. The weight of it feels good in my hand.

I ease down the hall toward the living room, sliding my back along the wall. There is no sound but the swishing of my shirt against the wall, the whisper of my breathing. I clutch the bottle with both hands. Soon I can see the television. The VCR is still on top of it. I step into the room, letting the bottle dangle at my side. I take a quick inventory—stereo, CDs, answering machine, telephone, Hannah's computer. The living room looks undisturbed.

I tiptoe back down the hall to the bathroom, even while I'm thinking, *No, you idiot, don't go in there,* and with the bottle raised in my hand I whip back the shower curtain. Nothing. In the bedrooms, I peer under the beds, check the closets, my heart pounding inside my ears. Nobody.

Then I sit on Hannah's bed and stare at the wall, rolling the champagne bottle between my hands. The adrenaline is fading, and I'm stunned by my own stupidity. There could have been someone in here with a gun. There could have been a man waiting in the living room to rape me and beat me, turn me into a police photograph Sergeant Morris would hand to Bishop in the morning.

The front door slams shut, and I jump up. I consider hiding in the closet, and then I think that it could be Hannah. But I can't call out, because if it isn't her, I don't want to give away where I am, so I stand out of sight just inside her door, with the champagne bottle raised, and when she walks in the room, she sees me and screams.

I drop the bottle on the floor. "It's just me," I say.

"What the hell," Hannah says, breathing hard. "You gave me a heart attack."

"Someone broke in here. Go look in the kitchen."

I listen to her footsteps go down the hall, stop, and then come back. "What a mess," she says. "Did you call the police yet?"

While we wait for the police, I tell Hannah what I did when I got home. I can't be still; I pace around the room while Hannah sits on the couch. Caught up in my own story I'm starting to believe I could have handled it. If I'd found people here I would have knocked them out with the bottle, stood over them until the police arrived. "I felt like a Charlie's Angel," I say. "I didn't stop to think. I was hardly even scared."

"But why did you take out your makeup bag?" Hannah says. "Wouldn't it have made more sense to hit them with your whole bag?"

I stare at her. "Jesus Christ, Hannah," I say. "I'm a fucking idiot, okay?"

"I just wondered," she says.

"Next time I'll remember that." I pretend to take notes. "Hit them with your whole bag."

"Fuck you," she says.

"No, fuck *you*," I say. Then to my embarrassment I burst into tears.

"My hero," she says, but nicely.

"Shut up," I say. "Don't you ever shut up?"

She stands up and puts her arms around me. "You were very brave," she says. "I mean it."

At first we thought nothing was missing. They went through my jewelry box and tossed things aside—real pearl earrings, savings bonds, my passport—but took none of them. Then we realized they'd taken a gold necklace of mine, some earrings of Hannah's, a case full of my mixed tapes and an old Walkman, two pairs of cheap sunglasses and some loose change that was on Hannah's dresser. They also took a bag of shake from Hannah's room. We didn't tell the cops about that. "Probably high school kids or junkies," one of the cops said. "Looking for quick cash, stuff they could stick in their pockets. It was probably an impulse break-in, too stupid or too high to plan it better. You said they answered your phone?"

"You got lucky," the other one said, looking around at our TV, our VCR. "You got the stupidest burglars in the state of Tennessee."

After the cops left I called David, and he came right over. Now he's fast asleep on his side, facing away from me. With one finger I write my name on his back. I've been awake half the night, thinking about what was on those mixed tapes, especially a particular one I made in college. I don't think I can re-create it. I know it was the greatest mixed tape I've ever made, but even so I can remember only half of the songs. To make the tape I borrowed some CDs from my roommates, and the sad fact is I don't even like those people anymore.

I get out of bed and go through my bag looking for the needle I found at Allison's. Sitting on the edge of the bed, holding the needle in one hand, I watch David sleep. I take the cap off and press the point of it with one finger, gently, not enough to break the skin. David rolls over toward me, murmuring something, and in that moment I accidentally press too hard. A drop of blood bubbles out. I rub it round and round between my finger and my thumb. I don't know what any of this means.

I'm going to find out.

11

In the morning David leaves before I'm fully awake, heading home to shower and let out the dog. He says in passing that he's going to call Allison's parents today, and I tell him not to say he knows me.

"Why not?" he asks, pausing at my bedroom door.

"I'm a reporter," I say. "They don't like me."

He nods. "I'll just say she sent me a tape." Then he's gone, a man with a mission.

Hannah calls our landlord to tell him he'll have to fix the back door, and I go into the kitchen to see what's left of the monster bugs. I spot some moths high up on the wall, near the ceiling, and my impulse is just to let them be, but I make myself climb up on the counter to catch them in my hands, one by one, so I can let them go outside. If I think too hard about their little wings beating against my palms it makes me shudder but as long as I keep my mind on the job I'm fine. I'm listening to the murmur of Hannah's voice in the other room, the gentle rhythm of the southern accent I almost never notice anymore. She laughs. I've known her so long, I could recognize her just by that sound.

Hannah comes in and watches me, leaning against the opposite counter. I'm trying to catch the last moth in my palm, it keeps fluttering away, and having an audience is making the muscles in my back tense up.

"Oooh, almost," Hannah says as I miss the moth again.

"What do you want, Hannah?" I say.

"Rude," she says, and crosses her arms across her chest.

"Sorry," I say. "This is frustrating." I get a wing between my thumb and forefinger. The moth flaps furiously, in a panic, and I'm trying as best I can to cup it gently in my hand without pulling its wing off.

"You got it," she says. I hold the moth between my hands and step backward, carefully, off the counter and onto a chair. Hannah opens the door for me and I open my hands to let the moth go. It just sits in my palm. "Go on," I say, shaking my hand out the door. It holds on. Finally I toss up my hand like I'm serving a tennis ball and the moth flies away.

"It liked you," Hannah says, and laughs.

I brush my hands together. "I wasn't so crazy about it." With the glass off the floor and the bugs gone, the kitchen almost looks normal. Hannah follows me out and down the hall into my bedroom. She sits in my desk chair and watches while I get dressed. She says, "What are you doing tonight?"

"I'll probably have a drink with the guys after work," I say, pulling my shirt over my head.

"Want to do something after that? I feel like I've hardly seen you lately."

"Sure," I say. "I'll call you."

She smiles at me and stands up. "Good," she says. At the door she pauses, holding on to the door frame. "Listen, you really were brave yesterday. I was impressed."

I pull a pair of pants off a hanger. "Thanks," I say, but she's already gone.

In the newsroom I'm a celebrity, everyone lingering at my desk to hear the story. After an hour, I'm making it funny, acting out the way I jumped to the side of the door, pretending that I brought my fingers up and together like a gun before I rotated into the room.

Peggy laughs and laughs, and then stops and looks serious. "Don't do that again," she says. "Next time call the police."

"Next time call me. I'll come right over," Bishop says. "I'll rescue you."

"That's okay. I'd rather be a Charlie's Angel than a damsel in distress," I say. "Next time I'll just get a real gun."

"You're not serious," Peggy says.

"Of course not," I say, though I can imagine how that would feel, the cold weight of a gun in your hand. "Anyway, I'm hoping there won't be a next time."

"Amen to that," Bishop says. He puts his hand on my shoulder and squeezes it before he ambles away.

"I'm glad you're okay," Peggy says. "Be more careful next time, okay, kid?" She grins. "I mean, there won't be a next time. Just be more careful."

As she turns to go, I remember the story I wanted to ask her about. "Wait, Peggy," I say. "I want to talk to you about a story you did on drug use."

She laughs. "You'll have to be more specific."

"It was about three years ago. You talked to a junkie named Paula."

She frowns, and when she speaks her voice is chilly. "What about it?"

"I was wondering if you could put me in touch with Paula, or if you know of any other sources. I'm looking for some background on heroin use in the city." The whole time I'm talking, Peggy's shaking her head.

"That was a while ago," she says. "I don't think I can help you. That culture, it changes by the minute."

"Anything you could tell me would be more than I've got now," I say. "It's important."

She sighs and leans forward against my desk. "There's a bar called the Lizard Lounge. That's where Paula made her connections."

That's where Allison Avery was supposed to be the night she died.

I write *Lizard Lounge* in my notebook. "I know the place," I say. "Thanks a lot."

She looks at me and nods slowly, not saying anything, a faint hint of a frown between her eyes. After she goes back to her desk, I sit and try to make notes. *AA was a junkie? Why wouldn't Angela know?* I chew on my pen for a minute, then write: *Why doesn't P want to talk about it?* The whole time I just keep thinking, *Next time, next time, next time.* I look at the page and see I've written that down. *Next time.* I drop my hands hard on the desk and push myself up. My chair rolls back, clattering into Evan's desk. The impact sends a stack of papers sliding. I stand perfectly still, realizing that everyone in the newsroom has turned to look at me. For a moment, I am at the center of a waiting silence, the eyes of all these curious people on me, watching, judging. Then I hear voices and the clicking of keyboards and I let out my breath.

Peggy is beside me. "Are you okay?" she says, her voice low with motherly concern.

I look around. Evan immediately begins gathering his papers. Bishop catches my eye and looks away.

"I'm fine," I say. "Why?"

"No reason," Peggy says.

"I'm fine," I say again, laughing a little. "I'm just going to the bathroom. I didn't mean to be so loud."

"Okay," she says, nodding at me. "Okay."

In the bathroom I lean in close to the mirror and look myself in the eye. I hold my gaze steady. Once again, I have newsprint on my face. I wet a paper towel and wipe it off.

Outside it's raining, beating faster and harder against the roof. I'm glad I'm in here, where it's cool and dry and nothing can touch me.

At lunchtime I head home for an hour, telling Evan that I just want to make sure no one's having a party in my living room. I say it like

I'm joking and he smiles. When I get home, I sit in the car for a few minutes, wishing I had one of David's cigarettes. I've been smoking too much lately. It's not raining anymore, and the street is quiet, the noon sun beating down on silent houses, toys abandoned in patches of unmowed grass.

I get out of the car and walk up to the house carefully, like it's an animal I don't want to startle. The front door is shut. I walk around to the back to see if the house looks secure. The screen door hangs open a little. I push it closed. It won't stay so I find a rock to prop against it. I walk back around to the front door, grab the doorknob and turn. It's locked. I throw my shoulder against the door. It doesn't move.

I step off the porch and cup my hands around my face to peer in the living room window. Nothing moves inside except the dust that floats in the sunlight. I pretend that I don't know the people who live here, moving my gaze over their ratty furniture, their piles of clothes and books and magazines, the CDs scattered across the floor. These people are young and messy and careless, the whole living room like the jumbled inside of somebody's junk drawer.

A car passes by, slowly, and I turn. How strange I must look to the neighbors, standing in the bushes with my heels sinking into the mud, a voyeur outside my own home.

Inside, I glance in all the rooms, holding my bag tight against my side. No one. In my own room, I peer into the corners of my closet. Nothing but a row of work clothes, suit jackets and blouses in muted colors. At the back I find a skimpy black cocktail dress I don't even remember buying. I've never worn it, the price tag still attached.

Under the bed there's a jumble of newspaper and, back by the wall, a shoe I thought was missing. On the desk, more newspaper. When I open the drawers I find old notebooks, a postcard from David saying he likes Paris though his parents dragged him to the Eiffel Tower, a letter from my mother asking if I ever think about rejoining the church. I run my finger down the line of books on my shelves: college textbooks, a few novels, the AP style manual. If I were writing about the girl who lives in this room, I'd say she thinks about nothing but her work.

I open my dresser drawers. In here the clothes are younger, brighter, tumbled together. Beneath a sweater I find my old pipe, a small gray one with the cold smooth feel of marble, a little ash still in the bowl. I turn it over in my hands. My mother, at least, would find this shocking, though I think if I were dead Hannah would get rid of it before my mother came to the apartment. If I were dead. I look around the room. What would be left in here to tell anyone who I was?

In the living room I sit on the couch, my bag in my lap. The weight of it reminds me of the videotape I borrowed from Allison's apartment. I pull it out. Allison 5, May 9, 1992.

I pop the tape in the VCR and rewind it to the beginning. When I press play, the TV fills with static, and then there's a click and a face appears, filling up the screen, so close I can tell only that the person is white. Then the face pulls back, features emerging. It's Allison. She is biting her lip, concentrating, while the camera moves up and down. Then she disappears to the side. The camera moves again, fitting a tall stool into the frame, and she is back. She walks backward, leans over to pick up a guitar, and perches herself on the stool.

Allison lifts her head and smiles at the camera. "May ninth, nineteen ninety-two," she says. "I'm Allison Avery." Her voice curls around the words, as though her name were part of the song. "Allison," she says again, her lips slowly shaping each syllable. "Avery." She laughs, a deep-throated, husky laugh, and then she begins to play. She lowers her head over the guitar, cradled against her stomach, her hair falling forward to hide half her face. Her body moves to the rhythm of the song, and she is beautiful. Then she begins to sing, and the room is full of that voice. I think of Angela playing the cassette for me and wonder why she didn't choose a video. Maybe she thought it would be too much, that the sight of Allison, her chest rising and falling with breath, her fingers flickering over the guitar strings, would shake her apart.

This is the first time I've seen the girl alive. I can't stop thinking of what awaits that lovely body, the way it will be broken and abandoned, emptied out.

Allison slips off the stool and walks toward the camera until her torso fills the frame. She bends down sideways, so that her face is visible, her long hair draped across her cheek, and then she says, "See you later." The screen goes blank.

I stand up and go over to the television, rewind the tape a little and press pause as Allison's tilted face fills the screen. She looks mischievous, as though she made this tape for someone who wanted her, someone she wanted to tease. A piece of her hair sticks to the corner of her mouth. Her lips curve in a half smile, the point of her tongue showing through her teeth. She is heavy-lidded, her lashes thick with mascara, her eyelids glittering with bronze shadow. It's an expression that suggests more to come, mysteries to uncover.

It's a face with secrets.

At the police station, I flip through the day's reports, almost shivering in the air-conditioned chill. Here are the things that happen in a day in the city. A hit-and-run. Two burglaries. The murder of a woman whose boyfriend shot her, then himself, while her five-year-old watched. The boyfriend is still alive.

I walk down the hall in a daze, writing leads in my head. "Five-year-old Sergio Davis . . . Lucille Davis, 29 . . . Bullet to the temple . . ." I don't even see Sergeant Morris until he speaks. "You heard?" he says.

"Yeah," I say. I have no idea what he is talking about. I know it's probably good. I flip open my notebook. "What happened?"

"A Mississippi state trooper found it abandoned off Highway Sixty-one." He leans in close, almost whispering.

"You're talking about the car," I say. "The dead girl's car."

"What else?" he says. He tells me they found the girl's missing shoe in the trunk of the car. Her purse was on the backseat. The wallet was gone, and her underwear was not in the car, which might mean the killer still has it. "Souvenir," Morris says grimly.

I take a stab. "Any drugs or paraphernalia in the car?"

He looks surprised.

"Heroin?" I say.

Morris shakes his head. "Morphine. How did you . . ." He stiffens, looking past me down the hall. I don't turn my head, just lower my notebook so that whoever is passing by won't see it. "Lieutenant," Morris says.

Lieutenant Nash passes us. He frowns, trying to place me. "Sergeant," he says, and keeps walking. I'll have to call him later to get confirmation and hope he doesn't make the connection to Morris. Morris makes as if to go in the opposite direction. I touch his arm. He turns, a look of warning on his face. He almost looks angry. I hesitate, a drug question dying on my tongue. "What kind of shoe was it?" I ask.

He frowns and takes another step away from me. "What's that got to do with anything?"

"It could be useful," I say, standing with my pen poised to write down his answer. He says, "If you say so." I can see him telling his buddies about this later. "Only a woman," he'll say, and they'll all laugh.

"What kind of shoe was it?" Bishop says. He snorts into his beer. "What the hell you ask that for?"

"That's the point," I say. "That's what I'm saying."

"She doesn't know why she said it," Evan says.

"What kind of shoe did you think it was?" Bishop says.

"A black sandal," I say. "I was picturing it, this one shoe sitting there when they opened the trunk. I bet she pulled up her foot and unbuckled it and took it off to bang on the roof, for all the good it did her."

Evan looks under the table. "You're wearing black sandals," he says.

"Don't psychoanalyze me," I say. "Half this town is wearing black sandals."

"Not me," says Bishop. "You, Evan?"

"Sneakers," he says. "White."

"Don't forget I saw the body," I say. "That's probably how I knew. Because it *was* a sandal. He told me."

"What color?" Bishop says.

"I didn't ask." I drain the rest of my beer. It's flat, acrid. "Her toenails were pink, if you want to know." In my head I see a foot, small, with toenails painted a shade called Innocence. I don't know if I'm remembering that color or making it up, but I know that shade of nail polish exists—my mother put a bottle in my stocking last Christmas. It's the color of Pepto-Bismol. I've never used it. Pink, the color of girls. Some women never stop being girls. I never wanted to be one in the first place.

"What else have you got?" Bishop asks.

"I'm running down a couple of leads," I say. "I found some interesting stuff at her apartment."

"Her apartment?" Bishop says. "How did you get in there?"

"Her friend Angela took me," I say. "She seems to think we're friends."

"That's a little weird," Evan says.

"I guess," I say. "She wanted someone to go with her."

"Hanging out with her friends," Bishop says. "It's above and beyond the call."

"What, you don't spend time with the people you're interviewing? When you're trying to get something from them?"

"It's different," Bishop says. "What are you trying to get? It's a stranger killing."

"You don't know that," I say.

"I befriend people while I'm interviewing them," Evan says. "It's over when I walk out the door. I don't call them up later and ask them to the movies."

"She asked me," I say. "And I learned something in that apartment."

"Like what?" Bishop says.

"Yeah, what?" Evan repeats.

They're both leaning in now, eager for the scoop. I realize I don't want to tell them yet. This is still my story. "She stole," I say. "She stole a sweater from her neighbor."

Bishops snorts. "I don't think *that* got her killed." He leans back in his chair, losing interest. "What else did you learn? The girl's shoe size?"

"Her taste in couches?" Evan says. "Whether she made her bed?"

"You," I say, pointing at Evan, "dig through people's trash." To Bishop I say, "You hung around a trailer park peering in windows."

"The suspect's windows," Evan says. "The suspect's trash."

Bishop says seriously, "It's a stranger killing. What do you think you're going to learn from the victim?"

"Why are you two turning on me?" I say. "You're the ones who taught me everything I know. You're the ones who showed me how to lie and cheat and steal."

"I could teach you to shoot a gun," Bishop says. "It's not my fault if you blow off a man's head." He points his finger at me and pretends to shoot.

We go outside, and it's only a moment before a sheen of sweat covers my skin. "Damn," Bishop sighs. "I'm moving to Alaska." He pulls his button-down shirt loose from his pants and fans his stomach with it.

"Send me a postcard when you get there," I say. "I'm going home." I pull my hair up into a ponytail and start walking back to the newspaper to get my car.

"Do you need a ride?" Evan calls after me. I shake my head and keep walking. Evan calls, "See you."

When I pass a pay phone two blocks later, I stop and dial into my voice mail. Three messages from Peter. I hunt in my pocket for more change and call him back. "Olivia," he says in a rush, when I'm only halfway through identifying myself. "My parents aren't here. Can you come?"

I park down the street and walk up to the Averys' house. Peter said he didn't want the neighbors to see my car in the driveway. "I know they're watching me," he said. "I heard my mother talking to Mrs. McAndrews on the phone." I'm not sure why I have to be a secret, but I oblige him. I have a strong feeling that there's something he can tell me, and I want to know.

When Peter opens the door, cool air touches my skin. He is wearing a white T-shirt and a pair of jeans, and he smiles when he sees me. "Come in," he says, and steps back inside. In silence, I trail behind him into the kitchen. "I just made coffee," he says. "You want some?" I nod and he takes two matching blue mugs from the cabinet and fills them. All of his movements seem slow, precise, as though he's drunk again and aware of how careful he has to be not to spill. I sit down at the kitchen table and he sets the mugs down in front of me. A few drops of liquid slosh out of one. "Shit," he says under his breath, and turns slowly to the counter for a paper towel. I watch him lay the towel flat on the table and press his hand against it. When the brown stain has soaked into the paper, I look up at his face. He's staring at his hand on the towel but he's not seeing it.

I touch his hand with a finger, and he starts.

"Sit down," I say. "I'll get it."

He eases into a chair. I move briskly, keeping my voice matter-of-fact while I ask him where the sugar is, opening and closing cabinets. I set everything on the table, pushing his mug toward him, dropping a spoon beside it, opening the carton of milk. The coffee is strong and bitter. "Good coffee," I say, nodding at him over my mug.

"What?" he says. He hasn't touched his.

"Good coffee," I say again. "Thanks."

Finally he picks up his spoon, adds sugar. "I'm glad you came," he says.

"Well," I say. I reach in my bag, fingering the metal rings of my notebook. "How are you?"

He meets my eyes and smiles. He actually looks grateful. "I'm okay," he says. He lifts his mug.

He tells me that he's been trying to keep busy. He hasn't wanted to see his friends much, they're nervous around him, he feels them watching him like he's become someone different, someone unpredictable and strange. They're afraid to laugh around him, afraid to talk about anything but Allison, and there's only so many times, he says, that he can listen to them say they're sorry. He tried going to work. Two women sat at one of his tables before he was finished clearing it, and he was awkward, trying to clear the dishes from the small table around them, their elbows and purses. As he walked away, he heard one of the women say, "I certainly hope the food is better than the service," and rage flooded his body. He dropped the bus tray to the ground where it crashed, silencing the restaurant, and then he turned toward that woman with his fists clenched. He got out, "If you think . . ." between his teeth before the manager grabbed him and hustled him into the kitchen, where she told him in a low, sympathetic voice that it would be better if he took a few days off. He's been watching a lot of television, he says. He's been working in his greenhouse. Even his parents are hard to talk to now, caught up in their own anger and grief.

"I feel like a crazy person," he says. "At least everyone treats me like a crazy person."

"People are afraid of you, because something terrible has happened to you." I stand up and go to the counter for the coffeepot. Leaning over him, I pour him another cup. For a moment I rest my hand on his shoulder.

"I guess you've been around a lot of people who've had something terrible happen to them," he says.

"Yes. A lot of people."

"And what about you?" he says. "Has anything terrible happened to you?"

"No," I say. I don't say that I wonder whether, when it does, I'll feel it like he feels this. Maybe I'll be one step removed, as though even my life were only another story I'm writing.

"You're lucky," he says. Then he takes the coffeepot from me and sets it on the table. "Do you want to see my greenhouse?" he asks. "It's in the backyard. I'd like to show you."

When he said "greenhouse," I pictured a lush jungle of tropical flowers and creeping plants, so many that they would block the cloudy glass walls, making it impossible to see in. But here are only neat rows of tiny trees, and the setting sun shines right in through.

"This one," he says, "is a maple grove. Forty years old." At first they look to me like leafy sticks planted upright in a pot, but then my vision swings around and I can see that they have the grace of whole trees. For a moment I feel that I am the one who is wrong, out of proportion, monstrously large. "Aren't you going to say how small they are? Some girls say"—his voice goes high in imitation—"'Oh, how cute! They're so tiny!'"

"I'm not a girl," I say.

He looks confused. "What do you mean?"

"I'm twenty-five. That's hardly a girl."

He grins, that mischievous grin, and throws his arm around me. "Come on," he says. "I'll give you the tour."

I try to ignore the weight of that arm on my shoulders. "This tree here is in the informal upright style," he says.

"What does that mean?"

"See, bonsai trees are sculpted into one of several different shapes. I forced this one to grow this way," he says. "Though it didn't take a lot of forcing. It's the most basic design because it follows the natural shape of the trunk." He draws a line in the air with his hand. "You want to develop a single line of the trunk, from the roots to the top, and you want the branch structure to look natural. The branches start about a third of the way up. But right here, see? I screwed up. Because there's not supposed to be any empty spaces."

"I bet you bring a lot of girls here," I tease. This is the first time I've seen his mood lighten. I move forward, out from under his arm, and run my fingers over the top of the tree.

"Of course I do, darling," he says, affecting a British accent. "But in the end there's only you."

"Of course," I say.

"Of course," he says.

I can't think of a joke to make. Against the tiny leaves, my fingers are clumsy as logs. When I look at him next he's not smiling anymore, and I know he's thinking about his sister. His sister. When I'm with him I find it difficult to think of her by name. Allison. He's thinking of Allison. He keeps his eyes on the tree while his hand finds a pair of tiny scissors on the counter, and then he snips off a miniature branch. "I have to keep them pruned," he says before he moves on down the row of trees.

I follow, watching him roll the branch between his fingers. "Can I have that?" I ask.

He looks surprised. "What for?"

"Because it's so small," I say. I think he'll take this as a reason; he can file it under the category of "girl."

He hands it to me. I drop it in my bag. "Maybe I should go," I say.

Chewing on his lower lip, Peter says nothing, and I wonder if he heard me. "Maybe I should go," I say again.

"You haven't asked me anything," Peter says. "About Allison."

"Another time," I say, taking a step backward.

He watches my face, considering something. Then he says, "Do you want to see her old bedroom?"

Yes. Of course I do.

❧

Upstairs in her bedroom the shades are drawn and half-dead plants are clustered on the windowsills. I don't know if I'm imagining the smell of some musky perfume. It must be her mother's scent, because it seems impossible that hers could linger so long. In the center of the room, I turn around and around. Peter watches me from the doorway. "She just moved out a year ago," he says. "I come in here sometimes, and it's almost like she's just left the room."

I have a feeling that he expects me to put on her clothes, curl up on her bed, go to sleep, maybe, with her pillow beneath my cheek. The thought doesn't frighten me as much as it should. I want to know her, the dead girl. I could learn so much about what happened to her, if just for a moment I could slip inside her skin.

I remind myself that this wasn't the room she lived in anymore, and that that explains the little-girl furniture—wood painted white, with tiny yellow and pink flowers—and the framed cross-stitchings on the walls. One is a sloppy picture of a house with a fence and purple flowers around it. "Bless This House" it says across the top in red, and at the bottom her initials "AMA" and the date. On the desk is another list of "things to do." *Pay credit card bill. Write Aunt Lucy. Make doctor's appt. B-day present for Pete.*

"When's your birthday?" I ask, and from behind me he says, "Valentine's Day." I turn, and he's standing close enough to kiss. Here in his dead sister's bedroom, he leans toward me like he's going to press his lips to mine. I start to step back, but all he does is hug me, bending down so that his head rests on my shoulder. "I miss her so much," he says, and we stand like this, my hands resting gently on his back. More than anyone I've met, this boy clouds my mind, leaves me hovering between the professional and the personal, sympathy and desire. I think, *I'm holding him like this so he'll tell me what I want to know.* But he's right—I haven't asked him anything since I walked in the door. "Just come in the room. Just fucking come in the room," he whispers, and I know he's not talking to me.

"You poor baby," I say, and I reach up a hand to stroke the back of his head. His hair is slightly damp with sweat. His head is heavy on my shoulder. "Allison," he says. I try not to stiffen. This is the second time someone has murmured that name into my skin.

"I want her back," he says. "I just want her back." He steps back and stares at me hard, as though he's searching for her in my face. "Nothing can make it better," he says. "I've never wanted anything so much that I couldn't have. Do you know what that's like?"

"What if they catch them? The guys who did it."

"I don't know if that will make me feel better," he says, his voice weary and adult. Then he asks, "Will it?" and now his voice is like a child's, like he really thinks I know the answer.

"I hope so," I say. "I'll do my best to help."

"Why are you so nice to me?" he says. I touch his cheek with my fingertips. "You haven't asked me anything about her," he says again. "Why did you really come here? Was it to see me?"

"You asked me to come." I lift my hand from his face.

He fingers a strand of my hair. "Why don't you wear your hair long, like you used to?" he says. "It looked good on you."

"You remember what I looked like?"

"Of course," he says. "I never forget a pretty girl." His hand slides to my shoulder and tightens there. "I really want to kiss you," he says, and his voice cracks, so that I can hear how much he wants it. "Is that okay?" Over his shoulder as he leans in toward me I see his sister's pink-and-white bed, and then I close my eyes and he slips his tongue inside my mouth. He tastes of coffee and faintly of cigarettes. Downstairs, the front door slams. Peter jerks away. "Shit, my mother," he says. He looks both frightened and defiant. "She's early." He goes to the door and looks down the hallway. "Stay here."

He slips out of the room. I hear his feet on the stairs and then voices below. In his sister's mirror I see my face. My cheeks and neck are flushed, my lips red.

Something pink is wedged behind the mirror where it's propped on the dresser. I pull it out. It's a wig—a bob, with bangs, in a brilliant pink. In the mirror I slip it on and tuck my hair beneath it. It looks good on me, though I feel distant from the image in the glass, like a cat thinking she sees another cat instead of her own reflection.

Someone is coming up the stairs. I yank off the wig and shove it in my bag, and when Peter comes through the door it's too late to change my mind.

"Come on," he whispers. "I'm going to sneak you out off the deck."

"Are you crazy?"

"Do you want my mother to see you up here?"

He hustles me down the hall into the upstairs den, out through the sliding glass doors onto the wooden deck. I let him help me up and over the railing, but when he tells me to reach for the thick branch of the tree that grows less than a foot away, I shake my head. "I can't."

"I've done this a million times," he says. "Allison showed me. You can do it." Then he wraps his arm around my waist and holds me, the muscles of his arm tense and hard against my stomach. He kisses my cheek. "Reach for the branch," he says, his breath warm against my ear. "I've got you."

"I must be crazy," I say, I reach out and wrap both hands around the branch like a gymnast on the parallel bars.

"Now swing," he says, and letting go, he gives me a little push. For a moment I'm just dangling, my throat full of a scream I can't let out, and then my frantic feet find the branch and I'm standing. My heart is jumping, and it's not with fear, it's with exhilaration. I look back at Peter leaning against the rail, his hair a golden brown in the setting sun. "I knew you could do it," he says. "It's all easy now."

Half-falling, half-climbing, I make it down the tree. I jump from a low branch and fall to my knees. When I'm standing, Peter leans over the deck railing and sails my bag down to me. A pink strand flutters out the side. I grab the bag and push the wig to the bottom.

"Cut through the neighbors' yard," he says in a stage whisper. "I'll meet you at your car."

The neighbors' dog barks at me from behind their screen door as I pass through the yard. I hear a voice ask the dog, "What is it, Apollo?" but no one comes to the door. I want to laugh at the idea of a dog named Apollo, and then just as suddenly I feel like crying. I break into a run, and reach my car sweaty and panting. The air inside the car is thick with heat, and my thighs stick to the vinyl seat. In the rearview mirror I pull my hair up into a tight bun, trying to breathe evenly. I fan the back of my neck with my notebook and wait for Peter.

When he comes, he opens the passenger door and sits in the car. "So Allison taught you that?" I say. "Was she a gymnast?"

"No, she was just brave. If she wanted something, she got it."

"Like what?"

He tells me that Allison had heard that a boy at her college was the son of a Nashville music executive. She found out what classes he took and went to one of them—it was something like advanced calculus, he says—and sat beside him and took notes. Then she asked if he wanted to study together. For two weeks she studied for a class she wasn't even taking, and then one night she put one of her own tapes in the stereo and waited until he asked who it was to tell him that it was her voice coming out of the speakers. He told her he would play the tape for his father. "I don't know if he did," Peter says. "I guess it doesn't matter now."

He tells the story in praise of his dead sister. I'm thinking about that poor kid, the way she manipulated and used him. Then I picture Carl, leaning in close across the table, the way I smiled as though I wanted him to touch me. I'm no better than Allison Avery. I'm just not as good at it as she was.

"You know a guy called today who wants to put out her CD?" Peter says. "I guess she'll finally get what she wanted."

"Your parents said yes, then?"

"I think so. He told my mother it would be tastefully done. A tribute."

"I know that guy," I say. "He'll do a good job."

"You know him?" Peter turns to look at me. "He sounded real interested in my sister. Did he know her?"

"I don't think so," I say. I should have just said no, but maybe David did meet her. Maybe he just didn't remember it until he heard her gorgeous voice, saw her pretty face. "If Allison always got what she wanted," I say, "why was she going to med school when she wanted to be a singer?"

"Did my mother tell you that?" I nod. He says, "She was never going to go to med school. It doesn't hurt for my mother to believe it. None of it matters now." He is quiet for a minute, and then he reaches over and punches in the cigarette lighter. "Do you mind?" he asks, pulling a pack from his pocket.

I tell him I don't mind and watch him take out the last cigarette, hold it in his mouth and reach for the lighter. These things seem to take a long long time. He inhales deeply, as though it's been a while since he's had a smoke.

"Can I have a drag?" I say. When he passes me the cigarette, his fingers touch mine. I inhale and pass it back. He has one arm folded across his stomach. The other lifts and lowers, lifts and lowers as he smokes.

This is what it's come to. I ask for another drag. His fingers touch mine. When he finishes the cigarette, he starts to talk. He tells me that he loved his sister, that she was pretty and brave and wonderful. The light outside fades while he remembers. He tells me that she got him through algebra, that she taught him to drive, that whatever he did, she had already done, and come back to show him the way. She always took care of him, no matter what.

"You sound like your mother," I say. "She tells me your sister was perfect."

"She wasn't perfect." He sighs. "But my mom refuses to admit it."

Peter says he's not even supposed to mention that she smoked, almost a pack a day, for a while, though she was trying to quit. He
says, "She got me that fake ID, you know. She used to take me out
sometimes." He shakes his head and says bitterly, "My mother
never really knew her at all." He falls silent, staring out the windshield at nothing.

This is the moment.

"Peter," I say softly. "Tell me about the morphine."

His jaw tightens. He doesn't look at me. "So you know," he says
flatly. "I should've known you'd find out." His voice grows sharp.
"The medical examiner said only the cops and the family would know,
but I guess nothing is sacred to a reporter. Who told you, anyway?"

What I say next has to be perfect, enough to make him go on. To
ask him directly what he means would be to reveal I don't know.
Medical examiner, he said. That means he's talking about autopsy
results, the tox screen, maybe drugs in her system. "Sometimes we
have a source," I say carefully.

"Well, that's vague." He shakes his head angrily. "They told my
parents the media would never know."

"I was only told about the morphine. Nothing else."

"That's enough, isn't it?" He turns to look at me. In the fading
light he looks years older than he is, his mouth strained, dark circles
under his eyes. "It was a lot of morphine," he says. "Enough to kill
her, maybe, if someone else hadn't."

"I'm surprised your parents told you," I say.

"They wanted to know if I knew why she had it."

"Did you?" I ask. "Did you know she was a user?"

His eyes widen and he laughs, a short, astonished laugh. "But she
wasn't, that's what's crazy. That's what doesn't make sense."

"You don't have to lie to me, Peter." I put my hand on his thigh and
give it a gentle squeeze. "It happens to a lot of people in medicine."

He stares at me, then speaks very slowly, as though to a child.
"What does?"

"Painkiller addiction." I'm weighing whether to tell him about the heroin. Maybe she was trying to move down the ladder, one rung at a time. Why else would she be using morphine when she still had heroin in her room?

"Olivia . . . ," he starts, then subsides. He returns his gaze to the windshield, his whole body gone oddly wooden. He doesn't move, doesn't speak. I can't even hear him breathe.

"Peter?" I reach out to touch his shoulder. With a sudden movement, like a cat pouncing, he grabs my hand and squeezes it. "Please don't print it, Olivia." His voice shakes, though he's trying to sound calm, reasonable. "It's not fair."

"Why not?" I say.

"It has nothing to do with . . . It doesn't even make sense."

I say gently, "If Allison was buying or selling drugs, it could have a lot to do with what happened."

"But she wasn't," he says, his voice rising with frustration. He snatches his hand from mine. "She wasn't. I know it."

"It's not just the morphine." I hesitate. He's staring at me now, so intently that I almost feel frightened. "I found heroin in her apartment."

"You found . . ." He looks away and for a long moment says nothing. When he speaks again his voice is calm. "How did the police miss it?"

"It was well hidden. I'm not even sure what made me look."

"Where was it?"

"In her bedroom."

"What did you do with it?"

"I left it there."

"I don't want my mother to find it."

"It's well hidden," I say again, reluctant to tell him where.

"This is hard enough already."

"I know."

"You won't print it, will you?"

"I can't promise that." He turns to look at me, his expression pleading. "I won't print it now," I say.

"People should be talking about what happened to my sister," he says bitterly. "Not about the things she did."

We sit without talking for a moment, the only sound the crinkle of cellophane as Peter unwraps a new pack of cigarettes. He slaps the pack hard against his hand. I watch him from the corner of my eye. He keeps his eyes down. He told me a secret. I told him one. Why do I feel like he came out ahead?

"When can I see you again?" he says abruptly.

"Peter," I say, "I know that you miss your sister . . ." I'm not sure how to finish the sentence.

"I want to see you," he says. "You don't believe that? Or you don't want to see me."

"I don't know what I want." My head is floating above my body like a balloon on a string, a cocktail of caffeine and nicotine and adrenaline pounding through my bloodstream. I'm tired of testing the water, trying not to scare him off. What I want is to ask him "What else can you give me?"

Peter lights another cigarette, his hand shaking. "You're the only person I can talk to," he says, not looking at me, his voice flat. "Nobody else understands."

"All right," I say. "All right."

He turns to me quickly. "When?"

"Friday," I say. "If we talk about your sister. I'd like you to take me to the places she used to take you. I want to meet the people she knew."

A smile breaks across his face. He nods. "Friday." He leans forward as though to kiss me, but I turn my face away and his lips meet my cheek. "Friday," he says again, and swings his long legs out of the car. He shuts the door gently and steps away.

I grip the steering wheel hard and pull away. He stands smoking, watching me go, and I know what I want. I want to stop the car and hold my hand out for that cigarette, just to feel him touch me again.

One thing I know, if you get what you want, the only thing that happens is you want something else.

❧

When I turn the key in my front door, I remember my plans with Hannah. The apartment is dark, and there's a note from her on the coffee table. "Waited for you until nine," it says. "Went to the movies with Linda from work. See you. P.S. Carl called."

I sit down heavy on the couch, fold the note into a square like the ones we used to pass each other in school. Then I unfold it again, turn it over and write on the back. "Hannah, I'm so sorry. I got hung up with work stuff. Wake me when you get in. Love, Olivia."

The sun wakes me in the morning. Hannah never did.

12

I'm in my car, strained forward over the steering wheel as though the movement of my body could translate to the line of traffic in front of us. Beside me Bryce mutters a steady stream of invective, most of it directed at the cop up ahead who just waved a Channel 5 van on through. The sun through the windshield pricks at my eyes, making them water. "Goddamnit," Bryce says. "God fucking damnit. Holy fucking shit. He's not going to let us through."

There's an accident on the interstate—a tractor trailer and at least three cars. We're trying to reach it.

Bryce rolls down the window and sticks his head out. "Officer," he says. "We're reporters, too. Newspaper." The cop just looks at him and doesn't say a word. "Come on, you let them through," Bryce says, and when the cop still doesn't answer, he says, "What's the deal, you like the way you look on TV?" The line starts moving. Bryce shouts out the window, "I could take your picture. You could get it framed."

"Forget it," I say. "We'll find another way."

Darting in and out of slow lanes of traffic, I get us onto the overpass that rises above the accident scene. I pull onto the shoulder and we get out. A line of people has already formed, leaning over the railing and shaking their heads or pointing. Newcomers slow their cars, pull over and get out, their faces eager with the question "What happened?" Bryce shoulders his way up to the railing, saying,

"Excuse me, media," and holding his camera before him as proof. Once up there he digs film out of one of the innumerable pockets on his photographer's vest and starts shooting pictures. The scene spreads out before us, an overturned tractor trailer in the middle of the road, one car in the ditch beside it, two more spun out away from it, one half crushed. Ambulances and cop cars with their lights going, cameramen readying their equipment. I can just make out Lydia McKenzie, combing her bleached-blond hair.

I lean way out over the railing. A few feet down is a grassy hill that slopes down to the interstate below. You have to be brave, I think, to get what you want. "Bryce," I say, "I'm going over."

He lowers his camera and leans out to look. "It's too far to jump," he says.

"That's why you're going to lower me," I say. I look around at the crowd. "Excuse me," I say, raising my voice. "Can someone help lower me down to the hill?"

A large black man steps forward, lifting his arm. "I'll help," he says. A slow grin spreads across his face.

"You picked the wrong day to wear a skirt," Bryce says as I hike my skirt up and clamber up and over the metal railing. I turn around, slowly, slowly, on the concrete until I am standing on the other side of the railing and gripping it with both hands. Then Bryce holds one of my hands, the man holds the other, and in unison they lean their bodies over while I push off with my feet. No one is watching the accident anymore, all their shiny faces turned down to look at me. Behind me an ambulance siren wails. I am dangling. The two men grunt, their hands gripping mine slick with perspiration, as they lean more and more forward, inching me toward the ground.

"That's as far as we can get you," Bryce says. He draws a deep breath. A drop of sweat falls from his forehead onto my face, and since I can't lift my hand to wipe it, it makes its way down my cheek.

"Okay," I say. "Let go." Bryce drops my hand immediately, and then I am dangling by one arm, the other man grabbing my hand with both of his. "It's too far," he says. "You'll get hurt."

My arm begins to ache. "Let go," I say. "It's okay. Let go."

He looks at me, frowning with effort and worry.

"Let go," I say. "Please."

He takes his hands away, and in that split second as his face rises up, up, I am afraid. Then I hit the ground, landing hard on my side, and start to roll. One of my shoes comes off, making its way down ahead of me. I keep rolling, closing my eyes like I did when I was a child so I wouldn't have to watch the green-blue whirl of sky and ground. I can feel myself collecting cuts and bruises, a rock thumps my shoulder, a stick scrapes my thigh. Then I stop rolling and open my eyes to the hot blue sky. I stand, brushing grass off my skirt, probing the tender place on my shoulder with my finger, and then I hear it.

Applause.

I look back up at the overpass, and see a blur of motion all along the railing, that long line of people clapping. I raise my arms like a gymnast dismounting and listen to someone cheer.

Behind me another siren starts up, and I turn, startled by the reminder. I find my shoe and put it back on. Then I clamber, half sliding, the rest of the way down to the interstate. The accident is on the other side of the concrete divider in the middle of the road. When I reach the pavement I see that the cops, too, are watching me, laughing and nudging each other and shaking their heads. I have to hike up my skirt to climb over the divider, and one of them whistles like a construction worker.

I straighten my skirt, smooth my hair behind my ears and walk up to the cops, grinning. An older man claps me on the back, still laughing. "Anything for a story, eh, little gal?"

"Just doing my job, sir," I say. The cops tell me two people were killed, three severely injured, including one pregnant woman. All have been rushed to the hospital. They say it looks like the truck driver was drunk, though I'm going to have to get confirmation before I can print that.

When I'm through I have to scramble back up the hill like a monkey on all fours. More people hold on to Bryce and the other man so they can lean way over to grab my hands, and then the people pull, and Bryce and the man pull, and I leave the ground. It's almost like flying.

When my feet are back on the concrete people gather around, patting my shoulder and shaking my hand. One woman says, "Honey, you still got grass on your back," and brushes it off with quick, firm strokes.

"You are crazy," Bryce says with admiration as we walk away. He holds up his camera. "Wait until you see the pictures. We should put you on the front page."

I imagine the cutline: "Anything for a story, reporter says." I turn and wave good-bye to the crowd. They wave back, smiles on all their shiny faces.

I'm just finishing the story when the phone rings. I pick it up and tuck it under my chin, still typing, and a male voice says, "Hi. I saw your stories today." I don't answer for a moment, and then I identify the voice as Peter's.

"Hey," I say, making my voice gentle. The story about his sister's car can't have been easy to read. "Had you already heard?"

"Heard what?" he says.

"About the car."

"No, no," he says. "Just what I read in the paper."

"I'm sorry," I say. There's a silence. I say, "Are you okay?"

He expels a heavy breath. "I guess." Then his voice brightens. "It was good to see you the other day."

"It was good to see you too." Then I laugh. "You wouldn't believe what I did today. I think swinging off your deck inspired me."

There's another silence, and the voice is different when he speaks again, puzzled, suspicious. "What are you talking about?"

I don't say anything for a minute. "Who is this?"

"This is Carl. Carl Fitzner," he says. "Who did you think it was?"

For a minute I just sit there with my mouth hanging open. Then I take a breath. "Hi, Carl," I say brightly. "Sorry about that. How are you?"

"I'm okay," he says, sounding irritated. "I wanted to know if you would meet me for lunch."

"Well—" I start.

He cuts me off, saying again, "Who did you think I was?"

"Sure," I say. "Where do you want to eat?"

When I get to the restaurant, Carl's at an outside table sipping a frozen margarita. He stands when he sees me, and leans forward to give me an awkward half hug. I sit down facing the sun and leave my sunglasses on. "Margarita?" Carl asks, waving the waitress over.

"I don't know," I say. "I have to go back to work." I flash him a smile.

"You should definitely have one then." He smiles back. "All the more reason."

I nod, and when the waitress comes I order one. "I'm sorry I didn't get back to you earlier," I say to Carl. "It's been a busy week."

"I've seen your byline a few times."

"You saw the story about Allison's car."

"Yes." Carl's face seems to sag. He looks down at his hands on the table.

"So how are you?" I say brightly. "How's the play going?"

"Good, good," he says, nodding. "Bob decided not to come back, so I've taken over his part permanently."

"You were the best actor there." I lean forward and touch the back of his hand.

He blushes.

When the waitress comes I pick up the margarita and hold the cool glass to my cheek before I take a sip. We order and while we wait for our food I tell him stories about the newspaper. I tell him about rolling down to the interstate this morning. I tell him Bishop's

Jack-off Daniel's story and pretend it's my own. Listening to me, he finishes his drink, and when the waitress brings our food he orders another. By the time we finish dessert he's on his third. I'm still nursing the first.

"You know what I really love about acting?" he is saying. "It's getting to be all those different people." He waves his arm expansively. "I've gotten to be a drug addict, a priest, a soldier . . . It'd be so boring just being Carl Fitzner, some guy. Every time I take a role, I'm someone else." He says it like he's amazed. "You must know what that's like a little," he says. "You're always finding out about something else, right?" His face is flushed with drink and the pleasure of having an audience. His grin is wide and sloppy. He's eager to listen to me. He's eager to talk.

"I'm having trouble finding out what I'd really like to know," I say.

"What's that?"

"What really happened to Allison. Who could have done this to her. What she was really like. I've heard a lot of conflicting stories."

"Like what?" he says, frowning.

"That she was a churchgoer," I say, watching his face. "That she was a heroin addict."

He laughs, a short, astonished bark, then frowns reproachfully. "That's not true," he says. "Who told you that?"

"Well . . . ," I say. I'm trying to decide how much I want to tell him. I put my bag on the table and pull out my notebook, pretending that I'm paging through it to see who said what. He's watching me intently, leaning forward as though to read what I've written, and his elbow knocks into my bag. It spills sideways onto the table and the empty chair below.

"Shit, I'm sorry," he says. I reach under the table to gather up pens and pieces of crumpled paper. When I sit up again he's clutching that pink wig, staring at it with a face as white as if Allison had just come walking onto the porch. "Where did you get this?" he says.

"It was Allison's," I say, too flustered to lie.

He turns his stricken gaze to me. "She used to wear this onstage sometimes," he says. "She said it helped her become a different person."

"I can imagine that."

He keeps staring at me, turning his eyes from my face to the wig and back again. "Did you steal this?"

I shake my head. "Someone gave it to me."

"Who?"

"Peter," I say, and wish I hadn't.

He frowns. "Why?"

"I don't know." I can't imagine why he would.

He nods to himself, running his fingers over the slick bright strands. "Maybe because you look a little like her," he says. He thrusts it at me suddenly. "Will you put it on?"

"Oh no," I say, leaning back in my chair and holding my hands out to stop him. He shakes it at me like a pom-pom. "I can't, Carl. It's too strange."

"Please," he says. He makes a choked attempt at a laugh. "Please put it on. I want to see what you look like." His voice is rising, and I glance around and catch the eye of an older woman. She's openly staring at us, her forkful of enchilada suspended in the air. I frown at her and she looks away. "Please," Carl says.

"All right," I mutter, snatching it from his hand. He's breathing so loudly I can hear the way the air shakes as he lets it out. I bend over and adjust the wig on my head. When I sit up, I flip my head back and lift my hands. "Ta da," I say, trying to make a joke of it. "It's a whole new me."

He stares at me. His face goes pale. His lips twitch. Then the color rises quickly back into his cheeks. He reaches for his glass and lets the margarita slide down his throat. "I'm sorry," he says, setting the glass down. "In those sunglasses, and that wig . . ." He swallows, his Adam's apple bouncing inside his throat. He's staring at his glass, turning it in his hands. He can't lift his eyes to mine.

I feel slightly sick, the way I did when I was ten after playing doctor with the neighborhood kids, wondering what inside me could make me do such things, knowing how my mother's eyes would widen, then narrow, if she caught me at it. I pull the wig from my head and put it back inside my bag.

"I'm sorry," he keeps saying, his voice wobbling on the edge of tears. "I know I asked you to do it. I don't know why . . ."

"It's all right," I murmur. "I know you were very close."

Finally he lifts his head to look at me, opening his eyes. "Oh," he says, a sound of surprise and disappointment. "You took it off."

I let a heartbeat pass. "You had been fighting when she died. That must be hard."

He nods. He's so shaken up he doesn't even ask me how I know about the fighting. "I'm so sorry," he says.

"Why are you sorry?" I say gently. "Tell me."

I watch his throat working. He begins to tell me about Allison's carelessness, how he saw her go home with one guy from a gig, and just a week later saw her with another guy, a black guy. "She said she was seeing this guy and she was going to keep seeing him." He presses the heel of his hand into his forehead, rocking a little in his chair. "She never knew how to keep herself safe. I wanted to protect her." His voice cracks over the word "protect."

"Carl," I say. "These men she was seeing? What were their names?"

"Names?"

"You never heard her mention them?"

He puts his hand on the table, and I take it. "Let me think, let me think." He squeezes my fingers. "One was white, one was black, that's all I know."

I think, *Russell Freeland.* I think of the note I found in her desk: *Where are you? I'm out looking for you. R.* "Was one of them Russell Freeland?"

"Russell? How do you know him?" he asks, his voice edgy with suspicion.

"I met him covering a story. How do you?"

"I never met him, but I remember her dating him in college," he says slowly. "I bet that's who it was." He moves his hand to grip my wrist. "You know what," he says. "I'm going to the police."

"Wait a minute, Carl," I say. He's hurting me. He's threatening to pull my story out from under me. I peel his fingers from my wrist. "What makes you think there's any reason to?"

"If he was seeing her, why hasn't he said anything? I think that's suspicious."

"We don't even know it was him."

"It's him all right. And I bet he knows something."

"Just let me find him first. Okay, Carl? Just let me find out."

He stares angrily past me, saying nothing. I take his hand again, rubbing one of his fingers with my thumb. "Please? Just give me a couple of days."

He nods. His face melts from anger back into sorrow and with his free hand he clutches at mine. "Thank you," he says.

"You're welcome," I say, though I'm not entirely sure what he's thanking me for.

For the next fifteen minutes I try to extricate myself, making half-hearted attempts to restart the conversation. All I can think about is letting Russell Freeland walk away across that parking lot. Carl doesn't want to let me go, and he doesn't want to talk. He just sits there nodding to himself, saying, "What?" whenever I ask him a question, and then, "I'm sorry," as though he's apologizing for something much greater than his inattention. At this moment, I don't even care what else he has to say. Like someone waking up after a drunken one-night stand, all I want to know now is how soon I can leave.

The phone is in my hand before I sit down. The girl who answers at the Freeland home says, "Russell? He's at work."

"That's right," I say. "I'll call him there."

"Okay."

"You know what?" I say. "I'm looking, and I don't have that number after all."

"Hang on," she says. "I'll get it for you."

I call the number she gives me, and a man's voice answers the phone with the name of a local law firm. I ask for Russell and wait while the man transfers me, drawing jagged lines across the page of my notebook, like bolts of lightning.

"Hello?" He sounds like he's speaking from inside a tunnel.

"Russell." I caress the name. *Russell.* Please be the one. "This is Olivia Dale."

Silence. "Hi."

"You said you wanted to talk to me about Allison Avery?"

"I did. But I've been reading your stories. I'm not sure there's anything I can tell you you haven't already printed."

"I'd like to talk to you, anyway. I think you might know her better than others." I wait a beat. "She is your girlfriend, isn't she?"

A long, long silence. I drum my fingers on the desk. I want to shout into the phone: "Tell me!" "Was," he says. "She *was* my girlfriend."

I can't keep the disappointment out of my voice. "You broke up?"

"No." His voice catches on a humorless laugh. "She died."

I can't help myself. My heart lifts at those words.

It's five-thirty, and two long hours remain before I'm to meet Russell Freeland at his father's church. I'm trying to pass the time reading the AP wire when I hear Evan shout my name. I look around. He's standing in the doorway to the TV room. "Hurry, hurry," he says. I half jog over there, Bishop and Peggy and two other reporters falling in behind me. Evan steps out of the way and I stand in front of the television. "Holy shit," Bishop says. "That's you."

On-screen, I'm dangling off the overpass, kicking my feet like I'm treading water, and then the hands holding mine let go and I'm falling. Watching my body drop, my stomach lurches and I feel the heat rising in my cheeks. The me on television hits the ground and starts rolling toward the interstate. Then she stops, and stands, stumbling a little, and straightens her skirt, and I hear the applause. The woman on-screen turns her back to the camera and throws out her arms, and the film freezes that way, in that moment of victory. I can't believe that's me, that woman with her body drawn up tight, her hands reaching up for the sky.

"There's a woman with real commitment to her job, Ted," Lydia McKenzie says, turning to her co-anchor. He chuckles. "Talk about persistence," he says. "She gets an A for effort." Lydia McKenzie giggles, and then they shuffle their papers and look seriously into the camera and say good night.

"Damn," Bishop says. He slaps me on the back. "You're a celebrity." I smile at him.

Peggy's shaking her head, grinning. "You're getting to be quite a daredevil," she says. She points her finger at me. "You be more careful from now on, kid. You're supposed to cover the news, not make it." She's still grinning.

"Just trying to do my job, Peggy," I say.

Evan says, "Remember when Bishop asked you how far you'd go for a story? I guess now you know."

"That? That was nothing," I say, laughing. "Just you wait."

When I get back to my desk, the phone rings. It's David. "Did you see me on TV?" I ask.

"What?" he says. "No. You were on TV?"

"On the local news. At an accident scene. You should watch tonight. Maybe they'll show it again."

"Can you tape it for me?" he says. "I might be busy."

"Sure," I say. "Okay."

"I called to tell you Allison's parents okayed the CD. Her mother's really nice, by the way. She's going to sort through her tapes and bring me some so I can figure out what should be on it."

"That's great, David."

"Yeah," he says. "I'm really excited. I can't wait to hear the other stuff, because if it's half as good as what she sent me, the only hard part will be figuring out what to drop." There's a pause. Then he says, "If this works, maybe I can do more than one."

"Maybe," I say.

"God," he says quietly. "What a voice."

Back in the basement of the Brighter Day Baptist Church, I sit with Russell Freeland in a pool of flickering fluorescent light, the room outside it a waiting darkness. I'm perched on the edge of my metal folding chair, my notebook on the seat behind me. We've been talking about how much he misses her, about the difficulty of his position, because to come forward would be to reveal the secret of their relationship and more than likely bring suspicion on himself. I'm trying to ease him into the more difficult questions, going as slow as I can stand, keeping my body still. I feel like a lit match.

Russell Freeland sits hunched over, his elbows resting on his knees, his clasped hands dangling between his legs, a reverse prayer. "We had issues," he says.

"Racial?" I prompt, and he flashes his eyes up at me. "No." It's a reproach. "I mean, yes, that was true for our parents. We had other issues."

He falls silent.

I take a guess. "She wasn't faithful?"

He smiles without humor. "Does everyone know about it?"

"It was something Angela said, about her wanting to touch the whole world."

"I guess you could put it that way," he says dryly. He drops his gaze to his hands. "Have you ever been around someone who was so . . . charismatic . . . I was just so happy when she was around, I tried not to think about what she did when she wasn't." He takes a few shaky breaths. I watch a tear run down the length of his nose and hang there. He knocks it off. "I don't know how to make you understand." He looks up at me and holds out his hand to me. I take it.

"I remember the first time I met her. She looks you in the eye like she *knows* you." He drops my hand.

I notice this is the first time he's used the present tense. "How did you know she was unfaithful?"

"She told me." I must look surprised, because he says, "Oh, she never lied. It was more like, this is me. Take it or leave it."

"Must be nice to have that kind of confidence." I didn't mean to say that out loud, but, when he answers, I know he must have thought about it too.

He says, "Some girls take it as a matter of course that every guy they meet will fall in love with them."

I'm trying to decide if that edge in his voice is bitterness. I say, "And that gives them power."

"Yes." He lets out a long breath. "I let her get away with . . ." He swallows the word. Murder.

I let Russell talk, about how he and Allison broke up in college over her infidelities, about how they met again last Christmas, when he came home on break from law school in Knoxville. These are the words he keeps using: *charisma, talent, electric, magnetic.* But he can't make me feel what it was like to be with her, any more than I can make him feel what it was like to see her dead, no matter how well I might describe her broken body in the dirt.

"Did your parents know about you?" I ask him.

"They knew we had seen each other before, you know, in college. But this time we decided to lay low until we were sure, because, why cause trouble. The mother . . . They ran these ads in the newspaper for the children's hospital? She was cradling this black child in her arms, looking all tender. But you think she wanted me in her white house? And my father . . . to him it's like abandoning everything he fights for."

I lean in close. "Is that why you didn't come forward before?"

"That, and . . ." He takes a breath. "I loved her."

He doesn't go on. I know what he means. To come forward will not be to assume his proper place as the grieving boyfriend. It will mean recriminations from his parents, most likely denials from Allison's mother, questions from the police. For a while this will be the lens through which everyone sees Russell Freeland, his image shimmery and distorted on the other side of his love for her, her terrible death.

He tells me she was beautiful, which she wasn't.

He tells me again that she was not a liar, which perhaps she wasn't. There's a difference between lying and not telling the truth.

He tells me she was a little bit wild, which she was, and I feel the moment has arrived.

"So you know about the drug use?" I study his face. He frowns.

"You mean like weed?"

I shake my head. "I mean the heroin."

His face is a picture of disbelief. "What are you talking about?"

I let a long beat pass. "Look, Russell, Peter told me about the morphine."

"Morphine?" he says. "Peter? I don't understand."

"The autopsy showed morphine in her bloodstream. Peter told me."

He jumps to his feet. Coming in and out of shadow, he paces behind his chair. "First of all, that kid is fucked up. I wouldn't believe a word he says. I don't know what his motivation could possibly be for telling you that, even if it were true, but I don't believe it."

"I got confirmation," I say quietly as he snaps, "What? What?" over the words. "I got confirmation," I say again calmly. "Morphine. Heroin."

He sinks back into his chair. "Maybe the guys who did this . . ." He swallows. "Maybe they gave it to her."

"Why?"

"I don't know," he shouts. He jumps to his feet again. "Jesus, why did they do any of it?" He presses his fingers hard into his eyes. "Peter." He shakes his head. "Why would he tell you that?"

"I don't know. He needs someone to talk to."

Russell laughs bitterly. "And he picked a reporter?"

Yes, I think. *And so did you.*

"Let me tell you something about Peter. The way he felt about his sister, it wasn't normal."

I frown. "What do you mean?"

"You know what I mean. He looked at her sometimes, and it wasn't like a brother. It was like a man."

This lodges like a rock in my throat. "You said she had that effect on men."

"He was her brother!" he bursts out. He sets to pacing again.

"Did he know about you?"

"I don't know. She could keep a secret when she wanted to, but they were close. She used to say he was like a part of herself. But for her, it was just sisterly. I don't know if she knew . . . the way he was about her. She never felt like her parents were really there for him, so she thought she had to be. She protected him. When he was little, she did his homework."

"When he got older . . . ," I prompt.

"I don't know. She introduced him to her friends. She loaned him her car." The mention of the car is a reminder; he stops talking, staring at the wall.

"Russell . . . those hours between when Allison left work, and when . . ." I stop and word it carefully. "When the neighbors say she got home. Do you know where she was?"

He shakes his head. "She was supposed to meet me for dinner. She never showed up. I called. She didn't answer."

"Did you leave a message?"

"Yeah, I . . ." He stares at me. "That means they know about me, doesn't it."

"What did you say?"

"Something like, I'm at the restaurant. Where the hell are you?" He grips the back of his chair. "I was pissed. I think I said, 'Who are you with?'" Swallowing, he closes his eyes. "Oh God. I said, 'Who the fuck are you with?'"

"You called from the restaurant. Did you say your name?"

"I don't think so. So they don't know who it is . . ."

"But they know you exist." I go over to him and lay my hand gently on his arm. "I think it's time you talked to the police."

"I know," he says. "I'm not looking forward to it."

"They're trying to figure out where she was those missing hours. It could be important."

"All I can tell them is she wasn't with me. So where was she?" We stare at each other. "You know where I'd start, if I were the one asking? I'd start with Peter."

I look away. He sounds jealous of Peter. I'm starting with the morphine in her bloodstream. I'm starting with the heroin nestled behind her bed.

"All right." He sighs. "You know these guys, the cops, right? Will you come with me?"

I hesitate. I have no idea whether my presence will help or harm him. I think, *It's the story. Follow the story.* "Sure," I say. "I'd be happy to." I think of what Morris said the first day, that they'd be looking for the boyfriend. Here he is, making this story so easy for me, a present in my lap.

One thing I know, for Russell Freeland, it only gets harder from here.

While Russell is with the cops, I make phone calls. First the newsroom to prepare them. Then the family. The mother leaves me in silence a few moments after I tell her. "All right," she says finally. "Here's what I want you to say. Are you ready to take it down?"

"Ready." I tuck the phone under my chin and prop my notebook on the metal box.

She speaks slowly, letting me get every word. "While we have no reason to consider this young man a suspect, we have confidence that the police . . ." She pauses. "What do you think? Something general like, police are doing everything they can? Or something focused on him. Police will . . . no. How about, we're sure he'll help the police in any way he can."

"Do you consider him a suspect?"

She sighs. "Don't write this down, Olivia, but I'll tell you. It makes me suspicious that he waited so long to say something. But if I accuse him, I might sound racist."

"Yes."

"And there's really no reason, other than his silence, to think he could have done it."

"Yes."

"So let's go with the general statement for now, don't you think?"

I nod into the phone, taking it all down.

"And could you add something about how we're sorry they felt they had to keep this relationship a secret?"

"Yes, ma'am," I say. "I'll put that in."

"Thanks, dear," she says.

After I hang up, I read over my notes. Tailor-made quotes, coming right up. There's a quality to that woman that I admire, even as I begin to despise her.

I'm sitting on the bench outside homicide, idly paging through my notebook, my eyelids heavy with exhaustion. The story is written, except for a comment from the police, which I'm unlikely to get at this hour. They cleared space for me on the front page by cutting one of Evan's Satanist stories.

Sergeant Morris comes out and crooks his finger at me. I follow him a little ways down the hall, and he puts his arm around my shoulders. We keep walking toward the exit. "Thanks for bringing him in," he says. "You can go home now."

"I'm waiting for a comment from you guys."

"It's too late for that," he says. "Tomorrow."

"Tomorrow it'll be all over the TV." I plant my feet, and he turns to face me.

"You don't have to say it," he says. "We owe you one. So we'll talk to you first."

"Promise?"

He laughs. "Promise."

"How long are you keeping him?"

He shrugs. "We're not charging him or anything. Just talking."

"Is he a suspect?"

He sighs, rolling his eyes up to the ceiling as he recites, "We're following all possible leads."

"Off the record. Is Russell a suspect?"

"Olivia . . ."

"Is he a suspect?"

He looks at me hard. I open my mouth. Nothing comes out. "What do *you* think?" he says. Then he turns and begins his slow progression back down the hall. "He's no murderer!" I want to shout after him. I don't. I picture Russell Freeland waiting by the phone, heart in his throat, asking himself where she was, who it was this time. Everyone keeps telling me any woman could be a victim. What does it take to make a murderer of any man?

13

Last night when I got home, Hannah was asleep on the couch in front of the television. The light on the answering machine was blinking and when I played it I heard David, Carl, and Peter one by one asking me to call them back. Carl mentioned he'd seen me on television, his voice warm with admiration. I didn't call any of them. I covered Hannah with a blanket and put the tape of Allison Avery in the VCR. With the sound turned down low I watched it over and over, pausing at various points to examine her expressions, as though each smile, each frown, were a possible answer to all the questions I wanted to ask.

When Hannah stirred and said my name I turned the tape off and we both went to bed. I don't know what Hannah dreamed about. All night I kept waking up in the dark hot room with no idea where I was, my heart racing, my body as heavy against my damp sheet as if I'd been drugged.

This morning I drank two cups of coffee and stood in the shower for twenty minutes. Despite my three trips to the newsroom coffeepot my head still buzzes with exhaustion. I've called Peter and David. I'm meeting Peter Friday night. I'm seeing David Saturday. I'm putting off returning the call from Carl.

The police, of course, aren't holding Russell, and all Lieutenant Nash will give me is that he isn't, at this time, considered a suspect. I write that down: *at this time.* I couldn't find Morris. Russell isn't at

work, and when I call the Freeland house I get his father. "Already,"
he tells me. "Already we're getting the calls."

"I'm so sorry."

"Stick to your own kind. And that's the mildest of it."

"I'm sorry," I say. "Is Russell there?"

"My son has spoken to you enough already, Miss Dale. He has
nothing further to impart."

"But he came to me in the first place," I say. "Are you sure he
doesn't . . ."

"He has nothing more to say," the Reverend Freeland says. "Not
even to you. I realize that this is your story, but Russell, Miss Dale,
is *my* son."

I write those words in my notebook. *Your* story. *My* son. I'd like
to hurl the notebook across the room, watch it slap against the wall,
all the heads in the newsroom turning to look in my direction with
the same motion, the same curious eyes. Russell Freeland is starting
to look like a dead end. I need something more. I am starved for information.

I keep thinking about all those tapes in the dead girl's apartment,
stacked precariously on the table and the floor. I need to see more
of them.

Angela is not at work when I call, so I try her apartment, hoping
that she's home. She answers on the fourth ring. I ask her how she
is, and murmur sympathetically when she says in a small voice that
she guesses she's okay. Then I tell her that I hate to bother her, but
I think I lost an earring at Allison's apartment. There is a silence
when I'm through speaking. Then Angela says, "I don't think I can
go back there today."

"That's fine," I say. "That's . . ." Perfect. "Can I just come and get
the key from you? I'll bring it back. I'm sorry to bother you about
this, but my mother gave me the earrings, so . . ."

"No, that's fine," she says. "Come on over."

Angela comes to the door in a terry cloth bathrobe. She's been in
the shower recently, and her hair clings damply to her head. Her

eyes are swollen, the skin beneath her nose chapped and red. She invites me in. When the door is shut I open my arms and she lays her head on my shoulder and lets out a long, shuddering breath. Over her shoulder I look around the living room. A pizza box is on the floor, dirty dishes stacked beside it. Papers and envelopes spill from the couch to the floor, and open photo albums lay on top of each other on the coffee table. Newspapers are strewn everywhere. The one on the couch is turned to the page with my story about the car. I can't quite read my byline from here, but I can recognize the shape of my name.

I pat her warm, damp back and she takes a deep breath. "I'm sorry I lied to you about Russell. I had promised her, and a promise is a promise."

"I understand."

She steps away and studies my face. "Do they think he did it?"

"Do you?"

She shakes her head decisively. "He loved her."

Yes, and isn't that his motive? I say, "I know. He's not a suspect."

"Good." She looks vaguely around the room. "I found some letters," she says, waving a crumpled tissue in the direction of the couch. "From when she went away to camp." I think she's telling me this to explain her emotional state. I wonder how many days she's spent like this. Her apartment, so neat when I first saw it, is starting to resemble mine in messiness. It's starting to resemble Allison's.

Angela drifts over to the couch and picks up one of the letters. "'There's a really cool girl in my cabin named Susie,'" she reads. "'She says she's already French-kissed three boys. She says it just takes practice.'" She laughs and folds the letter in half, then sinks down onto the couch. "She wrote, 'P.S. She's not as cool as you.' I guess she thought I'd be jealous."

If I could I would gather those letters up, take them home and pore over them at my desk. I'd like to put them in chronological order, use them to chart Allison's childhood, add them to the map I'm making of her life. This led to this led to this and that is why. Angela folds the letter again and presses it to her chest. I can't think of a way to take it from her.

"I saw your story about the car," she says. "Does it mean they're getting closer to finding them?"

"It helps," I say. "When they find them, the evidence in the car will help get a conviction."

"The cops think they still have her underwear," she says, her voice flat. "As a souvenir."

"They might have her wallet, too," I say. "If we're lucky it will get them caught."

Angela turns her face to me. "You're doing everything you can, aren't you?" she says. Her eyes well up.

I nod. A lump rises in my throat. I take a tissue from the coffee table and hand it to her. I ask her, as gently as I can, if I can have the key.

Alone in Allison's apartment, I move from room to room, turning on lights. Someone has been here and cleaned up. The furniture has been dusted, clothes and dishes put away, even the shoes in the foyer lined up in neat rows. I picture her mother here, kneeling on the floor putting pairs together. Silver boots. Pink sneakers. Red high-heeled sandals. It seems wrong that these things go on existing without her, as though all evidence of her life should have disappeared when she did. Now everything she owned is neat and organized, and the apartment feels like a museum, a historic home. I should be standing behind a red velvet rope, looking at a pair of glasses on the desk, slippers beside the bed, all those careful, eerie touches meant to suggest the person who lives here has only just stepped out of the room.

I walk in the bedroom and stop, clutching at the doorknob. Someone has cleaned it, just like the other rooms, but someone else has come after them and rifled through it. The dresser drawers are wedged open with bright pieces of fabric, as though the person were in too much of a hurry to fit the clothes back in. The bedclothes are rumpled, the mattress slightly askew, and a box of trinkets protrudes from underneath the bed. The wastebasket is empty. The papers on the desk have obviously been shifted since they were first stacked. The searcher didn't line them up properly before putting them back down. I don't know who it was—maybe the cops. Maybe Angela, Peter, Russell, or someone else, looking for some remembrance of Allison, looking for evidence of her misdeeds or theirs.

I check behind the headboard for the box. It's untouched. I pull it out and open it, touching the spoon, the needle, the foil with my fingertip. Then I close it and drop it inside my bag.

In the living room I find the videotapes stacked against the wall beside the television. Someone has put them in order, one through eleven. I run my finger down the stack. Two are missing. Five, the one I took, and nine. For a moment there is nothing I want more in the world than to know what is on that tape. I take number one off the top and put it in the VCR. For the next hour I sit watching tape after tape, the moments jumbling together in my mind.

Allison, wearing the pink wig and a short black dress, singing. She throws her head back and opens her arms wide to make room for the last enormous note, and then when she lifts her head again I can see it in her eyes, the triumph, the way her body tingles with the knowledge of her own power.

Allison and Angela sitting at the kitchen counter, smoking a joint and talking, with the long pauses and low voices of the very stoned. "I just have to be myself," Allison is saying. "I don't know how to be anything else."

Allison, onstage, beating out a rhythm with her hand on her guitar.

Allison, running her fingers through her hair.

Allison, laughing.

Allison. Allison. Allison.

The camera zooms in on Peter's face. He rolls his eyes, then puts a cigarette in his mouth and leans forward to light it.

Allison's voice says, "This is my baby brother, Peter. Isn't he adorable?" Peter's face fills the frame. He crosses his eyes and sticks out his tongue.

The camera shakes with Allison's laughter. "I'm teaching Peter to dance," her voice says. The picture bobbles as she sets the camera on the tripod and then she appears in the frame, holding out her hand to Peter. Peter shakes his head. "Come on," she says. "If you're going to the prom, you have to learn to dance."

"I do not," he says. "People don't dance this way at the prom."

"Come on," she says. "It'll be fun."

Peter sighs, and puts his hand in hers. I watch them dance, Allison leading, Allison singing, dee da da dee da da as they spin around the room. Peter joins in. Dee da da dee da da. They start spinning faster and faster, a blur of dark hair and smiling faces, until finally Allison collapses laughing on the couch, saying he's worn her out. He stands grinning at the camera. Then he holds out his hand to her. "One more dance?" he says.

She shakes her head.

"Please?" he says.

"All right," she says, and bounds up and into his arms. I watch them dance. I look at her hands clasped behind his neck, his hands on the small of her back. I see the way he's looking at her, and I know what it means. Russell was right. He whirls her around, and when they come to a stop he keeps on holding her. She laughs, and tries to step away, but he just tightens his arms around her waist. "Let go," she says, still laughing. She beats lightly on his shoulders with her fists. "Let me go, little brother."

He shakes his head and says nothing.

"Come on, Peter." She's not laughing anymore. "Let go of me. I know you're stronger than me. It's not funny."

He still doesn't speak, a strange smile frozen on his face. Allison begins to push as hard as she can against his shoulders. "Goddamnit," she says, breathing faster now with the effort. "Let go!" She throws all of her weight against the arms around her waist and in that moment he lets go of her and she stumbles back against the couch. I can't see her face anymore, just her torso and her thighs. "Jesus," she says. "Grow up."

Peter is still in the frame. He says nothing. A slow flush creeps up his neck and into his face, and he turns away like he's ashamed to look at her. "What is wrong with you?" she says, moving out of the frame so no part of her is visible anymore. Then the camera shuts off.

I sit for a moment watching the static on the screen. Whether he admitted it to himself I don't know, the desire that drove him to hold her like that. I don't know if now his sorrow is shaded with guilt. I don't know if the faint resemblance between me and that dead girl explains why he let me hold his hand at the funeral, why he kissed me that first night in the car.

There's one thing I do know.

I'm jealous.

I find Evan eating his lunch in front of the twelve o'clock news. When I walk in, Lydia McKenzie is promising surprising new developments in the Allison Avery murder case. "She's a little late, don't you think?" Evan nods at her serious face, his mouth full of sandwich.

"Unless they've got something else." A sick feeling rises in my stomach.

"What could they have that you don't have?" He pushes a bag of chips toward me.

"Nothing." I take a chip. "Sorry your story got bumped."

He shrugs. "Bishop wants us to go out with him after work." He glances at me, then looks back at the television. "To celebrate your big stories."

I watch him, trying to read in his face whether he's angry or jealous or mocking. His tone was neutral.

"It's coming on," he says.

We watch as one of the correspondents stands in front of 201 Poplar and relates the things everyone has already read in the paper. Cut to the Averys exiting the police station. Dr. Avery stops. A slight breeze lifts her blond hair away from her head like wings. Around her the shouted questions intensify. She calmly says, "I've given my statement to Olivia Dale. You can read it in the newspaper. That's all I'm going to say."

"Wow," Evan says, as we watch her walk away. "You're really the anointed one."

"Strange isn't it," I say. On-screen the correspondent's lines are almost word for word from the article I wrote. "She has a way of making me feel like we're in league together."

"For what?" Evan asks.

"I don't know," I say. "I'm trying to figure that out."

I find Dr. Gregerson standing in the hall outside his office, hands in his pockets. His mouth open a little, he's staring at nothing, and for a few moments I don't register in his view. Then he blinks, straightens up, and says, "Miss Dale? How can I help you?"

We sit in an exam room, the tools for a pelvic laid out on the table beside us. He tells me what he's already told the police, that Allison could somehow have gotten the keys to the med cart and stolen the morphine herself. Or Allison could have persuaded one of the nurses to do it for her. "We're forced to give everyone a lie detector test now," he says. "It's a real shame."

I think of Angela. She must top the list of suspects. I hope she passes that test.

The doctor says he never saw any signs that Allison was using. He says that it never occurred to him to wonder. Then he asks me, "If you already know all this, why hasn't it been in the paper?"

"I've had it in bits and pieces," I say vaguely. "I'm waiting."

He nods as though that makes sense. "I hope there's an explanation."

"So do I," I say.

Out in the hall, I put my notebook in my bag and shake his hand. Then I frown, as though a thought has just occurred to me. "Doctor," I say, "were you and Allison ever involved?"

He blanches. "What kind of question is that?"

"I'm sorry." I turn to go.

He touches my arm. "No," he says. "But I was very . . ." He searches for the word. "I was very fond . . ."

"I'm sorry," I say again.

When I was younger, scraggly-haired strangers with tattoos came to our church youth group to tell us they had had wild sex and done drugs and now they were reborn and sorry and here to tell us to keep going straight and true, take a bypass around that city of sin. They had done those things, though, tasted sin and survived to set it aside, and didn't that make them some kind of heroes?

If Allison Avery had lived, some day she might have had a husband who grinned when he said to the children, "Your mama had a wild youth." And she would have smiled and kept her secrets. But she died, and so in one version of her story she is stupid and reckless, she is a warning, a bad example.

I haven't written that version, and this is what I could have answered when the doctor asked me why.

This is America, land of rebels, land of puritans, land of hypocrites. I print that she did drugs, and Allison Avery is a bad girl come to a bad end.

I don't, and she stays what she is now. The perfect victim.

Bishop and Evan and I walk three abreast up the sidewalk to the M&O. I'm in the middle, my arms linked with theirs, and we're laughing. Bishop keeps calling me his "little girl," talking about how far I've come since the days when it made me nervous to approach somebody on the street with a question. At one point he bursts into a chorus of "Sunrise, Sunset."

Inside they insist on buying me a beer, and then Evan proposes a toast to the overpass, and then we toast Bryce for being so willing to let go of my hand. For the next two hours I rehearse my stories, my reaction to the break-in, my roll down the hill, my trip with Russell to the police station. I let them admire me. I don't tell them about swinging off the Averys' deck on a tree branch, Peter's arm around my waist. I don't tell them I'm thinking about going to the Lizard Lounge to talk to the people who might have known Allison, who sold her drugs or know who did.

When we say good night outside, Bishop hugs me and kisses me on the cheek. "You're a damn fine reporter," he says, his eyes a little misty. "I'm very proud."

Over his shoulder Evan rolls his eyes and grins. "Me too," he says. I hug him. "Just don't break your neck," he says, his breath warm against my ear.

I head back to my car, twirling my key chain on my finger and humming to myself. I'm as awake as if I had consumed an entire pot of coffee, my head buzzing and my cheeks flushed. I feel like I'm about to burst out of my skin. "Allison, Allison," I say under my breath. I'm going to go back to that bar, and maybe the people there will tell me what turn in her life took her to the place where I first saw her.

I'll tell them I'm looking for the best feeling in the world, and see what I can find.

Before I get out of the car I glance at myself in the mirror. My own face shocks me, it's so at odds with the way I feel. I look haggard— pale and plain. There are dark circles under my eyes, and my hair is limp against my cheek. In my button-down shirt and knee-length skirt I look nothing like the sort of girl a guy would walk up to in a bar. I look nothing like Allison Avery.

I dump my bag out on the passenger seat. The pink wig is a splash of brilliant color against the beige upholstery. I pick it up and turn it over, running my fingers over the slick strands. Then I put the wig on, looking in the rearview mirror to adjust it on my head. I open one more button on my shirt and pull off my dark panty hose. In my bag I find a never-opened tube of red lipstick. I run it over my lips, paint my lashes with mascara. "Hello," I say to the unfamiliar girl in the mirror.

Inside the bar it's almost as dark as outside, and I stand in the doorway for a minute while my eyes adjust. Cigarette smoke sits in the air. I glance into the side room, where the pool table is. A guy with long hair tucked behind his ears is lining up a shot. His opponent stands with his hands folded around the top of the cue. I can see how thick the muscles of his arms are beneath his skin. He glances at me and lets his gaze linger, looking at the wig. Immediately I duck my head and look away. Then I force myself to stand up straight, to turn and look right back at him. He's not watching me anymore. He's watching the other guy sink a perfect shot.

There's no band tonight and the place is not crowded. A couple sits at the bar, a group of college-age guys in baseball caps spills out from two tables. As I walk past them I watch them from the corner of my eye. They're drinking beer, smoking Marlboros, and paying no attention to me. One of them tells a dirty joke and the rest laugh uproariously, smacking the table with their open palms.

At the bar I swing myself onto a stool and order a bourbon on the rocks. With the cold drink in my hand I turn from side to side. A big-haired girl sits at the side of the bar next to a boy whose curly hair is damp against the back of his neck. He leans in close to her and she laughs, spluttering into her beer. He puts his hand on her shoulder. Her whole body inclines toward him, her eyes raised to his.

Behind the bar the bartender washes glasses, his face set and businesslike. "Excuse me," I say, leaning on the bar. He comes toward me, wiping his hands on a rag. "Can I get you something else?" he says.

playing pool with one of the boys now. "I'll be right back." Jerome lifts his head, looks me up and down, and grins. "Sure you will," he says.

He drives a truck with an oversized cab, jacked up on huge tires. He walks with me around to the passenger side and holds the door open for me. I stare up at the black leather seat, thinking maybe this isn't such a good idea. "Go on," he says. "Climb in."

When I'm sitting, he shuts the door, and goes around to his side. He's got a cross hanging off the rearview mirror. The cab is immaculate, no trash on the floor and just a baseball cap sitting on the seat. He swings himself in and shuts the door. Then he sinks back into the seat. "Like my truck?" he asks.

I nod, staring out the windshield at the dark parking lot. I glance at my door to make sure it's still unlocked. Casually, I rest my hand on the door handle.

"Let's see," he says under his breath. "'Scuse me." He leans across me to open the glove compartment. His arm brushes against my knee. His head is inches from my breast. I press my body back into the seat. He's whistling through his teeth, searching through the compartment. Now his arm is almost resting on my thigh. "It's in here somewhere," he says. I don't know what he's going to pull out of there. If I'm lucky it will be a small foil package. If I'm unlucky, it will be a knife, or a gun. I'm trying to breathe normally, keep my body from touching his.

"Here we go," he says. He straightens up. In his hand is a slender white joint.

"Marijuana?" I say. My voice is heavy with disappointment. "Don't you have anything else?"

He lowers his hand, frowning. "Like what?"

"Like heroin," I say.

He laughs. "Oh, girl, I don't do that stuff."

"I was just hoping."

"You don't look like a junkie," he says.

"I'm not." I turn my face to look out the window.

"What are you then, a cop or something?"

"No," I say. I must not sound convincing. He turns on the light and takes my chin in his hand, studying my face. "I don't think I know you after all," he says finally. "I thought you were a different girl."

"I'm sorry," I say. I push open the heavy door and jump down from the cab. Walking away, I pull the wig from my head and run my hand through my own damp hair. "A totally different girl," he yells after me. I don't turn around. I wipe the lipstick off with the back of my hand.

In my car I sit and watch him climb out of his truck and walk back to the bar, shaking his head. His hands are jammed down into the pockets of his jeans, and even from here I can see the outline of his triceps. When he opens the door to the bar a burst of laughter explodes into the parking lot, cut off sharp when the door shuts again behind him. Every turn I take just brings me to a dead end. It's like I'm traveling through a maze, the place where she died both the beginning and the end. She runs ahead of me, calling catch me if you can.

David finds me sexy in the wig. When I walk in his front door carrying it in my hand, he looks me up and down and says, "Have you been to a costume party?"

"I was undercover," I say in a teasing tone so he'll think I'm joking. I put the wig back on to show him, and he walks around me like I'm a car he's thinking of buying, running his fingers lightly across the middle of my back. "I like it," he says in my ear, then wraps his arms tightly around me. "Hey you," he murmurs. "Looking for a good time?"

"I don't even know you," I say.

"Want to?" he asks.

He leads me into the bedroom, where he takes everything off me but the wig.

❧

In the middle of the night, I wake up. The place is quiet, and when the air conditioner starts up it seems to roar like a jet engine. Even David's breathing seems too loud. I can't sleep anymore and I wonder what I've been dreaming. A faint light comes in the window, and I can make out that the closet door is open. When I look at it, my conviction that someone is in it is as strong as it ever was when I was a child. I sit up and stare at it, telling myself that it's empty. I crawl to the edge of the bed, trying not to disturb David, and reach out to push some shirts aside. Nothing but swaying clothes, shoes in a neat row. I ease back under the covers and pull the sheets to my nose, but my stomach still burns with stupid fear.

I get out of bed, and go to the closet, throwing the clothes to either side. I see nothing, but it's a walk-in closet, and someone could still be standing behind the coats all the way at the back. On hands and knees I crawl to the back of the closet, the heavy coats draped around my head. My hands find a stray belt, a pair of running shoes, then the back wall. The wall is cool and I press my face against it, remembering when I thought if I went into the back of my closet enough times I might eventually find a door. I always went looking for a way out when something frightened me. One night when I was nine and home alone, the phone rang and a man's deep voice asked for my mother. I said, as I had been taught, that she was in the shower. "Go get her, then," the man said, and when I said I didn't want to bother her and asked if I could take a message, he took a deep breath and said, "Do you want me to rape your mother?"

"No," I whispered. I was shot through with terror, the kind that turns your body cold.

He laughed and said, "I know where you live."

I dropped the phone and ran. When my mother came home she found me shaking at the back of the closet.

I can still hear it, the arrow in that disembodied voice, how much he hated me.

I close my eyes, and the thought flashes through my head: *The only thing we have to fear is fear itself.* It almost makes me laugh.

A hand touches my back.

I scream and scream. Arms wrap around my waist and haul me backward, and I fall against a body, still screaming. "Olivia, for God's sake," David shouts. "It's me. It's me."

I sit up. My pulse is pounding so hard inside my neck I can feel the skin above it is moving. "You scared me," I say.

"No shit," he says, running his hand up my arm. "What's the matter with you?"

"I don't know," I say. "I'm an idiot."

"Poor baby," he says. "Did you have a bad dream?" He takes me in his arms—and I have to put it that way, because when he wraps his six-foot-three self around my five-foot-two body, that's how I feel—taken, enclosed, held somewhere between security and fear.

14

For the thirty-fifth day in a row the temperature was above ninety degrees. Two old ladies were found dead in their apartments yesterday. I wrote the story this morning. Already this summer six people have died from the heat.

I'm waiting for Peter outside the Four Corners, fanning my face with my hand. It's been a long and frustrating day. I can't keep Allison on the front page. Forensic evidence has all but eliminated Russell Freeland as a suspect. I couldn't reach him for a quote and space was tight, so a small story is running on an inside page. Only suspects and murderers get front-page coverage, and often even murder's not enough.

Peter emerges from the restaurant, saying good-bye over his shoulder to someone inside. He's wearing his busboy outfit, a white button-down shirt tucked into black pants. He's got the sleeves rolled up to his elbows and his hair is mussed, his eyes are heavy-lidded with exhaustion. "I can't believe how hot it is," he says when he sees me waiting on the sidewalk. "It makes me want to lie down where I am and go to sleep. I read in the paper today some old lady died."

"There's been a couple," I say. "Old people with no air-conditioning."

"You wrote that story," he says. "It's weird to see your name in the paper."

"Wasn't much to it. I just talked to the cop on the phone." He's not really listening, pulling his shirt out of his pants and unbuttoning it. Underneath he's wearing a white T-shirt.

"Where are we going?" I ask him.

"Where my sister went. Isn't that what you said you wanted?" He shrugs out of the button-down and balls it up in his hand. "My car's just up the street."

When we get to his car, Peter opens the passenger-side door for me and grins, as though this is a trick he's just learned. His car smells of smoke and faintly of sweat. I glance in the back. The seat is covered with cassette tapes. Ratty gym shorts and a pair of old running shoes are on the floor. He gets in. "Sorry about the mess," he says. When he starts the car, the radio blares. "Shit," he says, switching it off quickly. "Sorry."

He pulls the car out onto the road. "So why do you want to do this?"

"I want to talk to people who knew her," I say. "I'm hoping someone can help us find a connection the police might have missed."

"You mean like someone who knows who killed her?" He swallows. "I thought the cops said it was a stranger killing."

"It probably was, Peter," I say. "I just want to check it out."

"I guess that can't hurt," he says as we come to a stop at a red light. "The police haven't found a goddamn thing." His voice fills with fury and he says again, "Not a goddamn thing," and drives his fist into the steering wheel.

I don't say anything. He lets out a long breath. Then the light changes and we pull on through. I watch the streetlights go by outside the window, wondering if anyone loves me as much as Peter loves his dead and buried sister.

"Are we going to the Lizard Lounge?" I ask, and when he nods I say, "I've heard a lot of drugs move through there."

He gives me a wary glance. "Are you still thinking about that?"

I reach inside my bag and pull out the box, holding it out to him in my palm. He looks down at it, then back at the road, gripping the steering wheel hard. "Where did you get that?"

"You recognize it?" He gives me a tight nod. All he says is, "It's Allison's," but something about his face tells me he knows what's inside. "You lied to me before about the heroin, didn't you?" I say.

"It's weird the way you say 'heroin,'" he says. "Her-o-in. So formal. Say junk. Smack."

"Junk," I say. "Smack. You lied to me."

"Yeah," he says, his voice heavy with sarcasm. "How'd you know?"

I open the box to show him the needle, the spoon and the tiny foil package nestled inside. He takes it from me and touches the needle with one finger, his face gone pale. "You know what this is, don't you?" I say.

"Of course," he mutters. He doesn't look at me. "Where was it?"

"Your sister's apartment," I say. "I told you."

I nod, and he lets out an aggrieved sigh. "Where?"

"That was you, wasn't it? You searched her room."

He doesn't answer. He runs his finger over the spoon and I wonder what he's thinking, if he ever saw his sister use it. "Why did you take it?"

I hesitate. "I didn't think your mom should be the one to find it."

"Thanks." He shoots me a grateful smile.

It gives me a pang of guilt, the way he believes whatever I say. "What can you tell me about it?" I ask him gently.

Shrugging, he lifts the foil package from the box and then drops it back in again. "Whatever you want to know," he says. "I'll tell you whatever you want to know."

"Can you show me where this came from?" I ask. "I want to meet the people you and your sister knew."

He stares at me as though this is not what he expected me to say. Then he nods, slowly. He smiles his transforming smile at me, and I wonder if I'm ever going to see it when his eyes aren't wet with tears. He stops the car at another light, and with his free hand he reaches for the back of my head and pulls me to him to press his lips hard to mine. "Thank you," he says, kissing me again and again. "Thank you."

I'm almost laughing, trying to say "You're welcome," though I'm not sure what he's thanking me for. Maybe for keeping his sister's secrets. Maybe for wanting to know what they were. By the time he lets me go I'm dizzy. My hand shakes when I reach for the box. Peter doesn't let go. "Maybe I should keep this," he says.

"I don't think so," I say. "What if your mother catches you with it?"

"I guess you're right." He lets me lift it out of his hand. "She sometimes searches my room," he says, and laughs without humor. "I even have to hide my cigarettes." While I tuck the box back inside my bag he lights a cigarette. I notice his hands are shaking, too.

The light turns to green, and Peter whips a U-turn in front of the oncoming cars. "Where are we going?" I say, bracing myself against the dash.

"You don't want to go to the Lizard Lounge," Peter says. "I'll take you where you really want to go."

A guy opens the door wearing nothing but a pair of shorts. He's pale and so thin that his ribs protrude. I have an urge to run my fingers along the first ridge of bone. He looks at me and his face is blank with confusion, his eyes small and rimmed with red. "Hi," he says. His face is familiar. He was there the night I took Peter home from that bar.

"Hi, Nate," Peter says, stepping up beside me.

Nate's face clears. "Mr. Avery," he says, offering him his hand. "How are ya, sir? Come in, come in." He moves aside so we can step into the apartment. We're standing in an entryway, carpeted in brown, with an open litter box in one corner. Ahead of us a long hall stretches away. When the door is closed Nate looks us up and down, smiling. "Hey," he says, pointing at me. "Friend of Allison's?" As her name leaves his mouth, he shoots a worried look at Peter.

"Olivia," I say to Nate, holding out my hand. Instead of shaking it he lifts it to his lips and leaves a wet kiss on my skin.

"Charmed," he says. Then he throws his arm around Peter's shoulders, still holding my fingers loosely in his other hand. "Pete, my good man," he crows. "Why haven't you brought this lovely young lady around before?" Peter's not looking at Nate, but staring down the hall. Inside his pockets his hands are balled into fists. "I know this little boy has a way with the ladies," Nate says to me in a confidential tone. "But wouldn't you prefer a man?"

I shrug. "I don't know any," I say. Nate throws back his head and roars with approving laughter. "Let's go in," he says. "The rest of the gang is in the living room."

We walk down the long empty hall to a nearly silent room. Six or seven people recline against cushions on the floor. I recognize two others from that night—Steve, who hails Peter, and the girl he was tormenting. She's sitting in a corner, her head back against the wall and her eyes closed. Every face in the room is flushed an unhealthy red, and then I notice that even the walls are glowing that same color. At first I think this is a trick my eyes are playing. Then Nate says, "You like my new bulbs?" and points at a lamp in the corner. It's a relief to see that the red light is real, and not some fever vision.

There are only three pieces of furniture, an armchair, a tiny sagging sofa, and a rickety coffee table. On the tiny couch is an electric guitar, a four-track on the coffee table. Nate sees me looking at it. "I just recorded something," he says, "Y'all want to hear it?"

"Sure." I stand looking around while Nate busies himself hooking the four-track up to his stereo. His walls are hung with rock and roll posters and glossy ads he's cut from magazines, most of them featuring the same thin, stringy-haired model. Peter sits on the couch. I perch on the edge of the ratty armchair and look around. There's a reddish-brown stain toward the bottom of one wall. "What is that?" I point at it.

"Puke," Nate says. "I don't clean if off as a reminder not to do speedballs."

"What's a speedball?" I wrap my arms around my stomach and lean forward, trying not to look at the stain. I wonder how much time Allison spent in this apartment, if she laughed or looked away when she first saw that mark on the wall.

"Cocaine and heroin," Peter says. I shoot him a look. He's staring at a Rolling Stones poster, his face a blank.

Nate nods. "Almost killed me," he says, and laughs. "It's ready." He sits on the couch beside Peter and presses play.

For a moment there's no sound but the faint whirring of tape casters. Nate closes his eyes, settling back against the couch. A guitar starts up, playing chords with the distortion turned up high, and then Nate's voice comes in, droning lyrics I can't make out. What seems to be the chorus starts, and Nate sings along with himself: "Oh, baby, I've been livin' on the edge, drivin' all night just to see you." Then the voice stops, and I hear the unmistakable gurgle of a bong hit.

Nate opens his eyes. "Isn't that cool?" he says. "I got the idea right before you came." He nods at me. He nods all the time, like a doll whose head is loose in its socket.

"It's really cool," I say. A pleased smile spreads across his face. It makes me sad. The sound of another bong hit comes out of the speakers, and he points at the stereo, grinning at me.

"Are you playing that shit again?" Steve groans from the floor. He clambers to his feet and comes over to stand behind my chair, leaning so heavily against it that I tilt backward, looking up into his face. His features are thick and droopy, as though the pull of gravity is stronger on him than the rest of us. "I know you," he says to me. "You knew . . ." He shoots a look at Peter and doesn't finish the sentence.

"Allison," Peter says sharply. "You can say it."

"How did you know her?" I ask, looking at Nate.

"College," Nate says. "We had a couple classes together. Chemistry." He gives a barking laugh. "I sucked at it. She let me copy her notes. She's cool." He frowns. "She was cool," he says softly. Then he touches Peter's arm. "I'm sorry."

"Goddamnit," Peter bursts out, jumping to his feet. "Stop fucking apologizing."

"I'm . . . ," Nate starts. He stops, uncertain. Peter strides out of the room. I hear a door slam.

"Shit," Steve says under his breath.

With some effort, because Steve's weight is still pulling the chair backward, I slide forward and get to my feet. Nate watches me, saying nothing, and I head to the back of the room and into the kitchen, looking for a closed door. When I see it, I go to it and knock. There's no response. "Peter, it's me," I say. "Can I come in?" I hear his voice on the other side, though I don't know what he's said. I open the door.

It's the bathroom, and Peter is sitting on the closed toilet, his arms wrapped around his stomach, rocking back and forth.

"Are you okay?" I say, because that's what you ask, even when you know the answer is no.

"I need something," he whispers. "I need something bad."

I go in and crouch beside him, my hand on his warm thigh. "What do you need?"

He runs his hand over my head, smoothing back my hair. Then he brings his hand around to my face, cupping my cheek. He's staring into my face like he's going to learn something there, and then in one motion he brings his other hand to my other cheek and slides forward off the toilet so that he's kneeling with me on the floor. Before I can think, he's kissing me, his hands are inside my shirt, and there's such urgency in him I can't help but feel it too, like an ache in the pit of my stomach, a buzzing in my skin.

"You'll do it, won't you?" he murmurs in my ear, and I lean back, frowning. His hand still cups my breast. "Won't you?" he asks, his voice imploring, and I don't say anything because I'm not sure what the answer is. Then he says, "I want you to do it too," and I realize he's not talking about sex.

"Do what?" I say. I pull on his arm to slide his hand out from under my shirt.

"Her-o-in," he says in a voice that suggests I should have known exactly what he meant.

"You want me to do heroin?" I say. I put my hand on his shoulder and push myself up to a standing position.

"Yeah," he says, standing too. "What else did we come here for?" We stand in this dirty bathroom staring at each other, and I wonder if this is like the first time he kissed me, if he sees something in my face I didn't even know was there. "What else?" I repeat stupidly.

"Don't you know?" he says, and then there's a knock at the door. "Peter?" Nate's voice says. "Olivia? Are you guys okay in there?"

Peter steps around me and whips open the door. Nate is standing there, his hand raised to knock again, his mouth a perfect O of surprise. "Listen, Nate," Peter says. "We'll be okay. But we'd like something to take our minds off it, you know?"

"I've got nothing, man," Nate says, spreading his fingers wide.

"We have some," Peter says. "Can you do the honors?"

"Yeah, sure, of course. Anything I can do to help," Nate says. "Jesus. All you gotta do is ask, you know that."

Nate and Peter leave the room, and I follow, because I don't know what else to do. I feel responsible for what he's about to do. I'm the one who showed him Allison's stash. I'm the one who asked him to bring me here to see her friends. Maybe he thinks when that heroin hits his brain he won't even remember her, and he can imagine nothing better than to forget her now.

Nate leads us into his bedroom, away, he says, "from the rest of those greedy fuckers." This room too is hung with posters and almost bare of furniture, just a little table next to a double bed in a surprisingly ornate wooden frame. Peter reaches for my bag and I let him have it. From the box he takes a small foil package.

Peter looks at me, hesitating.

"If this is the same stuff I had," Nate says. "It's pristine."

I rock back and forth a little on the bed. I keep swallowing, as though something is lodged in my throat. Unsure where to fix my gaze, I let my eyes drift from poster to poster. Only one is in a frame. I keep reading it over and over. Syd Barrett. The Madcap Laughs. Is this what I came here for, to find out what it feels like, to know what the dead girl knew? Being here is beginning to feel like a dream, like I can do anything because in the morning I'll blink myself awake and none of this will matter.

Nate puts some of the heroin in a metal spoon and heats it over a candle flame. I watch it turn to liquid amber. I watch him draw the liquid into a syringe and turn to Peter. Nate is smiling, heavy-lidded with desire and anticipation. "You want to go first?" he asks Peter.

Peter shakes his head. "Her first," he says. He fixes his gaze on me.

"Which arm?" Nate asks me, like a nurse giving a vaccine. I extend my right, then change my mind and hold out my left. I look down at my arm and imagine that I can see the pulse fluttering wildly inside my wrist, like a trapped moth. I resist the urge to switch arms again. Carefully, Nate sets the syringe down on the bedside table and wraps a black belt around my upper arm. He pulls it, tighter than any blood pressure cuff, and I watch a large vein rise to the surface of my skin. Nausea rises in my throat, and I look up to see Peter staring at my arm, his face white and sick.

Nate leans over and picks up the syringe, then crouches down in front of me, balanced on his toes. A little frown of concentration appears between his eyes. He starts to bring the needle to my arm, then hesitates, looking up at me. "First time?" he asks, and I nod. "This is going to feel like nothing you've felt before," he says in a teacher's calm and patient tone. "The important thing is to relax and enjoy it. It's the greatest feeling in the world." He turns his eyes to my arm again. "Like nothing you've felt before."

My heart pounds inside my ears. I think of Allison's face, her laugh, her enormous, aching voice. When I do this, in at least one way we will be the same.

"Clench your fist," Nate says. "That's right." Slowly he moves the syringe closer to my arm. I close my eyes and feel the prick of the needle entering my vein. I gasp. I think I feel my whole body melting. I see Allison again, not her face, but her body, her body like a broken doll.

I jerk my arm away, clamping my mouth shut to keep in a scream.

Nate rocks back on his heels. "Shit," he says calmly. "I didn't even touch you yet."

There is a silence. I stare at my unmarked arm, the purple vein plump and ready. "I . . . I," I say. I feel the blood rushing to my face, flushing my cheeks.

"It's natural to be nervous," Nate says. "I'll try again." He leans toward me. I take a deep breath, trying to calm myself. The needle comes closer. I watch, and I know I won't be able to let him put it in my vein.

I am a coward, and that is why I never get what I want.

"You know what?" I say. With my right hand, I pull at the belt, trying to undo it. It just gets tighter. I keep my eyes on my arm, afraid to look at Peter, afraid I'll see disappointment in his eyes. "I changed my mind."

"Oh," Nate says. He looks confused.

"So you go ahead," I say.

"But . . . ," he says.

"You go ahead," I say again firmly. I hold out my arm. "Take this off."

"All right." He seems cheerful again. He undoes the belt. I rub at the red mark left around my arm. Then I turn my eyes to Peter. His face is drawn. He closes his eyes and I notice that his hands are shaking. "Nate," he says, keeping his eyes closed. "I'm next."

Nate sighs. "I know it," he says. He lifts the belt to Peter's arm.

"Peter, don't." It's out before I meant to say it. He looks at me, his eyes gone dead. "We can't. This is stupid. I've got to tell the cops."

"Jesus," Nate says.

"Don't do it," I say, staring at Peter, and this time it sounds like a threat. "I mean it. I'll call your mother."

Peter closes his eyes. He looks beaten. "Fuck," he says under his breath.

"Look, this is too much controversy for me," Nate says. "I've got a joint you can smoke." He fishes a plastic bag out of his pocket and pulls a joint from it. "Wouldn't want you guys to feel left out."

Peter says nothing else to me. We sit pressed together on the bed, passing the joint back and forth, while Nate tightens the belt around his own arm. We watch Nate slip the needle under his skin. After a moment, Nate gets up and stumbles out of the room. We are silent. Nate returns, holding a clear plastic bowl. He sits, then calmly vomits into the bowl and sets it on the ground. I try not to look, feeling my throat constrict. "How's it feel?" Peter asks him.

Nate smiles, his head nodding gently. When he speaks, it's with a wheeze. Inside his blue eyes his pupils are tiny black dots. "Sorry," he says. "Just really high."

I keep my eyes trained on him, as though if I look at him hard enough I will catch some edge of the sensation he feels. I meant to feel it myself. Here I am again, just looking on.

We watch Nate float there for a while, then I take Peter's hand and stand up, and he stands too. Quietly, we file past the silent people in the red living room and let ourselves out.

Outside the apartment building the air is still and warm. A couple passes us, holding hands, the girl talking brightly about something, waving her free hand. Peter leans down and kisses me on the cheek. His cool lips feel good against my flushed skin. "What was that for?" I ask. "I thought you were angry."

"I was," he says. "But I know you were trying to look out for me. Allison was the same."

"She wouldn't let you?"

He shakes his head ruefully. "No one wants me to have any fun."

"I'm sorry."

"I wish everyone would stop saying that," he says. "Don't apologize to me again." He opens the car door. "You don't want to go home yet, do you? I feel like going for a ride."

The tension rushes from my body. I lean against the car for support. I am weak and frightened, and I'm glad he doesn't know it. "A ride sounds good," I say, and get in.

In the car, I'm half asleep, not paying attention to where we're going. When the car stops, I open my eyes. He's taken us to the crime scene. It seems inevitable that we should be here. Peter turns off the car and we sit and listen to the silence. He gets out, and after a moment I get out too. He's leaning against the front bumper, his arms folded across his chest. I walk over and lean back with him, his shoulder pressed to mine. "I know it's morbid to come here," he says. "I just keep thinking, this is the last place she was alive." He waves his hand. "Something here was the last thing she saw."

I can't think of anything to say. The image of her face on the television screen returns to me. Her dark hair slips across her cheek. Her lips move.

Peter turns toward me. I can feel him studying the side of my face. I don't move. "Olivia?" he says. He turns my name into a question.

I turn toward him. He searches my face, then reaches a hand up slow and brushes his fingers across my cheek. I'm holding my breath. "Eyelash," he says, and holds his fingers close to show me the lash resting there. "Make a wish." I close my eyes and blow the lash from his fingers. With my eyes still closed, I hear him say, "Your life stops." I open my eyes and watch him snap his fingers. "Just like that."

He looks terrified. I take his hand, locking my fingers with his. I want to throw myself open, feel everything as intensely as I can, the stars so bright out here where there are no lights, the air warm on my skin, the pressure of each of his fingers against mine. I could tell him the best you can hope for is these moments when you know it is you inside your skin. Your heart beats. You take a breath and warm air rushes into your lungs. There is no space your body cannot fill.

"Look how bright the stars are," I say.

He leans his head back. We are quiet. "Yes," he says. "Yes."

15

It's Saturday and I'm not supposed to be working. I snuck into the newsroom through the back door, because I knew if Peggy were here and she saw me she would turn me around and send me home. Luckily for me, another editor is on the desk. When I came in the room, he lifted his head from his computer screen just long enough to nod hello.

I feel sick to my stomach when I think about last night. Sitting at my computer, making phone calls, taking notes—these are balms to the painful memory of my own stupidity, these are the route back to control of my story and myself.

How Allison got the morphine is still a minor mystery. The lie detector tests are scheduled for next week. I've learned that the vial and the hypodermic were found in the trunk of the dead girl's car. Morris thinks that Allison gave herself a shot while she was locked in the trunk, knowing that pain was coming. I'm reluctant to accept this. She would have known that a high dose of morphine would impair her ability to fight. She would have known that it might kill her if her captors didn't. She would have been giving up.

Angela still claims to know nothing about the drugs, and though I couldn't say why, I believe her. I called Russell's house again, and to my surprise he called back to tell me he wasn't going to tell me anything more. He sounded weary, making a sad joke about going back to law school with firsthand experience with the law. They don't answer the phone anymore, he said, because of the media, but mainly because of the obscene phone calls, the threats. "I'm sorry," I said, for the thousandth time.

"I'm sorry too," he said.

I haven't called the Averys' house again. I don't want to talk to Peter, though I can't stop myself thinking about him.

Peter. I know him to be a strange and unstable person, too afraid of his mother, too much in love with his sister. Last night probably wasn't his first experience with heroin; he may not only have known about Allison's drug use all along, but have shared it with her. I don't want to believe it. I recognize my weakness when it comes to that boy. If I could find the root of it, I would pull it out and cut it into tiny pieces.

Perhaps they felt that way about Allison, the men who loved her. I write down their names. *Russell Freeland. Carl Fitzner. Peter Avery.* I add *Antonio Roberts.* This is the name of the man who tried to shoot his wife while I watched through the window. I add *Kenneth Obie.* This is the name of the man who put a bullet in his girlfriend Lucille Davis's head. I leave a blank line for the name of the unknown man who killed the prostitute Bernadette Smith.

I think about David, what he might do if he knew that I'd let Peter kiss me, that I'd let him touch my breast, that I'd not only let him but wanted him to.

One thing I know. Nothing kills like a man's love.

David stands in the center of the roof of the Peabody Hotel, calling after me, while I run laughing around the perimeter, as close to the edge as possible. "Why don't you catch me," I say, stopping in front of him, breathing hard. He looks like he doesn't want to play, but then he grins and lunges at me, arms out. I jump aside and dash back to the wall around the edge of the roof, leaning way out over it, just to see his eyes widen with fear for me.

"Come over here," I say. "It's a great view."

"I can see just fine from here," he says. "Please don't lean over the rail. You know it makes me nervous."

David is afraid of heights.

We've been to dinner downtown, where he told me all about his plans for the Allison Avery CD. "Gorgeous voice," he said over and over. "Such a pretty girl. So tragic. I wonder if I ever did meet her," he said. "You would think I would remember."

"Yes," I said. "Yes, you're right."

After dinner I coaxed him up here, which I can every once in a while, because I love the view, I love the little duck house, I love the way the air is thinner up here, breathable. Sometimes there are tourists up here, couples holding hands, loud clusters of drunken college kids. Tonight it's only me and David. I turn toward him and pose against the wall, arms out, head tilted. It's one of those nights when my whole body feels tingly, like there's magic in my fingertips and I could light the sky with one touch. "Come here," I say.

He shakes his head. "You come here."

"I want to kiss you under the stars."

"There's stars right here," he says, and folds his arms across his chest.

"Come on, David," I say. "You've got to confront your fears. Come to the edge and look over."

He shakes his head. I walk slowly toward him and he watches me warily. When I reach him I grab one arm and pull. His arms unfold, but he doesn't budge, bracing his weight against me. *"No,"* he says.

I put my whole weight into pulling on his arm. He snatches his arm free and I fall, hard, on my tailbone. Sitting on the ground, my feet sprawled in front of me, I look up at him frowning over me. "You always do shit like this," he says. Then he launches into a recitation of my crimes, the time when I leaned so far over the railing in a movie theater balcony that he grabbed me, certain I would fall. The time I let my father bully him into hiking up to a cliff, where his knees locked and my father and I had to half carry him back down. There's more, but I stop listening, focusing my gaze on his legs, the soft brown hairs on his knees. "You're not even listening to me," he says. He sounds tired. "Olivia," he says. "Are you even listening to me?"

The thought of continuing this conversation exhausts me. I wish I could be transported out of here, that I could click my heels like Dorothy and find myself somewhere else.

"What are you hoping to accomplish?" he says. "Are you trying to make me mad? Are you trying to give me a heart attack? It would be easier to just break up with me, you know." He nudges me with his foot. "Olivia? Are you okay?"

I look up at him. His face is in shadow. "I'm just trying to have a little fun," I say.

"Well, I've had enough fun. I'm going home. Are you coming?"

"Don't go home. I'm not ready."

"You can come or not," he says. "I'm leaving."

We are both silent. From the duck house comes the sound of rustling feathers, the contented quacking of one of the ducks. On the street below the cars whoosh past. Someone laughs. A sweet smell, like flowers, rises on the air. David holds out his hand to me and when I take it he pulls me up to standing. He drops my hand then, and we look at each other, inches apart. "I'm not going home," I say.

"Suit yourself," he says. We both turn. He walks away. I walk to the railing and lean on it. There is the city, like any city, beautiful on a summer night with the lights shining through the warm air and the people moving languorously on the streets below, calling out to one another, extending their hands. An urge to jump runs through me, a sensation so physical it's hard not to let my body move. I feel as though jumping from this roof would not be suicide, but entering the city like a diver enters a pool, a fast and clean arrival in the center.

The door to the roof slams. David is gone, and it's a relief to me. He makes me feel guilty, and I'm tired of it, tired of my uncertainty and fear. I'm tired of myself. I tighten my grip on the metal rail. Somewhere down there is the woman who broke into my house, the man who killed Bernadette Smith, the person who left Allison Avery dead on the ground. The summer's murderers hide their darkness inside them as they walk outside with their neighbors, looking up at the stars.

Inside the hotel I go to the bathroom and pull Allison Avery's wig from my bag. I couldn't bring myself to let Nate slip that needle in my vein, but at least in this small way I can be, if not who she was, at least someone different from myself. In the mirror I adjust the wig on my head, tucking the strands of my own hair away. Then I call Evan on the pay phone. He'll meet me on Beale Street, he says, in half an hour.

In the daiquiri bar at the end of Beale I order a strawberry daiquiri that comes in a child's sand bucket with a green plastic shovel. I offer Evan a shovel full. He shakes his head. He can't stop frowning at my wig. "You're in a weird mood," he says.

"I'm in a good mood," I say. I lean in and kiss him on the cheek.

"Your mouth is so cold," he says.

I kiss him on the other cheek, warm as the air. Then I kiss him on the forehead.

"What's with all this kissing?" Evan says. "Somebody might get the wrong idea."

"Or the right idea," I say, and wink at him. What I like about Evan is I can touch him all night and we will both know it doesn't mean a thing.

"You're on fire tonight," Evan says. "I'm getting nervous. Where's David?"

"He went home," I say. "It's just you and me." I take his hand and we step off the curb and enter the crowd moving along the middle of the street. We pass two men wearing dusters, the long coats of cowboys, their faces reflections of each other. I turn to look at them. They walk on by in perfect unison, matching each other stride for stride, the hair on each head parted at exactly the same point. "Did you see that?"

"I know them," Evan says. "They're identical twins, but they tell people they're cousins."

I stop and look hard at him. "You're full of shit."

He holds up his hands. "I swear," he says, laughing. "It's the God's honest truth."

"Why would they do that?"

"Why do people do anything?" he says. "To fuck with other people."

"You can't trust anybody," I say. I hold up my shovel full of daiquiri and this time Evan leans in and slides some into his mouth. He straightens up, his mouth stained pink, and I reach out to wipe the syrup from his lips.

"Allison?" a voice says behind me.

I turn, feeling like I'm moving in slow motion, like this is a scene in a movie, and there is a man behind me who starts when he sees my face. "I'm sorry," he says. "I thought you were . . ."

"Allison Avery?"

"You know her?" he says. He's a tall man in a T-shirt and jeans tight enough to show the long muscles of his thighs.

"I know her," I say. Evan frowns. He digs through people's trash, but he doesn't like to lie. "How do you know her?"

"I took her out a few times," he says. "Once she showed up in a wig just like that one. Did you buy them together?"

I tell him yes. I tell him Allison called us the pink ladies.

He says Allison turned to him in a bar and asked if he knew the difference between Ring-Dings and Ding Dongs and that when he explained she hugged him and said he had won her a bet and gave him her phone number. He said she dragged him to a ballroom dance place, he and she were the only couple under fifty and she didn't know the dances but she worked up a sweat trying and let a couple of the old men lead her through the twists and turns of the rumba. Allison told him she'd once waded into the Mississippi, fully dressed, on a hot day. "Bet she just dipped her foot in, and even that's dangerous. That girl," he says, shaking his head. "She couldn't stop moving. At a restaurant once, I bet her twenty bucks she couldn't sit absolutely still for ten minutes. She tried sitting there with her feet planted, her hands folded on the table. Her eyes were darting around, her lips twitching. She started chewing the side of her mouth."

Without my noticing, Evan has moved a few steps away. He stands at an angle from me, looking hard into the crowd as though to pick out a face he knows.

The man is looking around, too. I know he's looking for Allison and I imagine that she walks up behind me, complaining about the line at the bathroom. "Is she with you?" he asks.

"No," I say. And then I blurt out, "She's dead."

His face registers horror, disbelief. "My God," he says. "How?"

I shake my head, pressing my lips together like I'm trying not to cry. Tears burn beneath my eyelids; who am I fooling, this man or myself? "Somebody abducted her, killed her," I say. "Didn't you see it in the paper?"

Aren't you reading my stories?

"I heard a woman was dead," he says. "Never heard the name." He sounds so earnest when he says he's sorry. He fumbles in his pocket and hands me a handkerchief. I'm surprised. Not many men still carry them, especially not men his age. It's soft, white cotton.

"I don't need this," I say.

"You're crying," he says.

"I am not," I start to say before I decide it's better just to dab at my eyes. "Thank you."

"Keep it," he says. He looks so helpless, sagging like an unstuffed scarecrow, all useless, dangling limbs.

I look at the handkerchief. "You're right," I say. "I am crying."

At Evan's side I turn back and look at the man, slumping like a broken thing inside the moving crowd. His lips shape the words *my God my God,* still moving as we slip into the crowd and walk away.

"What was that all about?" Evan says, jamming his hands in the pockets of his jeans. "Did you get anything?"

"Just character stuff. Nice enough guy. He gave me his handkerchief." I wave it in the air as proof.

"Why did you say you knew her?"

"It just popped out," I say. "At any rate, it got him talking."

"I don't know," he says.

"You don't know what?"

"I don't know," he says, not looking at me. "I don't know."

"You never know what might be helpful," I say. I throw my hands in the air. "Who can understand that, if not you?"

Music bursts from the club next to us when someone opens the door. Inside the people bob and dip, holding each other close. "Let's go in," I say, taking Evan's hand and pulling. "I feel like dancing."

"No more talking to strangers?" Evan says, hanging back.

"You know me," I say. "I never talk to strangers." I bat my eyes. "I'm very shy."

He grins. "All right, then."

Inside we sit at the bar and order two bourbons. "On the rocks," Evan says.

"Straight up," I say, and Evan shoots me a look, eyebrows raised. When the drinks come Evan says, "To the news," and we clink our glasses together. I watch the dancers out of the corner of my eye while Evan talks about the story he's working on. I catch a few words, "terrible . . . dead . . . police . . . scoop." I lift my glass and realize it's empty. The bartender brings me another and I smile at him and tip him two dollars. Then I glance across the bar and see a woman staring at me. I look away, trying to listen to Evan talking. "You know?" he says. "You know what I mean?"

"Yeah," I say. "Sure." A few minutes later I look sidelong to see if she's still watching me. She stares right at me. This time I meet her gaze. She just keeps watching. In the darkness I can barely make out her face, but I see her eyes. I feel them on me. Evan is saying, "Are you listening to me?" Everyone keeps asking me that.

"Excuse me," I say, slipping off the barstool and taking a step in her direction, my pulse pounding inside my ears. She is standing too, her fists clenched at her sides, ready to accuse me of something. She's looking right at me. She knows me. I take another step toward her and then I realize.

She is me. It's a mirror.

The room whirls around me and I put a hand on the stool for support. "Are you okay?" Evan says.

"Oh yeah." I flash him a smile. "Just going to the bathroom." I lift my hand from the stool and squeeze his arm. "Be right back." It's a long trip through the crowd. Inside I lean against the counter and splash cold water on my face, avoiding the sight of myself in the mirror.

Head down, I come barreling out of the bathroom and smack up against a man's chest. "Sorry," I say. I look up, and see Carl's face, flushed red. "Oh," I blurt.

He cups my shoulder in his hand. "Are you all right?" he says, his voice gentle.

"Fine," I say, taking a deep breath and stepping back away from him. He leaves his hand on my shoulder. "I didn't see you."

"I know," Carl says. He lifts his hand from my shoulder and rubs the hairs on the wig between his fingers. "You look beautiful," he says. His voice is still soft and sweet when he says, "Who are you here with?"

"My friend Evan," I say. "He's at the bar."

"Would he mind if we had a dance?" He smiles at me and holds out his hand.

"Of course not." I put my hand in his and let him pull me out to the dance floor. As we reach the center the song comes to an end. We stand for a moment, smiling awkwardly at each other, and then a slow song begins. Blushing, Carl shrugs and reaches for me, his large nervous hands on the small of my back. I rest my hands on his shoulders. I don't know where to look. Carl keeps his eyes fixed on mine, a tiny smile playing over his lips. I smile back, and he takes that as an invitation to pull me closer, so that I'm pressed against his chest and there's nothing to do but rest my cheek against his shoulder. He's humming along with the song, one of his hands making slow circles on my back.

"Was Allison a good dancer?" I ask, and the hand stills. "You miss her, don't you," I say, leaning back so I can see his face. He nods, his mouth twisting like he's fighting back tears, and I sound as sympathetic as I can when I say, "I know it makes it worse that you can't apologize about your fight."

He nods and lets out a shuddering breath.

"What did you say to her that night?" I say. "I think you'll feel better if you tell me."

He shakes his head, pressing his lips together.

"Pretend I'm her," I say. "You can apologize to me." I wrap my arms around his neck and press my cheek against his shoulder. For a few moments we sway gently together, and I think it's not going to work, and then he begins to talk.

"When we were in high school," he says, "Allison got pregnant. It wasn't mine, but I asked her to marry me. She laughed. I asked her to marry me and she laughed." His hands tense against my back. "She had an abortion."

"But that's not what you were fighting about now," I say.

"No," he says. "It's just that sometimes it comes back to me, you know? What our lives could have been." Then he says, so softly I feel it more than hear it, a rumble in his throat, "She never even gave me a chance."

The song comes to an end, but I let him keep holding me. As a fast song starts and people split apart and begin to move, I take his hand and pull him to the side of the dance floor. "What happened that night?" I ask, keeping my eyes fixed on his face. He's looking at the floor.

"Think how different our lives would have been if she would have just let me take care of her," he says. "We'd have a baby, and she'd still be alive."

I imagine the two of them fighting, and in my imagination he calls her a whore, a baby killer, and then maybe he slaps her. I imagine Allison's face, flushing red with anger and hurt, the white mark of his hand across her cheek. She grabs Carl by the arm and pushes him to her door, and even once he is on the other side, shouting her name, she still wants to hit him so badly that she picks up a bottle of moisturizer and smashes it, listening to his heavy foot thud against her door, asking herself how he could call this love.

"She would still be alive," he says again, rubbing his fingers across his eyes. He sniffs, wiping his nose with the back of his hand.

"What's going on?" a voice says. I turn and see Evan standing beside me, an uncertain smile on his lips.

"Who's this?" Carl says, his voice sharp. "Your boyfriend?"

"This is my friend Evan," I say. "I told you, Carl."

"And who are you?" Evan says, irritation in his voice. He frowns at Carl.

Carl doesn't even look at him. He pulls me closer, lowering his voice. "I thought you said this guy wasn't a date."

"I'm not," Evan says.

"Then what do you want?" Carl says sharply.

"Jesus Christ," Evan says. "Who is this asshole?"

"Evan . . . ," I say, putting my free hand on his arm.

"Hey, Evan," Carl says, suddenly turning toward him. He drops my hand and squares his shoulders. "Back off."

Evan makes an incredulous face, looking at me. "Are you ready to go?" he says.

"No, she's not," Carl says. "We were talking." He looks at me. "Tell him."

Evan puts his hand on my arm. "Let's go, Olivia," he says. "I'm taking you home." With a quick motion, Carl knocks his hand away. "Are you her boyfriend?"

"No," Evan says. "Jesus."

"Don't touch her then," Carl says.

Evan shakes his head. He looks at me. "Are you coming?"

I don't say anything.

"Damnit, Olivia," Evan says. "What is going on here?"

Carl pushes Evan's shoulder with his hand. "Don't talk to her like that," he says.

"Fuck you," Evan says, his face turning red. He pushes Carl back.

Carl grabs Evan's shoulders in his hands and leans in close to his face. "Back off," he says.

"Olivia," Evan says, pushing Carl away, "will you tell this asshole to get lost?"

I don't say anything. Evan gives me a disgusted look and stalks off. Carl smiles and reaches for me. I step away. "I'll be right back," I say. I turn to go after Evan, pushing my way through the dancers. When I catch him, he stops and says, "What the fuck was that?"

"I'm sorry," I say. "I didn't want to piss him off. He's important to the story. I need to talk to him."

"I'm your friend, Olivia," he says. "Sometimes that has to come before the story." He looks up over my shoulder. "Here he comes," he says. "We're getting out of here." He wraps his fingers around my wrist and begins to pull me from the bar.

"Evan." I'm trying to speak calmly. "Evan. Let go of me. I've got to talk to him. I'm not ready to go home."

"I don't give a goddamn what you're ready for," he hisses. "You're drunk and we're leaving." He's pulling me through the crowd. I bump against an older woman in a halter top, knocking into one of her enormous breasts. "Sorry," I mutter.

"That's okay, sugar," she says. Her eyes follow me. She feels sorry for me, she wonders what I did to make my boyfriend, my husband, drag me out of the bar this way. She hopes he won't hit me when he gets me home, or maybe she thinks, from the wig and my short skirt, that I might deserve it.

I try to wrench my wrist from Evan's grasp, stumbling into a group of dancing college kids, who part around me and don't look me in the face. Evan tightens his grip and pulls harder. "Let go of me," I say.

"Keep your voice down," he says. He presses his lips together. No one wants to look me in the eye. He stares ahead. The crowd looks away.

"Look at me, Evan," I say. He keeps walking. "Look at me," I call, trying to plant my weight so he can't pull me through the door. He gives a final yank, and we're out in the hazy night, forcing the sidewalk traffic to diverge around us. I'm asking Evan to stop, to let go, to please turn around, but he just keeps walking, not saying a word to me, not even acknowledging that it's me he's got in tow. I see a headline: REPORTER HUMILIATED ON BEALE STREET. I'm staring at the back of his head, the muscles tight in the back of his neck, and then he yanks me around a group of people, so I stumble and almost fall and suddenly I hate him. "Let go of me," I shout. "Let go of me, you fucking faggot." As soon as the words are out of my mouth I feel sick.

Evan drops my wrist.

"Evan," I say, reaching for him. "My God, I'm so sorry." He says nothing. He stands for a minute with his back to me, clenching his fists at his side. Then he stalks off through the crowd.

"Fine," I shout after him. "Fuck you too." Above my head a blue neon guitar blinks on and off. A woman beside me takes off her tank top and runs laughing down the street in her bra. Her boyfriend picks up her top and goes after her. I pull my shirt away from my skin, sticky with sweat and the alcohol I can feel coming out my pores.

From behind me, Carl says, "Is he gone?"

"Yes, he's gone," I say, spinning around. I'd like to sink my fist into his pudgy stomach. "You shouldn't have talked to him like that."

"I was jealous," Carl says plaintively, reaching for me. "I'm sorry."

"He's not my boyfriend, Carl," I say. I step backward, leaving his grasping hands dangling awkwardly in the air. "He's not even my date."

"If he's not a date," Carl says, "why have you been with him all night? I saw you sharing your daiquiri with him. I saw how angry he looked when you were talking to that other guy."

"What other guy?" I ask, and then I realize he means the one who knew Allison. I take another step back. "Have you been following me?"

"I told you," Carl says. He catches my hand and holds it tight. "I'm watching out for you. Just like I did for Allison." He tightens his grip on my hand, pulling me toward him. He looks at me like he means to kiss me, inclining his face toward mine.

"You know what, Carl?" I say, panic rising in my throat. "I've got to go. I'll talk to you later." I pull my hand away.

"What do you mean?" he says. "We . . ." I don't stay to hear the rest. I turn and push into the moving crowd, almost running in the direction Evan went. I go until I reach the statue of Elvis at the end of the street. Evan is gone. Carl hasn't followed me. I stand there breathing hard. A man leaning against Elvis winks at me as he lights his cigarette. I stare at him. "All alone?" he says. He's got a tattoo of a dragon on his shoulder. I've never touched tattooed skin. He gestures at me with the cigarette hand. "Who are you supposed to be?" he says.

I've got the strangest sensation, like I'm running a fever, like this heat has slipped its way inside my head. The man's voice seems to come from very far away. "What?" I say.

"The hair," he says, gesturing again. "What's with the pink hair?"

I reach up and touch the wig. It feels slick between my fingers, not like real hair. "I don't know," I say.

"I like it," he says. He holds the cigarette in his mouth and talks around it. "Sexy."

I look back down Beale. I don't see Carl. The lights blink on and off. Crowds of people seem to be crossing and recrossing the street. A woman's voice rises from among them. "Can you believe it?" she is saying. "Can you believe it?"

"Hey," the man is saying, "Hey, pink girl."

I put my hands on my hips. "What do you want?"

He looks me up and down. "What do you got?"

"You can see what I got," I say.

"I sure can," he says. He grins and takes a step toward me. "I sure as hell can." He holds out a cigarette. "You want?"

I lean way forward and take it. "I don't smoke," I say, even as I'm putting the cigarette in my mouth.

"I can see that," he says, laughing. He strikes a match and lights my cigarette. "What are you doing here all alone?"

I take a step back and inhale. "I'm not alone," I say. He takes another step toward me. Panic flutters up in my chest. "Don't come any closer," I say.

"What's the matter, pink girl?" he says. "I just want to get to know you better."

"There's nothing to know." I take another step backward, then another. Then I drop the cigarette on the ground and step on it hard. When it's out, I spin on my heel and start walking as fast as I can back down the street. "Don't go, sugar," he calls after me. "I was just starting to like you."

A voice in my head is saying, *What are you doing? What are you doing?* and I don't know what to tell it. I'm moving through groups of college boys, couples, tourists, even a few children. They part around me, talking over my head, the same fixed grins on their faces. I am invisible.

In front of the bar where Evan left me, I sit on the curb and pull off the wig. My own hair is wet, plastered to my skin, and I run my fingers through it trying to shake out the sweat, trying to sober up and come back to myself. I've been down here talking to people for stories before. Once it was because a street artist who used to paint sidewalk portraits of tourists had died of AIDS. Every Christmas he

decorated all the windows of the bars and souvenir shops with pictures of Santa and elaborate, writhing ivy. I put on my reporter voice
and I went from place to place and told these bar people that their
friend was dead. Whatever they said to that, I wrote it in my notebook. I typed it in my computer. I saw it under my byline the next
day in three neat columns of text.

I can imagine myself in a story right now. I can hear these people
saying to a reporter, to someone like me, "I saw her, wearing that
pink wig. She was out of control, drunk, shouting on the street. I saw
her talking to some strange guy. I don't know what happened to her
after that."

I get up and start walking. Two blocks from Beale it's so quiet my
footsteps on the pavement pop like gunshots. A police cruiser flies
by, sirens wailing. Up ahead a tall figure crosses under a streetlight
and disappears around a corner. I keep walking. A man comes
toward me, watching his feet, his hands in his pockets. When he
passes me he looks up. I force myself to look into his face. He raises
his eyebrows and drops his head again. For another block I hear no
one, passing in and out of patches of light, past storefronts with dark
corners, past the mansion the Union Army used as its headquarters
when they took this city whole. Now it costs $8.50 to go inside.

I come upon a man sleeping in a doorway and stifle a gasp.
Somewhere off to the right, car brakes squeal and I jump. When a
car turns down the street, I step out of the way of the headlights like
a fugitive. Up ahead a woman walks quickly across the street,
glances over her shoulder, and disappears. I have the feeling that if
I turned my head just right I'd catch a glimpse of Allison Avery,
wearing her pink wig, a short dress, her silver boots, hurrying in the
opposite direction, turning her head back to look at me.

I turn in a wide circle. I am alone. Everyone on these streets is
alone, strangers clutching their fear and loneliness to them like a
purse they think someone wants to steal, hurrying home to lock
themselves away.

It takes me ten minutes to reach the newspaper building. A security guard lets me in the back. She looks at my outfit when I show her my press pass. "Late night," she says.

"Left my wallet here," I say cheerfully. "Pretty stupid." I hit the up button on the elevator.

"Someone waiting for you in the car?" she asks, and I nod. The elevator arrives. "You gotta be careful," she says, as I step in. "Did you hear what happened last night?"

"No," I say, holding the door open. "What happened?"

She nods out at the parking lot. "Woman from Circulation was held up in the lot," she says. "Guy made her perform oral sex on him."

"That's awful," I say. "Did they catch him?"

"Not yet," she says. "They've got a description. It's posted all over the building. From now on you should get one of us to walk you to your car when you're in the building late. Gotta be careful."

I nod at her. The doors close on her worried face.

On the way down the hall I pass the windows that look down into the production room. The presses are still. The building seems to vibrate with a high electric hum. In the newsroom I turn on all the lights and walk down the aisles, running my fingers along the sharp edges of the metal desks. I don't know what I came here to do. I feel in this moment that I am capable of almost anything, flying off a deck, rolling down to an interstate, running down Beale Street with my breasts exposed. Making the news, instead of just covering it.

I come to a stop at the wall. In front of me is a blue flier. I lean in to read it.

ATTENTION, it says. A WOMAN WAS SEXUALLY ASSAULTED IN THE PARKING LOT LAST NIGHT. PLEASE BE ALERT. DON'T WALK ALONE.

I go back to my desk. I pick up the phone and call a cab.

When I open my eyes, a figure is leaning over my bed. I take a breath to scream and Hannah says, "It's me." She's wearing a cardigan over a long T-shirt and she's holding that pink wig out over my face like she's going to smother me with it.

"Jesus, Hannah." I press my hand to my heart. "What time is it?"

"Four-fifteen," she says. "I woke up and I was worried you hadn't come home." She holds up the wig. "What is this?"

"A wig," I say. "A pink wig." Just the thought of explaining myself to her exhausts me. I know what's she's going to say, where did you get it, where have you been, what have you been doing, how much did you have to drink.

"I can see that," she says. "Where did you get it?"

"Somebody gave it to me," I say.

"Who?"

"Somebody I know from work," I say. "Why are you wearing that cardigan?" Her T-shirt says NO ONE CAN MAKE YOU FEEL INFERIOR WITHOUT YOUR CONSENT.

"I woke up cold," she says, sitting down on the edge of my bed and frowning at me. I can't understand how she could be cold. My skin, my sheets, are so wet with sweat it seems likely that I'm melting. I turn off the window unit at night because it makes a rattling sound that keeps me from sleeping.

Hannah turns toward the mirror and holds the wig up over her head to see what it would look like on her. In the half-light, without my glasses, it could be anyone's face reflected in that mirror, framed by that bright pink hair, and for a sharp and terrible moment I believe that it's Allison's. I have a vision of us all in pink wigs and cardigans, reflected side by side, the brilliance of the wigs washing out our faces until each pale circle is just an image of the others.

"Put it on," I say, though I don't want her to.

"No thanks," she says, still frowning. She lowers her arms and turns the wig round and round in her hands. "What . . . ," she starts.

I hold up my hand to stop her there. I say, "No comment."

She closes her mouth tight and drops the wig on the floor. For a long moment she stares at herself in the mirror, as though she's conferring with her reflection about her next move. She says, "I was going to say, what do you think this is made of, but I guess that's too painful to discuss."

Then she gets up to go, and I say, "I'm sorry, Hannah. I just want to forget this evening ever happened, okay?"

"You don't have to tell me anything you don't want to," she says before she shuts the door. "I'm not a fucking reporter."

16

Someone is ringing the doorbell. I come awake slowly and lie there listening for the sound of Hannah's footsteps. The house is silent, and then the sound of the doorbell comes again. I sit up and call Hannah's name. No answer. Pain pulses through my head. Every morning, lately, is worse than the one before. I swing my feet onto the floor and call Hannah again. When she still doesn't answer I get up and go down the hall. The place has a messy, abandoned look this morning, like a trashed motel room. The person is ringing the doorbell constantly now, not even pausing to give me time to answer.

I reach the door and look through the peephole. An enormous eye stares back at me through the hole. I jump back, knocking some shoes against the wall, and, hearing the noise, the person starts knocking on the door. I look through the peephole again and this time see a face. It's Carl.

I glance down at the deadbolt lock. It's open. I put my hand on the lever and click the lock into place as quietly as I can. Then I stand there, watching him through the peephole, trying not to make a sound. He turns away from the door, then back. "Shit," I hear him say.

I realize I've been holding my breath and let it out. It's quiet. I look through the peephole. No Carl.

Staying close to the wall, I creep over to the window and stand behind one of the open curtains. Slowly, I lean over just enough to look out. Inches from me, on the other side of the glass, I see his face. He's got his forehead pressed to the window, his hands cupped around his eyes. I jerk back behind the curtain. I don't think he saw me.

He knocks on the window with his fist. I press myself as far as I can into the corner. Every time I see a horror movie, every time I write a story about a woman assaulted in her home, I wonder what I would do in a situation like this. The truth is I'm terrified, my heart inside my throat, my hands shaking. The truth is I don't want to know what I'll do if he breaks that window open. All I want is for him to go away.

I hear his voice, muffled by the glass, as though he's underwater. He's calling my name. "Olivia," he says. "Are you in there? I want to talk to you. Olivia!"

I look around me for a weapon I could reach. There's a small lamp on the end table by the couch. I need something heavy in my hand. I dart toward the end table, and in that moment he sees me.

"Olivia!" he says. "I'm sorry about last night! I'm so sorry."

I look at him, his eyes wide, his forehead flattened by the glass, his lips shaping over and over the word *sorry*. I take a step toward the window, the lamp in my hand. "Get out of here," I say.

"What?" he shouts.

"Get out of here," I shout back. "Get the hell out of here."

For a moment he says nothing. He lets his hand slide down the window. It makes a squeaking sound. Then his face crumples and he starts to cry. His shoulders shake. His forehead bumps against the glass. "I'm sorry," he chokes out. It's not loud enough for me to hear, but I can read it on his lips. Finally he pushes himself away from the window and turns to go. I watch him walk to his car, his shoulders hunched in a position of defeat. He gets in the car and sits staring at my house for a moment and though I don't think he can see me now I take a step back.

Not until his car disappears up my street do I put the lamp back down on the table. Then I close the curtains on the living room window and go around the house making sure the doors and windows are locked, the blinds lowered. I go back in my room and get in the bed, shaking with nausea. I don't know how long I lie there, drifting in and out of sleep. When I finally sit up again my hair is plastered to my forehead with sweat.

I think about Carl's face, pressed up against my window. I pick up the phone and call Sergeant Morris. He answers on the first ring.

"Sergeant, it's Olivia Dale."

"Hello there, honey," he says. "What can I do for you?" He sounds like he's in a good mood.

"I wondered if you have any new leads on the Avery girl."

"Nothing I can tell you."

"What about the men she knew?" I ask. "Have you talked to Carl Fitzner?"

"I think Baker did," he says. "Friend of hers, right? Why do you ask?"

"I just thought maybe you should check him out," I say.

"Why?"

"He was in love with her," I say. "He never forgave her for rejecting him."

"That may be," Morris says. "But he didn't kill her, I'll tell you that much."

"Does that mean you have a suspect?"

"Ah, now, girl," Morris says, a laugh rumbling in his voice. "Are you asking me about Fitzner to trick me into telling what I know? You're a smart one."

"That's not it," I say. "I think there's something about him."

"Olivia, honey," he says. "Do me a favor. Leave the police work to the police."

"So you won't talk to him," I say.

"I don't need to," he says. "Don't worry about it. Everything's under control."

"Does that mean you have a suspect?" I ask again.

"Oh ho." He laughs. "Don't try that again. I got nothing to tell you." In the background I hear a low male voice say, "Morris, you got a minute?"

"You betcha," Morris says. Then to me, "Gotta go, honey." He hangs up the phone.

I'm still sitting there, staring at the phone, when it starts to ring again. I reach for it, then just let my hand dangle. The machine answers and the person hangs up. After a moment I pick up the phone, dial *69, and listen to the phone ring three times before a cheerful female voice says, "Black Horse Theater Company."

"Hello," I say. "May I speak to Carl Fitzner?"

"Sure," she says. "Hang on." I hear her sing out, "Carl, telephone."

I wait. Then he picks up. "Hello?" he says.

I hang up the phone and get out of bed. If Morris won't check Carl out, I will.

I'm driving into the sun, so bright through my windshield that it's hard to see anything else. I hope the stoplight I just drove through was still green. In ten minutes I'll be at Carl Fitzner's apartment building. I'm not sure what I'm going to do once I get there. I just want to take another look at the place where he lives. If he can come peer in my windows, I can go look in his.

The first time I looked at Carl Fitzner I thought I knew who he was, a lonely young man living in a basement apartment with failure wrapped around him like a blanket, angry with people like Allison for shining brighter, for being what he couldn't be and couldn't have. Then I saw him onstage, and he was the kind of actor so talented he didn't even seem to be acting, and now I wonder if he could be a murderer, someone for whom rage overcame everything else.

People are like those nested Russian dolls. There's always someone else hiding inside the person you think you know, layer after layer, each with the same painted face. I want to open someone up and hold that last solid little doll in my hand. I know all of Allison Avery's disguises, femme fatale, loyal friend, maternal and corrupting sister, virginal obedient daughter, performer, alive with the magic of her own touch. But who was she at the center? I don't know if I believe in the soul. I'm afraid of the darkness I see in all of us, every one of us a mystery.

I have looked in the mirror and not been certain that I saw myself. And what separates me from Allison Avery, from Carl Fitzner, but the features of my face?

When I get to Carl's building, I park my car in the farthest corner of the lot and walk back in the direction of the building. Heat rises off the asphalt in waves; I swear I can almost smell it, feel it filling my nostrils like steam from a kettle. I approach Carl's window from the side, staying close to the wall, and then I crouch near the living room window so I can look in. I've decided if anyone asks I'm going to say I think I dropped an earring here. I could even tell this story to Carl and be believed. I see only the living room I remember, spare and ratty.

Five minutes go by with no sign of Carl. My legs start to cramp from my crouched position. I study the room, trying to determine whether anything has been changed since I last saw it. On the bookshelf is a large framed photograph I don't remember seeing before. I lean in until I can feel the cool glass against my forehead, trying to make out the face in the picture. The long full hair indicates a woman, the face is pale—a white woman. I think it's Allison. I'm almost certain. I've come to know that face well.

A window around the corner opens into Carl's bedroom. He's not in there. The bedroom, too, is sparsely furnished. He has a twin bed covered with a blue blanket, tucked neatly under the mattress and pulled so tight it could be in a military barracks. The closet door is closed. There's a little loose change and a shoe box on top of the old white dresser, but nothing else to indicate anyone has ever lived in this room. I lean in, trying to peer into the corners of the room, and then I notice something. The window is unlocked.

I rock back on my heels. It would be so easy to slip inside. *Breaking and entering,* I imagine Evan saying. *Are you insane?* I picture Hannah's eyebrows raised, that look of contemptuous disbelief she perfected a long time ago. I shouldn't do it. I know that.

The window slides up without a sound. The screen squeaks, a small, barely audible noise. The frame is just large enough for my shoulders but with my torso half in I see that there's nothing to break my fall if I slide through headfirst. I wiggle back out and look around for any curious passersby. Nothing moves but the heat waves rising from the parking lot. I grab my bag and toss it through the window, aiming for the bed. It slips off and lands on the floor, pens and a notebook spilling out. Then I turn around and start easing my feet through, like I'm going cautiously down a slide. When my legs are all the way through, I take a breath and push off hard against the ground. My shoulder scrapes the metal frame and I land hard, wrenching my left knee. I crouch there until my heart rate slows. The air in here is still and heavy.

The room is just as monastic as it looked from outside. There's a television and VCR on a rolling cart at the foot of the bed. There's a desk and chair in the corner. I drag the chair over to the wall and stand on it to shut the window. I'm careful to leave things the way I found them; I move the chair back so its legs fit neatly in the indentations on the carpet. I pick up my bag and smooth the blanket.

On top of the dresser I find the shoe box full of playbills and scripts. I sift through them and find a clipping from the newspaper, a review of a local production that mentions a "promising performance from Carl Fitzner." Someone has inked in a huge exclamation point at the end of the sentence. In one script, Carl has written 1,233 on the last page in pencil. I flip through, trying to figure out what the number means. On other pages he has written smaller numbers, and I realize he was going through his lines, counting every word.

The dresser drawers are a turmoil of underwear and single socks, jeans and crumpled T-shirts. Underneath a sweater I find a book of monologues checked out from the library three months ago. I turn to a dog-eared page. It's one of Hamlet's. "O that this too too sullied flesh would melt . . ." I shake the book and a snapshot falls out—Carl in a black turtleneck, grinning into a dressing room mirror, his hand raised to apply foundation to his cheek, his eyes outlined in black. The reflection of the camera flash in the mirror beside him hides the photographer. On the back it says *Hamlet*, 1993 in neat print. I slip the picture into my pocket. In another drawer I find a wooden box. Inside is a jumble of high school yearbook photos. I sort through them, looking for Allison's face. They're all of girls, all with faces that seem plump and shiny with newness, emerging from clouds of glossy hair. I turn some over and read their curlicue handwriting: "To Carl, a sweet guy." "Carl, maybe I'll see you around this summer." "Dear Carl, it was fun being in French with you. Au revoir!"

I wonder if he sits here, reading these over and over, hoping to find more in these words. At the bottom I find Allison's picture, the same one we ran in the paper. I turn it over. "Carl, we've had our problems but I'm glad we worked them out cuz you're a nice guy. Wasn't driver's ed fun? I'll never forget how Coach Murdock screamed when I ran that stoplight! Oops! Love, Allison." I slip that in my pocket too.

On top of the television is an empty tape case. I push open the VCR with my finger, just enough so I can read the label on the tape inside. Allison 9, it says. I take my finger away and let the slot swing shut. Carl stole a tape from her apartment. I shudder, and then I think, *And so did I.*

I walk into the living room, and stop. The floor in front of the couch is littered with snapshots of Allison Avery. You could walk across them like a rug.

The picture on the bookshelf I saw from outside is also of Allison. It looks like a snapshot blown up to eight by ten. Allison is smiling, outside somewhere. Wearing a red shirt, she stands out in sharp focus from the trees behind her, their deep green leaves. Tucked inside the frame is a notecard. I open it. It reads "Dear Carl, I thought you might like to have this. Thank you for your thoughtfulness. Take care, Cynthia Avery."

I walk over to the couch and stand looking at all those faces on the floor. Then I drop to my knees and pick one up. It's Allison and Carl at a high school dance. Carl is thin and almost handsome. Allison is laughing, an enormous corsage at her wrist, her hair bountiful and stiff with hair spray. The picture is so soft to the touch I can only imagine he holds it in his hands every night.

I keep picking up pictures. Allison onstage in tight black pants and a tank top. Allison in a Betty Boop T-shirt, leaning forward and pursing her lips. Allison outside wearing a backpack and walking somewhere in a hurry, frowning at the ground. Allison as a little girl at the beach, her hair in pigtails. The little boy just behind her could very well be Carl. I hold on to that one for a moment, looking at their soft round cheeks, their brown legs coated with sand.

Some of the photos are as recent as a month ago, the date printed in the corner in blocky yellow figures. One of them, a picture of Allison curled up on her couch, frowning hard, is dated two days before she died. Her mouth is open, like she's telling him to get out, to go away, to stop.

I slide the pictures around with my hands. A foot away I spot one of Allison wearing that pink wig. I pick it up and bring it close to me, and my heart jumps.

The face in this picture isn't Allison's. It's mine.

I don't know how long I've been sitting here, surrounded by Allison, holding that picture in my hand. There's a sound—footsteps, the jingle of keys. I jump to my feet, scattering the pictures. Without thinking, I bolt back into the bedroom, where there's nowhere to go except the closet. As the front door opens, I pull the closet door closed. It clicks, too loud, and I hold my breath. I still have the picture in my hand. I shove it in my pocket. A long minute goes by. I'm imagining the door swinging open, Carl's shocked face, me blinking helplessly as the light rushes in. Nothing happens. I push through the clothes to the back of the closet, where there is barely enough space between the clothes and the wall for me to stand.

Footsteps approach, stop, approach. A light shines in through the crack at the bottom of the door. I clutch at his shirts and feel polyester, slick inside my hand. Then there's the sound of the bed creaking. Two thumps could be his shoes hitting the floor. I strain for more but hear nothing. The hot, close air inside the closet makes me want to gasp for breath. The line of light at the bottom of the door disappears.

Then I hear the sound of Carl's sock feet, padding across the carpet. The television goes on, a loud blare of sitcom laughter, and then a few clicks and silence. Then I hear a voice I recognize. "Hi," it says. "I'm Allison Avery. Thanks for coming."

Inside the closet I listen to Allison sing, and rub impatiently at the tears that come to my eyes at the sound of her voice. Then I listen to what must be the few moments after she comes offstage, the voices of her friends' congratulating her, her own giddy voice rising above the rest. I hear a male voice, murmuring something, and then Allison says clearly, "Well, thanks, Carl. Thanks for coming." Then she laughs. "Don't just stand there," she says. "Give me a hug."

The tape goes silent. I press my ear to the door. There's a faint whirring, and then I hear it again. "Thanks, Carl. Thanks for coming."

Three more times Carl rewinds the tape and plays those few words again. Then there's silence again and I wonder if he's paused the tape on her face, shaping her lips around his name.

What seems like a long time goes by before it begins, a sound I can't identify. It stops and starts, stops and starts. I push as quietly as

I can through the clothes and press my ear to the closet door. It's quiet, and then I hear the sound again.

Carl is sobbing.

He takes a ragged breath so loud I can hear it on the other side of this door and then he wails. The cry goes on and on, rising and falling. It chokes down into silence, then hiccups out again like the sputter of a motor. I sink down until I'm crouched on the floor of the closet, my ear tight against the door, and I listen to him cry. I notice everything about it—the high-pitched whimpers at the end of a long wail, the rapid exhalations that signal the start of another, even the tiny moans between those outward breaths—as though the quality of his crying can tell me whether this is the sound of sorrow or remorse. He sobs with abandonment, not even muffling the sound with his pillow, and I think the neighbors must be able to hear him, if they're home and listening.

I listen to him until he stops, trailing off into a series of sniffs and whimpers. I think I hear him whispering something to himself. Then he blows his nose, once, twice, and is silent.

I can just make out the face of my watch. I wait for half an hour. My knee aches where I wrenched it dropping through the window. I long to straighten out my legs. I recite lines of poems in my head—"In Xanadu did Kubla Khan/A stately pleasure dome decree:/ Where Alph, the sacred river, ran/Through caverns measureless to man/Down to a sunless sea." I say the alphabet, shaping my lips in silence around each letter. Something in my bag jabs me in the breast. I change my position with tiny, cautious movements.

When half an hour has passed I wrap my hand around the doorknob and turn it slowly, slowly, and with a tiny click the lock springs back and the door opens. I lean out into the dark room, bracing myself on the door knob, until I can see the bed, and Carl's figure on it. He is fully clothed, but stretched out, and his chest rises and falls with a sleeper's slow breathing. I straighten up. My knee cracks painfully. Carefully I close the closet door. For a moment something keeps me there, watching Carl, trying to see in his puffy red face, his curled-up body, the shape of a murderer. Instead what I notice is the place where his black shirt has pulled loose from his belt, the soft white roll of belly slipping out.

I let myself out the front door.

At home I sit on my bed, looking at that picture of myself. Hannah is still not here. Twice the phone rings but I don't want to answer it. The third time I hesitate for four rings, then snatch the phone off the receiver, but the person has hung up. I stare for a moment at the phone in my hand. Then I dial Angela's number.

She answers, and we talk for a moment about how she is. I bring the conversation around to Carl, and her voice tightens while she tells me again what a creep he is. "Angela," I say, "do you think there's any reason to consider Carl a suspect?"

There's a silence. I'm holding my breath. I'm hoping for a yes, because I need to know, because I want it to end. I'm hoping for a no, because Carl knows where I live, and I'm afraid.

"I don't think so," she says finally. "I think he was there the whole time."

"Where?"

"At the bar," she says. "Sitting at a table in the corner, pretending it was just a coincidence. He knew we used to go there and sometimes he would show up, looking for Allison. Sometimes he wouldn't even talk to her, just watch her from the corner. God, it was creepy. They'd even had a fight a few nights before about him following her around. But he didn't kill her. He was there all night, pretending not to wait for her." She sighs. "Sometimes I almost feel sorry for him."

"You do?"

She pauses. "No," she says, and her voice is sharp with hatred. "I don't."

17

The surface of my desk is an Allison Avery collage. Her high school picture in blurred newsprint. The back of the photo I took from Carl's, that looped handwriting, that girlish tone. Carl's face, grinning in theatrical makeup. The girl's dead body, curled up and smashed. The branch from Peter's bonsai tree. My notes. *Nice girl. Lilies. Rock and Roll. Wild. Sexy. Slut. Pothead. Junkie. Thief.* The picture of me, looking like her.

I'm picking up the phone to call the police station when I hear Peggy say my name. I look up, and she is standing beside my desk. "Can you come into my office?" she says. "I want to talk to you."

"I'll be right there," I say. "I need to make a phone call."

She shakes her head. "Make your phone call afterward," she says. She waits there until I stand up, and then we walk together across the newsroom into her office, my body jumping with impatience.

I sit down on the other side of her desk. "I'm going to get some coffee," she says. "Want some?" I nod, and she leaves the room. Peggy almost never uses this office; it's pristine compared to her desk in the newsroom. Framed articles circle the walls, one on political corruption that put her in the running for the Pulitzer fifteen years ago. I haven't been in here since I was first hired.

She comes back in and hands me a cup of coffee, saying it's hot. I sit and blow on it, waiting for her to talk. She seems uncharacteristically nervous, pretending to straighten papers on her desk, taking long sips of her coffee. Then she sets the cup down and leans forward, putting her hands palm down on her desk. "Look," she says. "I'm not going to pussyfoot around this. I need to know—are you using drugs?"

I just stare at her. Did someone know I was stoned that day in the office? It's not possible. "No," I say. "What are you talking about?"

"I'm talking about heroin," she says. "Are you using? Are you experimenting? Tell me the truth. I'll get you help."

I shake my head, flooded with relief. "I swear to you, Peggy. I don't know what you're talking about."

She sits back in her chair. "I can have you tested, Olivia. It's in the union contract. But I'd rather you just told me."

"Peggy, please tell me where you got this idea."

"Evan came to me," she says. She holds up a hand. "Now, don't be angry at him. He was worried about you, said you wouldn't talk to him, that you'd been strange lately." She sighs. "He saw you with needles. You've been so jumpy."

"My house got broken into!"

"I know. But one day, there was something about your eyes . . . I'm trying to give you the benefit of the doubt, but I have to agree that you just haven't been yourself."

"My God," I say. "Is everyone insane? The needle came from the story I'm working on. It came from Allison Avery's trash."

Peggy watches my face. "Why wouldn't you have told Evan that?"

I shrug. "I didn't want to talk about it until I was sure." Even to my own ears, that sounds like a lie. "Look at my arms," I say, leaning over the desk and extending my arms, palms up. She runs her fingers down my arms, then tilts her head up and looks into my eyes. "Pupils look normal," she murmurs. I straighten up. "You believe me now?"

She waves a hand. "It can be snorted now," she says. "It can be smoked. In the early stages of addiction, injection sites might not even be visible." She sounds as though she's quoting from one of her own articles. Then she says, "I'm going to tell you something." She takes a deep breath. "Paula, in the story. Her real name was Vivian, and she was my niece." She reaches a hand out toward me. "I've seen this thing drag people down. I don't want to watch it happen to you."

"It won't," I say. "I promise I'm clean. You've got nothing to worry about."

Peggy lets her hand fall on the desk. She says, "I want to believe you. So I'm not going to have you tested now. But I'll be keeping an eye on you, Olivia. One slipup and I'll have you peeing in that cup."

"I swear," I say again, standing up to go. "I'm clean."

She nods, her head bowed.

"What happened to your niece?" I ask her at the door.

She doesn't look up. "She's dead."

I stand in front of Evan's desk. I've never noticed before that bald spot forming at the crown of his head. "Can I speak to you?" I ask. He stands up and we walk in silence down the hall to stand near the window overlooking the presses. They're silent now, still waiting for the day's news.

"Peggy talked to you," Evan says, not even making it a question.

"Are you trying to get me fired?" I say. "Are you that angry about the other night? I know it was terrible, what I said to you, and I'm sorry."

"I didn't do it because I was angry. I did it because it was so unlike you. I was worried." He folds his arms across his chest. "You were out of control. The way you've been about this story, I thought you were crossing the line."

"It's a story," I say. "I'm covering it the best I know how."

"It's not about the story, Olivia," he says. "Admit that it's not about the story anymore."

"What's it about then, Evan? What's it about, if it's not about covering my beat?"

"I don't know," he says. "The way you told that guy on Beale that you knew her, that crazy lie you told him about the wig, you sounded like you believed it. You sounded like you thought she was your friend."

"The needle came from her," I say. "It came from Allison Avery. Are you happy now?"

"Did you tell Peggy that?"

"Of course," I say. "She might have me tested anyway."

"Well, if she does you'll come up clean," he says. "And everything will be fine."

"You idiot, I'm going to test positive for marijuana," I say. "You think they'll just let that slide? Remember Bob Anderson in Sports? He got fired for smoking dope."

Evan reaches out a hand toward me. I step back. "I'm sorry," he says.

"Maybe I should tell them to test you too," I say. I hear how my voice comes out, cold and sharp.

Evan recoils as though I'd struck him. "You were acting crazy, and I had seen the needles," he whispers. "I just wanted to help."

"Needle," I say. "One needle."

"I'm sorry," Evan says again. "It's just, in my experience, where there's one there's more."

"Two and two equals four," I say. "That rhymed. Did you notice?"

"Don't make jokes." He reaches for me again, and again I step away. "Please, Olivia."

I take a few steps backward, watching his face, those big brown eyes gone shiny with tears. He says, "You've been crazy lately. I just want to know what's wrong. Hannah says . . ."

"You've talked to Hannah?" I imagine the two of them, their heads together, whispering my name. "Are you checking all your sources? Have you talked to David? I bet he'd give you some good quotes. Maybe he already has."

"You know that's not fair." I take another step backward, then turn on my heel. He grabs my arm. "Don't go," he says. "We need to talk."

"We've talked enough," I say, wrenching my arm free. "I don't feel like being interviewed." I walk away. He calls my name. I don't look back.

Allison Avery is disappearing. Nothing I can come up with will put us back on the front page. I'm at the police station, paging through the day's reports without reading them. Morris isn't here, and Nash will only say that he has nothing to say. There was no mention of the girl on the twelve o'clock news. Things change. More people die, get raped, get shot, get robbed. It's the rare murder that lasts. I try to focus on the names in the stack of papers in my lap. The latest victims, the most recent offenders.

"Olivia Dale," a deep voice says. I look up and see Officer Smiley standing over me.

"Officer," I say. "How's it going?"

"Not bad." He grins. "I saw your story."

It takes me a moment to realize that of course he means the one about him. "Oh yeah? What happened with that? Is he in jail?"

"You didn't hear?" He shakes his head, eyes narrowed. "I thought you'd have followed up."

I feel stung. "I got busy."

"With that doctor's kid, right?" When I nod, he says under his breath, "Yeah," and that one soft word feels like an indictment.

"What happened?"

He shrugs. "She came in and paid his bail. I'm waiting to get the call that he's shot her."

"I'm going to do a series on domestic violence," I offer. I'd nearly forgotten that idea.

"Great," he says, his voice neutral. "I'm sure that'll help." He touches my shoulder gently. "See you around."

I watch Officer Smiley walk away down the hall, his powerful stride, his gun tight against his hip, his air of authority and purpose. I feel like a child, small and afraid.

❧

I spend the afternoon trying to let it go. I don't make a single phone call regarding the Avery investigation. Instead, I call David for the first time since Saturday night, and apologize like a good girl. He's not angry. He, too, sighs and talks about his worry for me. Then I write the stories I'm supposed to write. A two-year-old child run over by a truck. A liquor store holdup. I call the highway patrol to check fatalities. I am distant but polite with Evan. Maybe we're even now, depending on how you weigh our crimes.

At 5:35 my phone rings and before I touch the receiver I know it's Peter. "Can you come see me?" he asks as soon as I say hello.

"I'm really busy, Peter."

"I need to talk to you."

"We're talking."

There's silence. "Why are you being this way?" He sounds hurt. "Why would you be angry with me?"

I sigh. "I'm not angry. I've had a shitty day."

"Every day is a shitty day," he says. "I just want to see you."

I give in. I tell him I'll stop by on my way home.

No one answers the door at the Averys' white house. I walk around the house, looking up at the windows, searching for movement. No lights are on, no figures pass behind the windows. In the backyard I pull a leaf off a tree and shred it, tearing along the veins. I reach for another, and hear movement inside the greenhouse.

Inside, Peter stands with his back to me, running his fingers over one of his trees. His T-shirt clings to him, wet with sweat, and I watch the muscles in his back contract when he bends to clip a branch. *Ten minutes,* I think. *Then I'll go.* He turns, scissors in hand. "Olivia," he says. "You came."

"What did you need?" I ask, trying to sound brusque.

He smiles. "Let me just finish this," he says, and bends back to his tree.

My heart jumps wildly inside my throat. In this moment there is nothing but my desire, as though everything I am has contracted to a point. I could cross over to him, drop my bag on the floor, and lay both hands, fingers spread, on the small of his back, which would be hot and damp and tense with surprise beneath my palms. Then slowly, slowly, I could slide my hands around to his stomach, slip them up inside his T-shirt and touch his soft belly, skin against skin.

I cross my arms over my chest. "I've got to go home, Peter. What did you want?"

He turns, frowning, the sharp edge of his scissors pointed at me. "Why are you being such a bitch?"

What can I say? Because I'm worried I can't control myself? I say, "I'm in a hurry."

"Just get the fuck out, then, if it's so goddamn difficult to give me five minutes of your time."

"Fuck you," I say, suddenly blinking back tears. "You called me and I came. What do you want?"

He comes toward me now, waving those scissors. "The story's over, is that it? So I'm of no use to you now?"

"That's not . . ."

"What about all that *concern* for me?" He's right in front of me now. I keep my eye on the moving point of the scissors. "Was that faked?"

"My concern was real," I say slowly. At least it became real, and that's what matters now.

He mimics me. "My concern was real. Oh, Peter, how *are* you? I'm *so* sorry about your poor dead sister, at least as long as she sells papers."

"Listen to me." I reach for him but he steps back.

"I don't have to listen to you. I'm nothing more than a story to you, am I." He leans in again, bringing the scissors an inch from my hand. One quick jab and he could sink the point into my skin. "Fuck you," he says. "Fuck you."

Carefully I reach out my hand. I close my fingers around the scissors, and when I feel his grip slacken I take them from his hand. He stares at me. "Did you think I was going to hurt you?" He sounds as though he's going to cry.

"Of course not," I say, though for a moment anything seemed possible. Slowly I set the scissors down.

"I would never hurt you," he says. His eyes are filling with tears. He bites his lip. "I'm sorry," he says. "I don't know what's the matter with me."

"It's okay," I say. I pull him to me, his head against my shoulder, and he begins to shake. I hold him as tight as I can.

"Olivia," he says. "I think I love you."

"Oh, honey," I say. I think, *My God, he's seventeen*, as though I've only now learned it.

He lifts his head to look at me. "I mean it," he says. "I love you." His eyes keep searching my face, his hand clutching at my arm. The need is so naked in him, I can't help but say it. "I love you, too." He presses his lips against mine, hard, urgent, then leans back. That smile of his lights up his face, beautiful.

I feel about a million years old.

18

I leave Peter with promises that I'll see him again soon. He stands in the driveway and watches me go, his body leaning after my car. I drive all the way home with a lump in my throat and when I get there I go straight into my bedroom and curl up in a fetal position on the bed. I'd like to hold myself and sob, like I watched Carl do, but no tears come. This day has left me hollow.

The phone wakes me early in the morning. I lie there for a moment, my skirt twisted up around my waist. The ringing stops. I undo my bra and run my fingers over the painful red ridges it's left in my skin. I hear Hannah shout, "Wake up, Olivia. It's for you."

"Good morning, gal. Up and at 'em. It's gonna be a long day for you." It's Sergeant Morris and he sounds happy.

"What time is it?" I squint at my clock.

"Early. But you'll be glad I woke you." He pauses, letting the suspense build. "It's the Avery case. There's been an arrest."

I'm stunned.

"Olivia? Are you still there?"

"Who?" I say.

"Three kids in Bolivar," he says. "They tried to use her credit card at the gas station there. The Mississippi cops called us." His voice turns hard. "We've got them cold," he says. "We found her underwear in one of their bedrooms. The ringleader. Jared Gillespie."

"My God," I say under my breath.

"There's going to be a press conference this afternoon," he says. "Did they know her?"

"Doesn't look like it," he says. "Stranger killing, just like we thought."

"But why did they do it?" I say. "It doesn't make sense."

"Lord, I don't know," he says. "Thirty years I've been doing this, and I can tell you—it never makes sense."

When I'm off the phone, I run to the bathroom. For several minutes I kneel on the floor beside the toilet bowl. I feel like I'm going to be sick. Instead what comes out is a rush of tears. My whole body shaking, I put my face in my hands and sob, and that is how Hannah finds me, half-naked over the toilet bowl, my face a sticky mess.

She kneels beside me and holds me against her, and when she asks me what's wrong her voice trembles like she's going to cry too. I can't tell her. I just keep shaking. Hannah helps me stand. She helps me undress and turns on the shower. Underneath the stream of water I stand with my eyes closed, my face in my hands, until my body stills.

On the other side of the curtain, Hannah is asking me if I'm all right.

I open my eyes. There are the same blue tiles, the same green shower curtain I see every morning before I go to work. If this were any other day I'd be hurrying through this shower, singing while I washed my hair, anxious to follow up on the big break I'd just gotten. The scoop. So today I will finish this shower and get dressed and call Peggy and drive to Bolivar, Mississippi, in search of Jared Gillespie. I will find out how old he and his friends are and whether they have criminal records. I'll ask anyone who might know when they did it, and how, and where, and why.

This is my job. This is just my job.

The last time I was in Bolivar, it was to cover a story about the Board of Aldermen's attempt to get a local monument repaired. It was a

memorial for the town's Confederate dead, and the problem was
that in the forty years since its building, it had begun to lean. When
two aldermen went out and took measurements, they confirmed
what everyone had feared: the monument leaned, six inches to the
North. At the meeting, an old man with a beard stood up and said,
his voice breaking, "It's a mockery to the boys that gave their lives
fighting the Yankees. Our monument should be straight. Upright,"
and he snapped his legs together like a soldier coming to attention.

In this town there are three places of business, a general store, a
diner, and a gas station. When I pull into the gas station, a boy about
Peter's age comes out and motions for me to roll down my window.
He squints in at me. "What'll it be, ma'am?"

"Regular, please," I say. He starts the pump running and leans
over my windshield with a squeegee, methodically running it in neat
lines across the glass. I watch his face. He is whistling, eyes focused
on the water running down the windshield, never glancing at me on
the other side of the glass. I get out of the car. "Been a lot of excitement around here," I say, leaning against the door.

"Oh yeah," he says. He straightens up, puts the squeegee away,
and heads toward me. "'Scuse me, ma'am," he says, and I press up
against the door so he can get by. He whips the pump out of the car
and screws on the gas cap with a practiced air.

"You know those boys?" I let my voice slide into a drawl.

"Could you pop the hood?"

I lean inside the car and pull the lever. When I straighten up he is
under the hood of my car. His voice emerges, muffled. "The ones
killed that girl in the city, you mean?"

"Yeah," I say. "You know them?"

"I seen 'em around," he says. "This is a little town." He comes out
from under the hood, holding the dipstick. "You need oil."

I nod, and he goes about adding the oil. "You know where Jared
lives, then?"

"Oh yeah, I know," he says. He straightens up and lets the hood
drop, gently, then gives it a quick slam into locked position. "It's

hard to find." He wipes his hands on a rag. "I could take you." He doesn't look at me, pretending nonchalance as he runs the rag over each finger. His body is drawn up straight while he waits for me to answer. He wants to go. He's curious.

"Okay," I say. "Let's go." I get back in the car. He goes around to the passenger side and vaults into the seat. Then he holds out his hand to me. "Name's Mike."

"Olivia," I say, giving his hand a hard squeeze. He's covered in a fine layer of dust and his blond-brown hair falls in his eyes. He reminds me of my high school boyfriend, coming to my house after driving a tractor on his father's farm, his skin powdered with dirt and hot to the touch.

"What you want at Jared's house anyway?" Mike asks. "You don't look like a cop."

"I'm a reporter," I say. "I want to talk to his family."

"To get some insight and all?"

I nod, turning the key in the ignition.

"That's cool," he says.

He directs me off the main road down a series of dirt roads until we crunch over gravel and pull up to the house. It's a tiny house, no better than a shack, really, with nothing around but tall grass and weeds and the requisite auto parts piled to the side. A black dog sleeping inside a pen lifts its head to look at the car but doesn't bark. It yawns hugely and drops its head again. "They're not home," Mike says. "Car's not here."

For the first time it occurs to me that coming here alone with this boy was not the smartest thing to do. For all I know this isn't even the right house. I sit for a minute with the car running. Mike swings open the door and vaults out. He disappears from view around the side of the house and then reappears, leaning in my car window. His face shines with excitement. "I scouted it out," he says. "No one's here for sure."

Mike follows me around the yard as I circle the house. In the back, we press our faces to a window and peer inside at the living room. A few battered plastic toys lie in front of the television, which is the only thing in the room that looks new. "A kid lives here?" I say.

"Yeah," Mike says. "Jared's kid. A little girl." Then he disappears. I stand with my hands cupped around my face, looking for details. The ironing board in the corner, a child's pink dress waiting to be pressed. A ragged pair of women's slippers beside the sofa, which is orange and velour and shredded on the sides, probably by the tabby cat now watching me from the back of the couch. Even the cat looks battered and used, one ear bitten jagged, burrs caught in its fur. I tap on the glass and the cat's body stiffens. It leaps from the couch and disappears from view, then reappears suddenly on the windowsill, its nose working as though it can smell me through the glass. I scratch on the window with my finger and the cat puts its paw there, then looks at me, its eyes wide with curiosity, and meows. "What do you know about it?" I say, and it meows again.

"Hey!" Mike whoops from the side of the house. "Come here! I found something!"

Following his voice, I run around the house and smack into him. Together we stumble a step or two and then he puts his hands on my arms and steadies me, laughing. "Slow down, girl," he says.

I step back out of his grasp. "What did you find?"

He gestures at the ground. "This is where they burn their trash." The grass doesn't grow inside this circle, which is littered with scraps and bits of wood and plastic. I grab a stick and poke at it. The wind catches a piece of paper and it flutters away.

A car approaches, bumping down the dirt road. "It's them," Mike says softly, and I drop the stick and move to the front of the house, standing with my hands clasped in front of me as the car turns up the hill and comes to a stop next to mine. I feel myself growing calmer. I know my part now. When the car door swings open and a woman gets out with a bag of groceries I go toward her with a sympathetic smile. "You look like you could use a hand," I say, and wordlessly she hands me the bag. I balance it on one hip and extend my right hand. "Olivia Dale," I say, and when she takes my hand and gives it a limp squeeze, I say, "So nice to meet you, Mrs. Gillespie."

She nods, a sharp worry line appearing in her forehead. She is probably not long past forty, but she looks like an old woman. Her thin brown hair is pulled back into a ponytail, which she tugs on as she looks at me. Her pale flesh sags on her small frame—her breasts huge and ponderous inside her tank top, her legs lined with blue veins, her face puffy and pasty white. "Can I get another bag for you?" I say, and finally she finds her voice.

"That's all right," she says. "Only got a couple more."

I wait while she opens the back door and heaves out two more straining bags. From behind the windshield, a little girl watches me, her features small and sharp beneath a mass of curly hair. When I catch her eye, she looks away, and then she swings the passenger door open and gets out. When she stands, I see that she is not a little girl, but a teenager, in a T-shirt and a tight pair of cutoffs. Her face is heavily made up, and from beneath her purple eyelids she watches me for a minute, before she opens the back door and leans in. She stands up slow, a child of about four clinging to her neck, almost as big as she is. Under all this weight the two women move toward the house, and I follow. Mike appears at my side when I reach the front door. I had forgotten all about him. "You don't need to come in," I whisper.

He looks astonished. "But I want to," he says, and shuts the door behind us. The air inside the house is hot and close, and it's dark where we're standing. I follow Mrs. Gillespie into the kitchen and set the bag on the counter. She is putting her groceries away, milk and eggs in the ancient refrigerator, canned corn on the shelf on the wall. "Mrs. Gillespie," I say. "I'm so sorry to trouble you at a time like this. I wondered if I could talk to you for just a few minutes, about what your family is going through. About what they're doing to your boy."

"Jared's a good boy," she bursts out. She takes a paper towel and wipes her forehead. "They've got him locked up."

"I know," I say, moving in closer to lay a gentle hand on her shoulder. "I know how hard it is to see your boy locked up in that tiny cell. I'm sorry this has happened to you. You seem like a good woman."

She stares at me. "Who did you say you were?"

"Olivia Dale," I say. "From the newspaper. I won't take but a few minutes of your time. I want you to tell your side of the story." I squeeze her fleshy shoulder. "Jared's side."

"All right," she says, nodding. She waves her hand in the direction of the living room. "You just go ahead and sit down. I want to freshen up." She pulls her sticky tank top away from her breasts. "I won't be but a minute."

In the living room, Mike leans against the wall, hands in his pockets, talking to the girl. She sits with her feet up under her on the couch, absently petting the tabby cat. Mike turns his head when I walk in. "Teresa and I went to junior high together," he says. "She was a year behind me."

"I had to drop out in the ninth grade," Teresa says, her voice high and heavily accented. She's talking to Mike, but her eyes are fixed on me. "I got pregnant. I stayed until I couldn't fit inside the desks no more, then I had to drop out. I was fixing to graduate, too."

"How old is your daughter?" I ask.

"Almost four," Teresa says. "Her name's Annabelle."

"That's a pretty name," I say, easing down onto the couch. I touch the cat's tail, and it twitches away. I snap my fingers and hold my hand out, and the cat leans in to sniff me, then rubs its face against my hand and begins to purr.

"She likes you," Teresa says. "She's Jared's cat. She's been lonely without him. Haven't you, kitty?" she says to the cat. "Haven't you?"

"Jared's your boyfriend?" I guess.

"He's my fiancé," she says. "We've been engaged two years." She shows me her ring, a tiny gold band with a diamond—or imitation diamond—so small it's hardly even there. "It's real," she says, as though she knows I've been wondering, and then she strokes it with the tip of her finger. "We're supposed to get married in September," she says, her voice breaking. She lifts her head, gulping for air, and then she stares at me angrily while tears roll down her cheeks.

"I'm so sorry," I say. I reach out, slowly, and lay my hand on the back of hers where it rests on the couch. She stiffens. I keep my hand pressed on hers, and after a moment she relaxes. "Mike," I say, "can you find Teresa a tissue?"

"In the bathroom," she says, pointing. When Mike is gone, I say, "How can they think Jared did this awful thing?"

She shrugs, wiping at her face with her free hand. "I guess it's be-cause he was gone those days."

"He was gone?" I say, trying to keep my hand relaxed on hers.

"Yeah," she says. "He wasn't at work, and couldn't nobody find him." Mike comes back in, holding a wad of toilet paper. She thanks him, and slides her hand out from under mine to blow her nose.

"You didn't know where he was?"

She shakes her head, dabbing the tissue carefully beneath her eyes. "He left for work Friday morning like always, but then I guess he never got there, 'cause his boss called here to see where he was. He didn't come back until Saturday night."

"Why would he disappear like that?"

She shrugs again. "Sometimes he does," she says. "When he's been drinking and whatnot."

"Whatnot?"

"Well, you know," she says, leaning forward conspiratorially. "Sometimes . . ." Mrs. Gillespie's heavy footsteps sound in the hall, and Teresa shuts her mouth and sits up straight. She blows her nose again, then raises her eyes to Mrs. Gillespie's face. They stare at each other for a moment, and I wonder what there is between them. Then Mrs. Gillespie nods, once, as though she's decided something, and sits down in the tattered plaid armchair next to the couch. She has changed into a flowered dress with a wide neck and a short skirt that strains over her knees. No one speaks.

I lean forward, my elbows on my knees, and turn my head so I can look into the woman's downturned face. "Mrs. Gillespie," I say softly. "I'd like you to tell me about your son. I'd like to know what kind of person he is."

Mrs. Gillespie starts talking, telling me stories about Jared as a little boy, about the troubles that started when he was eleven. I don't even have my notebook out. I'm just nodding as she talks, and when she pauses, I say, "How awful," or "And then what?" or "I understand." I glance at Mike and see that he's closed his eyes, slumped back against the wall. Teresa stares out the window, petting the cat robotically until it gets up, shakes itself and jumps down from the couch. We all start when we hear a car motor, the crunch of tires on gravel.

"Are you expecting someone?" I say, standing, and Mrs. Gillespie shakes her head. I go to the door and open it a crack. Outside, Teresa's little girl, Annabelle, is standing, her feet apart, her hands clenched at her sides, watching a van with Channel 5 emblazoned across its side pull up. The van comes to a stop, and as the door opens and a high-heeled shoe appears at the bottom, Annabelle pulls her hands back and lets fly with a rock that thuds against the windshield. I hear a high-pitched "Oh!" and see the man behind the wheel instinctively duck his head. I open the front door all the way as Mrs. Gillespie and Teresa come to stand on either side of me. The van's back door opens and a young man in jeans and a baseball cap steps out. "It's Joe," Teresa says.

"Who's Joe?"

"He works at the diner," she says.

"Mrs. Gillespie?" Joe calls. "I've brought the TV reporters to talk to you."

Annabelle lets fly with another rock. Joe jumps to the side, and says, "Now, now, Annabelle." She says nothing, just bends and picks up another rock. Then Lydia McKenzie steps out, smiling, her hands up and palms out like she wants to show she's unarmed. Her camera man is right behind her. "Mrs. Gillespie," she calls. "I'm

Lydia McKenzie from Channel Five." She takes a step toward us. Annabelle's next rock strikes her foot. Lydia squeals and bends to rub her foot. Annabelle takes aim at the camera and comes within inches of hitting it. The camera man hustles his expensive equipment back into the van while Lydia hops out of the way of another flying rock. "Damnit," Lydia splutters. Then I hear a strange sound and look around to identify its source. It's Mrs. Gillespie. She's laughing, her face turning red, making a sound that's closer to choking. Teresa lets loose with a high-pitched giggle as Annabelle throws a shower of gravel in the direction of the van.

I stand at the door, waving good-bye, as Lydia McKenzie drives away. Annabelle keeps throwing rocks, watching them thud with a puff of dust into the place where the van used to be. Mrs. Gillespie touches my arm. "Come back inside," she says. "Can I get you some iced tea?"

The truth is, Mrs. Gillespie knows her son carries a darkness inside him. She knows he is sullen, and violent, and careless, that he can't hold down a job and doesn't always seem sober. With a hopeless look in her eyes, she keeps insisting that he's a good boy. It's too late to stop loving him now.

I ask her about the underwear found in his room and she says that they're probably Teresa's. I ask about the credit card and she says the real murderer left the wallet where Jared and his friends found it, that's all. I ask her about the DNA testing, and she draws herself up, and says, her voice shaking, that she knows it will prove her boy's not guilty. What I would really like to ask her is what it's like to love a monster. What is it like, Mrs. Gillespie, to carry a killer in your womb?

When we say good-bye at the door, she presses my hand and tells me she's praying for the poor girl's family. "I don't know what I'd do if something like that happened to my Jared," she says. "I hope they catch the real killers. I'm praying that they do."

❖

By the time I reach the afternoon press conference I've already learned more about Jared Gillespie than the police are going to tell us. I've learned, for instance, that since turning eighteen he's been picked up twice for drug possession. I take notes while the captain announces what I already know, that there's been an arrest, that the evidence is good. Flipping through my notebook I see Teresa's phrase "drinking and whatnot," and I can't stop thinking about that moment, the secretive look on her sharp face, the way she shut her mouth when Mrs. Gillespie came back in the room. I raise my hand and ask the captain about Jared's record. "Was it heroin?" I ask. "Was he dealing?"

The captain says it was heroin, but as far as he knows that has no relevance to this case.

This story will run front-page lead. THREE TEENAGERS ARRESTED IN BRUTAL RAPE, MURDER. Back at the newsroom I type their names into my computer and stare at them, the ordinary names of these young boys. Robby Shavers, 16. Cody Parker, 17. Jared Gillespie, 19. The last people to see her breathing, the boys who took her life.

At the end of the day I go down to watch the presses roll. I lean my forehead against the glass and watch those pages fly by. When I leave here, I'm going to go find Nate and ask him if he knows Jared Gillespie. It's my last possible answer to the question of why. When I close my eyes, I don't see the white pages or the neat type of my story. I see the needle in Nate's hand.

By now Allison's family has gotten the news about Jared Gillespie and his friends. I imagine her mother talking calmly about the death penalty while Peter slams his fist into the wall, picturing their faces. I wonder if he's thought of me at all today, if he knows I'm the one who wrote the story. What would he have thought if he could have seen me sitting in Jared Gillespie's living room, holding his mother's hand?

❖

I knock sharply on Nate's door. From the other side of the door I can hear music, but Nate doesn't appear. I lean in close and shout, "Nate, it's Olivia. Peter's friend," and then I hear him shout, "Come in."

Nate is sprawled out on his tiny couch. Again he's wearing nothing but a pair of gym shorts, his skin so pale it's almost translucent. "Hey," he hails me. "What's goin' on?"

"I wanted to ask you something." I stand over him.

"Shoot," he says genially.

"Do you know a guy named Jared Gillespie?"

He frowns. "The one who . . ." He lowers his voice, glancing behind him. I follow his gaze. There's no one there. "The one who killed Allison?"

"You know about it?"

He points with his chin in the direction of the kitchen. "Pete's here," he says as Peter emerges through the door. He stares at me like he's never seen me before, then moves slowly to the armchair and sits down, looking at the floor.

" 'Scuse me a moment," Nate says, slipping off to the bathroom.

I go to Peter and graze the back of his neck with my fingers. "What are you doing here?" I say.

He reaches up and grabs my hand. "What are *you* doing here? Looking for me?"

"What did you do today?" I ask. "After you heard?"

He is silent for a moment, playing with my fingers. Then he says, "For a while we sat around, my parents and me, and my mother talked about what will happen now, how there will be a trial and lots of media attention and how we need to stay calm and do everything we can to make sure these people get what they deserve. Then she and my father decided to go back to work. My mother said we have to keep doing what we do, and that she had patients to see."

"And you?"

He sighs. "After they were gone, I got in my car and drove to Mississippi. I drove around that shitty little town where they came from. I felt like I wanted to burn the whole place down."

"What did you do?"

"I found out where he lives, the one they think was the leader. I drove up and down past that house. It's a dump."

"I know. I saw it."

"You talked to those people?"

"I talked to his mother, his girlfriend," I say. "That's my job."

"I hate them," he says, his voice catching. "I know they're not the ones who killed her. But I hate them, all of them." He squeezes my hand. "When I was sitting outside their house today, I kept wishing I could make it explode, so the whole thing, all that junk in the yard, would just disappear like it was never there. I knew he wasn't there. I knew there wasn't anything I could do. But I wanted to do something. So I backed up, and then I slammed on the gas and drove my car into his mailbox." He laughs, a short, bitter laugh. "He killed my sister. I knocked down his mailbox."

"Did it make you feel any better?"

He looks up at me and shakes his head. "Now there's a big dent in my car," he says, and two fat tears spill out of his eyes. He brushes at them impatiently. "I came here to get high," he says abruptly.

"You mean to shoot up," I say.

"Yes," he says. "That's exactly what I mean." He looks at me like he's waiting for a lecture, but I don't give it.

"Olivia," he says, his voice choppy with desperation. He clutches at my hand. "Listen to me. It will make this all go away. Think about it. No pain, no anger." He presses my hand against his mouth and puts a kiss in the center of my palm.

No desire. No fear.

Nate returns before I say anything. "The thing is," he says, "I don't have any."

"Can you get some?" Peter says. "I've got money."

Nate stands up, reaching for a T-shirt crumpled in the corner of the couch. "In that case," he drawls, "I'll see what I can do." He pulls on his shirt, heading for the phone on the floor in the corner. I kiss Peter on the temple and slide my hand from his. Then I get up and go to the bathroom. It looks as though it hasn't been cleaned in months. Instead of a bath mat Nate has a crumpled towel on the floor. The bottom of the white shower curtain is stained with mildew, and some of the holes at the top have ripped, so that the curtain sags, barely holding on. The toilet seat is up and the rim of the bowl is stained yellow. With a piece of toilet paper in my hands I gingerly push it down. It lands with a clatter, and I think how ridiculous it is that I won't touch his toilet seat, but I'm considering letting him put a needle in my vein.

At the sink I wash my hands twice and splash my face with cold water. I look at myself in the mirror, letting the water drip off my face. I feel as though I should have put that pink wig on, painted my lips a deep red.

When I go back in the living room, Peter has sunk even lower into the chair, staring at the ceiling with a look that suggests he's trying not to cry. One of his legs is jiggling, the way David's does when he's itching for a cigarette. Nate is still on the phone. He has his back to me, and he's rising up and down on the balls of his feet. "Yeah, yeah, yeah," he is saying. "Tell me where?" He turns from side to side, looking lost. "Got a pen?" he says to me.

From my bag I take a notebook and pen and hand them to him. He flips to a blank page and writes something. "Take a left there?" he says, then writes something else. It's the most prosaic of conversations. "See you in half an hour," he says, and hangs up the phone. He rips out the page, folds it up and slides it in his pocket. "You ready?" he asks us, handing me the notebook and pen.

"Should we get some needles?" I don't know what the proper etiquette is, so I just ask him. "Do you have clean ones?"

"Brand-new," he says. He frowns. "I'm not stupid."

"Sorry," I say. "Just checking." I slip the notebook back in my bag.

"I've just got to find my shoes," Nate says, looking around. I follow, two feet behind him, as he hurries into the bedroom. I stand in the doorway and watch him crouch to peer under his unmade bed. His T-shirt rises, and I stare at his narrow lower back. I'm starting to feel a strange tenderness toward him, he is so thin and pale. At what moment did this become his life? I wonder if it was the first time he took a hit, or even earlier, the first time he skipped chemistry class, the first time he picked up a guitar he'll never really be able to play. "Shit," he says, straightening up. He comes out of the room so fast he almost collides with me in the doorway.

I watch him roam around the room, lifting newspapers and clothes and finding no shoes. He's chewing on his lip, and he stops and puts his hands on his hips. "Did you look under the couch?" I say. My voice booms out across the room. Nate drops to his hands and knees and peers under the couch. He gives a cry of triumph and stands up with a pair of old sneakers in his hand.

It takes him a long time to put the shoes on. I'd like to go over there and tie them myself. I just stand there, trying not to think.

"Olivia?" Peter calls from the other room. When I don't respond right away he calls my name again, his voice rising. I go back into the living room. He's sitting up straight, blinking hard, as though he's just woken up, and the look on his face is something close to panic.

"I'm here," I say, and he jumps to his feet and comes toward me. "What's the matter?"

"I didn't know where you were," he says. "I thought you might have left."

"Don't worry," I say. I give him a quick kiss. "I'm not going anywhere."

"We're doing this together," he says, sliding his fingers into mine again.

"I haven't decided yet." It's a lie. I've decided, but I don't want to think about it. I don't want to lose my nerve. I squeeze his hand.

Nate appears in the doorway and both of us turn. "You guys ready?" he says. "I'm getting antsy." He almost jogs to the door and we follow.

Outside, the night is soft and warm, like a gentle hand brushing your cheek. In the parking lot I stop and look around me like I have to memorize this scene. Peter stands here beside me. Across the street at Dolly's a giant neon doughnut blinks on and off. A girl's voice floats down the street, calling somebody's name. The moon is almost full, and in the air there's a faint electric hum.

"What are you waiting for?" Nate says. "Come on. We don't want to be late."

We take my car. I follow Nate's directions onto the interstate and outside of town. For a long time none of us speaks. I'm listening to the whirring of the tires on the road below, watching the headlights of other cars approach and recede. This is what I love about driving on the highway late at night, that you just keep moving.

I hear a faint rumbling and look at Nate in the rearview mirror. He's asleep and snoring, his head back against the seat, his mouth hanging open. I let him sleep until we reach our exit, and then I whisper his name.

He sits up with a start, blinking hard.

"We're here," I say.

He leans forward to peer out the windshield. There are not many lights off the exit ramp, no fast-food restaurants or truck stops, just an abandoned gas station with an old-fashioned pump and boards across its windows. "There it is," he says, and at the same moment I see it: a roadside motel with a blinking red vacancy sign. The place is U-shaped, with rooms that open onto the parking lot and an office at one end where, through the glass, I can see a fat woman reading a romance novel at the desk. Nate directs me to room 13, and I park in front.

"You got the money?" Nate says. I find my wallet and hand him a stack of bills. He tells us to wait in the car and gets out. I watch him knock on the door, dancing from foot to foot, until it opens and he disappears inside. Peter has his head turned out the window, his body rigid, with anticipation or anxiety, I'm not sure. I am not afraid now, because this isn't happening to me anymore. I'm watching it like a movie, and this is a movie set, this place that looks like a stopover for people on their way down. On the other side of that door is a room with bad green carpeting, and a bed too many people have slept in, and maybe a cheap TV and some indeterminate stain in the bathtub. It's number 13, just like Allison Avery's apartment, and Allison could be in there with Nate, smiling that mischievous smile as she hands some guy the money, her tongue just visible at the corner of her mouth.

I look at myself in the rearview mirror. There's that girl again, the one who is capable of anything.

Finally Nate emerges from the motel, one hand in his pocket. He flashes us a victory sign and hurries to the car. When he gets in he's as jumpy as if he'd consumed a pot of coffee inside. "Let's go, let's go," he says.

Once we're on the road he pulls his hand out of his pocket and shows us a small foil package. "Get us back as fast as you can. This is gonna be great." He slides the package back in his pocket and settles in against the seat.

"What was the guy like?" I ask. "The dealer?"

"He's just this kid from the suburbs in a baseball cap. But he gets great stuff. He doesn't cheat you like some people."

"You never said if you know Jared Gillespie."

Nate shakes his head.

"Why would he?" Peter says, his voice sharp.

"I'm just asking," I say. Then I say to Nate, "Are you sure? He's from Mississippi. He might be a dealer."

"Doesn't sound familiar."

"It's possible Allison knew him."

"She didn't *know* him," Peter says. He sounds furious. He crosses his arms over his chest and turns away from me to stare out the window.

"Sorry," Nate says, yawning. "Before today, I'd never heard of him in my life."

When we reach his apartment building, Nate takes the stairs two at a time. Peter follows him, and I bring up the rear, slowly. When I reach his living room, Nate is hunting for a candle. When he finds one and lights it, it's Peter who heats some of the heroin in a spoon over the flame. Sitting in the armchair, I watch him, humming under his breath as the little rock melts into a golden brown liquid. "Beautiful, isn't it," Peter says to me, and I nod. It is pretty, the color of amber. He draws it through a cigarette filter into a syringe.

I watch Peter slip the needle into Nate's arm like it's something he's done a thousand times before. I watch the red blood rush into the clear tube. I watch Nate's face contort in ecstasy. I watch his head drop backwards onto the floor. Peter looks down at Nate, satisfaction on his face, and then he unwinds the belt from Nate's arm and comes toward me on his knees. "Now you," he says.

These are the last moments before it happens. I think of Hannah, rocking me in her arms. David, pulling me to him through the crowded bar. Peter, telling me he loves me while his eyes fill up with tears.

Now he kneels before me, then reaches up and brushes his lips against mine. "You ready?" he says. I hold out my left arm. He leans in, the belt in his hands.

"Did you used to do this for Allison?" I say, looking down at his curly brown hair, his bent neck.

He shakes his head, tightening the belt around my arm. The vein pops out.

"Did Allison do this for you?" My voice catches over her name. I stare at the tender inside of my arm.

"What are you talking about?" He picks up the needle, touches my plump vein with a finger. "Allison and I never shot up together."

"Peter," I say, panic fluttering in my chest. "Didn't Allison do this?"

He glances up at me. "Allison?" he says. He looks down again, positioning the needle at my arm. "No, my sister was never a user."

"I don't get it," I say. My voice rises. "I found the stuff in her apartment."

"That box? That was mine," he says. "She took it from me so I wouldn't use it."

"But these were her friends."

"These are my friends," he says. "She just hung around to keep an eye on me. She pretended she was just spending time with me, but I knew what she was doing." With his free hand he reaches up and strokes the side of my face. "Don't worry," he says. "Everything will be fine." Then he plunges the needle into my vein.

I take a deep breath as he pulls the needle from my arm. He seems to be receding from me, though he is still there, kneeling at my feet and smiling.

I am warm.

I am calm.

I am sinking, heavy as a stone.

Someone is screaming my name.

I'm dreaming, and in the dream I'm cold and wet and the ground beneath me is shaking. Someone is screaming my name.

I open my eyes.

All I see is water. It's cold and it's beating down on my face.

I blink and try to lift my hand to wipe my eyes. I can't move. There's a weight on my chest, and pain. Someone is pounding on my chest so fiercely it jams my spine into the hard surface below me. I lift my head.

My skirt is bunched around my waist. A boy is straddling me, beating his hands against my chest. He is close to sobbing, calling out my name. We are in the shower. I stare at him, his red frantic face, his flying fists. He's hurting me. I think maybe this is still a dream.

"What . . . ," I try to say. My voice is so small.

The terrible pounding stops. The boy lifts his head and grabs my face between his hands. "Olivia?" he says. "Oh my God, Olivia?" I recognize him now, his face so close to mine I can see the pores in his skin. It's Peter.

"What . . . ," I say again. He clutches me to him, so hard it hurts. "I'm so sorry," he is saying, over and over, sobbing out my name. "I almost killed you." Then I turn my head and vomit over his arm. "Shit," I say. I realize that I'm crying.

"It's all right," he says. "It's my fault. Oh God, I'm so sorry." He eases back and helps me to a sitting position. He rinses his hand and arm under the water. With his other hand on my back, he holds me up. "How do you feel?"

"Terrible," I say. "I'm all wet."

"I know," he says soothingly, as though he's talking to a child. "Let's get you cleaned up." He takes off my wet, stained shirt and puts it in a ball on the edge of the tub. I can't even help him. I just sit here letting him lift and lower my arms like he's undressing a doll. I've never been so tired in my life.

Peter squirts shampoo into his hand and begins to wash the vomit from my hair. "You're all right now," he murmurs. "Everything's going to be fine." I lean forward and close my eyes. I feel as though I'm just now learning how to breathe.

"What happened?" I say.

"Your heart stopped," he says. He runs his hand through my hair to rinse it and it tilts my head back so that I'm looking him in the face, only inches from him, as though we're going to kiss.

"What do you mean, my heart stopped?"

"You died," he says. "I swear to God you died."

I shake my head. "That's impossible."

"Well, it happened," he says. "You were dead."

I try to speak but my voice lodges inside my throat.

"You were dead." He takes a choking breath. "Just like her."

I shake my head again.

He runs his hands through my hair. "Thank God you're all right. You scared the shit out of me. One minute you were fine, and then I was about to shoot up, and you just didn't look right. I could tell somehow, the life had gone out of you. I carried you in here."

"How long?" I manage to say.

"How long what?" The cold water keeps coming down, and I'm shivering.

"How long did it stop?"

"I don't know," he says. "It can't have been long, or I wouldn't have been able to start it again." He leans down and presses his ear to my chest, up against my wet skin. "It's beating now," he says. Sitting up, he takes my hand and lays it over my heart. "Feel that beating?"

I do feel it, my heart's faint rhythm against my hand.

Peter reaches over me and turns off the shower. "You're shivering." He rubs his hands rapidly up and down my arms to warm me. "Let's get out." While he climbs out of the tub I put my other hand to my neck and find that pulse with my fingers. Peter gets a towel and leans over to wrap it around me. Then he tells me to put my arms around his neck. I don't want to let go of my heart, but I do what he tells me. He half lifts me to a standing position. Leaning on him, I step out of the tub.

"Can you stand now?" he asks me, smoothing my hair back from my face. I nod. "Get out of those clothes and dry off then. I'll go get you something to wear." He leaves the room, dripping water.

Alone, I put both hands on the sink and lean in to stare at myself in the mirror. I look terrible. My shoulders are bare, my nipples showing through the wet fabric of my bra. There are dark circles under my eyes, and my pupils are enormous. My hair is wet and tangled. I run my shaking fingers through it. I see no resemblance to Allison in my face. This is just me who did this, pale lips, lank brown hair, skin drained of color.

I slip out of my wet clothes and wrap the towel around myself. I'm still shivering. A terrible sick feeling flashes through me, and I have to drop to my knees by the toilet and vomit again. This is all I can think about, each small movement I have to make. Put your hand on the sink. Pull yourself up. Turn on the water. Rinse out your mouth. Look in the mirror. This is just you, naked and afraid.

Peter comes back in with a T-shirt and a pair of boxers that must belong to Nate. "This is all I could find that's clean," he says apologetically. "Put them on and I'll make a bed for you on the couch."

"I've got to go home," I say.

He shakes his head. "You're not going anywhere. You've got to sleep this off, and I want to keep an eye on you." His tone is so firm, I don't argue. He watches me like he can't stand to move his eyes away. I drop the towel and put on the clothes. The T-shirt clings to me like a second skin. I feel like I should hang up Nate's towel. When I bend to pick it up another wave of nausea washes over me so I just leave it crumpled on the floor.

"I'm so sorry," Peter says again. He catches me up in a fierce hug. I don't have the energy to put my arms around him, so I just lean against him, like a rag doll. He helps me down the hall to the living room. He puts a pillow on the couch and hums to himself while he lays a blanket across the cushions. His fear is gone. He seems giddy with relief. All I feel is sad and tired and sick.

The couch is so small I have to curl up in a fetal position to fit, my body still shaking, with cold or fear or nausea. Nate is still spread-eagled on the floor, his eyes closed, his face a picture of bliss. Peter finds another blanket and tucks it around me. Then he kisses me on the cheek, and I close my eyes. "You didn't die," he whispers. Across my lids I see the headline: REPORTER DIES OF DRUG OVERDOSE. FRIENDS SAY DALE, 25, LED A SECRET LIFE.

I open my eyes again. Peter is sitting in the armchair, tightening the belt around his arm with his teeth. The needle is in his hand. I sit up. "What are you doing?"

He hesitates. "I don't want this to go to waste."

"I almost died," I say, my voice rising.

I almost died.

"I've done this before," he says. "It would take a much higher dose to kill me."

"You can't," I say, clutching at the blanket. "What if something happens?"

"Nothing's going to happen," he says.

"Please don't."

He sounds irritated when he says, "I know what I'm doing. Just go to sleep. It's fine." He sinks the needle into his arm. The color rises in his face and he slumps backward in his chair, nodding himself away.

I sit watching him breathe, terrified that the slow rise and fall of his chest will stop. It would break my heart if he died, because in this moment this boy feels like the only person in the world I really know. Not even Allison Avery would understand what I did tonight. All this time I never asked the right questions.

Peter is still breathing. I keep watching him, afraid to go to sleep. Later Nate rouses himself and stumbles off to bed. I stay awake, listening for the sound of my heart.

19

I have no idea where I am. It's dark in this room, and my legs are drawn up tight and cramping. There's a strange smell in here, both sharp and musty, like vinegar, and when I reach for the lamp that sits beside my bed my hand touches nothing but air. I sit up, my hands clutching at a blanket that doesn't feel like mine, and look around a large and nearly empty room with posters hanging on the walls. Then my vision clears and I know what all of these things mean. I know where I am. I remember, and the memory makes me shudder, brings back the sick feeling in the pit of my stomach.

I swing my feet onto the floor and stand up. My muscles ache as though after a hard run. My mouth is dry. Peter is sleeping on the floor beside the couch. I step over him and go down the hall to the bathroom to scoop water from the faucet into my mouth. On the floor in a pile are most of my clothes. I put on the skirt. It's still damp. The shirt, which is wet and crumpled on the bathtub, I leave behind.

Before I go I stand for a moment over Peter's body, watching him sleep. The faint sound of his snoring reassures me that he's still breathing. "Good-bye," I say out loud. I find my bag in the living room and leave.

Outside the sun is just coming up, and the sky is streaked with pink. The street is quiet. The sign over the doughnut shop is turned off. Everything is still and waiting. I put my hand over my heart and feel it beating. If my heart really stopped, shouldn't there be some kind of pain?

The drive home seems to take an hour. I listen to the radio without really hearing it. I put on my blinker and turn down streets and stop at red lights without ever thinking about where I'm going or how to get there. When I get home I let myself in as quietly as I can. It seems like a place I haven't seen in months, and I move around the room, touching the things I know to be mine, reminding myself that I live here.

In my bedroom I sit on the edge of the bed and think about going to work. I am sore and sick and dreadfully tired. I have no idea how long the signs will last, and I keep imagining Peggy peering into my eyes, noticing some mark on my left arm, and ordering me off for drug testing. The safest thing to do is call her voice mail and say I have the stomach flu and I'm not coming in. "Someone else will have to do the follow-up," I say into the phone. "I don't care who. Somebody else."

Then I take off my damp skirt and Nate's tight T-shirt and crawl into bed.

Later Hannah comes in and says I'm going to be late for work. I tell her I'm sick and she lays her hand on my forehead and says it feels like I have a fever. She brings me a glass of water and makes me sit up and take some aspirin. Then she leaves, saying she'll call later to check on me. After she is gone I sink back down into sleep. It is like going underwater, dropping like a stone to the bottom of a pool.

The sound of the doorbell ringing drags me from some terrible dream. I wake up drenched with sweat, naked and uncovered. I've kicked the bedclothes off. The doorbell rings again. I roll out of bed and find a T-shirt on the floor. Then I stumble down the hall to the front door, still half dreaming, moving on instinct. I reach the door and open it. For a moment I can see only a dark figure against the brightness outside, and in my half-dreaming state it seems like something out of a nightmare, a ghost, a visitation. Then the figure steps closer. It's Peter.

"I called the newspaper," he says. "They said you were sick." He touches my arm. "You look awful," he says, his voice colored with shock and worry. I put a hand to my cheek. I am hot to the touch. I know how I must look, damp and feverish, my hair tangled and wet. "Can I come in?" he says. I step aside. He comes in and shuts the door and the room is dark again. "Were you sleeping?"

I nod, leaning back against the wall. He shifts from foot to foot, looking around the room, the clothes draped over the couch, the magazines sliding off the coffee table onto the floor. "You're just as messy as . . . ," he says, but doesn't finish. He looks at me, biting his lip. I can't think of a thing to say. For a moment we are frozen here, staring at each other, and then he lunges at me and pulls me into a hug, holding me so tightly that for a moment I can't breathe, my face pressed against his chest. "I'm so sorry," he says. One of us is shaking.

He says that he wants to stay with me tonight, that he told his mother he was spending the night at a friend's. Then he is whispering something, that he's sorry, that he loves me, I think, and then he takes my face between his hands and kisses me, frantic, wet kisses on my forehead, my eyelids, my trembling mouth.

"Wait, wait," I say, taking my mouth from his.

"What's the matter?" he says.

I shake my head. A flush is rising through my body and I am so hot I feel as if I might faint. I clap my hand to my mouth and run down the hall to the bathroom to be sick again.

Afterwards I brush my teeth twice and stand in the shower under the cold water for five minutes. When I come out, tying my bathrobe tightly around me, Peter is waiting in the hall. "I'm so sorry," he says. "I don't know what's the matter with me."

"It's okay," I say.

"You're shivering." He rubs my arms with his hands. "You should be lying down." He puts his arm around me and we go into my bed-room.

We sit on the bed and he takes my hand. Cold water drips from my hair over my shoulders.

"Are you mad at me?" he says. I look at him, his face lined with worry as he asks the question again. He seems at once much younger than me and much older. I don't say anything. "I almost killed you," he says, his voice breaking. "I don't know what I would have done . . ."

"Why did you want me to do it?" I ask him.

"I thought that . . ." His voices trails away.

"Tell me."

"I don't know. I wanted you there." He looks at me, his eyes fill-ing with tears, and gives me that beautiful smile, just like the first time I saw him. "I wanted you with me."

"And Allison never did it?" I say. "Never once?"

"I tried to get her to," he says. "I told her it was the only way to really be in your body. Do you know what I mean? Sometimes everything seems gray to me, the people I know, school. Like my parents, just doing what they're supposed to every day. Life shouldn't be just day after day of doing your laundry, taking the car to the shop. It should be . . ." He looks up at the ceiling, searching for the right word. "It should be fierce."

"Why wouldn't she do it?"

"She said, all of that makes no difference if you die." One corner of his mouth slides up, somewhere between a smile and a grimace. "And I said, 'I'm going to die.'"

"What did she say?"

"She said, 'And if you don't?'"

For a long moment he is silent. Then he says, "There's something I haven't told you."

"That doesn't surprise me," I say. I almost laugh.

He says he'd been mainlining about two months when Allison found his stash and took it, then gave him the option of quitting or telling his parents. She stayed with him through the worst of the withdrawal, convincing his parents he had the flu. It was almost over when he woke up alone, overwhelmed with craving. When his sister came by after work to check on him, she found him headed out the door to Nate's. When she couldn't change his mind, she persuaded him to come back to her apartment with her, saying she would go get something to make it better.

I watch him as he tells his story, feeling oddly distant from him, as though there is a pane of glass between us. It doesn't quite make sense to me, why his sister would steal morphine for him, believing that it was better than heroin. He responds with impatience when I ask. "She was worried I would OD," he says. "Because my tolerance was lower. She wanted to control the dosage."

"Why didn't she give you the heroin?"

"She wouldn't have known how much to give me," he says irritably. "And maybe she didn't want me to know she still had it."

I nod, turning that over. "Did she give you the morphine?"

He shakes his head. "I never saw her again. She took me up to her apartment and made a bed for me on the couch. She kissed me on the forehead and she said, 'I'll be right back.'"

"But she wasn't."

"I don't know," he says. "I left. I just couldn't stand it, the waiting, so I left and I went to Nate's." He finishes the story in a rush. "I've thought about this a lot. And I think when she got back to the apartment and I was gone she went racing out after me, in a panic, and that's when they got her. That's when they killed my sister. And then when she was in that trunk, alone and trapped, she must have known they were going to kill her. Maybe they told her they were going to rape her, maybe she could just tell." He turns to me. "Think of it."

I'm shivering. "I have," I say.

"So she gave herself the morphine so there wouldn't be any pain. And she couldn't tell, in the dark, how much to use, so even if they hadn't killed her, she'd be dead." He takes both my hands in his and says very slowly, as though to be sure I don't miss a word, "It's all my fault. If I hadn't told her I was going to Nate's, if I had stayed in her apartment, she wouldn't have been there when they came by. I was weak. I as good as killed her." He shakes his head. "Nate wasn't even there. I just went home."

It's easy to believe it's his fault. He's right. He could have changed her path. I don't say that. I say, "If she hadn't taken a job at the doctor's office, if she hadn't gone home to check on you, if she hadn't met Russell in college and been in a hurry to meet him, if she'd left ten minutes earlier or later . . . a thousand things took her to that moment. You can't blame yourself." It's easy to believe that, too.

He sobs, his shoulders shaking. I know he wants to believe me. I pull him toward me, so his head is on my breasts, and I rock us both from side to side. "I'll never do it again, Olivia," he whispers, "I swear." He feels so fragile to me, his bones so close to the surface of his skin. I think about Allison Avery, how she would want me to hold her baby brother like this, to tell him it's not his fault. I know her secrets, the dead girl, but that is not what I want to remember, the facts of her life stripped bare and laid on the page. I want to remember how she felt, how much she loved this boy. When he stops crying, I ease him back on the bed, and he closes his eyes as though to sleep. I curl into him, my head in the curve of his shoulder. I listen to the warm thudding of his heartbeat inside his chest. We begin to breathe in unison. I close my eyes.

When I wake, one of us has rolled away. We are lying side by side on the bed, on our backs, Peter is still sleeping. I prop myself up and watch the gentle movement of his eyes beneath his lids, the flutter of his pulse inside his throat. I don't want him anymore, but I do feel, in this moment, that I love him. He sighs and murmurs something I can't understand. I would like to remember this forever, how it felt to be here now, the stillness of the room, the softness of his face in sleep.

I am certain of one thing. It will not be like this again.

20

When Peter and I walk into the kitchen, Hannah is sitting at the table, eating a bowl of cereal. She raises her eyebrows. "Well, hello?" she says, making it a question. I say good morning and introduce them. Then I pull out two bowls and some cereal boxes. Peter shifts nervously from foot to foot and says he's not hungry. "Do you want some coffee?" I ask, then I see Hannah hasn't made it yet.

Peter says he'll make some and busies himself with filters and grounds. I go outside to get the paper. As I leave the room I hear Hannah asking, "So how do you know Olivia?"

On the porch I unfold the paper and look for the follow-up story on the front page. There it is, WITNESS HEARD SUSPECTS PLAN-NING ROBBERY, with Evan's byline above the copy. I read the lead: "Samuel Peterson, 18, told police last night that he heard the suspects in the Avery slaying planning to steal a car and commit robbery," and then I make myself stop and go back inside.

When I walk back in, Hannah gives me the look I'm expecting, knowing, disapproving. I ignore her, and go over to Peter, where he is leaning against the counter and watching the coffee drip into the pot with a look of desperate concentration. I touch his arm and he smiles at me. "It's almost done," he whispers. I ask Hannah if she wants some, and when she says yes I reach into the cabinet for three mugs and set them in a neat row on the counter. Then I go to the refrigerator for milk. I retrieve the sugar bowl from the top of the fridge. I open a drawer and take out three spoons. This is the strangest moment of my life. I shot heroin into my arm. I spent the night curled up with a seventeen-year-old boy with a dead sister whose wig I have been wearing on the streets around Memphis. Now I am putting one spoon in each mug so that we can all have coffee and go off to work.

In silence the three of us sit at the table and drink the coffee. I reach for the paper again and read Evan's story. Samuel Peterson claims he heard Jared Gillespie and Cody Parker planning to drive to Memphis in order to steal a car and hold up a convenience store. He says he heard Gillespie suggest taking a car from the owner at gunpoint, because that way they could get the keys. The police now think that the abduction wasn't planned, that, as Lieutenant Nash says, "the whole thing just escalated."

That should be my byline above the first column, not Evan's.

"Olivia?" Peter says.

"Yeah?" I glance up. He's leaning toward me across the table, his empty mug pushed aside. With her head bowed over her bowl, Hannah is pretending not to watch us.

"I said, 'I'm going to go home now,'" he says. "My mother will be wondering where I am."

"Okay." I put the paper down, and he stands and comes around the table toward me at the exact moment that I scoot my chair back, so the leg of the chair rams into his leg. "Oh God, I'm sorry," I say, jumping to my feet. "Are you okay?"

He gives me a smile that looks more like a wince, and nods. Then he turns to go. I follow him down the hall into the living room, and at the door, we come together and hug. He kisses my cheek. I reach up to kiss him once on the mouth. I step back. We start to speak at the same time, and then we both stop, and then he smiles and says he'll talk to me later, and I nod and say good-bye, and that is all. He is gone.

I'm standing by the front door, my hand pressed to my mouth, when I hear Hannah's voice. "The dead girl's brother, Olivia?" she says. I turn to see her standing with her arms crossed at the other end of the room. "What is going on? How old is that child?"

I shake my head and say nothing. She must see that I'm on the verge of tears because she crosses the room and touches my shoulder gently. "Okay," she says, her voice softer now. "Okay."

When I walk into the newsroom, I feel as though everyone is going to fall silent and turn to stare. I stand for a moment at the front of the room. No one looks at me. Then Peggy lifts her gaze from the newspaper on the metro desk. She calls my name. I walk over to her, resisting the urge to tug on my left sleeve. She studies my face. "How are you feeling?" she says. I'm listening for a current of suspicion in her voice. I hear only a distracted concern. Now that I'm actually guilty of the thing she suspected, her mind is on other things.

"I'm fine now," I say. "Must have been one of those twenty-four-hour bugs."

"Good, good," she says, turning her attention back to the paper. "Glad you're back."

"About the story, the dead girl," I say. "I want to stay with it."

"That's fine with me," she says. "Just mention it to Evan. He took over yesterday."

"Okay," I say. "Thanks." She's not looking at me anymore. I stand here watching her. I have an urge to confess, to tell her the story of all the stupid things I've done, to show her the tiny mark on my arm.

"Don't stand there staring," she says without lifting her gaze. "Go back to work."

I walk through the rows of desks to Evan's. He watches me approach, playing with a pen in his hand. The front page is spread out on his desk. I point at his byline. "Good story," I say.

"Thanks." He touches my hand with his pen. "How are you?"

"Okay." We both nod. He looks down at the paper, chewing on his lip.

"You know it's my story, don't you?" I say. "Because I want it back."

He looks up and gives me a weary smile. "It's yours."

As I turn toward my desk he says my name. When I look at him, he says, "I'm sorry. I don't know how I could have thought . . ." He shakes his head. "I want us to be friends again."

"Don't worry," I say. "I'm sorry too." I touch the back of his hand, and he turns it over and grasps mine. We stand there for a moment, our hands locked across his desk. Then Evan's phone rings.

When Evan hangs up, he calls me and I roll my chair over to his desk. "That was my source in the DA's office," he says. "She says one of the boys has confessed." He hands me a piece of paper with a name and number. "I told her you would call her back."

I reach for the phone, my heart rate accelerating.

The woman in the district attorney's office reads me Robby Shavers's statement over the phone. At sixteen, Robby is the youngest of the boys, and he sobbed while he told the story. He didn't mean to kill anyone, he said, he just went along with the plan to steal a car. He thought they'd just go joyriding, something they had done before. They were cruising around in Cody Parker's car, trying to pick out one to steal, when Jared Gillespie saw the girl, walking toward the street, her car keys in her hand. Jared and Cody got out, and Robby Shavers slid into the driver's seat of Cody's car. Robby watched through the window as Jared and Cody forced the girl into the trunk of her car at gunpoint. The girl was shaking her head and trying to back away. Robby rolled down the window and he heard her saying, "Just take the car. I won't tell anyone." Jared hit her across the face, and she fell against the open trunk. Jared and Cody shoved her in. Then Robby followed them out to the park.

It was never part of the plan to kill anyone, Robby said, but they had trouble getting her out of the trunk, she seemed barely conscious, and during the struggle to lift her out she scratched Jared and he hit her. Then Cody hit her, and when she fell to the ground they were on her. They tied her hands. Jared raped her, Robby said. He didn't. He hung back, listening to her scream, and then he got back in Cody's car. He didn't look until he heard the other car's engine start. When he looked back, the girl's body was disappearing beneath the wheels of her car.

I hang up the phone. I put my hands flat on my desk. My fingers tremble slightly and are still. The picture of Allison Avery is still propped against my computer. She laughs. The boy in the baseball cap kisses her cheek. All the images I have seen of this girl alive can't erase the first one, the one of her dead. One thing I know, I won't forget this. I won't get over it. Some part of me will always be afraid.

For a moment I sit looking around the newsroom. A reporter stands up, grabs his jacket, and goes striding out of the room. Two editors stand close together, talking low, showing each other the papers in their hands. A woman leans into her phone, gesturing wildly, her voice rising. "I need to know," she is saying. "I need to know." I glance over at Evan. He's frowning at his computer screen, chewing on a fingernail. Around me the noise rises and falls, the clatter of keyboards, the ringing of telephones, the buzz of all these voices. Here in the center it is quiet.

I reach out and turn on my computer. I pick up the phone and dial the police station. While I'm waiting to speak to Lieutenant Nash, Bishop goes sauntering past, hands in his pockets. He's whistling through his teeth, a notebook in his breast pocket, his glasses sliding to the end of his nose. I catch his eye and smile. He smiles back at me and winks, welcoming me home.

21

In August, Jared Gillespie's attorney calls me and asks me to come to the jail and meet him. He wants me to sit in on an attorney-client meeting. He won't tell Jared who I am, he says, and everything I hear will be off the record. He wants me to see with my own eyes that Jared Gillespie is just a scared young boy.

Both of the other boys have now confessed, each claiming that he didn't rape her, that he wasn't the one who drove the car. The DNA evidence will prove at least one of them a liar about the rape. About the driver, everyone seems to agree. Jared Gillespie, scared young boy.

I meet the attorney at the county jail, just outside of Bolivar, Mississippi. Inside it's cinder block walls, and a few men dressed like inmates, just walking around. The attorney shakes hands with one and high-fives another, a man with a mustache who gives me a slow wink. Then he walks up to the woman manning the desk. She looks up and says, "Who do you want?" Half the prison population must be his clients.

I sign my name to a list at the desk. The woman doesn't even ask me who I am. She gets on the radio and says, "Bring in Gillespie." After a few minutes a man walks through the doors, alone, wearing handcuffs. I take a quick glance at him, then look at the lawyer, who motions for us to follow him into a side conference room. The room is so small that when I reach for a chair my arm brushes Jared

Gillespie's. There is no electric shock of revulsion. It feels like nothing. It feels like skin, warm to the touch.

We sit around the little table, the three of us, and I stare at the man across from me. Jared Gillespie is about six feet tall. He is thin but muscular, his biceps hard little lumps inside his long, slender arms. He sports a scraggly mustache. His stringy brown hair is long in the back and hangs over his eyes in the front. His face is young and round and soft. His eyes are black. He has a small mouth, lips so thin and pale they're nearly indistinguishable from his colorless skin. His overlapping teeth are stained a faint yellow from nicotine. He is nineteen years old.

He does not seem evil. His face is as blank as a doll's, even when he smiles.

The lawyer calls a guard to remove Jared's handcuffs. Jared rubs his wrists. He takes a cigarette from a pack and lights it, inhaling slowly. Then he pushes the pack in my direction across the table. "Want a smoke?" he says. It's the first thing I've heard him say. His accent is thick, lower-class southern. I nod and take a cigarette. He leans forward and lights it for me, and I look right into those black eyes. It's like peering through a window into a dark and empty room.

According to his friends' accounts, Jared Gillespie is the one who forced Allison Avery into the trunk of the car. He was the first to rape her, and he paced back and forth punching the air while the others took their turns. He was the one who began to hit her, and then he kicked her, said Cody Parker, until she stopped screaming. The other two say they started to run back to Cody's car, but Jared wasn't with them, and when they heard a car engine start up they turned back to see the blue Honda Civic backing away, then racing toward the curled-up girl, Jared at the wheel. "We just stood there," Parker said. "We couldn't do nothin'." When Jared pulled up beside them and ordered them to follow him, they did it, they say, because they were afraid he would kill them too. "He kept sayin' we couldn't let her go," Parker said. "He said she saw us and we couldn't let her go."

I can chart it out, now, exactly how it happened, who grabbed her, what they said, what they did, when they did it. I still don't know how it felt to be there, to be her, to be him, this boy who sits slouched in his chair smoking a cigarette, the picture of sullen youth. I'm watching him, trying to picture him doing the things I know he did, trying to picture his face contorted with rage, the desire to destroy. I would like him to be an evil genius out of the movies, leaning back in his chair and coolly regarding us while he explained his master plan. All I see is this blank-faced boy, and I can't feel anything about him, not fear, not even hate.

His lawyer begins to go over some of his strategy for defense, that the cops coerced the other boys into pinning the blame on Jared because he's the only one who will automatically be tried as an adult. Jared's claim is that he was there, but he didn't rape her, he didn't hit her, and in fact he got scared and took off running when the other boys climbed back in the car and gunned the engine. He says they came after him and demanded he get in the car. "I didn't want to hurt nobody," he says, his voice a monotone. "I thought we was just gonna steal the car."

"How are you feeling, Jared?" The lawyer leans forward, an expression of avuncular concern on his face. "Are you scared?"

Jared looks down at the table and shrugs. "Yeah, I'm scared, man," he says. He studies the cigarette in his hand, burned down almost to his fingers. "I'm really scared. There's no doubt about that."

"You know, Jared," his lawyer says, "that the district attorney will likely seek the death penalty."

"I know, man," Jared says, shaking his head. "I'm scared, too. Them other guys is lyin', and I'm the one who might fry for it."

The lawyer looks at me, as though to say, are you getting this? I raise my eyebrows. We stare at each other for a moment, and then he turns back to Jared. "I'm going to do everything I can to make sure that doesn't happen," he says. Then he pauses, leaning back in his chair. "Have you seen Teresa lately?"

"Yeah, she came to see me the other day."

"And how's your little girl? What's her name? Annabelle?"

"Annabelle, that's right. She's okay, I guess. I haven't seen her." He takes another cigarette from the pack.

"You miss your family, don't you?"

"Sure I do. I miss my mama, and Teresa, and my baby. What's she gonna think, her daddy locked up in a place like this?" He waves his hand to indicate the room. Then he lights his cigarette. "You want another one?" he says, looking at me. I look back at him, and he smiles, showing all his jagged yellow teeth. I shake my head, and he shrugs as if to say, your loss. He takes a drag and exhales slowly.

"You know Allison Avery's family misses her too," the lawyer says, his voice grave. He shoots me another look to see how I'm taking this.

"I do, and I feel real bad about that," Jared says. "I wish I'd never gone along with that plan. I read about her mama in the paper, and I'm real sorry for her. But she said she wanted me dead, and that's not right. I didn't kill her baby. I wasn't the one."

The righteous indignation in his voice when he says "that's not right" makes it hard to hold my tongue. Underneath the table I rub my hands up and down my thighs. Anything I could say to him would be like Peter ramming his mailbox, a useless, hopeless gesture. I want to say "You hit her. You raped her. You killed her." I want to ask him if there was any reason why.

I sit here listening to his lawyer feed him questions designed to provoke responses that will make me see him as human, as pitiable. I'd like to stop him and tell him that I've seen Jared Gillespie as human from the moment I walked into this room, and that it makes no difference. He is the reason I have to be afraid. He is death visited upon you without reason or remorse. He didn't kill her because she spurned him, because she cheated him in a drug deal, because he knew her and wanted her to die. He just killed her.

Jared Gillespie stands up to go back to his cell. His lawyer stands up, saying something I'm not even hearing anymore, and then I'm on my feet, too, and I hear myself saying, "Why did you do it?"

"Don't answer that, Jared," his lawyer says sharply. He frowns at me, his face a picture of righteous anger at my violation of the deal.

I ignore him, staring at Jared Gillespie. "Tell me why," I say. I can hear the note of pleading in my voice.

Jared looks at me for a long time. I wonder what he sees. I am the same height as Allison Avery, the same age. I have dark hair, the same shape to my face. Does he see her when he looks at me? Does he want to rape me, beat me, crush my bones? "Jared," I say, making my voice hard and sharp. "Tell me why."

"Lady," he says, finally, "I don't even know."

Epilogue

In Memphis, the end of the summer begins with Death Week. Every year thousands of people come from everywhere to line up outside the iron gates of Graceland and weep for a man they think they knew. Tonight I'm covering the candlelight vigil, moving through a crowd of solemn men and women in Elvis T-shirts, candles in their hands. Some of them are waiting to file through the gates behind the house and past the grave, strewn with flowers and love poems. Some of them have already been, and now they are just waiting with the others for the night to pass into the day that Elvis Presley died. A loudspeaker broadcasts his ballads, and some of the people sing along, tears streaming from their eyes. It's a hot, sluggish late August night.

When I'm through here, David wants me to come to Mud Island so we can talk. Two weeks ago I finally told him about the heroin, about my desire for Peter, about how completely I lost myself in the story. We were sitting on his front porch. Across the street a couple sat close on a porch swing, not talking, just watching the sun go down. Some mother's voice rose in the air after a tardy child. "I can't believe it," David kept saying over and over. "I thought I knew you. I had no idea."

"Neither did I," I said.

I don't know what else to say to him. I don't know what will happen to us. Perhaps he deserves someone more like himself, someone who takes people at their word. I'm not sure what I deserve. In the end I will probably go to my car and drive past all the yellow-painted homes, the porches, and hanging plants. A young woman riding her bike will lift her hand in a wave and I'll wave back. Then I'll drive onto the bridge off Mud Island, heading back over the river into town.

In the next week or so Peter will call to say that he's leaving for college. He'll say that he's going to write and I'll pretend to believe him. He's spent the last month in a drug-counseling program, and he'll swear to me again that he's stopped using forever. Neither of us will mention the fact that we'll both be at the trial, and most likely we won't speak there, just lift a hand in greeting from opposite sides of the room. What we have left between us now is a faint tenderness, a faint embarrassment. He seems like a dream I had, and when I remember it now it's not the words that passed between us I think of. It's the small sounds he made when I kissed him, somewhere between pleasure and pain.

As for Carl, sometimes I still catch a glimpse of him on the street or at another table in a restaurant where I'm eating lunch with Hannah. I pretend not to see him there.

I'm not going to put in the paper that Jared Gillespie doesn't know why he killed that girl. I'm going to keep reporting the things I've learned about him, that his father abused him, that he grew up poor and uneducated, that his father's departure and his own early parenthood left him blaming women for the problems in his life. I'm going to report that he was hopped up on pills and alcohol. When you read it you still won't understand how someone could do what he did, but the course of events will make a familiar, sad kind of sense, and you will know that everything happens for a reason.

I'm not going to put in the paper that I went looking for Allison Avery, that I thought I would find her in the heroin rushing through my veins. Instead I found her in the terror I felt when I woke up in the shower with a boy I didn't recognize screaming my name. I stopped my heart for her, and this is my secret, that I followed her as far as I could.

"Love Me Tender" comes over the loudspeaker, and on the chorus thirty thousand voices join in. There is no way to describe the sound except to say that it's beautiful, that it swells my heart. I look around me. A man beside me with dyed black hair and sideburns sways from side to side, his eyes closed. Two women hang on each other's necks, weeping. I am not as different from these people as I would once have thought, all of us just looking for some kind of meaning, a story to shape our lives. When I leave here I will go back to the newsroom and make these people into a story. I will describe them, and report the things they've told me here tonight. They come because Elvis helped them through some of the worst moments of their lives. They come to see how he lived and where he died. They come because he was pretty. They come because once they met him, touched his hand. They come to be swept up in emotion, to let the sound of his voice remind them what they're living for. When they see my story in the paper, when they see their names in print, they will feel a part of something so much larger than themselves.

One thing I know. I am still here. In the hot, thick night, I stand shoulder to shoulder with thirty thousand people. The tiny flames of candles flicker in their hands.

FOR THE BEST IN PAPERBACKS, LOOK FOR THE ⓟ

In every corner of the world, on every subject under the sun, Penguin represents quality and variety—the very best in publishing today.

For complete information about books available from Penguin—including Puffins, Penguin Classics, and Compass—and how to order them, write to us at the appropriate address below. Please note that for copyright reasons the selection of books varies from country to country.

In the United Kingdom: Please write to *Dept. EP, Penguin Books Ltd, Bath Road, Harmondsworth, West Drayton, Middlesex UB7 0DA.*

In the United States: Please write to *Penguin Putnam Inc., P.O. Box 12289 Dept. B, Newark, New Jersey 07101-5289* or call 1-800-788-6262.

In Canada: Please write to *Penguin Books Canada Ltd, 10 Alcorn Avenue, Suite 300, Toronto, Ontario M4V 3B2.*

In Australia: Please write to *Penguin Books Australia Ltd, P.O. Box 257, Ringwood, Victoria 3134.*

In New Zealand: Please write to *Penguin Books (NZ) Ltd, Private Bag 102902, North Shore Mail Centre, Auckland 10.*

In India: Please write to *Penguin Books India Pvt Ltd, 11 Panchsheel Shopping Centre, Panchsheel Park, New Delhi 110 017.*

In the Netherlands: Please write to *Penguin Books Netherlands bv, Postbus 3507, NL-1001 AH Amsterdam.*

In Germany: Please write to *Penguin Books Deutschland GmbH, Metzlerstrasse 26, 60594 Frankfurt am Main.*

In Spain: Please write to *Penguin Books S. A., Bravo Murillo 19, 1° B, 28015 Madrid.*

In Italy: Please write to *Penguin Italia s.r.l., Via Benedetto Croce 2, 20094 Corsico, Milano.*

In France: Please write to *Penguin France, Le Carré Wilson, 62 rue Benjamin Baillaud, 31500 Toulouse.*

In Japan: Please write to *Penguin Books Japan Ltd, Kaneko Building, 2-3-25 Koraku, Bunkyo-Ku, Tokyo 112.*

In South Africa: Please write to *Penguin Books South Africa (Pty) Ltd, Private Bag X14, Parkview, 2122 Johannesburg.*